Contents

Beer Lover's Mid-Atlantic

Bryan J. Kolesar

Globe
Pequot

Guilford, Connecticut

This book is dedicated:
to my father, Paul, a WWII Marine veteran and beer
drinker who gave me so much in so little time;
to my mother, Doris, full of nurturing love and a
likewise meticulous collector of information;
and to my wife, Patty, my love and barstool
partner in life.

Globe
Pequot

An imprint of Rowman & Littlefield

Distributed by NATIONAL BOOK NETWORK

Copyright © 2015 by Rowman & Littlefield

All photos by the author unless otherwise noted
Maps: DesignMaps Inc. © Rowman & Littlefield

British Library Cataloguing in Publication Information Available

Library of Congress Cataloging-in-Publication Data
Kolesar, Bryan J.
Beer lover's Mid-Atlantic : best breweries, brewpubs & beer bars / Bryan J. Kolesar.
pages cm
Includes index.
ISBN 978-1-4930-0155-2 (paperback : alkaline paper) — ISBN 978-1-4930-1594-8 (e-book)
1. Beer—Middle Atlantic States—Guidebooks. 2. Breweries—Middle Atlantic States—Guidebooks. 3. Microbreweries—Middle Atlantic States—Guidebooks. 4. Bars (Drinking establishments)—Middle Atlantic States—Guidebooks. 5. Food and beer pairing—Middle Atlantic States. 6. Cooking (Beer)—Middle Atlantic States. I. Title.
TP577.K66 2015
338.4'7663420974—dc23
2014050361

All the information in this guidebook is subject to change. We recommend that you call ahead to obtain current information before traveling.

About the Author

It all began with a Miller High Life. As barely a teenager, I recall smelling one of my dad's clear bottles of the "Champagne of Beers" and wondering what it was about beer that adults liked so much. It may have been "made the American way" with "purity you could see and quality you could taste," but I wasn't getting it.

When pouring a beer for Dad one summer afternoon, he hollered in from the patio wondering what I could be doing that was taking so long. Well, I figured if ice cubes are a part of other alchoholic beverages such as gin and tonics, then surely some crushed ice would be fine for this beverage too. After all, it was hot outside. By the time I unplugged the ice crusher and presented him with this beer, the damage had already been done. He was understanding, yet left me with no doubt that under no circumstances should I ever add ice to beer again.

Not much of my teenage years was spent thinking all that much about what "really good beer" meant. By the time college rolled around in the late '80s and early '90s, Dock Street in Philadelphia and Stoudts in Lancaster County caught my eye. Dock Street had its brewpub in Center City and bottles of their Royal Bohemian Pilsner, Illuminator Double Bock, and Amber Ale made their way into my refrigerator. Stoudts Gold Lager was another local beer of interest to me as was anything that was different and better tasting from what others were drinking. Not to sound above it all, there admittedly was plenty of nondescript, lifeless, uninteresting beer consumed during these years, but my mind and palate were quickly being awakened to the understanding that there was more to beer than lightly flavored pale yellow water.

Bars in Philadelphia like The Dickens Inn poured plenty of John Courage for me in the '90s. Bridgid's served gravity-dispensed Yards ESA in my neighborhood and, across town, Khyber Pass had live music and a diverse bunch of interesting beers. Sam Adams opened a brewpub in the Sansom Street space that Nodding Head later occupied. There's an unrecalled bar in Manhattan where I had a Chimay in the early '90s, but the experience didn't leave me with any marked memories other than that I'd ordered a weird, expensive beer from Belgium.

Beers that came to me from elsewhere in the States like Penn Brewery in Pittsburgh, Catamount in Vermont, and Breckenridge in Colorado also piqued my palate's curiosity and advanced my interest in different and fuller-tasting beers from smaller breweries.

If my math is correct, that means I've been on the hunt for great beer for over 20 years in both my backyard of southeastern Pennsylvania and around the world.

In 2005, homebrewer friend Adam Beck set me on the path to this book. Blogs were becoming the free and technologically easy thing to do and he asked if I would work with him on TheBrewLounge.com. Through the last 10 years and several different platforms for beer writing, I've enjoyed capturing the people, the places, the events, and of course the beer that makes the mid-Atlantic region one of the most diverse as well as one of the most fun in the country.

The Brew Lounge is still going strong and has led me to write this book expressing the richness of the mid-Atlantic beer scene as seen from Erie to the Eastern Shore, Hoboken to Hagerstown, Scranton to Solomons Island, Williamsport to Wilmington, and Pittsburgh back to my home turf of Philadelphia.

Acknowledgments

To everyone in the last 10 years who said I should write a book, this is for you . . .

To the extraordinarily high percentage of those owners, brewers, reps, distributors, and writers who provided insight and responded to requests for information, your cooperation reflects the best of what makes the beer industry great . . .

To those proprietors, bartenders, brewers, and customers who sent me away with more tips of new places to check out than I came in with, every opinion counted and the added workload was appreciated . . .

To a few specific fonts of beer information like Kevin Brooks, Chris Dilla, Mat Falco, and Suzy Woods, who took the time to create helpful lists of names and places worth checking out, the book wouldn't be the same without you . . .

To those such as Brian M., Deb and Steve B., Dennis W., Eric T., Greg G., Lloyd V., Mark L., and Tom Z., who met up with me along the journey and shared plates of food and glasses of beer, the camaraderie made the miles logged a bit easier . . .

To editor Tracee Williams, Lynn Zelem, and various staff at Globe Pequot/ Rowman & Littlefield, who apparently must be accustomed to dealing with first-time book authors because they handled my occasional crush of questions and requests for reassurances with professional ease . . .

To friends Matt M., for his legal advice, Jennie Hatton-Baver, for her all-around industry knowledge and marketing expertise, and established beer writers like Lew Bryson and Brian Yaeger, who provided insights from their own book-writing experiences, the shock of taking on such a project was made slightly less overwhelming with your counseling . . .

To my wife, Patty, who joined me on a few of the research excursions, assisted with the edit and review process, and, perhaps more importantly, helped our home life accommodate my disruption to our typical spring and summer . . .

To all the mid-Atlantic beer lovers who made this book necessary, I raise a glass to you . . .

. . . and I thank you all.

Introduction

Everyone has a starting point for their trip through the wild and wonderful world full of great beer experiences. Mine was told through my personal introduction a few pages ago.

For years, I was the guy the party with the "weird" beer, the "yuppie" beer, the "foo-foo" beer, or other adjectives to describe the not-so-typical beer.

Fortunately for most young adults coming of drinking age in current times, finding a satisfying beer to drink is much easier than in my early days. Now we see great beer options in stadiums, at airports, at fine-dining establishments, and at dive bars. They show up at family picnics and I see countless recycling bins filled with them when I go on my neighborhood runs.

The turning point came at some point in the last 5 to 10 years. My niece (who might not have been quite of legal drinking age so I'll withhold her name to protect the not-so-innocent) asked "Uncle Bryan, have you ever heard of Dogfish Head 120 Minute IPA?!" Family members and friends began sending newspaper clippings and web links related to something they saw on "the rise of craft beer" in the news or the next brewery opening in their neighborhood. Family in California's wine country began seeing beer show up at their wine parties and exclaimed "we had a beer that didn't taste anything like beer!"

Choices abound, information is more plentiful and flows more freely, and consumers appear open more than ever to local breweries making a more flavorful and more interesting beer. More, more, more. From my travels around this country I can safely state that good beer can be found at nearly every turn, in every city and rural town.

And while every region of the country is awash in beer more than ever, some have had it better than others with more of it for a longer period of time. The mid-Atlantic region has long been one of the richest beer regions in the country. German beers, unique Belgian offerings, English cask-conditioned ales, and a superb pub culture (particularly in the major cities) have existed and excelled in the mid-Atlantic region well before they took off in many other regions across the country.

But that doesn't mean there still isn't room for growth. I've been fond of saying that until every neighborhood has a brewing establishment like Earth Bread + Brewery (see also: Blue Canoe, Brewer's Art, Bullfrog, Dock Street, Forest & Main, Franklin's, Iron Hill, JoBoy's, Harvest Moon, North Country, Penn, Selin's Grove, Tired Hands, Voodoo, or Yorkholo—breathe—just to name a few) that weaves its food and beer as an integral component to a walkable, thriving community, there's plenty of room for more growth in the industry.

The process of getting the book to this final state was no small undertaking. Let's cover some ground rules. First, given the geographic range—the full states of Delaware, Maryland, New Jersey, and Pennsylvania—there was no way possible to cover every single brewing establishment and bar/restaurant that represents the craft segment well in under 400 pages. Covering all the brewing establishments alone would have been a challenge.

Therefore, judgment calls had to be made. My one major overarching principle was that no place could be listed in the book if I hadn't visited at least once—even if only for a 30 minute beer or a 2-hour meal and beers. It was too important to me to be able to personally say that I talked with people on both sides of the bar, drank the beer, tasted the food, breathed the local air, and saw the property inside and out in order to give the best and fairest possible representation.

So the list was whittled down from many potential hundreds to what turned into 379 visits to breweries, beer bars, and restaurants. This book is broken into geographic chapters and contains 320 establishments covered either by way of a profile entry or inclusion on a chapter-ending "pub crawl." If the related entities of establishments covered in this book are counted (e.g., The Belgian Cafe under the Monk's Cafe umbrella, or the multiple locations of DuClaw, Sharp Edge, Iron Hill, etc.) then around 370 total places have been mentioned in this book.

The research part of the project covered 9,444 miles driven, over 12,000 pictures taken, and many dozens of pages of both hand-scribbled and electronic notes. I've already described how the book is not meant to be an all-encompassing and exhaustive directory of every brewing concern and bar serving at least one non-macro beer. It can't be. My aim is to bring many of the usual suspects that most "Beer Lovers" would expect in these pages while hopefully shedding some light on less-discussed places that likewise deserve attention.

The book aims to present a little something for everyone—shiny new places, old historic spots; dive bar, sports bar, jazz bar, gay bar; barbecue, sushi, even a BYO (go figure); large-production brewery, small nanobrewery, urban brewery, farmhouse brewery. I look forward, I truly do, to hearing all of the objections to places included and cases made for those that were not.

As you read through this book and make your own experiences and traditions with beer, remember that it's not always about the beer. Well, of course, the beer certainly plays an important role and is a business, no doubt. But, it's so much more than that. It's there to celebrate the highs and soften the lows. I provide this book for you to enjoy in good taste.

How to Use This Guide

What is a brewery and what is a brewpub? Many considerable breweries have some level of food service included in the business. Does that make them breweries or brewpubs? Brewpubs, by definition, make their own beer so are they a brewery as well? It may not be an exact science, but I chose to make the distinction based upon the apparent significance that the kitchen plays at the establishment. Will that logic sync with yours on each entry in this book? It will vary I'm sure. But rest assured that establishments included in *both* the Breweries and Brewpub sections are viable brewing institutions and deserve the attention regardless of the label.

Getting past definitions, I encourage you to use this book to discover great beer in breathtaking upstate Pennsylvania and the way down southern reaches of Delaware and Maryland. Get out to stunningly beautiful western Maryland and northwestern Pennsylvania to sample beer in unique environments. How about New Jersey? You can drink beer near The Shore, in the vast expanse of the serene north-west part of the state, and amongst the hustle and bustle just across the river from New York City.

Visit the older places like Straub and Yuengling as well as the newer ones listed in the More to Come section near the end of the book.

As you discover these places new to you, remember it's not just about the beer. The beer, of course, is the beginning of the experience, but it's also about the people who made it and passionately sell it, the ingredients and farmers behind them, even the yeast that does its mysterious magic. Remember to appreciate all that goes into a great glass of beer in your journey to find it.

In addition to providing short guides for all the breweries, brewpubs, beer bars, and restaurants, you will also find chapters on:

Beer Is Going Places: Once relegated to the deserted wastelands of mass-market beer, airports of the mid-Atlantic now house bars with some of the most exceptional beer selections around. True to the spirit of airports, each tends to have its own regional flavor in the retail shops as well as on the tap towers. You'll even read about a pretty darn good train station bar. This section will help you find the best spots to relax with a beer during your next trip or layover.

Major Beer Festivals: Some of the finest beer festivals and events in the nation take place in the mid-Atlantic states. The festivals listed herein are ones that take place every year, almost always during the months under which they are listed. This section should help in planning out those beer events for the year, as many sell out well in advance. Keep your ears open for others, too, as new beer festivals are being planned all the time.

BYOB: Brew Your Own Beer: Almost all professional brewers got their start homebrewing on a much smaller scale. In this book's Brew Your Own Beer section, you will find a select listing of homebrew shops in the area and one of its contributed homebrew recipes.

In the Kitchen: Beer pairs well with a number of foods, and it can also be used to enhance dishes. The In the Kitchen section features recipes from area chefs that incorporate their beer both in the kitchen and on the table. You might be surprised at how versatile a cooking ingredient it is when used in everything from appetizers to entrees, dressings to desserts. Use the beer that is recommended when you can, but feel free to substitute a beer in the same style if the beer that is listed is not available to you.

Glossary of Terms

ABV: Alcohol by volume—the percentage of alcohol in a beer. A typical mass-market domestic beer is a little less than 5% ABV.

Ale: Beer brewed with top-fermenting yeast at relatively warmer temperatures than lagers. Ales are quicker to brew than lagers, which can require weeks of aging at cold temperatures. Popular styles of ales include pale ales, amber ales, stouts, and porters.

Barleywine: Not a wine but a high-alcohol ale that originated in England. English versions are more malt-forward. As with IPAs, American versions of barleywines often have been dosed with higher-than-traditional amounts of hops.

Barrel of beer: Production of beer is measured in barrels. A barrel equals 31 gallons and is typically abbreviated BBL.

Beer bar: A bar that focuses on a high quality beer selection.

Bitter: An English bitter is an English-style ale, more hop-forward than an English mild, but still more restrained than many IPAs.

Bock: A German-style lager, often stronger than the typical lager.

Bomber: Most beers are packaged in 12-ounce bottles. Bombers are 22-ounce bottles.

Brewpub: Typically a restaurant, but sometimes a bar, that brews its own beers on premises.

Cask ales: Also known as real ales, cask ales are naturally carbonated and are usually served with a handpump rather than forced out with carbon dioxide or nitrogen.

Clone beer: A homebrew recipe based on a commercial beer.

Contract brewery: A company that does not have its own physical brewery and pays someone else to brew and bottle its beer.

ESB: Extra-special bitter. A traditional malt-heavy English pub ale with low bitterness, a style that lends well to be served cask-conditioned.

Gastropub: A beer-centric bar or pub that exhibits the same amount of care selecting its foods as it does its beers.

Growler: A half-gallon jug of beer. 32-ounce growlers have also become popular in recent years. Many brewing establishments and bars fill growlers of beer to go.

Gypsy brewer: A company that does not own its own brewery, but rents space at an existing brewery to brew it themselves.

Handpump: Referred to also as a beer engine, whereby beer is manually "pulled" or pumped by the server from the keg to the faucet.

Hops: Hops are flowers used in beers to produce aroma, bitterness, and flavor. Nearly every beer in the world incorporates hops.

IBU: International bittering units, which are used to measure how bitter a beer is.

Imperial (or Double): A higher-alcohol version of a regular-strength beer, such as a double or imperial IPA.

IPA: India pale ale. A popular style of ale created in England that has taken a decidedly American twist over the years with a heavier emphasis on hops.

Kölsch: A light, refreshing German-style ale.

Lager: Beer brewed with bottom-fermenting yeast at relatively colder temperatures than ales. Takes longer and is generally regarded as more difficult to brew than ales. Popular styles of lagers include black lagers, doppelbocks, pilsners, and Vienna lagers.

Malt: Typically refers to barley malt, but sometimes wheat malt and other grains. Malt provides the fermentable sugar in beers. The more fermentable sugar, the higher the ABV in a beer. Without malt, a beer would be too bitter from the hops.

Microbrewery: A brewery that brews fewer than 15,000 barrels of beer a year.

Nanobrewery: A brewery that brews no more than a few barrels of beer per batch.

Nitro draft: Most beers that are served on draft using kegs pressurized with carbon dioxide. Occasionally, particularly with stouts, nitrogen is used, which helps create a creamier body.

Pilsner: A style of German or Czech lager, usually light in color. Many mass-produced beers are based on this style.

Porter: A dark ale, similar to the stout but with fewer roasted characters.

Quad: A strong Belgian-style ale, typically sweet and high in alcohol.

Russian imperial stout: A stout is a dark, heavy beer. A Russian imperial stout is a higher-alcohol, thicker-bodied version of regular stouts.

Saison: Also known as a Belgian or French farmhouse ale. Ranging widely in flavor and aroma, it can be fruity and it can also be peppery. Usually refreshing.

Seasonal: A beer that is brewed only at a certain time of year to coincide with the seasons.

Session beer: A low-alcohol beer, one you can have several of in one long drinking "session."

Stout: A dark beer brewed with roasted malts.

Tap takeover: An event where a bar dedicates a significant number of its taps to one brewery.

Triple (Tripel): A Belgian-style ale, typically lighter in color than a dubbel but higher in alcohol.

Wheat beer: Beers, such as hefeweizens and witbiers, that are brewed using a relatively higher percentage of wheat malt along with barley malt.

Yeast: The living organism in beer that causes the sugars to ferment and produce alcohol.

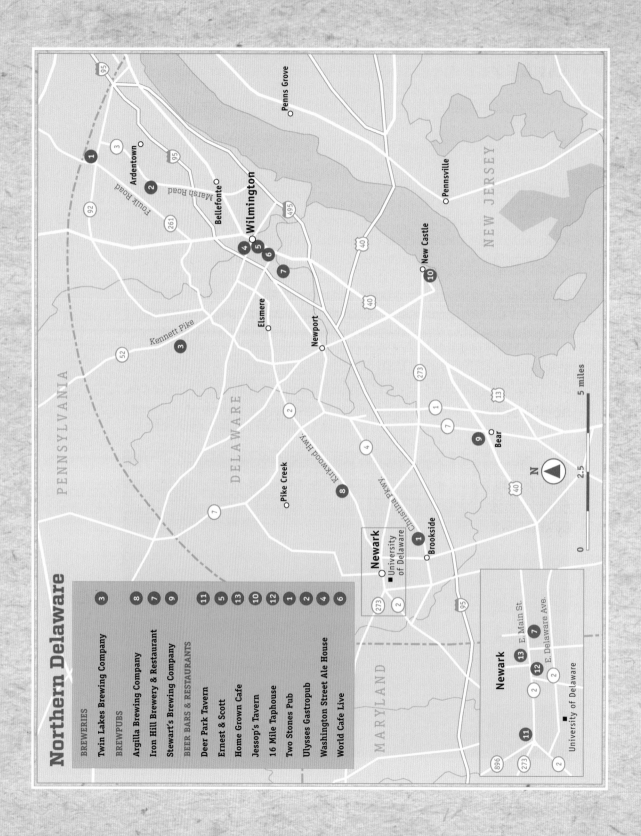

Northern Delaware

BREWERIES

Twin Lakes Brewing Company	③

BREWPUBS

Argilla Brewing Company	⑧
Iron Hill Brewery & Restaurant	⑦
Stewart's Brewing Company	⑨

BEER BARS & RESTAURANTS

Deer Park Tavern	⑪
Ernest & Scott	⑤
Home Grown Cafe	⑬
Jessop's Tavern	⑩
16 Mile Taphouse	⑫
Two Stones Pub	①
Ulysses Gastropub	②
Washington Street Ale House	④
World Cafe Live	⑥

Northern Delaware

Delaware is known as the Blue Hen State, the Home of Tax-Free Shopping, and the First State (with regard to signing the Constitution). Drivers who pass through on I-95 understand why it's also referred to as the Small Wonder. From the entrance just north of Wilmington to the exit just beyond Newark, I-95 travelers spend only 25 miles in Delaware.

From a beer perspective, let's first take a look at Northern Delaware, roughly defined as being above the C&D Canal in St. Georges. There's plenty in Wilmington, Newark, and the neighboring communitites to satisfy your thirst for great beer.

When traveling through the area, be advised that New Jersey has its Noo-erk; in Delaware, it's New-ark, cleanly and crisply enunciated like many of the beers encountered while exploring the northern end of the state.

Breweries

TWIN LAKES BREWING COMPANY

4210 Kennett Pike, Greenville, DE 19807; (302) 658-1826; twinlakesbrewingcompany.com; @TwinLakesBrews

Founded: 2006 **Founder:** Samuel S. Hobbs (CEO) **Brewers:** Robert Pfeiffer and Julia Christie-Robin (assistant) **Flagship Beer:** Greenville Pale Ale **Year-Round Beers:** Route 52 Pilsner **Seasonals/Special Releases:** Winterthur Wheat, Oktoberfest, Tweeds Tavern Stout **Tours:** Wed 5 p.m. and Sat 1 p.m.; $22 to tour; tasting complimentary **Taproom:** Yes **Naming Inspiration:** Named after the seventh-generation Twin Lakes Farm property

A brewery like Twin Lakes tugs at the heartstrings and palates of beer lovers, foodies, and historians. From the approach off Route 52 to the brewery tour to a walk around the property, one cannot help but be taken by the preservation of the lightly farmed 252-acre property run by a seventh-generation family member, Sam Hobbs.

The 90-minute tour focuses on the historical aspect quite a bit in addition to the actual beer-making process. It certainly is an informative and integral component to the story for a brewery with as much history as Twin Lakes.

The story begins with the British landing at Elkton and includes General Washington passing through the area and drinking from the well. Ken, an affable tour guide and über beer guy, will go on during the tour to weave in historical tidbits related to the region and the brewery property including the "Washington Pear Tree," the Battle of Brandywine, and how Vice President Joe Biden and his now-wife, Jill, are from just over the hill and, when dating, ice-skated on the

property lake in front of the brewery. But, for all of the interesting history and side stories, there is still the beer to discuss.

Under the motto of "Fresh, Delicious, Local," solar-powered Twin Lakes endeavors to use something from the land and it begins with water sourced from beneath the farm. In the future, they would like to use part of the property to grow and source their own hops as well.

The brewery, like many, has responded to market demand by adding fermenters in the last couple of years. Anyone who has been on the tour knows that this is no small undertaking given the tight quarters of the brewery on the lower floor of the converted farmhouse.

And while the brewery has stuck close to their usual lineup of beers, which have included the **Pale Ale** and **Pilsner**, a **Stout**, an **English Ale**, and an **Oktoberfest**, they also are listening to the market and considering an IPA and a Belgian variety in 2015.

Beer Lover's Pick

Greenville Pale Ale
Style: American Pale Ale
ABV: 5.5%
Availability: Year-round; 12-ounce cans

The brewery's affection for all things local continues here with a nod to the local municipality. This year-round, medium-bodied beer has continued to grow in popularity, especially once it became even more portable in 2011 with 12-ounce cans. This light copper-colored ale has a slightly sweet malt aroma—similar to the kind you get when you walk into a brewery—and delivers a pleasant balance of graham cracker sweetness balanced with light citrus from whole-leaf Cascade hops. This is an equally great beer to kick back with on the hammock in the heat of summer as well as paired with beef stew on a chilly winter night.

Brewpubs

ARGILLA BREWING COMPANY

2667 Kirkwood Hwy., Newark, DE 19711; (302) 731-8200; argillabrewing.com;
@ArgillaBrew
Founded: Pietro's Pizza opened in 1978 and the brewery was added in 2012 **Founder/ Owners:** Rodger Powell (founder), Steve Powell, Candace Powell **Brewers:** Steve Powell and Bryan Taylor **Frequent Beers:** Blonde on Belgian, Golden Goldings, and rotating Pale Ales **Naming Inspiration:** Steve's middle name is Clayton and his mother is Italian. Argilla is Italian for "clay."

Owner Steve Powell is following in his father's footsteps of over 35 years in the pizza business on the outskirts of Newark.

The menu is filled with a variety of foods like beer grain breadsticks, ale-battered onion wings, a slow-roasted pulled pork with broccolini, sharp provolone, and basil aioli, and the extensive list of pizzas.

At Argilla, there's a very well-made basic Margherita pizza. The pizza menu begs for further exploration and, in some cases, a bit of trust to find a pie full

of flavors that may not be readily apparent. Take, for example, the bacon and apple pizza. Described as being made with "bacon and Red Delicious apples and house smoked cheddar/mozzarella and topped with apple butter on an olive oil base," it may not sound like anything you have ever had on a pizza.

Take that leap and, better yet, order it with a beer like **Blond On Belgian** (5.8% ABV) for a beer-pairing delight. This beer is clean and crisp with mild fruitiness that drinks nicely by itself but also complements the apples on the pizza well without being too "big" to overwhelm the pizza.

The Porkette Pie, with slow-roasted pork, broccolini, and mozzarella is another winner. Even with the creatively delectable pizzas coming out of the oven, it is quite possible that Argilla today is known even more so for the beer coming out of its small operation in the brewhouse adjoining the kitchen.

Given the small 1.5-barrel brewing operation, Powell has plenty of latitude to experiment while brewing approximately five barrels per week. Therefore, the beer list is likely to frequently change and often not repeat specific beers for quite some time.

Powell is looking to double his brewhouse size to three barrels in early 2015. But, don't expect Argilla beer to wander too far offsite, as they "aim to be an East Coast pizzeria establishment that also serves and brews great beer." Head to the restaurant for the freshest beer, a dinner, and their family-friendly spring and fall festivals.

IRON HILL BREWERY & RESTAURANT

147 E. Main St., Newark, DE 19711; (302) 266-9000; ironhillbrewery.com/newark; @IronHillNewark
Founder and Owners: Kevin P. Finn (President), Kevin Davies (Director of Culinary Operations), Mark Edelson (Director of Brewing Operations) **Opened:** 1996 **Brewer:** Justin Sproul **Brewing Output:** 8.5-bbl brewhouse; 1,000 barrels/year

710 Justison St., Wilmington, DE 19801; (302) 658-8200; ironhillbrewery.com/wilmington; @IronHillWilm
Opened: 2003 **Brewer:** Brian Finn **Brewing Output:** 10-bbl brewhouse; 1,300 barrels/year

Iron Hill has nearly a dozen locations across Delaware, New Jersey, and Pennsylvania. Depending upon when you read this book, the number could still be less or it might be more. Iron Hill has continued its impressive growth to complement its equally impressive run of award-winning beer.

The brewpub's locations are strategically located to feed off lively surrounding activity. The two Delaware locations are no exception. The Newark location was the company's first and was remodeled in 2012. It is located in vibrant downtown Newark, just steps from the University of Delaware's main campus. On any given day, students, families, professionals, and university staff can be found enjoying the brewpub's kitchen and beer offerings.

Iron Hill keeps its company headquarters in nearby Wilmington and its fourth location is located along the Christina River, where a Riverwalk connects downtown and the train station to exciting options along the river. Case in point: You can park once (or come into the downtown train station) and easily walk between the Iron Hill, Frawley Stadium (home to the minor league Blue Rocks baseball team), Riverfront Market, and the Delaware Children's Museum.

Once inside Iron Hill, though, you may be hard-pressed to leave. Each location (and Wilmington is no exception) devotes plenty of attention and investment to the kitchen with staffs that focus on creating exceptional food selections that can stand on their own or be expertly paired with beers.

Some of the most popular and well-done menu items include the Asian lettuce wraps, cheesesteak egg rolls, Southwestern black bean burger, and a variety of hearth-baked pizzas on malted barley dough. They have also taken into account customer dietary needs and created low-calorie and gluten-sensitive menus. The atmosphere that Iron Hill has created shows that while the beer is exceptionally good, it need not hog the spotlight.

At Iron Hill, the core group of beers (**Iron Hill Light Lager**, **Ore House IPA**, **Pig Iron Porter**, **Vienna Red Lager**, **White Iron Wit**, **Witberry**, and a seasonal **Belgian Ale**) is made to corporate standards by each location's brewing team. Each location then has the latitude to add to the list of available draft beers to showcase their individuality and creativity in the brewhouse.

Head brewers Justin Sproul (Newark) and Brian Finn (Wilmington) have both won awards for the work they've done at Iron Hill. Sproul has a hand in the most

The Hills Are Alive

Something is always happening at Iron Hill. It could be a beer-pairing dinner, held nearly monthly at each location. Many of each location's new beer releases are turned into special events, sometimes paired with special food offerings.

At Wilmington's waterfront location, the "backyard" affords an enticing venue for beer events. Perhaps none is more anticipated than the annual bocce showdown, typically held in August, between the host brewery and other Delaware brewery-based teams.

Customers come to witness fun, games, and frivolity along with the lineup of interesting beers that each participating brewery brings. By dusk, sometimes later, a champion brewery bocce team is crowned and the post-competition action moves to the lawn chairs.

award-winning beer in the Iron Hill family, the **Russian Imperial Stout**, while he worked at the Media, PA, location with head brewer Bob Barrar; Finn recently took home a bronze medal from the 2012 Great American Beer Festival for his **Black IPA**.

Rounding out the Iron Hill mission is community involvement. They took a popular concept and applied it to all locations, available any Monday through Wednesday. They call it the Give 20 fund-raising opportunity, where a group can dine out to benefit a specified charity with Iron Hill donating 20 percent of the food check to the organization. Just another example of how eating and drinking well can go for the greater good.

STEWART'S BREWING COMPANY

219 Governors Pl., Bear, DE 19701; (302) 836-2739; stewartsbrewingcompany.com
Founded: 1995 **Owner/Founder:** Forrest Allen Stewart (Al) and founded with Greg Stewart **Brewer:** Ric Hoffman **Flagship and Year-Round Beers:** Governor's Golden Ale, Wacky Wheat Ale, Irish Red Ale, Stewart's IPA, Highlander Stout **Seasonals/Special Releases:** Oyster Stout, McBride's Strong Ale, Windblown Blonde **Naming Inspiration:** Family name

Stewart's can be many things to different people. For some, the brewpub is a family gathering place for dinner. To others, it's a popular place to gather with friends for Sunday afternoon football. And yet for others, like you and the presumed reason you're reading this book, it's a place to hunker down at the bar and savor a variety of award-winning beers.

Northern Delaware

Brewer Ric Hoffman (pictured below in his 7-barrel brewhouse) has been with the brewpub since 1998. During that span he has brewed up 14 medal-winning beers, two wins each for his **Oktoberfest**, **Smoked Porter**, and **Windblown Blonde Kölsch**. The **Stumblin' Monk**, a fruity and sweet Belgian tripel which drinks deceivingly easy for over 9% ABV, alone has brought home three medals and a variety of others have tallied six medals toward Hoffman's total.

One beer in particular worth noting is the **Oyster Stout**, a silver medal winner at the 2012 Great American Beer Festival in the Irish Dry Stout category. This beer, especially when served on nitrogen, is a seasonal crowd pleaser with a smoothness that takes just the briny edge off the beer to make it go down perfectly with a Scotch egg or all by itself.

In 2010, Executive Chef Dan Dogan arrived in the kitchen and showcased a revamped menu during the popular anniversary dinner held in August. On a daily basis, the current balance of the old usual and creative food items on the menu is just about right and provides for interesting complements to the beer menu.

Take, for example, the pulled short rib and bahn pita, which incorporates the Highlander Stout and is a satisfying plate of food on its own but shines even more when paired with the **Highlander Stout** (obvious choice) or the **McBride's Strong Ale**.

Hoffman brings a diverse lineup of beers to the year-round lineup, but shines even more so with some his seasonal/occasional brews like the refreshing springtime **Windblown Kölsch** and the wintertime **McBride's Strong Ale**, which weighs in at 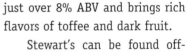 just over 8% ABV and brings rich flavors of toffee and dark fruit.

Stewart's can be found off-site most often at festivals like Brews by the Bay in Lewes, DE, and other tasting events. But for the full experience and widest selection, stop by the pub and soak up the good times and beer. By the time you read this, Stewart's should have completed a major restaurant renovation to provide an even more comfortable experience at one of the region's hidden gems.

Beer Bars & Restaurants

ERNEST & SCOTT

902 N. Market St., Wilmington, DE 19801; (302) 384-8113; ernestandscott.com;
@ErnestAndScott
Draft Beers: 20, plus two handpumps **Bottled/Canned Beers:** Around 30

Ernest & Scott's will catch your wandering beer eye with some old familiars like Allagash, Dogfish Head, Sixpoint, Southern Tier, and Tröegs. They may even surprise you with some smaller, younger guys like Baltimore-Washington Beer Works (aka Raven) and Eastern Shore Brewing. 16 Mile and Twin Lakes make the list as well.

The soaring ceilings and stylish interior design of a former bank building make the restaurant a comfortable and enjoyable place to enjoy the F. Scott Fitzgerald and Ernest Hemingway inspired restaurant and bar.

The menu is split down the middle between the "Hemingway" and the "Fitzgerald Way" to reflect the difference in personalties of the two. The menu changes seasonally but some regular favorites include pulled pork tacos with pineapple relish, Thai curry mussels, the rabbit sausage grinder with broccoli rabe and spicy marinara, and pan-seared scallops with wild mushrooms.

Ernest & Scott is a sister establishment to Chelsea Tavern, barely a block away and across from the historic Grand Opera House. Either of these would make fine choices for a pre- or post-performance visit.

HOME GROWN CAFE

126 E. Main St., Newark, DE 19711; (302) 266-6993; homegrowncafe.com
Draft Beers: 13 **Bottled/Canned Beers:** Over 50

Home Grown started in 2000 as a T-shirt shop near the University of Delaware and has grown into local favorite for "vegan, vege, carnivore, and gluten-free lifestyles." Fans of great beer love to stop here as well.

Whether stopping in for a weeknight dinner or weekend brunch, customers find a spacious and comfortable atmosphere either indoors or on the front covered patio, plus a list of fine beers from which to choose. The bar's beer list includes local favorites like Dogfish Head, Fordham & Dominion, and Twin Lakes along side popular out-of-region breweries like Lagunitas and Sixpoint.

If your brunch more likely begins with a Bloody Mary, you'll be in luck with an excellently balanced one served up with a sultry sriracha punch. A beer or a bloody will go well with something like a BLT (served with an over-easy egg and aioli sauce), buffalo chicken and Belgian waffles, or a long lineup of omelettes made with eggs from nearby Powers Farm.

For the vegan lifestyle, there is no shortage of options on the menu with the likes of homemade vegan egg substitute, vegan sausage, tofu scramble, vegan cheese, and vegan bacon either in prepared dishes or available as substitute.

The beer goes down easily late night as well, often with live, local bands playing. Jazz comes to the microphone for easygoing Sundays. You dig?

JESSOP'S TAVERN

114 Delaware St., New Castle, DE 19720; (302) 322-6111; jessops-tavern.com; @Jessops_Tavern
Draft Beers: 18 **Bottled/Canned Beers:** Over 250

There are plenty of towns across the Eastern Seaboard of the US that ooze history at every turn in their colonial-era streets. One such example that might escape broader attention is New Castle.

A walk around the streets of this river town founded in 1640 serves up images of merchants and longshoremen going about their daily work. A place like Jessop's is where you might imagine finding them repairing after a day's hard work over a few grogs of beer. This historic section of town, during early colonial days, reportedly had more than 60 such establishments.

Jessop's sits on a property that dates to 1674, and in 1724 the property was home to Abraham Jessop's barrel-making business. The original, much smaller

building began its time as a restaurant in the mid-1900s and was expanded to its current footprint.

That history still lingers in the walls at Jessop's in its current incarnation under proprietor Justin Day. The owner since 1996, Day endeavors to serve up a bit of the old and the new, the Belgian and the Dutch together under one roof. For these efforts, they have received numerous "Best of Delaware" awards.

With staff dressed in colonial garb, Jessop's serves a beer list that skews more to the non-local end of the spectrum, and includes an impressive bottle list filled with over 250 Belgian beer varieties, available for both on- and off-premise consumption.

Taking up near-permanent residence on the draft tower are choices such as New Castle Brown, Jessop's Wheat (from Leinenkugel's), Hoegaarden, Gulden Draak, and, fittingly, the Yards Ales of the Revolution Series. All provide excellent dinner companions for a menu teeming with mussels, tavern steak, shepherd's pie, and baked crab imperial.

After such a feast, New Castle's streets and proximity to the water provide the perfect opportunity to walk off the dinner while taking in the city's colonial riverside charm.

TWO STONES PUB

2502 Foulk Rd., Wilmington, DE 19810; (302) 439-3231; twostonespub.com/main-W.php; @2StonesNaamans
Draft Beers: 24, plus one handpump **Bottled/Canned Beers:** Around 75
2 Chesmar Plaza, Newark, DE 19713; (302) 294-1890; twostonespub.com/main-N.php; @2StonesPub
Draft Beers: 24, plus one handpump **Bottled/Canned Beers:** Around 80
843 E. Baltimore Pike, Kennett Square, PA 19348; (610) 444-3940; twostonespub.com/main-K.php; @2StonesPub
Draft Beers: 20, plus one handpump **Bottled/Canned Beers:** Around 75

The staff and customers alike at Two Stones put their knowledge and love of great beer on display at any of the three locations. The original location in Newark sports a metal feel, Wilmington an industrial motif, and the newest location in Kennett Square, Pa. incorporates plenty of wood into the interior design.

No matter the interior design, the beer list is what brings the most praise to this multiple location beer business. Two Stones is big on great beer and brings focus to the locals doing it well like 3rd Wave, Dogfish Head, Evolution, Fordham & Dominion, Victory, and Yards.

To sweeten the deal, happy hour lasts for 3 hours on weekdays and allows the customer to pick from three beers for $3, or $5 wines, Dogfish Head-based cocktails, and light snacks.

A cheese board featuring two cheeses, cured meat, fig jam, and toast is a good deal as well for exploring the beauty of beer and cheese.

Two Stones does plenty of promotional events throughout the year from simple tastings to full-fledged dinners that showcase the staff's knowledge and passion for great beer.

ULYSSES GASTROPUB

1716 Marsh Rd., Wilmington, DE 19810; (302) 691-3456; ulyssesgastropub.com/ulysses
-gastropub; @UlyssesGastro
Draft Beers: 24 **Bottled/Canned Beers:** 150+

A bar whose chalkboard not only lists the ABV percentage of each beer, but also pays attention to details like the umlaut in Tröegs, the spelling and capitalization of Dogfish Head, and the apostrophe in He'Brew gets just a little extra beer credit.

The original founders of the Dead Presidents Pub in Wilmington and current owners of Six Paupers in Hockessin bring out this evident level of beer geekery at Ulysses in the tap handle decor lining the walls and bartender knowledge of specific beers and breweries.

Like nearby Two Stones Pub, there's obvious support of the local guys from established Dogfish Head, Stoudts, and Yards to the newer upstarts like 3rd Wave, Evil Genius, and Mispillion.

The open and square-shaped bar is conducive to socializing over beers and the dining rooms provide a comfortable space to sit down and enjoy a full dinner. On Tuesday, the deal gets even better when, with an entree purchase, wine and large-format beer bottles are marked down by 50 percent.

A menu that serves up hearty portions of beef, chicken, and pork dishes as well as "mussel pots" and chicken wings served a number of ways including a sriracha glaze and a "hellfire" sauce is sure to keep the hunger at bay while enjoying a night of beer at Ulysses.

As they like to say, "all craft, no crap." You'll, no doubt, agree.

WASHINGTON STREET ALE HOUSE

1206 N. Washington St., Wilmington, DE 19801; (302) 658-2537; wsalehouse.com
Draft Beers: 24

Even before you set foot inside the award-winning Washington Street Ale House, a free parking lot behind the restaurant is the first thing this downtown Wilmington establishment (est. 1997) has going for it. Inside, the typical bar scene reflects a customer base from all walks of life including sports enthusiasts, group parties, day laborers, and after-work professionals and hospital staff. Good thing the tap list is likewise large and diverse.

The Ale House was one of the first in the Wilmington area to pour a large and diverse lineup of beers, which today typically includes some local usual suspects from the likes of Dogfish Head, Stoudts, Tröegs, Twin Lakes, and Yards. From out of state, California heavyweights such as 21st Amendment, Bear Republic, Green Flash, and Sierra Nevada plus Allagash (ME), Schlafly (MO), and Sixpoint (NY) can often be found pouring from the taps.

When out on a beer excursion you'll find that the Ale House's kitchen provides plenty of belly-filling food including half-pound burgers (Kobe and chorizo meat loaf are two standouts), other sandwiches (a stellar Cubano, for example), and the typical bar lineup of fried delights, wings, fingers, and pretzels to ensure your beer drinking doesn't go down on an empty stomach.

WORLD CAFE LIVE
500 N. Market St., Wilmington, DE 19801; (302) 994-1400; queen.worldcafelive.com
Draft Beers: 8 **Bottled/Canned Beers:** Around 25
3025 Walnut St., Philadelphia, PA 19104; (215) 222-1400; philly.worldcafelive.com
Draft Beers: 11 **Bottled/Canned Beers:** Around 25

In addition to being impeccable music venues that have become must-stops in the region for primarily small and independent acts, both World Cafe locations also host numerous beer events throughout the year.

Full-fledged beer festivals, beer events with a musical tie-in, and food-and-beer-themed dinners and events routinely show up on the calendar at both locations. Both spaces include two performance stages and bars across two floors in which to enjoy good beer and music.

While World Cafe Live rolls out great beer for the unique events, the day-to-day draft selections are considered just adequate at both locations. The bottle selection is much more to the beer lover's interest and focuses largely on local craft breweries like 16 Mile, Dogfish Head, Evolution, Flying Dog, Flying Fish, Sly Fox, Stoudts, Tröegs, Victory, Weyerbacher, and Yards.

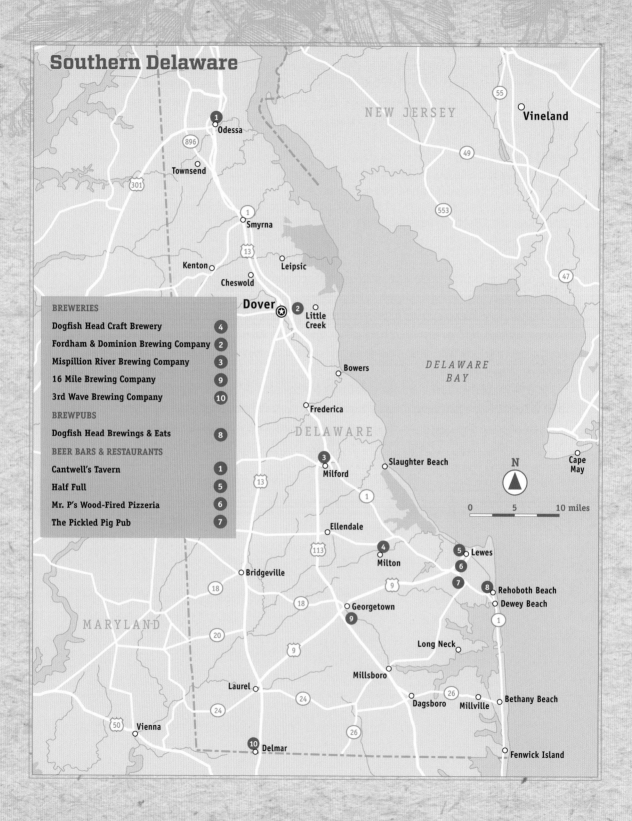

Southern Delaware

BREWERIES

Dogfish Head Craft Brewery	4
Fordham & Dominion Brewing Company	2
Mispillion River Brewing Company	3
16 Mile Brewing Company	9
3rd Wave Brewing Company	10

BREWPUBS

Dogfish Head Brewings & Eats	8

BEER BARS & RESTAURANTS

Cantwell's Tavern	1
Half Full	5
Mr. P's Wood-Fired Pizzeria	6
The Pickled Pig Pub	7

NEW JERSEY

Vineland

DELAWARE BAY

DELAWARE

MARYLAND

Cape May

N

0   5   10 miles

Odessa

Townsend

Smyrna

Kenton

Cheswold

Leipsic

Dover

Little Creek

Bowers

Frederica

Slaughter Beach

Milford

Ellendale

Milton

Lewes

Rehoboth Beach

Dewey Beach

Bridgeville

Georgetown

Long Neck

Millsboro

Laurel

Dagsboro

Millville

Bethany Beach

Vienna

Delmar

Fenwick Island

Southern Delaware

When I first learned of the Slower Lower Delaware moniker to describe the geographic territory of Delaware south of the C&D Canal, I learned that while some see it as a pejorative, most seem to embrace it. It's almost like a badge of honor worn to demonstrate pride in embracing life at a slower pace than that of nearby Wilmington, Newark, Philadelphia, and Baltimore.

If the overall pace of life seems slower in the mostly rural countryside and beach towns, don't think for a minute that the breweries and bars are slouching. What follows is a rundown of the breweries, brewpubs, bars, and restaurants that are representing beer well in the Slower Lower.

Breweries

DOGFISH HEAD CRAFT BREWERY

6 Cannery Village Center, Milton, DE 19968; (302) 684-1000; dogfish.com; @DogfishBeer
Founded: 2001 (production brewery in Milton) **Founder:** Sam Calagione **Brewer:** Tim
Hawn **Year-Round Beers:** 60 Minute IPA, 90 Minute IPA, Burton Baton, Indian Brown
Ale, Namaste, Midas Touch, Sixty-One, Tweason'ale, Palo Santo Marron **Seasonal Beers:**
Aprihop, Festina Peche, Piercing Pils, Punkin Ale **Tours:** Free tours, no reservations.
Includes four samples. Mon through Wed 11 a.m. to 4 p.m., Thurs 11 a.m. to 7:15 p.m.,
Fri and Sat 11 a.m. to 5 p.m. **Taproom:** Yes **Naming inspiration:** Named after the jut
of land in Maine where Sam spent summers growing up.

As the Dogfish Head brand (founded in 1995) nears its 20th anniversary and continues to grow by leaps and bounds, it is just as "off-centered" as always. Sam Calagione is just as energetic and charismatic as he was when he began with not much more than a homebrew kit.

This passion that started small in a cramped apartment now employs 180 equally passionate people (and some almost as appropriately "off-centered" as

Calagione) that have taken the belief in great-tasting, and typically unusual, beers to the masses. Going into 2015, Dogfish Head beers can be found in 30 states and Washington, DC.

The completion in 2013 of the $52 million expansion at the Milton headquarters, where they continue to add fermentation capacity, has taken them not only well past the 200,000-barrel output of 2013 (with plans in 5 years to at least double the current production output), but has expanded the tasting room and the retail shop, created a permanent parking spot for Bunyan's Lunchbox, and enhanced the overall experience for visitors who come from around the world to sample and socialize in the Dogfish Way.

Events at the brewery they are most proud of include the Weekend of Compelling Ales and Whatnot and Analog-A-Go-Go. The "Weekend" is filled with a staggering amount of beer (including many vintage-dated Dogfish beers), live music, and

Beer Lover's Pick

Indian Brown Ale
Style: American Brown Ale
ABV: 7.2%
Availability: Year-round; 12-ounce bottles

Dogfish Head brews so many beers across the flavor and style spectrum (and some that fall outside of traditional styles—the off-centered way!) that it's not easy to boil down the brewery's offerings to one recommended pick.

I'd love to feature the Festina Peche for its tart refreshing nature or the Palo Santo Marron for its big and rich flavors coming from the aging in the South American wood barrels or the Midas Touch for its equally Asian food–friendly and dessert-friendly qualities in the "Ancient Ales" series. Others swear by and eagerly anticipate the annual release of the Punkin Ale. The 60 Minute IPA is a staple in many a beer fan's cooler.

But, pin me down and I'll stick a claim here to Indian Brown Ale as the Beer Lover's Pick. This long-running beer that dates back to 1999 is a delight to drink on its own or with dinner next to a plate of barbecued meats.

food between both the brewery and the pub in Rehoboth Beach. Analog-a-Go-Go is a weekend of live music, record selling and swapping, and, of course, beer. Cask-conditioned beer is on display as well for this celebration of sound and suds.

The annual Dogfish Dash includes 5-K and 10-K options and has enabled the brewery to contribute more than $150,000 to the Nature Conservancy over the past few years. The race is extremely popular as it gives runners more than one reason to make the trip to Dogfish Head. At the conclusion of the race, medals are awarded personally by Calagione, and live music, food, beer (naturally), and fun 'n' games give participants and supporters a perfect Sunday morning at the brewery.

As Dogfish Head continues to grow in beer production, the accompanying experience promises to be as unusual as always. As long as the trip remains off-centered, the crowds will be sure to follow.

FORDHAM & DOMINION BREWING COMPANY

1284 McD Dr., Dover, DE 19901; (302) 678-4810; fordhamanddominion.com; @FoDoBrewing
Founded: lineage to 1989 **Founders:** Bill Mulhaueser (Fordham founder and current owner) and Jerry Bailey (Dominion founder) **Brewers:** Daniel Louder, Chris Gordon, Justin Colatrella **Flagship Beer:** Dominion Oak Barrel Stout and Fordham Copperhead **Year-Round Beers:** Dominion's Double D, Morning Glory, and Hop Mountain; Fordham's Gypsy Lager, Route 1 IPA, and Rams Head IPA **Tours:** Fri 4:30 and 6 p.m., Sat 11 a.m., 12, 1, 2, 3 p.m. **Taproom:** Yes **Naming Inspiration:** Old Dominion is Virginia's nickname and Fordham's name pays respect to the first man to brew beer in Maryland, Benjamin Fordham.

The old adage of the whole being greater than the sum of its parts certainly applies at the Fordham & Dominion Brewing Company in Dover. Since officially combining the two breweries under one roof in 2009, the company has continued brewing fan favorites from each of the respective brewery's pasts and introduced new beers to keep up with market demand of current times.

Take, for example, the **Dominion Oak Barrel Stout**, a favorite throughout the years that still drinks as smoothly as ever and, at 5.5% ABV, is a beer that helps bust the myth that all dark beers are high in alcohol. Another longtime favorite is the **Millenium Barleywine**, a beer that commemorated the brewery's 1,000th batch and, if a recent tasting of a 2000 vintage is any indication, is a 10% ABV beer that stands the test of time rather well. Judges too have taken notice, most recently awarding the **Candi Belgian Tripel** a gold medal at the 2014 World Beer Cup. Later in 2014, judges at the Great American Beer Festival sent the brewery home with a silver medal for its **Spiced Harvest** in the pumpkin beer category.

Dominion Oak Barrel Stout
Style: American sweet stout
ABV: 5.5%
Availability: Year-round; 12-ounce
    bottles

This beer is a reminder that color is neither a flavor nor an indication of strength. It's both a dark beer and a beer with oak barrel flavor that is low in alcohol. Double head turn for some, I know.

The brewery uses vanilla beans and oak chips to simulate the wood barrel and plenty of dark malts to bring out the roastiness. With a great taste and smooth finish, you'll probably want a few of these before the night is over.

Other relative newcomers in the brewery's portfolio are making a splash. The spring seasonal, **Cherry Blossom Lager**, is first and foremost a solid lager, albeit one that has the pleasant addition of 300 pounds of Michigan cherries to lend a refreshingly mild tart kick.

The **Double D IPA** is refreshing as well, just in a different way. When the time calls for a 9% ABV mouth-filling burst of tropical citrus hops, this is the Dominion brew to reach for. And, the **Fordham Doppelbock** is likewise a beer big on flavor, delivering the characteristic rich chocolate of a decent doppelbock.

The combined brewery had a capacity for 35,000 barrels of output at year-end 2013 and contract brews for the Easton-based **National Premium** brand (barely 2 percent of F&D's total output). Supporting the local community, the brewery hosts regular meetings of the Bottles & Pints Craft Beer and Homebrew Club and throws the annual celebration called R2Hop2, a festival of local food, beer, and music.

By the way, have kids with you when arriving at Fordham & Dominion? No worries, they can take the tour with you and hang around the tasting room as there are four all-natural sodas made on-site. Not a bad way to introduce kids to a healthy approach to beer consumption and education.

Southern Delaware

MISPILLION RIVER BREWING COMPANY

255 Mullet Run St., Milford, DE 19963; (302) 491-6623; mispillionriverbrewing.com; @Mispillion
Founded: 2013 **Founders:** Eric and Megan Williams
Brewer: Ryan Maloney **Flagship and Year-Round Beers:** Greenway IPA, Beach Bum Joe Belgian Pale Ale, Praetor Imperial Porter, and Double Chin Double IPA
Seasonals/Special Releases: too many to list in addition to the Single Hop Series, Once & Done Series, and Tasting Room Exclusives **Tours:** Sat 1 to 4 p.m. on the hour
Taproom: Yes **Naming Inspiration:** The Mispillion River separates Kent and Sussex Counties. Historically, Milford was a ship-building town, hence the sailing-ship logo.

Mispillion River is one of the newest breweries to take the small state of Delaware by storm. Located approximately 25 miles northwest from that other brewery that started even smaller and grew into a powerhouse, Mispillion River exploded on to the scene in November of 2013 with a reported 400+ people passing through its doors on opening day.

The brewery is located in a former metal shop and was renovated in less than 6 months. After clearing the regulatory hurdles with relative ease, they came out of the gate swinging with eight styles available on opening day and have kept the taps flowing with over 85 different beers brewed in less than 2 years since opening.

Supplementing the 15-barrel brewhouse is a 1-barrel system with converted freezers regulated for fermentation. The tasting room has always had 10 beers on tap since day one and aims to continue to do so.

In addition to the **Double Chin** discussed as the Beer Lover's Pick, the **Beach Bum Joe** and the **Greenway IPA** are sure to catch the beer lover's attention. The Beach Bum is a crisp and dry Belgian pale ale that works perfectly as a summertime beer picked up en route to the beach. The judges at the 2014 World Beer Cup agreed, awarding it a silver medal as an American-Belgo style.

A typical night in the tasting room is standing room only with beers continuously being passed across the bar and food brought in from local food trucks like Mr. Bar-B-Que. Two televisions are muted, card games are available at the tasting room tables, and occasionally live music plays from the corner of the room.

Double Chin
Style: Double IPA
ABV: 8.0%
Availability: Year-round; draft only

No one new craft beer on the Delaware beer scene seems to generate more enthusiasm than this double IPA from Mispillion River. Owner Eric Williams says this is his answer to the West Coast IPA. He pretty much nailed it.

There are spicy, floral, and earthy notes all bursting from this beer with 65 bittering units—which makes it just about the perfect beer to pair up with some smoked meats and barbecue from a food truck parked outside the brewery or your backyard smoker, whichever is closer.

Based upon the popularity of the tasting room and market demand, the brewery cannot slow down. Plans for 2015 include the addition of new fermenters in order to keep pace with a frantic and frequent brewing schedule. This will serve the brewery well as they look to grow into Pennsylvania and Maryland in 2015.

Southeastern Delaware may still look like it's dominated by one very large craft brewer, but times are changing and places like Mispillion River bring more options and more availability of great beer served in a great atmosphere.

Southern Delaware

16 MILE BREWING COMPANY

413 S. Bedford St., Georgetown, DE 19947; (302) 253-8816; 16milebrewery.com; @16Mile
Founded: 2009 **Founders:** Brett McCrea and Chad Campbell **Brewers:** Mike
Pfaffenhauser, Chad Campbell, Brett McCrea **Year-Round Beers/Flagship Beers:** Blues'
Golden Ale, Amber Sun Ale, Responders Ale, Tiller Brown Ale, Inlet IPA, Old Court Ale
Tours: Fri and Sat 12 to 3 p.m. on the hour **Taproom:** Yes **Naming Inspiration:** As the
centrally located county seat of Sussex County, Georgetown is 16 miles or less from the
border to any neighboring county and became known as being 16 miles from anywhere.

After opening in a 200-year-old farm building on an 8-acre piece of land and making a splash with their predominantly English-inspired beers (and many of the "session" strength), 16 Mile expanded in 2012. Not only did the brewhouse roughly double in size, but the expansion also brought a large new tasting room capable of handling large groups of "beer tourists" and private parties.

Two beers that are great introductions to what 16 Mile is up to are the **Tiller Brown** and **Old Court**. The former is a solidly built English Brown Ale full of rich malty flavors and a touch of burnt coffee and the latter is a pale ale with toasted bread notes and bright hoppy aroma.

16 Mile has its hands in many different projects and endeavors. The brewery has a line of collaborative beers with Yorkshire, England–based Copper Dragon, with whom they've released numerous beers in the Heraldry series, including **Battle of Waterloo** (with recipe references to Napoleon) and **1872 Licensing Ale** (a very well-made porter profiled as a Beer Lover's Pick) among others. The most recent was late last year called **The Soul Cake Ale**, an imperial amber with added cookie spices. For their combined efforts, the breweries were recognized as the Brewery Partnership of the Year at the 2014 International Beer Awards in Rome.

1872 Licensing Porter
Style: English Porter
ABV: 8.1%
Availability: Limited

Tiller Brown and Old Court are always available and extremely good representations of their respective styles. But keep an eye open for the Heraldry series discussed earlier.

The third in the series, 1872 Licensing Porter was a solid porter with roasted notes and a slight bit of chocolate. Even though the beer weighed in at 8.1%, the booziness was kept in check. Adding to its interesting back story, ingredients included Gilbey's gin, juniper berries, and a touch of sea salt. The deft balancing of the ingredients shone in the finished product of this great drinking porter with a nod to history.

The brewery likes experimenting and testing the boundaries of beer and food and has intriguing projects on the horizon to further explore the topic. In 2014, an Old Court-infused scrapple produced by Kirby & Holloway Provision Company in Harrington, Delaware, was made commercially available and went over quite well, as did a hops-infused coffee in conjunction with The Point Coffee House in Rehoboth Beach.

The Georgetown Fire Company Annual Oyster Eat is a point of significant pride for the brewery as they teamed with the local fire company in support of a great cause. After the firefighters took a liking to 16 Mile's beers, the **Responders Ale** became a part of the annual fire company fund-raiser and throughout the year a percentage of sales at the brewery goes to the National Fallen Firefighters.

Finally, in 2013, to supplement its continued growth, the brewery partnered with a restaurant group to open the 16 Mile Taphouse in Newark, in the downtown space that the legendary Stone Balloon live music venue used to call home. In addition to the brewery's own and guest beers, they offer a moderately priced food menu with interesting and varied selections such as salads, wings, and entrees. The Jamwich is a highlight on the menu and can either be a beef, chicken, or black bean burger topped with red pepper jam, blue cheese, lettuce, and tomato.

Plans back at the brewery have them adding more fermentation tanks into 2015 and beyond as continued growth dictates.

Southern Delaware

3RD WAVE BREWING COMPANY

501 N. Bi State Blvd., Delmar, DE 19940; (302) 907-0423; 3rdwavebrewingco.com; @3rdWaveBrewing

Founded: 2012 **Founders:** Lori L. Clough and Suellen Vickers **Brewers:** John Panasiewicz, Jerry Franklin **Year-Round/Flagship Beers:** ShoreBreak Pale Ale, 1st Wave IPA, Big Reef Porter, Bombora Double IPA **Seasonals/Special Releases:** Beach Juice Berliner Weisse, Frisco's Beach, and the Paddle Out Series (small batch) **Tours:** Sun 12:15 p.m. **Taproom:** Yes **Naming Inspiration:** In surfing parlance, the third wave in a set is the best to take.

3rd Wave Brewing Company provides a great reason to drive almost as far south in Delaware as any other brewery likely will ever sit.

The young brewery is located in a converted grocery store, the original location of Evolution Brewing Company, which moved on a few years ago to a larger facility just down the road and across the state line in Salisbury, MD. While 3rd Wave is still comparatively small, they have some adjoining properties that they purchased with plans to expand.

The 10-barrel brewhouse is manned with talent brought in from Iron Hill (Panasiewicz) and the local homebrew store, Xtreme Brewing (Franklin). The talent will come in handy as 3rd Wave continued its growth strategy in 2014 by adding a covered patio in the front parking lot and pushed its distribution into all remaining untapped counties in Maryland. In 2015, the brewery expects to add a bottling line, extend the loading dock, and, importantly, add a storage building.

In addition to solid year-round beers like the **1st Wave IPA** (see Beer Lover's Pick), the amped-up **Bombora Double IPA** (a more intense IPA experience), and **Shorebreak Pale Ale** (well-made pale ale capable of pleasing the masses), 3rd Wave dabbles in some seasonal beers that fans of the brewery hope to see on a regular basis.

The **Tennessee Wild** begins as a well-balanced brown ale with a wonderful spectrum of additional flavors contributed by toasted coconut, Madagascar vanilla beans, and six months of aging in sour mash whiskey barrels. Another popular offering is a seasonal that many hope will come around each mid to late winter. The release of **Irish Whiskey Stout** is synced up with St. Patrick's Day and is their Dawn Patrol (a coffee and cream stout; see the homebrew clone recipe in the BYOB: Brew Your Own Beer section) made with local Indian River Espresso & Coffee Company in nearby Millsboro and Jameson-soaked oak staves. A breakfast stout, anyone?

If, in surfing terms, the third wave is the best to catch, based upon their successful track record through the first wave, the future certainly looks bright for a long ride.

1st Wave IPA

Style: India Pale Ale

ABV: 6.2%

Availability: Year-round; draft only, bottles anticipated in future

Hopheads who appreciate an IPA that shows moderation in citrus, in bitterness, and in mouthfeel will find this a great example of a balanced IPA. 1st Wave can be a summertime thirst-quencher that will beg for growler refills before the day is over. The second growler fillup will go great on the picnic table with fish and vegetables coming off the grill.

Brewpubs

DOGFISH HEAD BREWINGS & EATS

320 Rehoboth Ave., Rehoboth Beach, DE 19971; (302) 226-2739; dogfish.com
Founded: 1995 **Founder:** Sam Calagione **Brewer:** Ben Potts

Before there was the super-sized, beer tourist destination 15 miles away in Milton, there was Rehoboth Beach. Remaining true to its roots, the Dogfish Head Brewings & Eats pub on the main strip in Rehoboth Beach is still in operation nearly 20 years after opening as an experimental lab of sorts. It's the kind of lab where seasoned brewer, Ben Potts, is able to brew up small 2-barrel batches of off-centered beers in keeping with the company philosophy and serve them up to a seemingly never-ending flow of vacationers and beer tourists.

These fun and interesting brews might be cooked up with wild carrot seeds, black garlic, spruce tips, wild mint tea, roasted chestnuts, or spotted dick. Yes, you can look up that last one; it was named *Just Richard*. And some go on to garner awards like in 2014 when Choc Lobster—concocted with Maine lobsters, dark cocoa powder, and basil—brought back a silver medal in the indigenous/regional beer category from the Great American Beer Festival.

The point is that the Dogfish pub is a fun place to go where you can certainly toss back one of a dozen or so production beers made up the road in Milton. Adding to the experience of sitting among the tap handles and company decor inside or casually alfresco on the outdoor patio, though, is the ability to drink a beer that will never be available outside the pub, one that changes your mind about what and how beer can be, or one before it goes into full year-round production. The latter has been the case for a handful of beers over the years including Noble Rot, Namaste, Palo Santo Marron, and Immort Ale.

If you're looking for a break from the beer side of the menu, you might also be interested to know that upstairs you can look in on the small distillation room from which a number of Dogfish Head spirits including rum, vodka, and gin are produced. The bottles are available for takeout or served as individual drinks at the bar.

As mentioned in the brewery's Milton profile, sitting still is not something Dogfish Head intends to do anytime soon. In addition to the recently completed major expansion at the brewery, a unique lodging experience called Dogfish Inn is now open in Lewes and a brewpub expansion into an adjoining available space is in the works for 2015. Change, but always in an off-centered manner.

Beer Bars & Restaurants

CANTWELL'S TAVERN

109 Main St., Odessa, DE 19730; (302) 376-0600; cantwells-tavern.com;
@CantwellsTavern
Draft Beers: 12 **Bottled/Canned Beers:** A vintage cellar with over 25 beers

The Northern Delaware chapter had its nod to history, and here in Southern Delaware another nostalgic trip to colonial times can be found in Odessa.

Cantwell's makes its residence in a building that dates back to 1822 and was home to Cantwell's Bridge Hotel and Tavern for nearly 100 years. The age of the property fits in amid this charmingly historic town, which was settled in 1662 and where other buildings display plaques and markers with years as early as 1700.

Inside Cantwell's, however, it's anything but old-fashioned. Numerous photographs and relics line the walls, but the menu smacks of modern-day flair.

At its relatively young age, Cantwell's has already developed a loyal following and is particularly popular for Sunday brunch. In addition to a MYO (make-your-own) Bloody Mary bar, the brunch food menu is full of quiches, burritos, omelettes, and a delectable 8-ounce "Breakfast Burger" topped with egg, scrapple, cheese, and hollandaise sauce.

On the beer side of the bar, the locals are represented well with Dogfish Head, Tröegs, and Yards making regular appearances alongside out-of-region favorites like Allagash, Green Flash, Lagunitas, Smuttynose, and Unibroue. Yards Love Stout matches up quite nicely with a selection of oysters off the raw bar. The restaurant hosts occasional beer events including brewery-focused dinners, and the quaint town provides a perfect setting for a post-dinner walk through history.

Cantwell's is owned by a group that also operates the equally historic Deer Park Tavern (established 1851) in Newark near the University of Delware and the popular McGlynns Pub in Newark and Dover. Both have a similar focus on serving great beer.

HALF FULL

113 W. Market St., Lewes, DE 19958; (302) 645-8877; halffulllewes.com
Draft Beers: None **Bottled/Canned Beers:** 10 to 15

A bar that leads with wine and no draft beer in a beer lover's book? In yet another historic Delaware waterfront, Half Full definitely belongs on the list. If you've arrived by way of the Lewes-Cape May ferry, it will be one of the first quality stops for a bite and a beer that you can make after disembarking.

The tempting pizzas gracing the menu beg to be ordered and paired with either a glass of wine or beer. Well-chosen wines they are, and some in your group may appreciate them. But, as the reader of this beer lover's book, you should know that although this place plays up the pizza and wine concept, they haven't forgotten the beer, with roughly a dozen bottles and cans of tasty beers available to accompany the pizzas.

Take the Dublin Pig and its toppings of slow-cooked pork, sliced apple, and balsamic drizzle. Then taste the North Coast Old Rasputin Stout and see if isn't one of the best examples of beer paired with food.

MR. P'S WOOD-FIRED PIZZERIA

1004 Kings Hwy., Lewes, DE 19958; (302) 645-1900; chrisandjenna.com/pizza
Draft Beers: 19, including 1 cask and 1 nitro **Bottled/Canned Beers:** 10

Continuing with the pizza and beer theme, on the outskirts of Lewes sits Mr. P's, a local favorite that has been turning out nearly 25 different pizzas since owner Rick Thomas reopened and imported an Ambrogi wood-fired oven in 2007.

Recognizing the public's rapidly expanding palate for different beers, Mr. P's took on 12 traditional CO2 lines and one handpump of many local beers and in 2014 added an additional five CO2 lines.

The beer list is typically split with around half the taps occupied by locals like 16 Mile, Dogfish Head, Fordham & Dominion, Evolution, and Mispillion River. A sign

hanging by the oven explaining in large print the beauty of cask-conditioned beer further evidences the love for great beer.

Pastas, subs, salads, and appetizers round out a menu at this casual roadside stop that makes it a year-round favorite for both locals and vacationers.

THE PICKLED PIG PUB
18756 Coastal Hwy., Rehoboth Beach, DE 19971; (302) 645-5444; pickledpigpub.com; @PickledPigPub
Draft Beers: 14 **Bottled/Canned Beers:** 50

The lively and friendly atmosphere at The Pickled Pig makes it a perfect respite from the seemingly endless glut of surrounding outlet shopping or a beer-and-a-bite pit stop when heading either in or out of downtown Rehoboth Beach, just a few miles down the road.

The pub goes to great lengths to showcase local beers from Delaware and Maryland like 16 Mile, Dogfish Head, Eastern Shore, Mispillion, and Twin Lakes. The cheese board is sure to satisfy all the non-lactose-intolerants at the bar. Playing up the beer-and-cheese pairing concept, the Chef's Cheese Board fits the bill, complete with eight cheeses, fig jam, cured meat, candied walnuts, and toasted baguette pieces.

For the hungry beer-seeker, the bacon jam and blue burger (blue cheese, bacon shallot jam, and red onion), the spicy Thai drunken noodle dish, and the warm pretzel turkey sandwich (shaved turkey with red onion and cranberry cream cheese on a toasted pretzel roll) make perfect beer-drinking companions.

If you spend your summers in Rehoboth Beach, the Pickled Pig could certainly become one of your regular hangouts. With frequent beer tastings and pairing dinners, and a Pub Club (more beer, less to pay) to boot, this is a top-five beer experience in the Rehoboth Beach area.

Management also runs the popular Pig + Fish in the heart of Rehoboth Beach where you can "eat like a pig and drink like a fish." The food menu there is dominated by pork and seafood as the name suggests and a small, but well-crafted draft list of a dozen beers including nearby Dogfish Head and Evolution and out-of-state favorites like Jolly Pumpkin, Dieu de Ciel, Schlafly, and Weyerbacher.

Between the two spots, take your pick or pick both. You can't lose.

Rehoboth Beach—Pub Crawl

Rehoboth Beach is a beach town; therefore it should be of little surprise that it's a highly walkable town—one with plenty of great options for eating and drinking along the way.

Your pub crawl around Rehoboth Beach is so conducive to walking, you will even have time to browse the endless retail shops, take off your flip-flops to walk along the surf, and maybe even catch a few winks to help get you through the rest of your pub crawl. Surf's up, pints up!

TOTAL WALKING DISTANCE: 1.5 miles (or 1.0 mile if you don't take the extended boardwalk option)

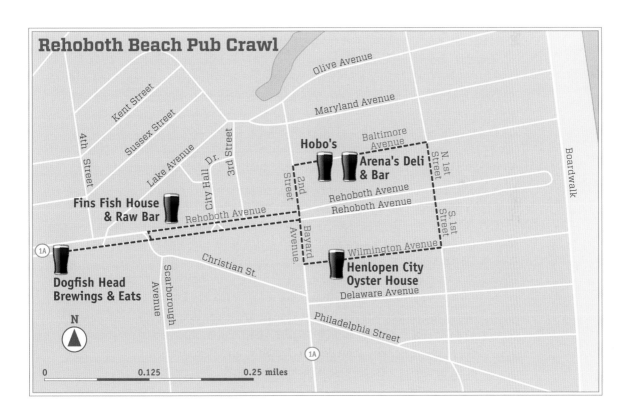

Directions: You barely need a road map to find Hobo's. Simply look up while strolling the main drag in town—Rehoboth Avenue—and spot the water tower. Hobo's is on Baltimore Avenue, which runs parallel to Rehoboth one block to the north, and just a stone's throw from the water tower.

Hobo's Restaurant + Bar, 56 Baltimore Ave., Rehoboth Beach, DE 19971; (302) 226-2226; myhobos.com

Start your day with brunch at Hobo's, where proprietor Gretchen Hanson (see her recipe contribution in the In the Kitchen section) has been serving up great vegan fare that is interesting for even the most fervent carnivore. And the carnivore side of the menu is good enough to get vegans thinking twice about their dietary restrictions.

Local beers from 16 Mile, Dogfish Head, and Evolution are available most of the time to enjoy on the comfortable front patio, where the street scene is not too distracting on this relatively quiet side street away from the busyness of Rehoboth Avenue. The food menu is organized into Nibbles and Noshes (small plates), Flat (quesadillas), Leafy (salads), Wet (soup), Starters, and Sandwiches and Wraps.

Popular and recommended dishes, most with varying combinations of local, ethically conscious, and organic inspiration, include crab beignets with crab and brie dip, wild mushroom quesadilla with brie and truffle oil, Blue Hill lobster sandwich with fresh arugula and red pepper cream, and Rehoboth Girlfriend roasted eggplant sandwich with tapenade and peppers. The menu is always subject to change, as should be expected, with the seasonality of available ingredients.

Your pub crawl could end here with several more beers while lounging on the front porch. But you have some work to do, so settle the check and vow to come back for a full dinner on another day.

Directions: Take a left off Hobo's front porch, turn left on 2nd street, walk one block to cross over Rehoboth Avenue, and proceed barely four blocks to arrive at the Dogfish Head pub.

Dogfish Head Brewings & Eats, 320 Rehoboth Ave., Rehoboth Beach, DE 19971; (302) 226-2739; dogfish.com

Many of the production beers from the Dogfish Head brewery in Milton are available at the pub. While many reading this book likely have ready access to much of Dogfish Head's production portfolio of beers, it would be a mistake not to take up pub brewmaster, Ben Potts, on his handful of very interesting (and, naturally, very off-centered) beers made behind the bar on the pub's 2-barrel system.

Although there's no telling what creative concoctions may come out of Potts's brewhouse next, you can bet they'll be bursting with both flavor and creativity. Earlier in 2014, a collaboration with Florida's small, but exciting and growing, Funky Buddha was called Nano-Nano and presented a full flavored beer thanks to the deft blending of grilled habañeros, sea salt, and chocolate in a 7.6% ABV porter.

If you need a light bite from the menu, look for a spent-grain soft pretzel, Namaste chile calamari (with a Namaste and Thai basil glaze), or a cup of crab and corn chowder. For something equally tasty but more substantial, try the short rib cheese fries, lamb sliders, or one of the house-made pizzas.

Directions: After Dogfish Head, you'll be a few beers into your pub crawl at this point, so be a good pedestrian and cross to the other side of Rehoboth Avenue at the nearest allowable intersection. From DFH, you'll only need to walk approximately ¹⁄₁₀ mile back toward the ocean once you've crossed the street.

Fins Fish House & Raw Bar, 243 Rehoboth Ave., Rehoboth Beach, DE 19971; (302) 226-3467; finsrawbar.com; @RawBar
Fins to the left! Or, if you're coming from the direction of Dogfish Head, Fins to the right. A bit of Jimmy Buffett lyrics knowledge comes in handy being in Rehoboth Beach, so hopefully that reference was not too obscure.

Any of the stops on this pub crawl are worthy of becoming an enjoyable lunch or dinner spot. Fins is no exception—sporting a menu replete with fresh fish fillets, shellfish, and other fish-centric entrees. If you do find yourself with a hankering for a small plate of food, the tempting appetizer menu will present you with solid options like bruschetta and shrimp and crawfish spring rolls to tide you over until dinner.

Saddle up to the bar and get set up with a fine beer. It seems there's always something enticing available from the out-of-state Schlafly Brewery or regional favorites like Flying Dog and Evolution.

Directions: Before heading off to dinner at the Henlopen City Oyster House, depending upon the time of day, you might like to head a few blocks east to walk along the boardwalk and surf. You could stop back at your place, clean up, maybe even catch a few winks. If you head directly from Fins, go left out the front door, a short walk east on Rehoboth Avenue to take a right on Bayard Avenue, and then one block to turn left on to Wilmington Avenue and the front door of Henlopen City Oyster House.

Henlopen City Oyster House, 50 Wilmington Ave., Rehoboth Beach, DE 19971; (302) 260-9193; hcoysterhouse.com; @HCOysterHouse

In its short history, Henlopen City Oyster House has developed much attention and praise for both its kitchen and beer selection.

Executive Chef Bill Clifton's food menu presents plenty of ocean goodness from bouillabaisse, grilled scallops, and a lobster roll to at least 8 varieties of oysters on the raw bar that makes this the perfect place to sit down for a dinner after a solid day of sampling the best beer Rehoboth Beach has to offer.

The beer menu is no slouch either, carefully arranged to present options of draft beers, bottles, cans, and "big bottles to share." Depending upon the current selection of around 50 bottles and 9 draft lines (including one cask-conditioned), among the typical lineup of locals you could spot are far-flung stellar brews from De Halve Maan, De La Senne, Dieu Du Ciel, Fantome, or Mikkeller.

It will be easy to fill up here on a satisfyingly appropriate beach town dinner and a couple of excellent beers. Save room, though, for that one last beer at your final stop of the evening.

Directions: You could head directly to the last stop, Arena's, which is just around the block from the Oyster House. However, if you didn't get in some board walking earlier, you could take the opportunity now to walk off dinner by heading toward the ocean, turning left, and walking the boards until coming back down to street level at Baltimore Avenue. Then walk west until you reach Arena's between 1st and 2nd Streets.

Arena's, 149 Rehoboth Ave., Rehoboth Beach, DE 19971; (302) 227-1272; arenas deli.com; @ArenasDeli

After dinner, if you're looking for one last place to kick back, it's tough to go wrong at Arena's. Now with seven locations (the most recent opening in Newark in 2014), this is the 25-plus-year-old original and perhaps the most relaxed of them all.

Tucked away off Rehoboth Avenue in the middle of the block, the feeling of a beachside getaway pervades. With the requisite surfboard and beach theme, you'll find a beer list showing off 21st Amendment, Crabbie's, Goose Island, Malheur, New Belgium, Oskar Blues, Samuel Smith, and Uinta in a pretension-free zone. In the beer menu section of the chalkboard cordoned off for locals, 16 Mile, Evolution, and Twin Lakes are often found taking up tap handles putting local and fresh beer front and center.

If somehow after this pub crawl, which presented so many great food options along the way, you still find yourself hungry, Arena's is a great place for a soup and salad or sandwich.

Baltimore

BREWERIES

19 Heavy Seas Beer
5 Peabody Heights Brewery
2 Union Craft Brewing Company

BREWPUBS

6 The Brewer's Art
9 Dempsey's Brew Pub & Restaurant
10 Pratt Street Ale House (Oliver Brewing Company)
20 Red Brick Station (White Marsh Brewing Company)

BEER BARS & RESTAURANTS

8 Alewife
17 Annabel Lee Tavern
3 Birroteca
4 Golden West Cafe
11 Heavy Seas Alehouse
15 Hudson Street Stackhouse
16 Mahaffey's Pub
12 Max's Taphouse
18 Of Love & Regret Pub & Provisions
7 The Owl Bar
14 Smaltimore
13 The Wharf Rat
1 Woodberry Kitchen

Baltimore

Baltimore, like Philadelphia, is steeped in brewing history. It's the new scene, however, that is grabbing ahold of the city in both old and new neighborhoods, from touristy downtown and Inner Harbor to the no-nonsense neighborhoods.

The city is fairly walkable and has some decent transportation options to help get you around to some of the farther-flung neighborhoods. Grab your camera, take some tours, and then get out there—hon—and belly up to the bar.

Breweries

HEAVY SEAS BEER

4615 Hollins Ferry Rd., Halethorpe, MD 21227; (410) 247-7822; hsbeer.com; @HeavySeasBeer

Founded: 1995 **Founder:** Hugh Sisson **Brewers:** Chris Leonard (Brewmaster/Operations Manager), Chris Schultz (Brewing Team Lead), John Eugeni (Production Manager), and a team of 7 others **Flagship Beer:** Loose Cannon IPA **Year-Round Beers:** Gold Ale, Powder Monkey Pale Ale, Cutlass Amber Lager, Small Craft Warning Uber Pils, Peg Leg Stout **Seasonals/Special Releases:** Black Cannon, Riptide, Red Sky at Night, Winter Storm, and the Uncharted Waters series **Tours:** Most Sats 11 a.m., 12:30, 2, and 3:30 p.m. Open to all ages. For $5, the tour includes a souvenir pint glass and five beer samples. **Taproom:** Yes **Naming Inspiration:** The brewery's original Clipper City name commemorated Baltimore's role in designing and building the first clipper ship. When looking for a new name to reflect a "higher gravity brand, Heavy Seas seemed a good segue from Clipper City."

To help bring a bit of balance to the brewery side of this chapter, it's a bit of cheat to include Heavy Seas in the Baltimore chapter as the brewery technically resides just outside the southern city line in Halethorpe.

The history of Heavy Seas does have actual roots in Baltimore proper (Federal Hill) and begins all the way back in 1989 when owner Hugh Sisson first launched into the beer-making world at his family-run Sisson's Restaurant & Brewery. Those early years led him to the opening of Clipper City Brewing Company in 1995, which later was rebranded Heavy Seas, and established him as one of Maryland's brewing pioneers and leading voices of the past 25 years.

The Heavy Seas Tap Room (updated and rebuilt in early 2014) is a fairly large and comfortable room and typically presents tastes of all year-round beers as well as some limited releases and a few cask-conditioned offerings. Samples, as well as full pours at regular price, are available of the 10 beers typically on tap—8 on draft and 2 on the handpump.

Beer Lover's Pick

Loose Cannon
Style: India pale ale
ABV: 7.25%
Availability: Year-round; 12-ounce bottles
The Loose Cannon is a well-balanced IPA, even with an American kick at 7.25% ABV, that goes down easily, replete with citrus and pine notes from the Simcoe hops.

Heavy Seas stakes its claim as the largest producer of cask beer in US and you may find it around town "custom-hopped" for retailers' special events. When at the Tap Room, I was fortunate to encounter a delicious version with an extra dose of Amarillo hops and pear wood.

The Loose Cannon is a great beer to begin with; the fun things the brewery does with the beer in firkins can go in any number of rewarding ways. Given the sturdiness and full flavor of this beer, on the table it can work well with a big gumbo or spicy chicken wings.

Baltimore

A good place to start is with the **Gold Ale** (4.5% ABV), a bronze medal winner at the 2014 Great American Beer Festival, that awakens your palate with an ever-so-slight hop aroma and crisp and refreshing finish.

Move on to a sample of **Cutlass Amber Lager** (5.25% ABV), formerly known simply as Märzen, which is an easy-drinking, smooth lager with pleasant toasted malts. Great American Beer Festival judges have bestowed a medal in 5 consecutive years, making it the brewery's most award-winning beer.

The **Peg Leg Imperial Stout** (8% ABV) is a great beer to drink any time of the year in my opinion. It's a smooth and surprisingly easy-drinking beer, particularly if you like notes of coffee, chocolate, and hops intermingled in a big malty beer.

For extracurriculars, the brewery hosts the annual Beer & Oyster Festival, Real Ale & BBQ Festival, Burgers & Brews Festival, Beer & Bacon Festival, and Chili & Cheese Festival. Off-site, a Heavy Seas Alehouse can be found in Baltimore (plus a new one in Rosslyn, VA); see Beer Bars & Restaurants section in this chapter.

PEABODY HEIGHTS BREWERY

401 E. 30th St., Baltimore, MD 21218; (410) 467-7837; peabodyheightsbrewery.com; @PeabodyHeights

Founded: 2012 **Founders:** Stephen Demzcuk, J. Hollis B. Albert III, and Patrick Beille **Brewer:** Ernie Igot **Contracted Beers:** Baltimore-Washington Beer Works, Full Tilt, and Public Works Ale brands and select distribution packages for Fin City, Monument City, Mountain State **Tours:** Seasonally or by appointment **Taproom:** In conjunction with tour dates **Naming Inspiration:** The brewery is located in the Charles Village neighborhood, which previously had been called Peabody Heights.

Full Tilt Camden Cream
Style: Cream Ale
ABV: 4.8%
Availability: Year-round; 12-ounce bottles

Many beers flow through the tanks at Peabody and one that has been nicely timed and is catching on with the market has been the Camden Cream from Full Tilt. As the baseball on the label suggests, this is a great beer—a crisp, lager-like beer with a slight floral aroma and citrus hop note that goes down smoothly like a well-made cream ale—that can carry you through a baseball game or whatever activities the spring and summer months throw at you.

Peabody Heights has a growing reputation as a solid contract brewery primarily for Full Tilt, Public Works, and Baltimore-Washington Beer Works (aka the Raven Beer). Full Tilt is showing up most in the market with its **Camden Cream** (4.8% ABV) and **Baltimore Pale Ale** (6.3% ABV). Baltimore-Washington Beer Works sends the **Pendulum Pilsner** (4.5% ABV) and **Tell Tale Heart IPA** (7.25% ABV) around the region. Public Works gets some exposure with its **Red Cent Amber** (5.25% ABV).

All of these have diversity in styles that the brewers at Peabody Heights have demonstrated they can handle in production quite well. In addition to these three significant relationships, the brewery has also done work with Fin City, Monument City, and Mountain State for their distribution products.

UNION CRAFT BREWING COMPANY

1700 Union Ave., Baltimore, MD 21211; (410) 467-0290; unioncraftbrewing.com;
@UnionBrewing
Opened: 2012 **Founders:** Kevin Blodger, Adam Benesch, and Jon Zerivitz **Brewer:** Kevin Blodger **Year-Round Beers:** Anthem Golden Ale, Balt Alt Altbier, Blackwing Lager, and Duckpin Pale Ale **Seasonals/Special Releases:** Foxy Red IPA, Old Pro Gose, and Snow Pants Oatmeal Stout **Tours:** Sat 1:30, 2:30, and 3:30 p.m.; Free **Taproom:** Yes **Naming Inspiration:** A reference to how beer is "the union of water, barley, hops, and yeast."

Since opening the city's first production brewery in over 30 years, Union has been winning fans at every turn in the beer-loving city and creating quite a buzz along the Jones Falls River, straddling the burgeoning Hampden and Woodberry neighborhoods.

For those not familiar with these neighborhoods, they are situated around the large city park—Druid Hill—that contains the Maryland Zoo, a disc golf course, and the Rawlings Conservatory & Botanical Gardens.

The brewery's large sign is visible from I-83 and the parking lot is ample. The Jones Falls Trail is a recreational path (city streets in certain sections) that provides a scenic bicycling trip to the brewery. There is yet a third way to conveniently arrive at Union Craft: The Hunt Valley/BWI Marshall Airport light rail line makes a stop at the Woodberry Station a mere 308 feet away.

Once inside the brewery's tasting room, order some beers and learn what all the fuss is about. The **Perfecta Pils** (5.4% ABV) is a wonderfully refreshing way to begin

Balt Alt

Style: Altbier

ABV: 5.6%

Availability: Year-round; 12-ounce cans

Awards: Great American Beer Festival (Gold, 2012); World Beer Cup (Bronze, 2014)

At Union Craft, the copper-colored Balt Alt is an extraordinary melding of rich malts, even a touch smoky with noticeable, but not obtrusive, hop bitterness. It comes together as a very well-balanced altbier that works well on the dinner table with German bratwursts.

Maybe it's the translation of the word Alt ("old") from German that gives brewers or consumers a hang-up with this underappreciated style, but don't let that get in your way of trying this excellent beer.

a visit to the brewery, while sitting outside by the food truck. The beer has a pleasant crispness, making it easy to drink with just a touch of fruit sweetness. **Duckpin Pale Ale** (5.5% ABV) takes a solid pale ale and gives it a good dose of in-your-face citrus hops flavor.

Wintertime in Baltimore usually calls for snow pants to dig out cars and shovel sidewalks. Union has its own **Snow Pants Oatmeal Stout** (8% ABV) in a glass. If you're visiting the brewery at the right time of year, this smooth, chocolate, and roasty beer balanced with a good dose of piney hop flavor can be found on draft in its original form and also in aged form from Heaven Hill bourbon barrels. Summertime visiting, however, should have you reaching for the 2014 silver medal–winning **Old Pro Gose** (4.2% ABV), an excellently tart example of the German style.

Union Craft has certainly upped the city's brewing game in its first couple of years. Their beers can be found at most bars with credible craft beer lists around the city, but time spent at the brewery drinking at the source is time well spent.

Baltimore

Brewpubs

THE BREWER'S ART

1106 N. Charles St., Baltimore, MD 21201; (410) 547-6925; thebrewersart.com; @BrewersArt

Founded: 1996 **Founder:** Volker Stewart **Brewer:** Steve Frasier **Year-Round Beers:** Beazly Belgian Strong, Birdhouse Pale, and Resurrection Abbey Brown **Seasonals/ Special Releases:** Charm City Sour Cherry, La Pétroleuse, Tiny Tim, Le Canard, Green Peppercorn Tripel, Haymarket, and many others

Brewer's Art has been around since 1996 and has been a destination for both fans of great beer and foodies for much of its history. Parking can be tough in this popular, mostly residential, neighborhood, so keep in mind the nearby Metro station (State Center) and Amtrak's Penn Station. As a point of reference, the Metro would hook you up quite nicely with the beginning of the Baltimore Pub Crawl at Alewife, described at the end of this chapter.

Set inside a classic townhome/mansion in the Mt. Vernon neighborhood, for a casual night on the town, people-watching out the large front windows is a relaxing way to socialize and imbibe.

Those looking for a meal will find the dining room is not-quite-casual but not-really-formal. The menu presents diners with options spanning the more expected like striped bass and steak frites to the more unusual, like stuffed quail, steamed cockles, and rockfish tartare.

Dishes like these have the beer-and-food-pairing mind creating interesting combinations. Take the **Tiny Tim** (5% ABV) as one example whose hibiscus petals and rosemary pairs nicely with a fish dish like the rainbow trout. The **Green Peppercorn Tripel**, a smooth and slightly spicy Belgian tripel (9% ABV), has what it takes to stand alongside the meaty lamb osso buco. Finally, the rich dessert menu bursts with fruit and chocolate sweetness and **Le Canard** is just the superbly malty beer (8.5% ABV) to work well with a selection such as the pecan and almond tart with chocolate drizzle or the *tres leches* with strawberries.

For the late-night crowd, there may not be a more perfect hangout than the pub's subterranean lair. Getting into a great Belgian strong ale like the slightly boozy **Beazly** (a 7.25% golden colored beer formerly known as Ozzy), the rich and slightly sweet **Resurrection**, or the **Birdhouse Pale** (using one of the more recent rock-star hops, Citra) over conversation in the hip hideaway is a perfect place to do just that.

DEMPSEY'S BREW PUB & RESTAURANT

Oriole Park at Camden Yards, 333 W. Camden St., Baltimore, MD 21201; (410) 843-7901; dempseysbaltimore.com; @DempseysBrewPub
Founded: 2012 **Founder:** Delaware North Sportservice **Partner:** Baltimore Orioles
Brewer: James DeQuattro **Year-Round Beers:** Rain Delay IPA, Rick's Red Ale, The '83 Golden Ale, and Wild Pitch Wheat **Naming Inspiration:** Orioles catcher Rick Dempsey who played with the team from 1976-1986

Catcher Rick Dempsey played on the World Series–winning Orioles team of 1983. I wasn't there but am betting that there were no craft, or "micro" if you prefer, beers served at stadium concessions during the championship season.

Dempsey now has his name on the restaurant and brewpub that turns out a handful of beers made just a foul ball's bounce down the first base line. Over the years, the selection has improved around the ballpark to now include area beers from the likes of Dogfish Head, Evolution, Flying Dog, Fordham & Dominion, and Heavy Seas. For a full sit-down meal during any given game or non-game day, Dempsey's offers a dining experience among photographs and memorabilia from across the years of Orioles history.

A few dozen bottled beers, including a Maryland-only section, are available in addition to the Dempsey-inspired beers. An insider's tip will tell you that game day prices are more than double non-game day prices.

First up on the beer list is the **'83 Golden Ale** (4.8% ABV). My 1983 Phillies bias aside, this is an easy-drinking beer that will have you sitting back nice and easy awaiting the next pitch. The **Wild Pitch Wheat** (4.9% ABV) may not be so far and outside, but it's got a refreshing orange kick to it that goes nicely alongside a baby arugula salad with honey port vinaigrette dressing, Danish blue cheese, toasted pecans, sliced pear, and craisins.

The **Rick's Red Ale** (5% ABV) has a bit more malt backbone to

it and will have you taking a swing at the grilled three cheese and tomato sandwich. Finally, the **Rain Delay IPA** (5.2% ABV) has a firm malt balance to the slight bitterness that works very well with the soft-shell crab sandwich (when in season, of course) and the Dempsey's fish tacos with jalapeños and red pepper aioli.

PRATT STREET ALE HOUSE (OLIVER BREWING COMPANY)

206 W. Pratt St., Baltimore, MD 21201; (410) 244-8900; prattstreetalehouse.com; @PrattStAleHouse

Founded: Oliver Brewing Company in 1993; Pratt Street Ale House in 2008 **Founders:** Bill Oliver of Oliver Brewing Company 1993-2008; current owner Justin Dvorkin **Brewer:** Stephen Jones **Year-Round Beers:** 3 Lions Ale, Blonde, Dark Horse, Draft Punk, Ironman Pale Ale, Modern Life Is Rubbish, Sea of Spears **Seasonals/Special Releases:** Cherry Blossom, King Of The Night Time World, Winters Wolves

The abridged history lesson here goes something like: 1) Wharf Rat has had two locations, one at its current Fells Point address and one previously where Pratt Street Ale House now resides; 2) Bill Oliver still runs the Wharf Rat in Fells Point, but no longer the Oliver Brewing Company, which he founded over 20 years ago; 3) Justin Dvorkin opened the Pratt Street Ale House in 2008 when he purchased and

took over the space and, along with it, Oliver Brewing Company; 4) the future for Oliver holds potentially great things as the new, greatly expanded production facility should be open on Shannon Drive in the eastern side of the city with the capacity to at least double production by the time this book hits the shelves.

Fortunately, the beer does not take as much explanation. Fans of English-style beers will be pleased when visiting the bustling Pratt Street Ale House (particularly on game days for the Baltimore Orioles) and taking in its well-made Oliver Ales. On any given day, most of the beers on tap are brewed by Oliver, including five hand-pumps. The remaining are guest brewery taps that could be pouring anything from Stillwater Artisanal to Jailbreak to Unibroue or Left Hand.

The Oliver "session" beers that garner the most deserved attention include the **Best Bitter**, a classic weighing in at 4.8%, **Dark Horse**, an extremely nice English mild at 4%, and the **ESB**, big on flavor and admittedly stretching the "sessionability" term a bit at 6%.

While the more sessionable and English side of the spectrum is well represented, the brewery hasn't forgotten about those who like to immerse themselves in bigger flavors and bigger aroma. Try a **3 Lions Brown** (an Americanized English Brown Ale at 7.5%) or **Draft Punk** (an American IPA pulling no punches at 7%) for just such a treat.

The kitchen turns out equally pleasing food to accompany the fine beers on tap. It seems only appropriate, but also a wise decision, to order a fish-and-chips plate of beer-battered haddock. A shrimp po' boy sandwich (marinated in Cajun cream and served with an Old Bay tartar sauce) and the Pratt pear salad (with dried cranberries, candied pecans, Gorgonzola cheese, pears, and grilled chicken) also make worthy beer-pairing companions for an all-around solid session at the pub.

Whether heading to an Orioles game or pub hopping around Baltimore (see recommended Pub Crawl stop #3 at the end of this chapter), Pratt Street Ale House is a required destination for great atmosphere, beer, and food.

Chesapeake Real Ale Festival

One of the mid-Atlantic's significant cask ale festivals is held at Pratt Street Ale House. The festival features a handful of house-made Oliver beers as well as a few dozen other local and regional firkins.

The event is an afternoon of beer, food, and live music on Pratt Street and is sponsored by the Society for the Preservation of Beers from the Wood—SPBW, for short—the UK-based organization that endeavors to promote their traditional serving format of beer.

RED BRICK STATION (WHITE MARSH BREWING COMPANY)

8149 Honeygo Blvd., White Marsh, MD 21236; (410) 931-7827; redbrickstation.com; @RedBrickStation

Founded: 1997 **Founders:** Bill Blocher and Tony Meoli **Brewers:** Michael McDonald, Pat Coffman, and David Thompson **Year-Round Beers:** Daily Crisis IPA, Avenue Ale, Honeygo Light, Something Red, and Spooner's Stout **Naming Inspiration:** The LLC name fits the local theme of the White Marsh neighborhood and Red Brick Station reflects the buildings in the community and is meant to evoke a small-town feeling.

Since I cheated a bit by including Heavy Seas in the Baltimore chapter, Red Brick Station likewise sits just outside the city border in Baltimore County and will be included here as well.

In the bustling town center of White Marsh, Red Brick Station has been a model of consistency over the years. A component to the success is head brewer McDonald, who has been with the company since day one, brewing on the 14-barrel Peter Austin open fermentation system.

The **Avenue Ale** (4.1% ABV), a clean and crisp golden ale, gets a visit to Red Brick started rather nicely and goes quite well with the locally recognized beer battered fish-and-chips. **Something Red** (5% ABV) is a sturdy, malty beer capable of working well with any of the burgers, particularly the Kona Burger, 100% Angus beef seasoned with "special spices" and topped with pineapple.

No beer, however, may be hitting the mark better than the **Daily Crisis IPA** (6.1% ABV). It's no crisis at all when this malty English-leaning IPA joins the dinner table alongside either the crispy fried chicken–topped mac-n-cheese or the Prince Edward Island beer mussels that have their own spicy kick from jalapeños and garlic.

From the firehouse-themed design of the restaurant and bar to the fresh and local beer and food menus, it's obvious the degree to which Red Brick Station has integrated itself within the community. Fans of the Baltimore Ravens will know that Red Brick Station's designation as "Ravens Roost #52" suggests that the bar is a very popular place to watch the football game. For guests staying at one of the local hotels, the free town center trolley provides convenient service. Every town center should be so lucky.

The town of Abingdon—just north a bit off I-95—is about to become lucky as Red Brick Station plans to unveil a new location. Future guests of the new location will be impressed with the 10,000 square feet of dining and drinking space that intends to capitalize on the success of the White Marsh location.

Beer Bars & Restaurants

ALEWIFE

21 N. Eutaw St., Baltimore, MD 21201; (410) 545-5112;
alewifebaltimore.com; @AlewifeBaltimor
Draft Beers: 40 **Bottled/Canned Beers:** Approximately 100

Alewife occupies a former bank building at the corner of Eutaw and Fayette and puts the space to comfortable use. The restaurant is spread across two floors and multiple rooms, where walls are filled with colorful and eclectic artwork. The energetic bar sits prominently inside the entrance with large people-watching windows fronting the room.

The attention to detail on the draft list is evident with a handful of locals and a bevy of out-of-towners spanning the style spectrum. Brewer's Art and Heavy Seas might be two obvious local examples; to newcomers, Raven and Full Tilt maybe not so much, but still equally local and befitting a good Baltimore beer list. From farther afield, Drie Fonteinen, Dupont, and Mikkeller are known to make occasional showings on the well-developed draft list.

In addition to the food menu items mentioned later in the Pub Crawl section of the chapter, Thai peanut wings with cilantro sriracha (how about a Dogfish Head Indian Brown?) and a black bean burger (thinking: Full Tilt Baltimore Pale Ale) provide interesting variety on the menu. The blue catfish tacos in particular, pulled from the Potomac River served with chimichurri-chipotle cabbage slaw, present themselves nicely, particularly with the aforementioned Saison Dupont.

Alewife occasionally hosts special events like special releases and themed tap takeovers, but excels at presenting great food and beer in a comfortable setting with great service on a daily basis.

ANNABEL LEE TAVERN

601 S. Clinton St., Baltimore, MD 21224; (410) 522-2929; annabelleetavern.com;
@AnnabelLeeMD
Draft Beers: 4 **Bottled/Canned Beers:** Around 20

Ask around Baltimore about cultural touchstones and anything from the Chesapeake Bay to "hon" to Natty Boh to the Colts leaving town might come up. Chances are good that Edgar Allan Poe will as well. Poe spent time living around the country, Baltimore being one place for a few years, and he died there mysteriously in 1849.

After working as general manager at The Brewer's Art, Kurt Bragunier opened the Annabel Lee Tavern in 2007 in the Canton neighborhood. It exists in a building that dates to 1905 and was named after the last work Poe penned prior to his untimely death at the age of 40.

The tavern exudes Poe in its dark and brooding manner. Yet it's approachable, comfortable, and friendly in nature making it one of the most unusual pub experiences in the city—and quite possibly the hidden gem in the whole of this Baltimore list.

It's not as if the locals don't know. This tavern is equally popular for its beer, wine, and cocktails at the bar as it is for its creatively solid kitchen turning out interesting plates of food like Southern-style meat loaf and roasted duck breast. Several vegetarian options, like a spinach and portobello burrito and mango vegetable curry, are available as is a daily rotating set of at least a half-dozen specials.

Fans of long draft lists may be disappointed with just four taps, though Brewer's Art Resurrection is a dependable resident on the draft tower. The bottle list, however, is where the pub shines with a modest, but well-chosen, selection of beers spanning from Saison Dupont and Tripel Karmeliet to Union Blackwing Lager, Blue Mountain Über Pils, and Left Hand Nitro Milk Stout.

To quote from two of Poe's works: at this little "kingdom by the sea," ". . . what care I how time advances? I am drinking ale today." You should as well.

BIRROTECA
1520 Clipper Rd., Baltimore, MD 21211; (443) 708-1934; bmorebirroteca.com; @BmoreBirroteca
Draft Beers: 24 **Bottled/Canned Beers:** Approximately 30

To find Birroteca is to know Baltimore's old mill corridor, where the beer-centric bar and restaurant now resides in a building that dates back to 1883. This definitely is not downtown or Fells Point or any other similar city-like neighborhood.

The drive from downtown takes nearly 15 minutes and wraps you scenically around the prominently situated Amtrak station, past the neighborhoods of Mt. Vernon and Charles Village, and upon arrival lands you along the Jones Falls River in the shadow of I-83.

Inside, plenty of original stonework shows off the building's history. The large square bar seats approximately 25, a small outdoor area provides an alfresco option, and multiple dining rooms across two floors are tastefully decorated to provide a comfortable atmosphere.

Birroteca and its bar manager, Nick Ramey, have put a great deal of effort into creating a beer program that has a heavy focus on breweries of the mid-Atlantic region with the likes of Brewer's Art, Burley Oak, Evolution, Flying Dog, Heavy Seas, and Union. With the help of Chef Melanie Molinaro, the restaurant has been conducting fun and educational dinners around both beer and wine, in addition to pint nights, whiskey classes, and special beer releases.

The food menu features a staggering number of mouthwatering pizzas like the Duck Duck Goose (duck confit, fig-onion jam, and duck egg) and Cipolla (pancetta marmalata and roasted Vidalia). Not to be outdone by the pizzas, the pasta menu will help those beers along as well. A wide noodle dish like pappardelle with wild boar Bolognese and pecorino or golden beet ravioli with goat cheese and spiced pistachios will fit the bill quite nicely.

With all of these pieces in place in such a short period of time, it should not be much surprise that the *Baltimore Sun* named it a Top Bar in 2013 and Top Restaurant in 2014. The success of Birroteca has helped spawn sister establishment, Nickel Tap House, in November 2013 just a few miles up the road in one of Baltimore's last neighborhoods to the north—Mt. Washington—with a similar concept and dedication to interesting beer and food.

GOLDEN WEST CAFE
1105 West 36th St., Baltimore, MD 21211; (410) 889-8891; goldenwestcafe.com; @GoldenWestCafe
Draft Beers: 15

Here is yet another entry promoting great breakfast or brunch, with a solid bar menu that includes great beer.

Located in the Hampden neighborhood, Golden West moved into its current location over 10 years ago. The move allowed them to flourish and grow into what they are today. The menu shows that location and diversity are important to Golden West. Local, all-natural, free-range eggs are used and every section of the menu has vegan options.

Evident from the crowds that stream through the door on Saturday and Sunday morning, it's a fun place to go with the family and friends. The dining room is spacious and has room for three window tables, perfect for people-watching.

At the bar, Irish coffees, mimosas, and Bloody Marys are poured seemingly without pause. The beers get attention too and are sure to cover locals like Baltimore-Washington Beer Works, Brewer's Art, Flying Dog, Heavy Seas, and Union while stellar out-of-town guests on the draft tower often include the likes of Allagash, Boulevard, and Yards.

The brunch menu is full of delectable items spanning the sweet to the savory. Be careful of the eyes-are-bigger-than-the-stomach syndrome here. The zucchini brie pancake is a scallion and zucchini flapjack topped with brie and house-made honey butter and goes great with a Boulevard Tank 7.

El Guapo serves up chorizo, jack cheese, and scrambled eggs on a ciabatta roll with hash browns and is perfect with a Yards Brawler. Lox Stock & Bagel is a "deconstructed" case of smoked salmon, tomato, onion, cucumber, greens, cracked pepper, capers, hard-boiled eggs, and cream cheese and is served masterfully with an Allagash White on the side.

The strawberry rhubarb french toast calls for a Union Anthem Golden. And the Hangover Burger—served with bacon, jack cheese, guacamole, and a sunny-side-up egg—gets you ready for an afternoon nap when paired with Flying Dog Gonzo Porter. Oh my.

Breakfast (and beer): Because it's the most important meal, and drink, of the day.

HEAVY SEAS ALEHOUSE
1300 Bank St., Baltimore, MD 21231; (410) 753-1403; heavyseasalehouse.com; @HeavySeasAleHse
Draft Beers: 8 **Bottled/Canned Beers:** 25

If you've visited the brewery (profiled in the Breweries section of this chapter), you've tasted the fresh variety of year-round beers and perhaps a few seasonals. In Fells Point, technically Little Italy by a block or two, get further immersed in a Heavy Seas experience with a decor in keeping with the brewery's image.

As in many cities of the Eastern Seaboard, the Alehouse's neighborhood is steeped in history. Heavy Seas is located inside the old Holland Tack Factory, which called the location home for over 90 years. Holland fasteners were found in every-

thing from major league baseballs to school bulletin boards and sofas, and during the Civil War, the building served as a hospital for Confederate soldiers.

A restaurant group that works closely with the brewery to promote the Heavy Seas brand runs the Alehouse. It's exemplified in the motto "where great beer meets great food."

The Alehouse provides a decent setting to learn more about the intersection of beer and food. Off the small-plates menu, the grilled sausage sliders are made with the brewery's Über Pils and Old Bay seasoning and go perfectly with the same beer. Likewise, the Peg Leg Stout used in the 8-ounce Bank Street Burger with smoked cheddar cheese provides the perfect accompaniment in a glass.

The schooling continues with the full lineup of available beers from Heavy Seas, and the Alehouse conducts events to showcase them on a weekly basis. One extra-special event worth noting is the biannual Guest Chef Dinner to which chefs come from around the country to help raise money for the Ulman Cancer Fund for Young Adults.

HUDSON STREET STACKHOUSE

2626 Hudson St., Baltimore, MD 21224; (410) 342-0592; hudsonstreetstackhouse.com; @HSStackHouse
Draft Beers: 36 **Bottled/Canned Beers:** 150+

Fittingly located across the street from the smokestack of the old American Can Company, Hudson Street Stackhouse is a high-quality neighborhood joint in the popular Canton neighborhood and sports a perfectly comfortable feel with exposed brick walls, backed up by friendly and efficient service at the bar.

The Stackhouse loves its locals and Burley Oak, DC Brau, Flying Dog, and Union can often be found on tap among a bevy of Belgians both from the bottle and on tap. Adding to the comfort level is the happy hour, which knocks $2 off every draft beer and runs conveniently long from opening until 7 p.m. on weekdays and until 5 p.m. on Saturday and Sunday. Thursday night after 11 p.m., all Belgian drafts are likewise reduced by $2.

To help with all the great beer, the kitchen serves up some of the meatiest and tastiest wings around. Beyond the appetizer menu, the list of burgers is sure to tempt with ten locally sourced half-pound Black Angus offerings, including a Bay Burger topped with homemade crab dip for a taste of the region. "The Dom" sandwich is served on a Milano roll and stuffed with prosciutto, capicola, and fresh mozzarella,

and is tough to turn down. From the pizza oven, there's an excellent Hornario's Hot and Spicy, which mounds taco-seasoned ground beef, mozzarella cheese, and hot sauce atop a piece of flatbread.

Locals have it pretty good in the Canton section of Baltimore.

MAHAFFEY'S PUB

2706 Dillon St., Baltimore, MD 21224; (410) 276-9899; mahaffeyspub.us; @MahaffeysPub
Draft Beers: 20, plus two cask handpumps **Bottled/Canned Beers:** Around 90

Every city has its share of neighborhood joints that are integral to the community. Mahaffey's is one of Baltimore's. It's a long narrow bar pouring great beer and telling great stories of friends and good times. It's one of those places where the local neighborhood feel is strong, but outsiders are not turned away.

It's also home to some of the best food and beer prices in town. Most food selections come in under $10 and are great deals for items like a 10-ounce Angus burger, a Caribbean jerk chicken sandwich, or a super-sized BLT that contains a whopping half-pound of bacon.

Mahaffey's also puts the happy face on happy hour pricing. With generous hours that cover 3 p.m. until 7 p.m. and on Monday until close, the happy hour deal for all to enjoy is three 10-ounce beers for $6. That is not a misprint.

Sunday at Mahaffey's tends to be more of a locals day than any other and you'll likely see more of the 100 Beer Club members toting their mugs and relaxing with friends. Customers get credit for each of 100 unique beers consumed and on their birthday get their name on the beer list for the day.

Just a bunch of small ways that add up to big fun, and sometimes big savings, at the Canton neighborhood bar.

MAX'S TAPHOUSE

737 S. Broadway, Baltimore, MD 21231; (410) 675-6297; maxs.com; @MaxsTaphouse
Draft Beers: 103, including five handpumps **Bottled/Canned Beers:** Roughly 2,000

Not unlike other Fells Point establishments, Max's building has a long history as a bar near the port and reportedly has ghosts that inhabit the building.

Current owners took over the property in 1986 and have, over time, turned a total of five properties into what Max's Taphouse is today. It was named after owner Ronald Furman's grandfather.

Most employees have at least 10 years under their belts. It pays off in terms of both front and back of the house operations. Cellarman and GM Casey Hard is well known and respected throughout the industry. By tasting every beer that comes through the establishment, he can keep both staff and consumers on their toes and informed about the many hundreds of beers available both in draft and bottle format.

It's not happenstance that even the seemingly simplest piece of brewery or alcohol-related swag gets turned into artwork. Much of the place's design and its sometimes eclectic artwork comes from so much that they receive and don't discard. Max's envisions opening up space currently closed off to customers as something almost like a breweriana museum, potentially with parts of the collection for sale.

Jason Hard and Jason Scheerer keep the draft hardware in good shape and the complex gas system flowing to push the beers properly out to the customers. Bob Simko has been day bartending for nearly 20 years and has a knack for names, even of relative strangers, and the beers they like to drink.

So, what about those beers, you ask? The draft and bottle counts listed above tell the story. Ask for just about any local beer or any beer imported to the state and chances are very good that Max's carries it in some form.

Ones that have near-permanent residence on the tap towers include Delirium Tremens and La Chouffe, both served through a custom beer tower from Belgium. Other fan favorites regularly available include Allagash White, Flying Dog Double Dog on nitrogen, Heavy Seas Loose Cannon, Hofbräu Hefeweizen, Lindemans Framboise, Steigl Lager, and Union Duckpin.

The Taphouse remodeled the side bar in 2011 and christened the new version "Notre Passion," serving mostly Belgian and Belgian-styled beers. They claim to be "bringing a new look to Max's almost daily" and the statement does not seem far off the mark.

Max's hosts a major event almost every month and brings attention to a style of beer or an

origin of beer that goes beyond the simple tap takeover. As would be expected with the recent explosion in demand for Belgian and sour beers, the annual Belgian extravaganza in February is now capped by an all-sour day to end the 4-day event.

Getting into the food side of things here is something like the beer experience at Max's; it's nearly impossible to list in succinct format the many ways they find to impress. On a menu stuffed with sandwiches, flats, wraps, quesadillas, tacos, pretzels, nachos and other assorted pub grub, the Tater Bowl (tater tots topped with pulled pork, jack cheese, sour cream, and bacon), Eastern Shore sliders (crab sliders with a creole aioli sauce), mussels (particularly with the bacon and Irish stout cream sauce), and the fried pickles (dill and sea salt chips with chipotle aioli) temptingly rise to the top.

It's evident that not only the beers and food are special to the business, but the employees and customers are as well. It is all part of what makes Max's a beer lover's destination.

OF LOVE & REGRET PUB & PROVISIONS
1028 S. Conkling St., Baltimore, MD 21224; (410) 327-0760; ofloveandregret.com; @ofLoveandRegret
Draft Beers: 23 **Bottled/Canned Beers:** Around 60

Where can the popular gypsy Stillwater Artisanal brews from Brian Strumke be found usually more often than anywhere else? If anywhere in Baltimore, it will be at his Of Love & Regret (OLAR) on Brewers Hill across from the old Natty Boh (National Bohemian, if you prefer) facility at the eastern edge of the equally popular Canton neighborhood.

It didn't take long after OLAR's unveiling in 2012 for fans of the Stillwater Artisanal lineup of beers to discover this gem away from the more compact and congested areas of downtown, Fells Point, and Federal Hill.

As a gypsy brewer, there really is not a singular brewing location to tie all of the Stillwater beers together. At OLAR, Stillwater beers find their way onto more than half of the taps, making it the perfect beer bar for fans of the gypsy brewer to find obscure, limited-production beers that can rarely be found anywhere else. For example, collaborations with Mikkeller, DC Brau, Oxbow, and Hof Ten Dormaal are just a few that have been known to flow from OLAR's taps.

Non-Stillwater taps that show up could range from a few miles away (a special seasonal from Dog Brewing or a cider from Millstone Cellars) to a few thousand miles away (La Baladin from Italy, Freigeist from Germany, or Trois Dames from Switzerland).

Cellar Door, Stateside Saison, and Why Can't IBU are three of Stillwater's most popular and are most regularly found on the draft menu. Generally speaking, which is always a dangerous thing to do when talking of a brewer like Strumke and his beers, Stillwater's beers tend to gravitate to the middle of the road alcohol-wise, averaging around 6.5%, and favoring saisons influenced heavily by yeast that turns out highly aromatic and flavorful beers. It should be mentioned that the 23rd tap handle is a brew by Stillwater as well; however, it's an iced coffee that's described as a "dark French roast from High Grounds, cold brewed on French oak, and addictive."

In the kitchen, with Keith Curley at the helm, there is no shortage of tempting bites of food to accompany the well-made beers that scream out for pairing. (See Curley's contribution in the In the Kitchen section later in the book on the topic of beer and food.) The menu is split between smaller plates and more substantial dishes like crab cakes, flatiron steak, ravioli, burgers, and brisket.

The vegetable banh mi burrito is one entree that pops off the menu with its array of ingredients including black beans, ginger, Asian slaw, sriracha sweet chile aioli, basil, and cilantro that make it work perfectly with a beer such as Cellar Door or the Of Love and Regret.

One attention-grabbing small plate that stands out if you only have time for one is the grilled dates stuffed with goat cheese and pecans. The dates are wrapped in speck and served with honey mustard. Think about pairing this tasty plate of food with As Follows or Existent, both of which carry a richer, maltier base and a higher alcohol level that works quite nicely with the big flavors coming off the plate.

When it comes time for leaving, OLAR/Stillwater can go along for the ride. The second floor "Provisions" shop stocks a decent amount of beer and related accoutrements for takeaway. If on a schedule, be sure not to be ensared in "The Jaded Lounge" upstairs bar, which serves up its own beer menu, draft cocktails, draft spirits, and a few beer-and-a-shot specials. Don't say you haven't been warned that leaving Of Love & Regret is difficult.

THE OWL BAR

1 E. Chase St., Baltimore, MD 21202; (410) 347-0888; theowlbar.com; @OwlBar
Draft Beers: 20

Large East Coast cities are no strangers to history. Around the corner from The Brewer's Art sits what was formerly The Belvedere Hotel (today a mix of condominiums and office space) where inside resides the legendary Owl Bar. The hotel dates back to 1903 and has kept the original bar top, floors, walls, booths, and some of the stained glass.

The naming of the bar refers to the statues of owls at the bar whose eyes, during Prohibition, would blink to indicate that alcohol was on premise and being served. Today, with a belief that the best beers come from the United States, the bar stocks a draft list that is predominantly from the US and many from the local region.

The kitchen serves up what passes for very good food, a notch above standard for the typical pub. Standouts include the duck-fat fries and Mini Crabbies on the appetizer menu and the crab dip pizza, ahi tuna BLT, and Umami Burger with truffle garlic aioli from elsewhere on the wide-ranging menu.

For a more upscale experience from the management team behind The Owl Bar, take the elevator to The 13th Floor, where the dining and views are equal in grandeur and a smaller but well-chosen list of beers can be found.

It's no longer a secret and there is no need for decoding the owl's eyes. The Owl Bar is a must-stop classic when in Baltimore.

SMALTIMORE

2522 Fait Ave., Baltimore, MD 21224; (410) 522-1421; smaltimorebaltimore.com; @SmaltimoreMD
Draft Beers: 48

Smaltimore burst onto the local bar scene in mid-2013 and quickly made a name for itself with a large, mostly Maryland-themed, beer menu, a rollicking sports bar atmosphere, and a friendly nature among both the staff and the customers.

The one unique feature that also turned heads was the installation of the Drink Exchange system, whereby beer prices fluctuate with demand. A ticker board keeps track of current price and daily highs and lows. Therefore, perhaps on certain game days, it's not inconceivable to find, say, a Natty Boh priced higher than a Jailbreak, Stillwater, or Heavy Seas.

Customers are drawn not only for the beer and sports at Smaltimore, but for the food as well. It's not exactly the most common food menu that juxtaposes burgers, tater tots, wings, and mac 'n' cheese with sushi, but they pull it off, and dining guests appear to appreciate it.

THE WHARF RAT

801 S. Ann St., Baltimore, MD 21231; (410) 276-8304; thewharfrat.com; @WharfRatFells
Draft Beers: 20, plus 4 handpumps

The waterfront Fells Point neighborhood oozes charm around every corner as well as history that dates to the 18th century. History for the current tenants, the Oliver family, of 801 S. Ann St. dates to 1987.

History buffs will enjoy visiting for a meal and a few drinks to learn about how certain sections of the building, and its ghosts, can be traced to the late 18th century. According to owner Jennifer Oliver Martin, after fires in 1795 and 1835 destroyed many wood buildings in the neighborhood, it is believed at that point the property's exterior was lined with brick. Inside, the floors trace roots to Pennsylvania Dutch barn walls circa 1850.

Before you get too wrapped up in the history and storytelling, grab a beer. The Wharf Rat serves up a wide range of beers across its 20 taps and 4 handpumps. The passionate beer advocates within ownership and management claim to taste, rate, and plan the draft beer menu roughly 2 months in advance allowing, of course, for the unannounced arrival of anything special.

Several local breweries, like Heavy Seas, Oliver, Union, and Red Brick Station can be found on tap from time to time. However, it's the relationship with Yards Brewing that is special to the pub. In addition to the regular availability of IPA, Love Stout, and selections from the Ales of the Revolution series from the Philadelphia-based brewery, the ESA is the only beer to have permanent residency on the tap tower at The Wharf Rat.

Out of the kitchen, to accompany these fine beers, are solid plates of food like lump crab and artichoke pizza, fish-and-chips (orange roughy), and mini burgers. A bit more unusual, not to mention tasty, is an interesting twist on the soft pretzel by stuffing it with crab meat and topping it with a cheese blend.

For fans of a cozy atmosphere, friendly service, neighborhood vibe, the ability to choose from 4 handpumps of cask-conditioned beer, and food served with a good dose of history and ghost stories on the side, The Wharf Rat is the perfect place to hang out in Fells Point.

WOODBERRY KITCHEN

2010 Clipper Park Rd., Baltimore, MD 21211; (410) 464-8000; woodberrykitchen.com; @WKRestaurant
Draft Beers: 8

We've been down the road to Hampden a couple of times already in this chapter. Here is one last entry to round out the neighborhood. Birroteca, Golden West Cafe, and Union Craft Brewery all reside nearby. Nepenthe Homebrew is also just a stone's throw away.

Woodberry Kitchen is highly touted for its kitchen, as well it should be. The open-air kitchen is on display for all to see in this comfortable and tastefully designed two-floor restaurant space.

The kitchen loves its locally sourced ingredients like the Cape May dayboat scallops, Tilghman Island crab cakes, local farm vegetables, and Lancaster County chickens. The resulting presentation and flavors come through masterfully and reflect a high attention to detail.

They also maintain an acceptable beer list to accompany the stellar food. As with the locally and freshly sourced ingredients, the beer list changes to provide

a wide variety of flavors to match up to the diverse food menu. Think dark malts in nearby Frey's Dark Rye, a spicy and floral display from Ommegang's Fleur de Houblon, a soft and fruity wheat from Jailbreak's Blackberry Wheat, and a flavorful and slightly bitter brew in the Raven Tell Tale Heart IPA.

The flatbread menu makes for a great opportunity for matching up the likes of a croque monsieur flatbread (ham, cheddar, and mustard cream) with Victory's Prima Pils and a sausage/red onion/mustard cream flatbread with a Freys Dark Rye. They also keep a small selection of local ciders and meads, which likewise are growing in popularity.

Come for the food and the atmosphere and the beer certainly follows at this great example of bringing the two together for the best possible outcome.

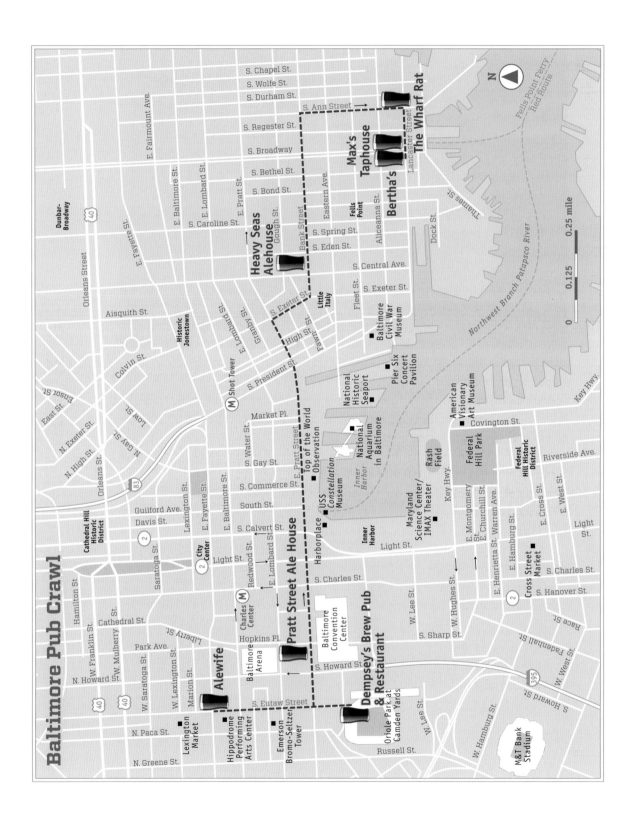

Baltimore Pub Crawl

Baltimore—Pub Crawl

The Baltimore pub crawl takes advantage of the highly walkable streets and visually appealing scenery along the way. If the stretch from the Inner Harbor over to Fells Point poses too much of a challenge, there's a free shuttle called the Charm City Circulator that runs different downtown routes and can easily pick up and transport you free of charge between the two destinations.

TOTAL WALKING DISTANCE: 2.50 miles
FERRY COST: $7 one-way; $12 all-day
CIRCULATOR BUS: Free

Directions: To get things started in Baltimore, find your way to Alewife, north of Camden Yards and the Inner Harbor where there are plenty of parking garages. Alternatively, the bar is just a couple of blocks from a number of light rail and subway stations.

Alewife, 21 N. Eutaw St., Baltimore, MD 21201; (410) 545-5112; alewifebaltimore .com; @AlewifeBaltimor

Alewife makes sense as the first stop on this downtown-based pub crawl. For starters, it's very close to public transportation, which is a convenient mode of transportation around the often busy city streets.

As with any good prolonged pub crawl session, the first stop or two should have a dose of food included. At Alewife, the beer lover's suggestion will steer you in the direction of the Smoke Burger, an 11-ounce local beef blend topped with applewood smoked bacon and smoked Gouda, gruyère, and chipotle aioli, all perfectly nested inside a brioche bun. Did someone also say duck-fat fries?

The beer you'll want to chase this with might be something from local Flying Dog, Brewer's Art, or the Full Tilt Baltimore Pale Ale, made at Peabody Heights Brewery on the north side of town. This 6.8% piney, hop-forward beer is a very nice crisp beer that stands up well to and complements this, dare I say, epic burger.

Directions: The walk to Dempsey's will burn off a couple ABVs and calories. Turn left from the front door of Alewife, head south for 4–5 blocks. Cross over Camden Street to enter the stadium complex and Dempsey's. Game or no game, Dempsey's will be open.

Dempsey's Brew Pub & Restaurant, 333 W. Camden St., Baltimore, MD 21201; (410) 843-7901; dempseysbaltimore.com; @DempseysBrewPub

Recall the point I made earlier about game day versus non-game day prices at Dempsey's; don't shoot the messenger. Also, if it's within 3 hours of game time, you can only enter Dempsey's with a ticket to the game. So, do plan carefully.

When at the bar, the best way to experience Dempsey's is typically with a flight of their four beers and then, if time permits, a full pour of your favorite. The experience is heightened if you happen to be an Orioles fan, or perhaps just a baseball fan in general. Walk around the restaurant checking out the memorabilia on the walls and taking peeks into the playing field area.

Directions: Pratt Street Ale House is but a two-block walk by leaving Dempsey's and turning right on Pratt Street. Before you know it, you'll be sipping on Oliver Ales.

Pratt Street Ale House, 206 W. Pratt St., Baltimore, MD 21201; (410) 244-8900; prattstreetalehouse.com; @PrattStAleHouse

Pratt Street Ale House serves up a combination of house Oliver beers as well as five guest taps on average. The real stars here are the cask-conditioned ales. Choose from one of the four handpumps and go all session-out with something along the lines of a Back to Basix (2.8% ABV) or Dark Horse (4% ABV).

Fear not high alcohol lovers, these beers deliver on the flavor. Each of these puts the hallmark English malts, hops, and yeast on full display and should serve as a good way to mix up the pub crawl here on the third stop.

Directions: Baltimore is quite walkable, so don't let this 1.1-mile walk deter you from spending the extra 20 minutes. You could take either a taxicab, the free Charm City Circulator, or a water taxi, but you would miss the scenery of the USS Constellation, the National Aquarium, and the Shot Tower along the way. Turn left from Pratt Street's front door and head east for just under a mile on Pratt Street. Make a right on South Exeter Street, a left on Bank Street, and you'll arrive at Heavy Seas Alehouse.

Heavy Seas Alehouse, 1300 Bank St., Baltimore, MD 21231; (410) 753-1403; heavy seasalehouse.com; @HeavySeasAleHse

Located inside the old industrial Tack Factory building, the restaurant group that runs the restaurant showcases all of the Heavy Seas beers from the taps to the food menu and even to the cocktails.

Opt for the proprietary Loose Cannon IPA cask offering at this stop on the pub crawl. If you haven't caught on to beer cocktails yet, this could be the place to do it. The Sea Shandy adds blueberry-mint lemonade to the Gold Ale for a refreshing twist on one of the brewery's standard beers. The Cannon Fuse is equally enjoyable where the Loose Cannon serves as the base to which hop vodka is added along with house-made ginger syrup and fresh lemon. Enjoy, but behave, or they might make you walk the plank.

Directions: Make a left out of Heavy Seas' front door. Head east for just under a half mile on Bank Street into the heart of Fells Point. Turn right on South Ann Street and walk four blocks. The Wharf Rat sits at the corner of South Ann and Lancaster Streets.

The Wharf Rat, 801 S. Ann St., Baltimore, MD 21231; (410) 276-8304; thewharfrat .com; @wharfratfells

At the Wharf Rat, cozy and cask is the name of the game. The handpumps are occupied by cask-conditioned ales from the likes of Heavy Seas, Yards, Raven/Baltimore-Washington Beer Works, to name a few.

The ceilings are low, the twinkle lights are strung, and the conversation is pleasant. Perfect for gathering around a table with your pub-crawling constituents to plan the rest of the evening.

Directions: Head out the front door and walk a bit more than a tenth of a mile west on Lancaster Street—resist the urge to stop at Max's quite yet—Bertha's will be directly in front of you at the intersection of South Broadway.

Bertha's, 734 S. Broadway, Baltimore, MD 21231; (410) 327-5795; berthas.com; @EatBerthas

It's difficult to miss Bertha's. From the Broadway Market (est. 1786) across the street, the signs simply say "Bertha's" or "Bertha's Bar." From closer to the water taxi landing, a large green wall screams out "Eat Bertha's Mussels." When you know that the bar is serving up a few different Heavy Seas, it's worth a quick stop on this pub crawl to have yet one more Heavy Seas beer that you'd previously not.

If the timing is right, you may luck out and find the Heavy Seas Powder Monkey on the handpump. It's an English-style pale ale that presents itself beautifully on cask and, at Bertha's, it's on a private label called Bertha's Best Bitter. That now, in case you've tired of my fondness for "real ale," is my last cask recommendation on this pub crawl.

Directions: Walk out Bertha's front door. Look directly east toward the direction you came in. Max's is barely 100 average-person strides across the street from Bertha's.

Max's Taphouse, 737 S. Broadway, Baltimore, MD 21231; (410) 675-6297; maxs.com; @MaxsTaphouse

If all you previously knew about Baltimore's beer scene was Max's, you can't be judged too harshly for that. They've been doing what they do with great beer for quite some time. The reason the Pub Crawl ends, and does not begin, here is because if you began here, you might never make it to the rest of the places on the itinerary.

Not to take anything at all away from the other stops on this tour. Max's, though, is so overwhelming in its presentation of beer across the board and serves it up with a variety of standard and not-so-standard pub options.

Check out a couple of locals off the beer menu like Burley Oak 'Merica or DuClaw Neon Gypsy and be sure to stop at the Belgian bar in the smaller adjoining room to the main downstairs bar. There you will find whatever suits your need at this point of the night—a low-alcohol beauty like Thirez Extra (4.5%) or the barrel-aged Alvinne Melchior Monbazillac, which weighs in at a hefty 11.5%.

Directions: How are you getting home? If you parked downtown or took the train, walking may not be your first option after a day of drinking and walking. Ideally, you might be staying in a nearby hotel room. Taxis are plentiful in Fells Point and can get you back downtown, as can the water taxi, which could provide a scenic end, with hopefully no choppy waters, to your pub crawl.

The Rest of Maryland

Annapolis (inset)

BREWERIES

1. McHenry
36. Backshore Brewing Company
22. Baying Hound Aleworks
34. Burley Oak Brewing Company
30. Eastern Shore Brewing Company
35. The Fin City Brewing Company
6. Flying Dog Brewery
11. Frey's Brewing Company
41. Jailbreak Brewing Company
10. Milkhouse Brewery at Stillpoint Farm
9. Monocacy Brewing Company
31. Mully's Brewery
12. Pub Dog Brewing
14. Ruhlman Brewing Company

BREWPUBS

4. Antietam Brewery & Restaurant
7. Barley and Hops Grill & Microbrewery
8. Brewer's Alley Restaurant & Brewery
15. DuClaw Brewing Company
33. Evolution Craft Brewing Company
Franklin's Restaurant, Brewery, &
27. General Store
39. Frisco Tap & Brew House
21. Gordon Biersch Brewery & Restaurant
13. Johanssons Dining House
1. Mountain State Brewing Company
24. Rock Bottom Restaurant & Brewery
32. Ruddy Duck Brewery & Grill

BEER BARS & RESTAURANTS

38. The Ale House—Columbia
2. Always Ron's
18. Brasserie Beck
5. Dan's TapHouse
19. Dogfish Head Alehouse
23. Gilly's Craft Beer & Fine Wine
16. The Judge's Bench
40. Kloby's Smokehouse
29. Lures Bar & Grille
20. Mannequin Pis
45. McGarvey's Saloon & Oyster Bar
42. Metropolitan Kitchen & Lounge
25. Mussel Bar & Grille
28. Old Line Bistro
17. Pub Dog Pizza & Drafthouse
26. Quarry House Tavern
44. Ram's Head Tavern
3. Schmankerl Stube
43. Tsunami
37. Victoria Gastro Pub

The Rest of Maryland

Maryland is an odd-shaped state that does not necessarily lend itself, therefore, to easy beer exploration. Baltimore is fine enough with its dense neighborhoods and public transportation. But once you get out of the city, you're looking at criss-crossing waterways that lead in one direction to the Chesapeake and the Eastern Shore of the state and all the way clear to West Virginia in the other direction. Heading south will take you to the doorsteps of the nation's capital.

So grab a trusted driving companion and hit the road. For a relatively small but densely populated state, there's plenty to discover out there on the road to great beer.

Breweries

BACKSHORE BREWING COMPANY

913 Atlantic Ave., Ocean City, MD 21842; (410) 289-0008; facebook.com/Backshore; @BackshoreBrewCo

Founded: 2013 **Founder:** Danny Robinson **Brewer:** Adam Davis **Flagship Beer:** Boardwalk Blonde **Year-Round Beers:** Downtown Sugar Brown, Intergalactic IPA **Tours:** Too small for tours, but basically the entire operation can be seen from the barstool **Taproom:** Yes **Naming Inspiration:** The part of the beach beyond where the waves hit, "It's basically the land that our brewery is built on."

No other brewery in this book is as close to the Atlantic Ocean as Backshore. Cape May Brewing Company might come to mind in New Jersey. East Coast Beer in Belmar. Nope. No one else sits along the boardwalk with the boards, sands, and crashing ocean surf as its front yard.

Having finished its second summer season at 10th and the Boardwalk, the location holds promise for the future of the brewery. Good thing the beer does as well. Under the watch of brewer Adam Davis, who joined the team in 2014, the beers,

particularly the **410 Kölsch** (4.7% ABV) and **Downtown Sugar Brown** (6.0% ABV) have made a splash (pun definitely intended) with beachgoers. Big beers tend not to go over too well at the shore, especially in the heat of summer.

Space is at a premium in both the 1-barrel brewhouse (2-barrel fermenters and brite tanks) and around the tasting bar, with some extra room to mill around out front on the boards. So it makes sense that nearby Tall Tales Brewing Company has been employed to help meet the growing demand. The sample "platter" is a rigged up skateboard, adding to the location-appropriate decor. A small pizza and pretzel menu can help with the hunger and both 32- and 64-ounce growlers are available to go.

Not yet convinced? How about some closing words from Danny Robinson?

"Brewing beer a few steps from the beach ensures a laid-back, free-spirited atmosphere at our brewery and in our beer styles. We brew our beer in the salty air, with our toes in the sand, and the sun on our faces. We spend serious time together creating our beer, and have a ridiculous time with our customers enjoying it."

Beer Lover's Pick

410 Kölsch
Style: Kölsch
ABV: 4.7%
Availability: Warm-weather seasonal; draft only

None of the solid choices when you visit Backshore will likely exemplify a refreshing low alcohol and stylistically accurate summertime beer like the 410 Kölsch.

Stop in between your shore-side activities to cool off and hydrate with a glass of this easy-drinking

German-style Kölsch with a subtly balanced array of fruit flavors and a small hop dosage just enough to remind you it's made in the States.

BAYING HOUND ALEWORKS

1108 Taft St., Rockville, MD 20850; (301) 637-9322; bayinghoundales.com;
@BayingHoundAles
Founded: 2010 **Founder:** Paul Rinehart **Brewers:** Paul Rinehart, Christopher Kuhn
(head of pilot brewing), and Justin Messimore **Year-Round Beers:** Lord Wimsey Pale Ale,
Taj Mahound Brown IPA, Rockville Golden/ Kölsch, Long Snout Stout, and Hop Shot IPA
Tours: Thurs, Fri, and Sat **Taproom:** Yes **Naming Inspiration:** Marmalade, the owners'
bloodhound

For a tiny 4-year-old Rockville brewery that turned out roughly 200 barrels in 2013 and self-distributes in Maryland, Baying Hound has made it onto the map. The small nanobrewery has a growing presence in DC and good representation in area bottle shops like Gilly's, Belby's, and The Bottle Shop.

Part of the allure is due to the nano nature that affords them a bit more flexibility to routinely give customers something new and unique in addition to the handful of year-round beers that they offer.

Another draw for beer fans is the thematically appropriate collaborations that Baying Hound has done with Dog Brewing. Called Scratch 'n' Sniff, these may likely be each brewery's most popular beers. They are seasonal IPAs and have included Black IPA, Red Rye IPA, White IPA, and a fresh hop harvest IPA—a fun take on both the company names and a very popular style in recent years.

Beer Lover's Pick

Rockville Golden
Style: Kölsch
ABV: 5.5%
Availability: Year-round; 22-ounce bottles

My good fortune here allows me to share two breweries in a row that make a mighty fine Kölsch, a beer with roots in Köln, Germany. As with the take on the style at Backshore Brewing in Ocean City, this refreshingly crisp and slightly fruity Kölsch works well as a summertime thirst quencher but can also work quite well on the dinner table, perhaps with a cranberry, walnut, and feta salad or a cup of shrimp ceviche.

BURLEY OAK BREWING COMPANY

10016 Old Ocean City Blvd., Berlin, MD 21811; (443) 513-4647; burleyoak.com; @BurleyOak

Founded: 2011 **Founder:** Bryan Brushmiller **Brewers:** Bryan Brushmiller, Aaron Miller, and Justin Sherman **Year-Round Beers:** Just The Tip, Pale Ryeder, Rude Boy **Seasonals/Special Releases:** Too many to list **Tours:** Free, Sat 3 p.m. **Taproom:** Yes **Naming Inspiration:** A derivation of the town's name combined with the cooperage (oak barrels and baskets) business that resided in the building circa 1900

Burley Oak is one of those places that it seems everyone is talking about. It was noteworthy how many people I talked to along the way (both customers and those "in the biz") who wanted to ensure that I make my way to Berlin. The brewery sits close enough to the road to be difficult to miss and, once you're parked and inside, the comfortable and friendly atmosphere and exceptional beers make it difficult to leave.

The tasting room sits in full view of the brewery inside a former cooperage. The tasting room is open to all ages and four-legged canine friends are often spotted there as well. Live music happens most Saturdays and, judging from the calendar, various other activities or entertainment on any other given night.

Rude Boy

Style: Imperial red ale, has also been referred to as a "sessionable barleywine"

ABV: 8.1%

Availability: Year-round; 750-milliliter bottles

With other beer names such as 'Merica, Just The Tip, Cougar Juice, Assawoman Amber, Fat Kid, and Golden Sex Panther, it might not sound as much fun to order something as boring-sounding as Rude Boy. But do so.

Dark fruit, moderate level of booziness, a hint of chocolate, and a touch of smoke give the beer a complex depth that makes it wonderful to explore sip after sip. Pairing works well with a crème brûlée dessert or a rich cheese plate with gruyère, almonds, and prunes. The beer is bottled once a year in 750-milliliter bottles and holds up nicely with time.

They run 13 draft lines of the brewery's beers plus a root beer for the kids. Burley Oak, like many places, serves up small-glass flights and that's a good thing here. The 13 taps cover a range of styles and alcohol levels that typically includes Berliner weisse, sour, kölsch, barleywine, IPA, Belgian dubbel, saison, pale ale, and porter . . . to name just a few.

The **Sour Trip Berliner Weisse** delivers just the right amount of mouth-puckering refreshment and, at 3.3% ABV, will be found pouring again in your empty glass in no time at all.

Just The Tip (5% ABV) **Kölsch** is just the ticket as a nicely balanced easy-drinking session beer with soft, sweet fruit notes.

Quality brown ales in the States can be difficult to come across, but that is slowly changing. **'Merica** (6.9% ABV and 50 IBUs) definitely pushes away from the English-style, but yet it's very well done and worth a second pint.

In the few short years that Burley Oak has been open, they have ingratiated themselves with local residents as well as the business community. Not only do customers flock here seemingly nonstop to hang out and to get growlers to go, but the brewery plays host to numerous events throughout the year that celebrate their locals—from the farmers who help source the grains to the food vendors and musicians who add to the events.

Next time you're wandering through southern Maryland and wondering where good beer can be found, wonder (and wander) no longer.

EASTERN SHORE BREWING COMPANY

605 S. Talbot St., St. Michaels, MD 21663; (410) 745-8010; easternshorebrewing.com
Founded: 2008 **Founders:** Adrian ("Ace") and Lori Moritz **Brewer:** Zack Milash **Year-Round Beers:** St. Michaels Ale, Knot So Pale Ale **Seasonals/Special Releases:** Duck Duck Goose Porter, Magic Hefeweizen, Brewmasters Reserve series **Tours:** Available upon request **Taproom:** Yes

The brewery on the southern end of Talbot Street leading into the mostly tourist town of St. Michaels has been around for more than 5 years and has found itself in a triangle of boozy delights in an historic mill complex—beer from Eastern Shore Brewing, wine from St. Michaels Winery, and most recently, behind the brewery and winery, a distillery. It is worth making mention of Lyon Distilling Company if not for its well-made rums, but for the distiller and co-owner Ben Lyon, who moved from Massachusetts and his former job at Cisco Brewery in Nantucket.

Beer Lover's Pick

Back Creek Blonde
Style: Blond Ale
ABV: 4.8%
Availability: Warm-weather
    seasonal; draft only
Back Creek is a nice and clean beer perfect for the summer weather of the Eastern Shore. It contains a touch of fruitiness and slight hop bitterness, along the lines of a

kölsch. A couple growlers of this well-made, low-alcohol blond ale go perfectly with the summer heat and the fresh catch of the day.

Eastern Shore continues to do what it has been doing, giving locals and vacationers something different to choose from other than the mass-produced offerings at local retail shops. The brewery is creating a local product and the public seems to appreciate it judging from the crowds that come through the doors, particularly on the weekends.

Be on the lookout for the **Magic Hefeweizen**, which is straight-up banana and just a touch of clove and hops. The **Knot So Pale Ale**, an IPA dry-hopped with Columbus hops, has shown recent improvement over earlier versions with its pronounced bitterness and noticeable grapefruit and orange citrus flavor. The **Permanent Midnight**, an imperial porter, goes in an entirely different direction with a huge addition of local blackstrap molasses and a touch of licorice.

Eastern Shore's beers can be found locally at popular establishments in St. Michaels like the Harbour Inn Marina & Spa and St. Michaels Crab & Steak House as well as around the Eastern Shore. Recently, keg distribution expanded into Annapolis and Baltimore.

THE FIN CITY BREWING COMPANY (AT HOOPER'S CRAB HOUSE)

12913 Ocean Gateway (Highway 50), Ocean City, MD 21842; fincitybrewing.com; @FinCityBrews

Founded: 2012 **Founder:** Vince Wright **Brewers:** Vince Wright, Michele Wright, Patrick Brady (Operations Director), and Michael Glavich (Cellarman) **Flagship Beer:** White Marlin Pale Ale **Year-Round Beers:** Angler Ale—Light Golden Ale, Jackspot Amber Ale, Sneaky Wheat, and Black Fin Black IPA **Seasonals/Special Releases:** Captain Jack's Pumpkin Ale **Naming Inspiration:** A nod to the rich fishing history of Ocean City, particularly as it's referred to as the "White Marlin Capital of the World"

Fin City owner, Vince Wright, moved his family to the Ocean City area in 1996 and quickly became enamored with the seashore life and its history. Wright is a homebrewer who got his start in 2007 with help from Xtreme Brewing (see BYOB: Brew Your Own Beer section later in this book), where kitchen/laundry room

Beer Lover's Pick

Jackspot Amber
Style: American Amber
ABV: 5.8%
Availability: Year-round; 12-ounce bottles

A beautiful balance of toasted malts and slight hop bitterness, the Jackspot Amber goes down clean and easily enough to beg another sip and a plate of hard cheeses, mild buffalo wings, or gumbo.

Most Fin City beers are named after something related to the fishing and nautical nature of the area. In this case, Jackspot is the sweet spot approximately 20 miles off the coast of Ocean City named after Captain Jack Townsend where he helped Ocean City lay claim more than 75 years ago to being the "White Marlin Capital of the World."

brewing led to garage brewing followed by a very short video clip on the Discovery Channel's *Brew Masters* show, an invitation to pour at a beer festival at Hooper's Crab House, and finally a proposal to brew and serve on-site at Hooper's.

Today, beers served at Hooper's are made on-site on a 7-barrel system and distributed products are contracted out of Peabody Heights Brewery in Baltimore. Distribution is growing in 2015 to include Delaware, DC, Virginia, and eastern Pennsylvania.

At Hooper's, the home-turf bar for Fin City, the beers can be enjoyed at the inside bar or dockside at the restaurant's Sneaky Pete's bar. There may not be a more perfect setting for grabbing a well-balanced Fin City **White Marlin Pale Ale** (6% ABV) to wash down an order of crab claws and a bucket of clams.

The slightly tart citrus from the **Sneaky Wheat** (5% ABV) makes a nice accompaniment to salads on the menu such as the scallop salad (with sun-dried cranberries) or the apple chicken salad (with sun-dried cranberries and green apples).

A visit to Hooper's is fun for the whole family, from the Dale Earnhardt tribute car and 1920s caboose to the waterfront dining. Tasty, fresh, and local beer is now part of the experience.

FLYING DOG BREWERY

4607 Wedgewood Blvd., Frederick, MD 21703; (301) 694-7899; flyingdogbrewery.com; @FlyingDog

Founded: 1990 in Aspen (brewpub), 1994 in Denver (brewery), 2009 consolidated all production in Frederick, MD **Founders:** George Stranahan (1990) and Richard McIntyre (1994) **Brewers:** Matt Brophy, Ben Clark **Year-Round Beers:** many, including Double Dog Double IPA, Gonzo Imperial Porter, Oh Scratch Amber Lager, Pale Ale, Pearl Necklace Oyster Stout, Raging Bitch Belgian-style IPA, Snake Dog IPA **Seasonals/Special Releases:** Many, one of the most recent being Dead Rise Old Bay Summer Ale **Tours:** By reservation only Thurs through Sat **Taproom:** No

Turn off English Muffin Way and down Wedgewood Boulevard on the southern side of Frederick to find the massive Flying Dog brewery. Flying Dog moved its brewing operations from Colorado in 2008 to the home of the former Frederick Brewing Company, which brewed the popular Wild Goose brand and had been acquired by Flying Dog in 2006.

Flying Dog's popularity seems to grow with each beer release that carries the artwork of Ralph Steadman (introduced to the brewery by author Hunter S. Thompson) and, considered by some, suggestive or profane bottle-label language. The brewery turns out a long list of beers across the style spectrum. For a "style" that can be difficult to master, the **Raging Bitch** is a Belgian-style IPA (8.3% ABV) that strikes a good balance between the fruity yeast profile and the floral and citrus hop notes.

Dogtoberfest (5.6% ABV) has deservedly won more medals than any other Flying Dog beer in recent years. Between 2008 and 2013, this German-style märzen has been awarded two golds and a silver medal at the annual Great American Beer Festival. It's a solid malt-forward beer that goes well with sausages and burgers topped with caramelized onions at the backyard barbecue.

The **Horn Dog** (10.2% ABV) is, like the Gonzo profiled below, a beer big on flavor and alcohol. This is a barleywine that screams out for cheese. This could be a plate of strong blue cheese or smooth, rich brie along with some candied walnuts. Or it could be paired with a decadently sweet dessert like cheesecake topped with blueberries or a caramel drizzle. Like the Gonzo, the Horn Dog has won medals both for the "regular" (Gold, 2011 GABF) and the aged version (Gold, 2009 GABF; Silver, at both the 2014 and 2012 World Beer Cup).

Beer Lover's Pick

Gonzo
Style: Imperial porter
ABV: 9.2%
Availability: Year-round; 12-ounce bottles
Awards: Great American Beer Festival (Gold, 2009) and Silver for the barrel-aged version at both GABF (2009) and the World Beer Cup (2010)

This beer is not for the faint of heart, nor liver. It is, however, for those looking for a big beer experience. Big in roasted and chocolate malt, big on hops, and, if you get the barrel-aged version, big on whiskey booziness. The latter is aged for at least a half year in oak whiskey barrels.

The Gonzo porter can go equally as well with a mushroom swiss burger as it can a chocolate ganache cake.

Gonzo journalism, as exemplified by the man honored in this beer—Hunter S. Thompson—may no longer be an outrageous concept, but the beer, time and again, holds up as an outrageously delicious experience.

If you want to see and taste Flying Dog in person, do not procrastinate. Make tour reservations early as they are popular and fill up quickly. Grab a Flying Dog and "let's party"!

FREY'S BREWING COMPANY

8601 Mapleville Rd., Mount Airy, MD 21771; (301) 639-7146; freysbrewing.com; @freysbrewing

Founded: 2013 **Founder:** Adam Frey **Brewer:** Adam Frey **Flagship Beers:** Whack Truck McDonkey, Pussy Pilot Parade **Year-Round Beers:** Bulletproof Mustache, The Recruit, Backwoods Brigade, and ¡Viva la Revolución! **Tours:** No **Taproom:** No

Here at the first of three farm-based breweries in this Maryland chapter, Adam Frey wears many hats as owner, brewer, and hop farmer on his family farm property called Libertytown Hops.

As Frey correctly refers to the operation as a "farmhouse brewery," he "never set out to be a mass-producer, our genuine craft beers are exactly what we claim they are: farmhouse."

Beer Lover's Pick

Backwoods Brigade
Style: Smoked American Farmhouse Ale
ABV: 4.2%
Availability: Year-round; 22-ounce bottles
At an open fermentation farmhouse brewery, as owner Adam Frey will disclose up front, each beer's subsequent brewing has the potential to be different from the last. It's not a fallback; rather it is a nod to farmhouse brewing history.

This smoked beer has the potential to be the right crossover beer for those not inclined to like smoked beer. The smoke element is only lightly noticeable in the aroma and barely moderate in the flavor. Drink this around the campfire with some s'mores; seriously, give it a try.

The usual suspects being turned out of this 2.5-barrel brewery are a Pale Ale, Session Ale, American IPA, Black Rye IPA, Imperial IPA, and a Smoked American Farmhouse Ale. Almost all of the names give a playful nod to veterans and active military and come from the creative mind of Frey himself.

The **Whack Truck McDonkey** is not whack at all but will whack you upside the head with a potent dose of earthy and bitter hops. Yet, at 7.5% ABV, you'll likely be asking for another one of these drinkable Imperial IPAs. The **Pussy Pilot Parade** is fun to ask for at a bar and fun to drink. It's got a hefty dose of rye and dark malts and a good wallop of Columbus hops for some pungent earthiness and citrus characteristics.

If working farmhouse breweries in Maryland are going to catch on, Frey's is a good starting model.

JAILBREAK BREWING COMPANY
9445 Washington Blvd. N., Laurel, MD 20723; (443) 345-9699; jailbreakbrewing.com; @JailbreakBrewCo
Opened: 2014 **Founders:** Justin Bonner and Kasey Turner **Brewer:** Ryan Harvey **Select early beers:** Big Punisher, Made Wit Basil, Welcome to Scoville **Tours:** $10, Sat 1, 3, 5 p.m. **Taproom:** Yes

As the first production brewery in Howard County, Jailbreak made quite a splash in 2014. Throughout this book project, there may not have been one new brewery mentioned to me more than Jailbreak, by both consumers and industry folk. That indicates something good must be going on in Laurel.

Jailbreak refers to the owners breaking away from the tech and business world into something for which they truly feel passion. Sharing the passion is their head brewer, Ryan Harvey, who came over from Dogfish Head to get something much

Beer Lover's Pick

Welcome to Scoville
Style: IPA
ABV: 6.9%
Availability: Year-round; draft only
This beer deftly balances the bittering units from the generous hop additions with the scoville units and vegetal presence from the jalapeño peppers. The heat is barely perceptible and creates a great drinking experience.

smaller in scale off the ground. Given the early track record at Jailbreak, brewing outside the *Reinheitsgebot* norms should not be that much of a stretch for Harvey.

Jailbreak is located in a low-rise business park and has a spacious tasting room with a clear view into the brewing operations and a comfortable setting in which to taste their lineup of beers. Live music and food trucks are another appealing reason to make the visit.

I normally may not have given much thought to including such a young brewery in this book. But after tasting several of the Jailbreak beers and talking with owner Justin Bonnor, I'm making a not so wild assumption that they will be around when it comes time for a second edition of this book.

MILKHOUSE BREWERY AT STILLPOINT FARM

8253 Dollyhyde Rd., Mount Airy, MD 21771; (301) 829-6950; milkhousebrewery.com; @MilkhouseBrew
Founded: 2013 **Founders:** Tom Barse and Carolann McConaughy **Brewers:** Tom Barse, Thomas Vaudin **Year-Round Beers:** Coppermine Creek Dry Stout, Red-Eye Porter, Dollyhyde Farmhouse Ale, Best Bitter, Harvest Pale Ale, and the Stairway IPA series
Tours: No **Taproom:** Yes **Naming Inspiration:** A nod to the dairy farm roots of Frederick County and the Stillpoint Farm

A safe hunch is that there is much of Maryland undiscovered by many outside of the major cities. A detour off any of the major roads linking these urban areas delivers one of the mid-Atlantic's most visually appealing and relaxing rural settings.

In recent years, great beer can be added to the list of diversions worth making into the Maryland countryside. Take Milkhouse, for example.

Tom Barse has been homebrewing since 1972 (March 9 to be exact; he still recalls the day fondly), growing commercial hops since 2007 (at least a thousand plants in the ground), and operating his farm on the picturesque rolling property since 2006 with horses, honey, sheep's wool, and hay to show for it.

With a hop farm on site and as president of the Northeast Hop Alliance—not to mention his extensive homebrewing background—Barse had a head start in getting the first licensed farmhouse brewery in the state off the ground. His mission since then has been to help present the best farm-to-table beers to consumers.

In the tasting room and outdoor pavilion that was added in early 2014, guests can get sample-size and full pours of at least a half-dozen available beers, depending upon the current brewing schedule. Barse aims to brew at least once a week, as schedules and demand dictate. Meats and cheeses from local farms are available to provide the perfect accompaniment to the beer tasting.

Coppermine Creek

Style: Dry stout

ABV: 4.5%

Availability: Year-round; draft and occasionally in 22-ounce bottles

Milkhouse Brewery does turn out some
well-made beers over 5% ABV. Thinking
about farm life, relatively lower alcohol
beers rule the day and most nights.

    Two sub-4% beers were discussed above and the featured Beer Lover's Pick goes
to the Coppermine Creek Dry Stout. This smooth, pitch-black stout with a tan head
snaps with a dry roastiness, slight bitterness, and hints of chocolate whose flavors
hold up decently when poured from a nitrogren tap as well. For food pairing, you can
opt for the traditional oyster partnership on the table or go for a simply seasoned
grilled steak.

A typical lineup of available drafts might include any of the year-round regulars like the excellent **Dollyhyde Petite Farmhouse Ale**. It's referred to as a "delicate, Belgian-style Patersbier" and, at 3.4% ABV, is an extremely soft, refreshing, and easy-to-drink beer full of wonderful hints of sweetness, spiciness, and earthy hop flavor, none of which stand too far out to get in the way of wanting to have multiple glassfuls.

The **Goldie's Best Bitter** likewise comes in very low in the sessionable realm at 3.9% ABV but delivers a bit more of a hop kick with dry hopping courtesy of Stillpoint Farm Chinook hops. It's a perfect beer to sit outside watching fieldwork in process.

The tasting room has local farm and vendor products available for sale in addition to the brewery's bottled and growler beer. Books, cheese, wool products, or artwork are available for purchase to remind you of your visit to the Maryland countryside.

By the time you read this, Milkhouse may be well on its way to opening indoor "brewhouse seating" overlooking the 10-barrel brewery. They recently began self-distributing, so word is getting out and that means the tasting room will likely be more crowded than ever. So, shh, don't tell anyone.

MULLY'S BREWERY
141 Schooner Ln., Prince Frederick, MD 20678; (443) 968-9426; mullysbrewery.com; @MullysBrewery
Founded: 2013 **Founders:** Cindy and Jason Mullikin **Brewers:** Jason Mullikin (brewer), Cindy Mullikin (cellarwoman) **Year-Round Beers:** Marc Six Blonde, Jack Straw IPA, Carmelite Wheat, Shucker Stout, and Patuxent Pale Ale **Tours:** Sat and Sun; $5 includes six 3-ounce samples **Taproom:** Yes **Naming Inspiration:** It's the family nickname.

Mully's is on the Calvert Peninsula of Maryland, bounded by the Patuxent River to the west and the Chesapeake River to the east. If you've never been down this stretch of Maryland, once you have, you will probably swear to return to this beautiful piece of country soon thereafter.

The Mullikins have gone big right out of the gate as Mullikin, a former home-brewer, has a 15-barrel brewhouse and a combination of 15- and 30-barrel fermenters. There is room in the building to potentially do contract brewing for others, but they are first concentrating on growing their own business.

The **Patuxent Pale Ale** (4.75% ABV) is a nod to the Patuxent River, the life source of the region, which flows into the Chesapeake Bay. This is a wonderful summertime low-alcohol thirst quencher that is high on citrus hop flavor, yet with a firm but not overwhelming malt backbone.

On the other hand, **Jack Straw IPA** takes the hops and runs with them. A big, crisp, and dry IPA coming in around 6.5% ABV and 85 IBUs means that the piney

Beer Lover's Pick

Shucker Stout
Style: Dry stout
ABV: 5.25%
Availability: Year-round; 12-ounce bottles

Imagine that, two dry stouts featured back-to-back here. It certainly was not planned.

The Shucker Stout, like its Irish cousins, is a dark beer myth buster. While many dry stouts come in between 4% and 4.5% ABV, this dry stout from Mully's is still low enough to consider drinking several in a session. The beer is full of bitter, roasted, and chocolate notes but disappears quickly enough to beg another sip. Try dark chocolate-covered pretzels as a tasty companion.

hops are jumping up and down for attention and that it will go perfectly with a heaping plate of nachos.

As the brewery has grown out of its first year, it added Small Batch Sunday along the way and helped begin Zymurgists of the South, a homebrew club that meets at the brewery. Small Batch Sundays occur the last Sunday of each month and give customers a firsthand opportunity to see a brewing demonstration on the pilot system and taste the previous month's batch.

RUHLMAN BREWING COMPANY (AT CREEPING CREEK FARM)

2300 Harvey Gummel Rd., Hampstead, MD 21074; (410) 259-4166; ourales.com; @RuhlmanBrewery

Founded: 2012 **Founder:** Henry Ruhlman **Brewers:** Henry Ruhlman, Jesse Ballard
Year-Round Beers: LeWac Amber, Rebel Rye, Black Knight Imperial Stout, IPA, Buzzard Brown, Milk Stout, Red Ale, and Ruhl's Lager **Tours:** Sat and Sun; $5 includes sample of all beers on tap **Taproom:** Yes

Henry Ruhlman would love to have you stop by Creeping Creek Farms and try his beer, sold under the name Our Ales. Take a tour and sample all of the beers, typically around 10 to 12 mostly ales with maybe a lager or two thrown in. You can feel free to walk the property, in and among 1,600 hop plants, give or take. Bring your dog, too.

If you'd like to toss some Frisbees around the disc golf course, as well as in and among the hop plants, you may do that for a small charge. Down the hill from the 10-barrel brewhouse, or brewbarn might be more accurate, there's an outdoor facil-

ity that can be used for private parties complete with a food truck, games, and beer garden–like tent and tables.

The brewery hosts a summer concert series and a major "Concert at the Creek" in August. If a few hours of revelry and beers leave you not wanting to drive, camping is permitted by the pond.

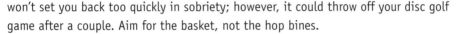
IPA

Style: American India pale ale

ABV: 5.8%

Availability: Year-round; draft only

A wonderfully crisp and refreshing IPA that's an exercise in balance and stays below 6% is quite an IPA treat. It's got a firm malt backbone to counterbalance the bitter Centennial hop punch and has the wonderful citrus aroma of the Cascade hop.

Drinking quite a few of these around the pond while camping overnight on the brewery's property won't set you back too quickly in sobriety; however, it could throw off your disc golf game after a couple. Aim for the basket, not the hop bines.

All of this is the long way of saying that a visit to the home of Our Ales is a comfortable one. It further underscores the logic of beer as agricultural product being produced on a piece of farmland.

Yes, the beers, of course. The four most deserving callouts include the **Milk Stout**, the **Rebel Rye**, the **Buzzard Brown**, and, yes even at Our Ales, the **Ruhl's Lager**.

The **Buzzard Brown** (take note of the buzzards drying themselves on a nearby dead tree and cell phone tower) and the **Milk Stout** each use whole flower Cascade flowers grown on site for just a little extra hop floral aroma boost where the former has a nice balance of nutty and chocolate notes and the latter is a smooth, just-sweet-enough version of the traditional Milk Stout.

The **Ruhl's Lager** has the traditional markings of a well-made, malty American lager. The **Rebel Rye**, on the other hand, uses molasses and barley and rye malt milled by Union Mill Homestead in nearby Westminster. The beer was brewed to commemorate the 150th anniversary of the Corbit's Charge in the days leading up to the Battle of Gettysburg.

The Rest of Maryland

Brewpubs

ANTIETAM BREWERY & RESTAURANT (AT BENNY'S PUB)

49 Eastern Blvd. N., Hagerstown, MD 21740; (301) 791-5915; antietambrewery.com
Opened: 2013 (Benny's opened in 2007) **Founder:** Bill Skomski Sr. **Brewer:** Daniel Maerzluft **Year-Round Beers:** General's Golden Ale, Lil' Ben's Milk Stout, Kelly's Red River IRA, Prickett's Porter **Seasonals/Special Releases:** Winter Ale, Otto's Orchard Series (wheat beer seasonal) **Naming Inspiration:** Local battlefields and nearby Antietam Creek

Benny's had a pretty good restaurant for several years when they decided to add a brewery operation. They brought in veteran brewer Daniel Maerzluft to quickly ratchet up their brewing game. After just a year in the brewing business, 2014 brought an expansion into additional brewing space and a bottle shop provided customers even more ways to enjoy great beer in Hagerstown, including a PEGAS CrafTap growler filler to deliver an even better growler of take-home beer.

Rising to the top of the list is **Kelly's Red River IRA** (7.5% ABV). It's got all the pleasure of a well-made malty red ale along with a bigger dosage of American citrus hops (they took it to 75 IBUs) than usual for the style, hence the Indian Red Ale.

Lil' Ben's Milk Stout also impresses. It's a 5% ABV smooth sipper with significant coffee and chocolate notes in the flavor profile.

Sandwiches on the food menu play with the Austin Powers theme a bit with nods to Shagwell (turkey, bacon, ham, and basil mayo), Fat Bastard (ham, swiss cheese, and crabmeat salad), and the Mustafa (a take on an Italian sub), the first two of which may just happen to be the best two on the menu.

Benny's hosts live music on occasion with the brewery serving as an appropriate backdrop. With a few other beer stops to make in Hagerstown, Antietam/Benny's gives a decent representation on the eastern outskirts of the city.

BARLEY AND HOPS GRILL & MICROBREWERY

5473 Urbana Pike, Frederick, MD 21704; (301) 668-5555; barleyandhops.net; @BarleyAndHop
Founded: 1999 **Founder:** Gary Brooks **Brewers:** Larry Pomerantz, Jake Knill **Flagship Beer:** Annapolis Rocks Pale Ale **Year-Round Beers:** Catoctin Clear Blonde Lager, FSK IPA, Tuscarora Red Irish Red Ale, Schifferstadt Stout **Seasonals/Special Releases:** Lunch Break Series (session beers) and Myth and Monster Series (tying local folklore to beer)

Head brewer Larry Pomerantz has a background that includes a culinary degree and many years as a homebrewer. It shows in the quality of beers being made at the brewpub with the ideal location across from the Francis Scott Key Mall near the busy intersection of I-70, I-270, and Urbana Pike.

Pomerantz, assistant brewer Jake Knill (former coworkers at nearby Flying Dog), and their Czech-built 15-barrel coppertop brewing operation are on full display for customers to see. With recent legislation, the brewpub is able to move some of its beer to off-premise retail accounts.

The pub keeps around 13 of the brewery's beers on tap with 2 typically reserved for guest beers. The **Highway to Helles Maibock** (6.7% ABV) is an extremely well-made beer with a firm maltiness that works quite well with wings or potato skins. A recent entry on the list of **Lunch Break** series of beers, a Brown (4% ABV), makes for the perfect midday beer, as the name suggests, and goes nicely with a Stuffed Burger (cheese on the inside). With beer-battered shrimp or the crab cake platter, consider the flavorful and easy-drinking **Catoctin Clear Blonde Lager** (4.7% ABV).

It's obvious from the everyday menu that serious thought is put into the practice of food and beer together on the table. The kitchen and brewery take the brilliant idea to yet another level with recurring beer dinners. From the quality of the product coming across the bar and out of the kitchen and the dozens of brewery awards won at multiple competitive venues, it's obvious that Barley and Hops continues what it strives to do very well.

BREWER'S ALLEY RESTAURANT & BREWERY

124 N. Market St., Frederick, MD 21701; (301) 631-0089; brewers-alley.com; @BrewersAlley

Founded: 1996 **Founder:** Phil Bowers **Brewers:** Tom Flores (Brewmaster), Todd Perkins (Head Brewer), Daryl Eisenbarth (Brewer), Maggie Lenz (Quality Assurance Manager), Jess Dixon (Cellar Technician) **Year-Round Beers:** Kölsch, India Pale Ale, 1634 Ale, Oatmeal Stout, and Nut Brown Ale **Seasonals/Special Releases:** Hefeweizen in spring and summer, Dunkelweizen in fall and winter **Naming Inspiration:** A row of breweries near Carroll Creek, the last of which closed in 1904

They may have sold off the restaurant's brewing equipment to Shmaltz Brewing Company in 2012 as they transitioned the brewing operations to Monocacy Brewing Company just a couple of miles up the road. Since existing brewmaster Tom Flores and staff are running the show at Monocacy (plus, there's the plan of installing a 3-barrel brewhouse back at the restaurant in 2015), I am inclined to leave

them here in the brewpub section until further notice. Monocacy Brewing Company is open for tastings, tours, and growler fills on Friday and Saturday. Year-round beers produced under the Monocacy name include: Riot Rye Pale Ale, Brewtus Coffee Imperial Stout, and H.L. Rex American Session Pale Ale.

Flores came to Brewer's Alley in 1997 after putting some time in at Wild Goose and Clipper City and produced approximately 1,800 barrels of beer in 2013. His English-style **India Pale Ale** (5.6% ABV) most recently garnered a silver medal at the World Beer Cup in 2010 and a bronze medal at the Great American Beer Festival in 2009. The balance between the solid malt flavor and the hop aroma is what this style of beer should exhibit.

In addition to the IPA, grabbing attention at the brewpub are two beers at polar extremes of the style spectrum. First, the **Kölsch** (5.1% ABV) exhibits all of the expected attributes of a well-made and clean German kölsch. This mild yet flavorful and lightly hopped beer works nicely with the shrimp, avocado, and grapefruit salad.

Going in the other direction is the **Resinator Double IPA** (8.4% ABV), which arrives in the wintertime with a big malt backbone, enough to support the powerful impact of the aggressive hopping. This well-balanced beer is warming and works well with a Nuevo Mexican Chorizo Pizza from the wood-burning brick oven.

DUCLAW BREWING COMPANY

16 Bel Air South Pkwy., Bel Air, MD 21015; (410) 515-3222; 7000 Arundel Mills Circle, Hanover, MD 21076; (410) 799-1166; 4000 Town Center Blvd., Bowie, MD 20716; (301) 809-6943; duclaw.com; @DuClawBrewing
Opened: 1996 **Founder:** Dave Benfield **Brewer:** Jim Wagner **Year-Round Beers:** Bare-Ass Blonde Ale, Euforia, Hellrazer, Misfit Red, Serum, Sweet Baby Jesus! **Seasonals/ Special Releases:** 31 Pumpkin-spiced Lager, Black Jack Stout, Celtic Fury, Devil's Milk, Funk, Mad Bishop, Naked Fish, Old Flame, Oz, Repent, Retribution, Snake Oil, Twisted Kilt, and the eXile series

The production brewery is not open to the public, but the full lineup of DuClaw beers is on display at all three pub locations plus, for thirsty travelers passing through, the Baltimore/Washington International Thurgood Marshall Airport. The Bel Air location was the first when the beer landscape was much bleaker than in current times.

As the brewpub has grown into a super-sized production brewery with its supporting pubs around the area, the beer coming off the lines can still be just as interestingly different as it was nearly 20 years ago for suburban Maryland.

Take, for example, the **Sweet Baby Jesus!** (6.5% ABV) chocolate peanut butter porter. One of the first to commercially brew this type of beer—and certainly to experience the level of commercial success—DuClaw quickly had a new best-seller on its hands not long after brewing it in 2011 and a bronze medal award-winner at the 2014 Great American Beer Festival. The beer that elicits wrinkled brows from many (for either the name or the ingredients or maybe both) is rather well done—the beer is still identifiable as a beer and the chocolate and peanut butter come along for the ride, a very tasty ride.

At the pubs, the **Bare Ass Blonde** and **Euforia Toffee Nut Brown Ale** (both 5% ABV) are two of the most popular and both are excellent takes on their respective styles. Two seasonals that are sure to warm and delight in the cooler months are the **Black Jack Russian Imperial Stout** (8% ABV) and **Devil's Milk Barleywine** (10.5% ABV). Both are part of a growing lineup of DuClaw beers packaged also in bottles.

EVOLUTION CRAFT BREWING COMPANY

200 Elmwood St., Salisbury, MD 21801; (443) 260-2337; evolutioncraftbrewing.com; @EvolutionBeer
Founded: 2009 **Founders:** Tom Knorr and John Knorr **Brewers:** Michael Piorunski and Kerry Williams **Year-Round Beers:** Lot 3 IPA, Primal Pale Ale, Exile Red, Lucky 7 Porter, and Lot 6 Double IPA **Seasonals/Special Releases:** Sprung, Summer Session Ale, Jacques Au Lantern, Secret Spot Winter Ale, and the Migration Series

Evolution scored a swell spot when they moved across the state line in 2012 from Delmar to Salisbury along a rail line adjacent to the old Reddy Ice Factory. Not only did they significantly expand brewing capacity and distribution reach, but a restaurant (Public House) became part of the equation as well.

There's a reason why fans of Evo beer (the popular shortened form of the brewery's name) flock to the Public House. Some combination of events, specials, and entertainment each day of the week. A fantastic menu of meats and cheeses. A staggering list of beers on tap and in special vintage bottles. Plus, maybe even a guest tap or two from someone local and special, like 3rd Wave Brewing Company who opened in Evolution's former Delmar space.

On the brewery side, free tours of the brewery are offered Friday, Saturday, and Sunday and give visitors a behind-the-scenes look at where the brewing takes place one or two times a day, four days a week. The brewery side has its own bar for tastings and growler fills, but settling in to a table on the Public House side provides a full gastronomical experience not to be missed.

Assembling a "simple" platter of meats and cheeses (served also with pickles, bread, fruit, and jam) is a treat in and of itself. For something more substantial, the local Virginia clams, Chesapeake cobb salad (with soft-shell crab when in season), duck confit burger with gruyère cheese, and a Brewhouse Ribeye with blue cheese mashed potatoes should take proper care of any nagging hunger.

It's nearly impossible to run down the myriad of beers brewed at Evolution, but **Evo Sprung** (4.9% ABV) is mild in flavor, aroma, and leans toward the lighter body side. Light floral notes and a touch of earthiness become more pronounced when paired with something like lightly seasoned chicken breast or an herbed goat cheese.

Lot 3 IPA is often the Evo beer that many first encounter. Perfectly in line with typical American IPAs, it grabs attention with 6.8% ABV and 65 IBUs thanks in large part to the Columbus and Chinook hops. It goes down all too easy and makes a perfect tablemate in the Public House with a Bacon Johnny Burger on brioche.

From the darker, roastier side of the beer list, **Lucky 7** (5.8% ABV) is an excellent porter that comes in relatively light on the alcohol, but big on a balance of roasted bitter and chocolate malt flavors. Do not miss **Rise Up Stout** (6.7% ABV) when it's available during winter months. It's an appropriately warming beer balancing great flavors of a full-bodied roasted stout with organic coffee from the local Rise Up coffee shop.

Finally, the **Migration Series** is limited and available periodically throughout the year on draft and in 750-milliliter bottles, giving fans of barrel-aged beer yet another reason to flock to Salisbury.

FRANKLIN'S RESTAURANT, BREWERY & GENERAL STORE

5123 Baltimore Ave., Hyattsville, MD 20781; (301) 927-2740; franklinsbrewery.com;
@FranklinsBrwry

Founded: 1992 (brewpub added in 2002) **Founders:** Mike and Debbie Franklin **Brewer:**
Mike Roy **Year-Round Beers:** Bombshell Blonde, Private IPA, Rubber Chicken Red,
Twisted Turtle **Seasonals/Special Releases:** Too many unique offerings to list

Franklin's is three properties stitched together serving three purposes: a restaurant, a brewery, and a general store. The original building dates back to the late 19th century and served as the Hyattsville Hardware Store for over 75 years.

Brewer Mike Roy had an equally unique brewing atmosphere when he came from Milly's Tavern (Manchester, NH) in 2010. His beers at Franklin's all come across as very clean and span the style spectrum from basic low-alcohol blondes, reds, and pale ales to higher alcohol and more flavor-bending wheat wines, double IPAs, and barrel-aged browns.

The restaurant, with a small kitchen counter downstairs and a modest-size bar upstairs, bustles with the energy from a local crowd, particularly during the dinner hours, and a friendly staff that is schooled in both the kitchen's and the brewery's menus.

Being a small-sized brewing operation—though creating 1,350 barrels of beer in 2013—affords Roy the ability to do a lot of different things in different ways. Some must-trys include the Mic Czech, Miami Weiss, Psychedelic Smokehouse, Me So Hoppy, Guardian Angel, and 97-Pound Weakling. They have a knack for naming beers as well as making them.

Go Brewpubbing, Come Home with a Gift for the Kids

Be sure not to leave Franklin's—in their words, the "world's first toy store brewery"—before browsing through the General Store. Not only is Franklin's beer bottled and available to take home for later enjoyment but the eclectic and quirky store is full of everything from candy to jewelry to small stocking stuffer gifts perfect for the holiday season and birthdays alike. For those who are shopping-averse, Thursdays in the General Store feature wine tastings.

Tops of this bunch, however, goes to the **Mic Czech Pilsner**. Weighing in around 5% ABV and sporting a spicy Noble hop kick, the Mic Czech is the kind of beer that reminds you what good, locally crafted beer is all about. It does its tip of the cap to Old World brewing and reminds you that at the cornerstone of every wild American tap list should be a well-made pilsner, the kind of beer that most brewers freely admit is one of the toughest to master.

The kitchen does a great job at sourcing local, fresh, and interesting. The North African Nickel Curves are perfect for when you need something tasty to eat but are not looking to get stuffed. They are all-lamb merguez sausage burgers along with tzatziki sauce and come three to a plate. If meat is not your thing, then try the Noodleless Lasagna, which is a fun vegetarian approach to replace noodles and beef with meaty eggplant.

Expect to see more of Franklin's beyond Maryland and DC as the addition of new fermenters, a new glycol cooling system, and larger cold box will help them increase their in-house draft lines to 20 and their distribution.

FRISCO TAP & BREW HOUSE

6695 Dobbin Rd., Columbia, MD 21045; (410) 312-4907; friscogrille.com; @ FriscoTapHouse
Opened: 2010 (in its current location; brewery since 2012) **Founder:** Adam Carton
Brewer: Chris Myers **COO/Beer Director:** Alex Taylor

The home of the growing Push American Brewing name is at Frisco Tap & Brew House, which also is home to a stupendous list of great beer on tap from near and far. Nearly 50 beers (including two on nitro and two cask-conditioned) can be found flanking four Push beers on the digital draft board behind the bar. More than 100 mostly high-end bottles are available as well.

With all this good beer available, Push Craft Brewing looks to grow beyond its current 7-barrel setup to a 30-barrel system with the aim of taking more tap handles both at home and at retail accounts across the state and region. The owner's love of motorcycle racing fuels the branding and passion for the good beer fuels the brewing.

Push has tended to gravitate toward bigger beers and the IPAs have gone over well with consumers. The **Reckless Ascension** (7.1% ABV), for example, is an extremely flavorful and drinkable American IPA.

The restaurant turns out the ubiquitous wings, nachos, salads, pizzas, burgers, and fish tacos. Noteworthy on the menu are a very good chili, Natty Boh–steamed mussels, burritos, fajitas, and spicy grilled chorizo sausage with queso. If the latkes pop up on a specials menu, be sure to check them out as well.

Frisco has big plans for the Maryland beer scene. Late in 2014, a new Frisco Tap House opened in Crofton, Anne Arundel County near Annapolis, with a whopping 106 craft draft lines.

JOHANSSONS DINING HOUSE
4 W. Main St., Westminster, MD 21157; (410) 876-0101; johanssonsdininghouse.com
Founded: 1994 **Founder:** David Johansson **Brewer:** Jay Lampert **Year-Round Beers:** Hoodle Head Pale, Whistle Stop Amber, and Honest Golden Ale **Seasonals/Special Releases:** Alt, Saison

Johanssons is a pleasant place to visit, particularly for Sunday brunch when the set price includes drinks and a stunning food buffet. Perhaps surprising to some, it is also a place to try some rather well-crafted beers.

The bar has a comfortable tavern-like feel with vertical ceiling paddle fans and is a good place to sample the beers made on premise.

The standard lineup includes a crisp and fruity **Honest Golden Ale** (5% ABV) that works quite nicely particularly in warmer weather, a slightly citrus hop–leaning **Whistle Stop Amber** (5.3% ABV), and the **Hoodle Pale Ale** (6% ABV) which with British hops has the beer mimicking an English IPA.

The kitchen does a full array of sandwiches, burgers, salads, standard appetizers, plus escargots as an interesting twist, and a half-dozen pizzas. More compelling still are the weekly specials that can include 50-cent oysters on Friday, $5 burgers on Monday, and extended happy hour specials Monday through Friday from 3 p.m. to 7 p.m.

MOUNTAIN STATE BREWING COMPANY

6690 Sang Run Rd., McHenry, MD 21541; (301) 387-3360; mountainstatebrewing.com; @MtnStateBrewing

Founded: 2005, brewery in WV; 2008, pub in MD **Founders:** Brian Arnett and Willie Lehmann **Brewers:** Mike Supak, Kate Lane, Michael Singer, Tyler Elliott (Cellerage) **Flagship and Year-Round Beers:** Almost Heaven Amber Ale, Cold Trail Ale, Miner's Daughter Oatmeal Stout, Seneca Indian Pale Ale **Seasonals/Special Releases:** Black Fork IPA, Dolly Suds, Rumsey Rock Porter

John Denver aptly described West Virginia as "Almost Heaven" and one cannot help but sing along when driving south from Pittsburgh to McHenry where Mountain State has its Maryland location.

I took a bit of liberty including Mountain State here under the brewpub section of this chapter. The beer is all made roughly an hour to the southwest at its West Viriginia brewery in Thomas on the edge of Canaan Valley State Park where they host the annual 2-day Brew Skies Music Festival. However, since it turns out to be pretty good beer and there may come a day when they set up a small brewery operation next to the hop field in McHenry, I figured you should know about it.

The restaurant seats around 200 people along with some patio space for outdoor dining and has one of the most picturesque settings imaginable. So far, this book has spotlighted urban oases, strip-mall settings, working-farm brewery properties, and, now here, a rustic spot overlooking the rolling countryside surrounding Deep Creek Lake in Western Maryland.

It's fitting, therefore, to begin a tasting session at Mountain State with **Almost Heaven Amber Ale** (5.2% ABV). It has the hallmark caramel malty flavors of a decent amber and works very well with one of the more than 20 flatbreads, like The Cuban with pulled pork, coming out of the hand-built oven near the bar. Fire on the Mountain is another flatbread that screams for attention with its sausage, pepperoni, and chipotle heat.

The other three core Mountain State beers continue the sessionability theme with the **Cold Trail Ale** (a 5.6% ABV soft and light blonde, perfect after a day of Deep Creek Lake activities), **Seneca IPA** (a 5.4% ABV India Pale Ale, big on flavor, moderate on bitterness, and easy on the sobriety), and **Miner's Daughter** (a 5.5% ABV smooth and roasty oatmeal stout that reminds you dark beers can be easy to drink and low in alcohol).

Whether you come by two wheels, four wheels, or by horse—yes, there is a hitching post because that does happen from time to time—you're guaranteed a relaxing stay with a solid meal and tasty beers.

ROCK BOTTOM RESTAURANT & BREWERY

7900 Norfolk Ave., Bethesda, MD 20814; (301) 652-1311; rockbottom.com/locations/bethesda; @RockBottom
Founded: 1991 **Founder:** Frank Day **Brewer:** Geoff Lively (at Bethesda) **Flagship and Year-Round Beers:** Kölsch, White, Red, IPA **Seasonals/Special Releases:** A rotating dark beer and a Brewmaster's Choice

Rock Bottom and Gordon Biersch came together in 2010 under the corporate umbrella called CraftWorks Restaurants and Breweries. Brewmaster Geoff Lively, at the Rock Bottom location, has been there through it all for more than 15 years.

Along the way, he has brewed up multiple award-winning beers like **Right on Rye** (a silver and two bronze medals for this rye beer at the Great American Beer

Festival between 2004 and 2008) and the **Highland Courage** (three gold medals combined at the World Beer Cup and Great American Beer Festival for this Scottish-style ale between 2008 and 2010) in addition to the company standard beers.

Up the road 15 minutes or so is the Rockville location of Gordon Biersch where brewer Christian Layke puts out an excellent "house" **Czech Pilsner** and a **Rauch Märzen** that placed third in the smoke beer category of the 2014 World Beer Cup. This

Gordon Biersch location was the former home of Kevin Blodger, who went on to open the Union Craft Brewery in Baltimore.

Back at Rock Bottom, the food menu has interesting takes on burgers (e.g. Bourbonzola Burger and 2 a.m. Burger) that make for nice pairings with the malty and slightly noticeably hoppy **Red Ale** (5.7% ABV) or the citrusy **IPA** (6.6% ABV). On the lighter side of the menu, the **White Ale** (5.3% ABV) and the **Kölsch** (5% ABV) are well-suited for the mini "street fish tacos" and chicken Waldorf salad. If you're visiting during hotter weather, the **Hot As Helles** (5% ABV) is a perfect thirst-quenching beer with light toasted malt flavor.

The company as a whole fosters an award-winning atmosphere and, with its roughly three dozen Rock Bottom locations, took home the Brewpub Group of the Year award at the 2013 Great American Beer Festival. See the Pennsylvania chapters for more about the Rock Bottom locations near Pittsburgh and Philadelphia.

RUDDY DUCK BREWERY & GRILL

13200 Dowell Rd., Dowell, MD 20629; (410) 394-3825; ruddyduckbrewery.com; @RuddyDuckGrill

Founded: 2009 (Piney Point in 2013) **Founders:** Carlos Yanez and Michael Kelley **Brewer:** Matt Glass **Year-Round Beers:** India Pale Ale, Festbier, Helles Lager, Rud Light, and Biere Nouveau (gluten-free) **Seasonals/Special Releases:** Apricot Wheat, Irish Stout, Coffee Toffee, Scottish Ale

Ruddy Duck is a gem in one of the farthest points from anywhere in Maryland. Past Mully's Brewery in Calvert County, all the way down in Solomons just before the lovely Solomons Island, sits the brewpub with Argentinean roots. Entering the establishment to the sight of soccer balls, World Cup decor, and the like confirms this. Finding a beer cocktail menu that contains a Caipbeerinha, among other very well-crafted beer cocktails, is even further proof.

The pace of life and the approachability of fellow men and women in this laid-back area is evident and makes it easy to sit back for a couple of hours and enjoy the beers. The year-round beers offer a solid **IPA** (7.2% ABV) and gluten-free option—in the spring, a **Peach Nouveau** (4.8% ABV) that brings forth a deliciously dry peach flavor in a beer brewed with honey, sorghum, and quinoa.

From the rotating taps, the **Falconer's Flight Pale Ale** (a 5% ABV medium-bodied with big hops), **Coffee Toffee Stout** (a 5% ABV dry stout with bold flavors), and **Irish Stout** (another dry stout, this one at 5.2% ABV and a bit more traditional) are all standouts and, at their respective alcohol levels, can get you through a couple of games on the television or an afternoon of Adirondack chair–sitting, relaxing in

the backyard at home. Speaking earlier of Mully's, keep an eye open for the occasional collaboration brew with these Calvert County neighbors.

The food menu offers up plenty of options from light fare to more substantial dishes. The namesake duck finds its way into a few tasty dishes including Duckadillas, duck spring rolls, and BBQ duck pizza. Joining the meat parade is a wonderful dish of boneless short ribs and chimichurri. Vegetarians are in luck, as well, with a couple dozen items to choose from on a specially tailored menu.

When it comes time for dessert, it's back to the beer cocktail menu where the Signature Chocolate Cake (filled with marshmallow cream and topped with chocolate ganache and salted toffee) goes absolutely perfectly with a **Chocolate Covered Cherry**. This cocktail uses either the Irish Stout or Coffee Toffee Stout as a base and with the cake covers all the bases of sweet, bitter, and salted to tease all the corners of the palate.

Ruddy Duck opened a sister establishment with incredible views called Ruddy Duck Seafood & Alehouse in St. Mary's County on a small strip of land near where the Potomac dumps into the Chesapeake.

Beer Bars & Restaurants

THE ALE HOUSE—COLUMBIA

6480 Dobbin Center Way, Columbia, MD 21045; (443) 546-3640; thealehousecolumbia
.com; @alehousecol
Draft Beers: 25, plus 4 handpumps **Bottled/Canned Beers:** 50+

In the small universe of beer destinations in Columbia, The Ale House is at the fortunate center of it all. In one direction is Victoria Gastro Pub and in the other are Frisco Tap & Brew House (Push American Brewing Co.) and Maryland Homebrew. Good beer is not lost on the locals, or at least not access to it. The traveling beer geeks are catching on as well.

With roughly a dozen Oliver beers on tap and a few more on the handpumps, there's no doubt that this is part of the Pratt Street Ale House (Oliver Brewing Company) family. Late October 2014 saw Severna Park—just north of Annapolis— add Park Tavern as the newest location to the family with over 30 draft lines and a dozen dedicated to Oliver.

Stone, The Bruery, New Belgium, and Weyerbacher all find their way to the bar here at The Ale House. As do local upstarts like Freys and Jailbreak.

The food menu has nice touches such as the mussels (jalapeños & prosciutto and pork belly & Granny Smith apples are two interesting twists) and the tacos (confit duck and adobo pork with roasted pineapple are two versions that should grab your attention).

With the planned move and growth in Oliver Brewing Company and the new Park Tavern, the stage is set for even more great beer in the suburban Baltimore region.

ALWAYS RON'S

29 N. Burhans Blvd., Hagerstown, MD 21740; (301) 797-71778; alwaysrons.com;
@AlwaysRons
Draft Beers: 30 **Bottled/Canned Beers:** 30+

Basically, it's always been Ron's. The current incarnation dates back approximately 10 years, but it goes back even longer as Ron's Deli. The good beer and beer-geeky bartenders who know their stuff are something of even more recent times.

While the food menu sports a solid and approachable list of classic tavern standards, the beer list will please the most hard-to-please beer geek. Area breweries like Brewer's Alley, Devil's Backbone, Dogfish Head, DuClaw, Flying Dog, and Pub Dog are well represented alongside the likes of Allagash, Malheur, Schlafly, Tröegs, Uinta, and Victory.

The bar is clean and tastefully decorated without being pretentious. In addition to live music on Saturday night, Ravens fans will recognize that, as a "Ravens Roost" (#124 to be exact), this is the place to be on game day.

BRASSERIE BECK

311 Kentlands Blvd., Gaithersburg, MD 20878; (301) 569-4247; brasseriebeck.com;
@BeckKentlands
Draft Beers: 16 **Bottled/Canned Beers:** 150+

Brasserie Beck has been serving up Belgian fare and beers in the nation's capital since 2007 and is named after Chef-Owner Robert Wiedmaier's son. Since then, his Mussel Bar & Grille has opened in Arlington and Bethesda. Wiedmaier has been named in Belgium as a Chevalier du Fourquet des Brasseurs, a high honor for those playing a role in protecting and promoting the wonders of Belgian beer.

Now comes a second Brasserie Beck. Having just opened in May 2014, the restaurant and bar atmosphere can be best described as stylishly casual in this mixed residential and retail suburban community. A semiprivate patio is available for comfortable outdoor seating.

For starters, the Antigoon house beer crafted for Wiedmaier by Brouwerij de Musketiers in Belgium is a very smooth, lightly-hopped, and drinkable "double blonde" with notes of apricot that weighs in at 6.8% ABV.

Beyond the unique house beer, expect to find anything from area breweries like Devil's Backbone, Dogfish Head, Evolution, Flying Dog, and Port City. From farther afield, look for Allagash, Firestone Walker, Great Divide, and high quality Belgians such as Chimay, Orval, Rochefort, and St. Feuillien.

Beef carbonnade, asparagus salad, and a croque monsieur are sure bets on the food menu, full of flavor and satisfying. Mussels come prepared a half-dozen different ways and the wild mushrooms, smoked bacon, and truffle cream are an interesting twist. Sometimes keeping it simple is the way to go and the braised meatballs with tomato sauce and Parmesan is right on the mark in that regard.

DAN'S TAPHOUSE
3 S. Main St., Boonsboro, MD 21713; (301) 432-5224; drnth.com; @DansTapHouse
Draft Beers: 24 **Bottled/Canned Beers:** Around 50

I wish I could recall all of those along the way who tipped me off to great beer destinations, so I could thank them. Dan's was not on my initial list but was whispered to me somewhere in Maryland. It was added to the travel itinerary between Frederick and Hagerstown. And that turned out to be a very good detour indeed. A

detour to what I later learned could be referred to as the town that romance author Nora Roberts built.

In 2012, Roberts's son opened Dan's TapHouse and promptly put it through a remodel and rebuilt the bar space. The result is a tasteful and comfortable atmosphere where the focus is as local as possible. On the beer menu, that means DC Brau, Flying Dog, Monocacy, Fordham & Dominion, Heavy Seas, and Tröegs. From the kitchen, it means regional farm meats, produce, and seafood.

It's always interesting to peel back small-town layers, often finding deeper stories than you could have ever imagined. In Boonsboro, it looks like good taste is one of the layers.

DOGFISH HEAD ALEHOUSE
800 W. Diamond Ave., Gaithersburg, MD 20878; (301) 963-4847; dogfishalehouse.com; @Dogfish_Ale
Draft Beers: 20

From the omnipresent tap handles in Delaware (and 30 states, for that matter), to their brewpub in Rehoboth Beach, to a recently opened boutique hotel in Lewes, to a television show, it's difficult to deny the once-small brewery out of the small state of Delaware and the role it has played in shaping the craft-brewing industry as we know it today.

In 2005, a private restaurant group entered into a licensing agreement with the brewing company to create an extension of the Dogfish Head experience. Gaithersburg was the first, as subsequent locations in Falls Church and Fairfax, both in northern Virginia, followed.

Save for the tap takeovers with brewery staff and Sam Calagione's appearances around the region, stopping in for a bite and a brew at a Dogfish Head Alehouse will probably be the next best way to be immersed in all things Dogfish Head.

They've got the branding covered at the Alehouse from the floor mats to the wall decor to the swag available for sale. Of course, they've got the beer covered as well.

In addition to a full lineup of production beers, the exclusive Ale House 75, not to be confused with the production version of 75 Minute IPA/Johnny Cask, is simply a 50/50 mix of the 60 Minute IPA and 90 Minute IPA off the taps.

The kitchen puts out a full menu of options ranging from the most basic appetizers, soups, salads, and entrees to more complex fare including jambalaya, a portobello and Gorgonzola burger, a lamb burger, and an Alfredo Cajun pizza. Most of the main menu items are listed with a recommended beer pairing.

Live music is offered on a regular basis, sometimes outside, and beer dinners are conducted occasionally to further heighten the Dogfish Head experience.

In a small bit of irony, the off-center-themed Dogfish Alehouse is located in Gaithersburg, across from the National Institute of Standards and Technology.

GILLY'S CRAFT BEER & FINE WINE
2009 Chapman Ave., Rockville, MD 20852; (301) 770-5515; gillyscbfw.com; @JTGilly
Draft Beers: 19 **Bottled/Canned Beers:** Hundreds to choose from on the shelves

First-timers to Gilly's may find it a bit disorienting. Is it a take-out beer shop? Yes it is. Is it a deli/sandwich shop? That too. Is it a bar? Well, perhaps not in the traditional sense, but why not? Let's call it that as well. Nearly 20 beers are available on tap for pours by the pint, half-pint, and growler.

The staff is friendly and welcoming and armed with tons of beer knowledge, so venture in and make yourself at home; you'll likely stay longer than you expected. Brewery reps also like stopping by for the educated staff (like managers Tom Gilchrist, Matt Splain, and Paul Stonebraker), some of whom work at breweries and others who have close relationships with them and have even brewed special releases.

Plus, being able to sit down at the small bar to sample from a menu of 10 cheeses and over 20 interesting sandwiches is, all can agree, a pretty good thing indeed. Tempting sandwiches include standards like Bonnie's BLT, Turkey, and Roast Beef Sammy and those a bit further from the mainstream like Nancy's Country Pâté

(pâté, tarragon mustard), Bacon Berry Brie (bacon, strawberry jam, and brie), and Tommy's Tummy Buster (where two grilled cheese sandwiches are substituted for bread in any other sandwich!).

Not only does Gilly's keep both day and late-night hours, with some advance notice they can also fulfill keg orders. Tastings and tap takeovers are conducted on a frequent basis. Sundays are special days for growler club members who get half-price growler fills. Lots going on and worth checking out.

THE JUDGE'S BENCH
8385 Main St., Ellicott City, MD 21043; (410) 465-3497; judgesbenchpub.com; @JudgesBench
Draft Beers: 17 **Bottled/Canned Beers:** 50+

The Judge's Bench is a perfect nightcap kind of place. As Ellicott City begins to shut down after dark and dinner hour, The Judge's Bench is heating up with great beer and entertainment. They have light bites to eat here as well, but the experience is quintessential beer, single-malt whiskey, live music, and hanging out.

The draft and bottled-beer list has a decent representation of breweries from all across the country, plus a respectable list of Belgian and Belgian-style beers. On any given night, Heavy Seas Below Decks, 21st Amendment Bitter American, Schlafly Pils, or even Dogfish Head 120 Minute IPA could be on tap. The whiskies here are so popular, and plentiful, that there's a Whisky Club available to join for special access and pricing.

The bar's name was inspired by the 1800s grocery store that formerly stood on the property and on whose bench judges from across the street would come to sit to enjoy a cool beverage in the shade. Air-conditioning and fans are plentiful these days and the beer and good times are better than ever.

KLOBY'S SMOKEHOUSE
7500 Montpelier Rd., Laurel, MD 20723; (301) 362-1510; klobysbbq.com; @KlobySmokehouse
Draft Beers: 20

Let's get this out of the way first. Kloby's does a popular thing called a Jar-B-Que. It's a mason jar stuffed with layers of pulled pork, beans, and cole slaw. For $2 more, a little something extra comes in the form of topping the jar with smoked pork belly and bacon. Take a minute to, shall we say, digest that.

Then we can move on to talking about the way in which great barbecue can go so well with great beer. Kloby's does both at their restaurant. Plus, they take the show on the road with local catering and a food truck that has been known to show up at the new brewery, Jailbreak, on the other side of North Laurel.

A slam-dunk recommendation, while talking about Jailbreak, is pairing its Welcome to Scoville Jalapeño IPA with the Jalapeño Pork Balls. The strength of the beer and firm malt backbone match up well with the chile heat. From the more traditional side of the menu, a trio slider sampler of classic wood-smoked pulled pork, brisket, and chicken will work perfectly with a Tröegs Troegenator.

There are smokehouse wings done more than a dozen different ways, signature smoked burgers, and a page full of ice cream soda and sundae options. You're not leaving here hungry, or thirsty.

LURES BAR & GRILLE

1397 Generals Hwy., Crownsville, MD 21032; (410) 923-1606; luresbarandgrille.com; @LuresBar
Draft Beers: 26 **Bottled/Canned Beers:** Around 25

The beer and food alone are enough to lure you here. The spacious parking, indoor bar areas, and outdoor dining patio are appeals of Lures just outside of Annapolis and up the road from the Maryland Renaissance Festival.

Lures has been open since 2008 and has established itself as one of the premier beer destinations in the area. If you become a regular customer at Lures, you'll probably like to consider becoming a member in the Beer Club (or Wine Club, if you wish), in which you get a free beer each month and an annual free birthday dinner.

A great way to start a visit to Lures is with an order of Rockfish Bites, which are beer battered and served with a spicy plum dipping sauce. Tuna tartare with sea salt, jalapeños, and sweet chile vinaigrette is another fantastic, tasty way to begin. Grabbing a Victory Summer Love or local beer like Jailbreak Berry'd would work as a nice accompaniment.

For a meal platter, it's hard to go wrong with the Black & Bleu Steak Tacos, filled with filet tips and blue cheese crumbles and paired with a Brewer's Art Resurrection. The Sushi Burger takes diced sushi-grade tuna, forms it, blackens it, and serves it on a roll topped with sweet chile mayo. A Jolly Pumpkin Bam Biere works nicely here.

Dessert is not something to skip at Lures, as they bring in fresh nine-layer Smith Island Cakes—referred to as "Maryland's State Dessert"—from the Eastern Shore. Flavors vary by day, but if you luck into the Double Chocolate version, no doubt the Stone Imperial Russian Stout, Lagunitas Cappuccino Stout, or Jailbreak Dusk Till Dawn will cap off a memorable visit to Lures.

MANNEQUIN PIS

18064 Georgia Ave., Olney, MD 20832; (301) 570-4800; mannequinpis.com;
@MannequinPis
Bottled/Canned Beers: 50+ Belgian-only beers

Mannequin Pis, the restaurant in Montgomery County, MD, that is, has been around for over 15 years, long before many were aware of the wonders of great Belgian beer. The statue in Brussels has been there much longer.

The restaurant (be forewarned that there is no bar) and its cozy dining room are tucked away unassumingly in a small strip of storefronts in the heart of Olney's retail center. The experience at the restaurant is pure Belgian assembled by a passionate ownership and kitchen staff that know the cuisine and the beers from trips to Belgium and, quite simply, practice. The front-of-the-house staff is regularly trained to speak knowledgably about the importance of glassware, the food and the beer, and the intersection of the two.

The bottled-beer menu will typically feature at least four Trappists and a wide array of Belgian beers including De Dolle, Kwak, St. Bernardus, St. Feuillien, and Urthel. I'm not going to reprint it here, but if you'd like to know how retailers in Montgomery County feel about local liquor control, read the bottom of the beer menu.

The experience of a full Belgian menu of beer and food is well worth it. On the food pages of the menu, delicious classics spill forth such as Belgian endive salad, seafood waterzooi, carbonnade Flamande, and a kilogram serving of mussels served any of 17 different ways.

Twice a year, special dinners are held to further underscore the beauty of a well-paired beer dinner. Places such as Mannequin Pis, like hidden restaurant and bar gems in Belgium, make it clear that some of the best experiences are just around the next corner.

McGARVEY'S SALOON & OYSTER BAR

8 Market Space, Annapolis, MD 21401; (410) 263-5700; mcgarveys.net
Draft Beers: 6 **Bottled/Canned Beers:** Around 50

Judging McGarvey's from the outside looking in, as well as by a walk around inside, it's the same as it's always been for 40 years. That means a lot of wood, Tiffany lampshades, stained glass, and the ubiquitous oyster bar.

It means classic menu items like French dip sandwich, surf and turf, Caesar salad, and carrot cake. By stating all the ways in which the bar is the same is actually a compliment. It has stayed the same without showing its age. Its location and its longevity mean that it has remained recognizable and relevant to at least a couple of generations passing through the area for work, play, or residence.

A major difference, however, is the overhaul of the beer menu that shows much more life than it has in the past. Located a block from the Naval Academy and a couple of blocks from the Maryland State House and Governor's Mansion, this harborside classic bar is now serving up quality beers from the reliable locals like DC Brau, Dogfish Head, Fordham & Dominion, Flying Dog, Heavy Seas, and Union Craft. A lot of the old with a shot of the new at McGarvey's.

METROPOLITAN KITCHEN & LOUNGE

169 West St., Annapolis, MD 21401; (410) 280-5160; metropolitanannapolis.com;
@Metropolitan3
Draft Beers: 6 **Bottled/Canned Beers:** 30+

Metropolitan by night and by day are two different animals. At night, it exudes the hip nightlife side of Annapolis. By day, it's a bit more low-key and diverse.

The establishment is 4 years old and the attention to the beer program began around January 2014. Customers have flocked for the small but carefully chosen draft beer list and much larger bottle list that typically has at least a couple of locals and a couple from the West Coast.

The likewise carefully built food menu focuses on quality over quantity. The categories of "small plates," flatbreads, and soup, salad, and sandwiches each present a handful of solid options like the curry chicken salad, tilapia tacos, and "Fists of Greece" flatbread are perfect beer-friendly accompaniments. For breakfast, Metropolitan has the bases covered as well with sriracha breakfast tacos, pork belly eggs Benedict, and breakfast-based flatbreads and burritos.

A few blocks away sits Metropolitan's sister restaurant, Tsunami, who get their own shout-out as well for putting some fine craft beer on the menu alongside a menu consisting of sushi, pan-Asian cuisine, and some more "traditional" steak and seafood.

I was told Annapolis has some catching up to do in the world of different and interesting beer. These two stops make it seem like they're on their way.

OLD LINE BISTRO

11011 Baltimore Ave., Beltsville, MD 20705; (301) 937-6999; oldlinewine.com;
@OldLineWine
Draft Beers: 15 **Bottled/Canned Beers:** Plenty to choose from on the retail store shelves

If it were just the wine and spirits and beer, Old Line wouldn't make this book. Not that they don't stock one of the largest selections of craft beer around. My rule for the book is no distributors or bottle (only) shops. But, they do have that five-letter word, bistro, at the end of their name. If you walk past the well-kept displays of local beer and beers of the world, you'll come upon a bistro in a room unfair to call a back room.

The bistro pours 15 lines of beer and is known to serve up a whole lot of locals like Burley Oak, Starr Hill, Devil's Backbone, Jailbreak, Union, Evolution, and Flying Dog. They just so happen to pour some pretty darn good wine as well, if you are so inclined.

The food pages of the menu are not lacking either. This is not your typical (is there such a thing?) beer-store food menu. Think fried brussels sprouts, steak ciabatta with sriracha mayo, steak frites, a list of TV show–themed 8-ounce burgers, and fish tacos.

College Park and the University sit squarely between Franklin's (see Breweries in this chapter) and Old Line. If you're in the area, this is a stop you want to make.

PUB DOG PIZZA & DRAFTHOUSE

8865 Stanford Blvd., Columbia, MD 21045; (410) 872-0364; pubdog.net/columbia.html;
@PubDogBrewing
20 E. Cross St., Baltimore, MD 21230; (410) 727-6077; pubdog.net/federal_hill.html;
@PubDogBrewing
Draft Beers: 12

Every day is a dog day at Pub Dog. The two locations are serving Pub Dog Brewing beers from Westminster, brewed on the old Clay Pipe Brewing equipment. The pub approach at the two is basically the same, with the difference being the original Federal Hill location (est. 2001) is much more urban in its total space and narrow storefront layout. The newer location in Columbia (est. 2007) has more open bar space, plus an outdoor patio where canines are permitted to mingle with their two-legged friends.

Initially, Pub Dog was contracting its beers out of Old Dominion before they closed up shop. Now, in a twist, Pub Dog is doing contracted beers for other brewing establishments. As for their own beers, the pubs typically have a dozen beers on tap that cover most of the basic colors and styles.

The blond, orange wheat, and English ale are all easy and refreshing. The black, brown, and amber all pick up the malt and roast to another level. There is an IPA and a double IPA for the hopheads. And a few fruit beers like peach, blueberry, and raspberry that are better, particularly the peach, than might first be imagined.

Don't be shocked, however, when two mugs are delivered. The "Dog Deal" is that two of the same kind at the same time cost a total of $4.50. Basically that means 20 ounces of beer in two glasses for $4.50. Not necessarily the steal of the year, but still a pretty good deal, especially if you want to share the second glass with a fellow drinking partner.

QUARRY HOUSE TAVERN

8401 Georgia Ave., Silver Spring, MD 20910; (301) 587-8350; quarryhousetavern.com;
@QuarryHouseTvn
Draft Beers: 8 **Bottled/Canned Beers:** "Hundreds"

As the last interesting place in Maryland to get a good beer before hitting the state line with DC, the Quarry House Tavern seems like neither a house nor hardly any other tavern. Well, maybe the basement of a house. That is if you can find it on your first pass along Georgia Avenue just a couple of blocks from the Silver Spring Metro station stop.

The "front door" is at the bottom of a long flight of stairs from street level. Once inside, it might be difficult to leave. Subterranean bars seem to have that effect on people.

The atmosphere comes across as classic dive bar. Dark, low ceilings, weekly live music, popular theme nights like quizzo, hot dogs, tacos, and assorted other reasonably priced pub grub. But, here's the catch: For all of its dive-bar goodness, the drinks menu excels with a stellar list of eight drafts and plenty of bottles from DC, Maryland, the States, Italy, Germany, the UK, and Belgium. Plus, a whiskey list the length of both arms.

Dive bars shouldn't be talked about too much lest we ruin the good times for those who are in the know. Now you are as well but, shhh, don't tell anyone else.

RAM'S HEAD TAVERN

33 W. St., Annapolis, MD 21401; (410) 268-4545; ramsheadtavern.com/annapolis; @RamsHeadGroup
Draft Beers: 30+ **Bottled/Canned Beers:** Around 140

Annapolis dates back to 1649 and is a state capital renowned for sailing, brick, and history. This can be discussed while walking the streets and seeing the sights of the picturesque city. Or you could grab a pint of beer at Ram's Head and transport yourself back hundreds of years.

Brewing in Annapolis dates back to pre–Revolutionary War years and Benjamin Fordham's brewery. The dots are connected through the years when Fordham Brewing Company opened in 1995 inside of the Rams Head Tavern. **Gypsy Lager** was the first brew and still today, with Fordham's brewing all handled in Dover (see the Southern Delaware chapter), is a popular component of Fordham's core brands. The Lager, a German helles, in addition to the **Copperhead Ale** and **Route 1 Session IPA**, are routinely served on tap at Ram's Head. The **Ram's Head IPA**, a bigger IPA at 7.5% ABV and 75 IBUs, is brewed as a nod to the history with the Annapolis establishment and can likewise be found regularly at the bar. A sister beer from the brewery,

typically the wonderfully sweet Dominion Oak Barrel Stout, can usually be spotted as well.

Ram's Head is a sprawling patchwork of dining rooms, bars, and a live entertainment stage. The Ram's Head On Stage has developed into a premier destination for musical acts touring through the region. In the dining rooms, tater tots are all the rage these days and a meal could easily start off with the kitchen's spin on them, served with a crab dip. The menu sports a lot of the standard tavern fare you might expect but the Roasted Pear Salad and the Rasta Pasta are two entries on the menu that deserve attention.

After a meal and listening to some live music, sipping an Oak Barrel Stout in the below street level cozy pub is a great way to close out a visit to Ram's Head.

SCHMANKERL STUBE

58 S. Potomac St., Hagerstown, MD 21740; (301) 797-3354; schmankerlstube.com
Draft Beers: 5 **Bottled/Canned Beers:** 10

Schmankerl Stube is to German beer and food as Mannequin Pis is to the Belgians a few pages back. Hagerstown has a real treat in its midst with a Bavarian-themed restaurant over 25 years old and still going strong.

This local fixture serves up the requisite fare in a town founded by a German immigrant, Jonathan Hager. From German to English, Schmankerl Stube roughly translates to a small, cozy room in which to eat something small and delicious, and the restaurant has pulled it off.

The restaurant is run by a Bavarian, Charles Sekula, and there is an intense pride reflected in the service and the authenticity of the menu. A handful of draft and bottled beers typically includes selections from Ayinger, Bitburger, Erdinger, Hacker-Pschorr, Hofbräu, and Paulaner. Making sure you get just enough beer to drink, the serving sizes range from a small glass to 0.5 liter, 1 liter, and up to a 5-liter mug.

The kitchen cooks up German delights like *Käsespätzle, Schweinshaxe, Sauerbraten, Wiener Schnitzel,* and various plates of wurst. Whether eating and drinking indoors or outside in the biergarten, *Gemütlichkeit* is surely the rule of the day.

VICTORIA GASTRO PUB

8201 Snowden River Pkwy., Columbia, MD 21045; (410) 750-1880; victoriagastropub.com; @VictoriaGPub

Draft Beers: 24 **Bottled/Canned Beers:** Around 250

This place gets its name in part from the downtown London train station, and since the term "gastropub" has its roots in England, it makes sense. It also makes sense to stop here in Columbia when looking for good beer and food. The relentless focus from day one has been on quality food and beer menus. The restaurant also holds special events like well-conceived monthly brewery-centric dinners.

The beer menu pulls from all corners of the world, but a special Maryland section deserves special attention. Evolution, Flying Dog, Heavy Seas, and Union are regularly found on the draft towers at Victoria. The kitchen, in its role, presents a dizzying list of interesting plates such as duck poutine, grilled asparagus with speck, lobster and grilled brie, white truffle popcorn, and Allagash beer-battered fish-and-chips.

Between the multiple dining rooms, the comfortable bar, and the friendly and efficient service, in this little hotbed of quality beer stops in Columbia (Frisco, Maryland Homebrew, and The Ale House are all within 3 miles), Victoria is playing its part quite well. The ownership expects to add a farm brewery to its playbook in 2015 with Manor Hill Brewing Company to be located in Ellicott City (see More to Come later in the book).

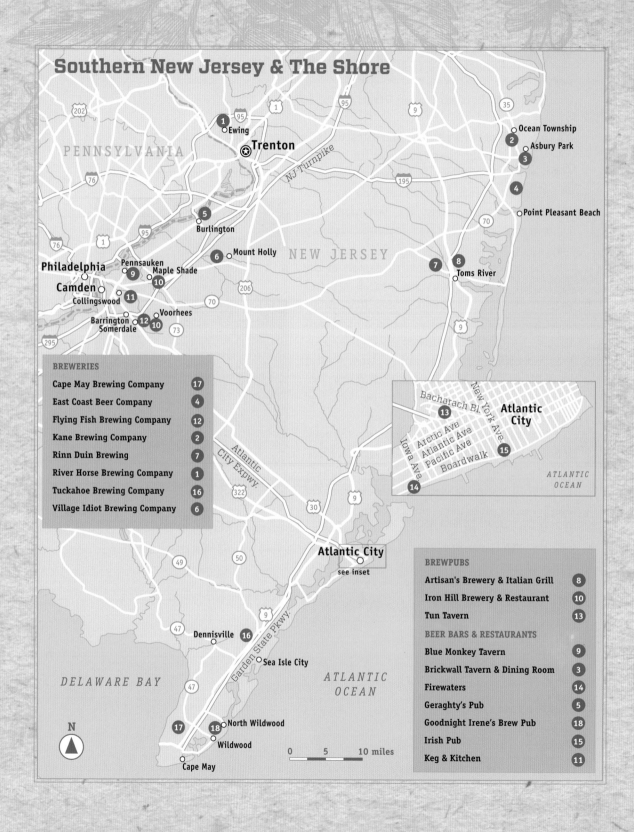

Southern New Jersey & The Shore

PENNSYLVANIA

1 Ewing

Trenton

NEW JERSEY

5 Burlington

6 Mount Holly

Philadelphia
Pennsauken
9
Maple Shade
Camden 10
Collingsworth
11
Voorhees
Barrington 12 10
Somerdale

Ocean Township
2
Asbury Park
3

4

Point Pleasant Beach

7 8
Toms River

BREWERIES

Cape May Brewing Company	17
East Coast Beer Company	4
Flying Fish Brewing Company	12
Kane Brewing Company	2
Rinn Duin Brewing	7
River Horse Brewing Company	1
Tuckahoe Brewing Company	16
Village Idiot Brewing Company	6

Atlantic
City Expwy.

322

30

Atlantic City
see inset

49

50

Dennisville 16

Sea Isle City

DELAWARE BAY

North Wildwood
17 18
Wildwood

Cape May

0   5   10 miles

Bacharach Bl.
New York Ave.
Atlantic City
13
Arctic Ave.
Atlantic Ave.
Pacific Ave.
Iowa Ave.
Boardwalk
15

14

ATLANTIC
OCEAN

ATLANTIC
OCEAN

BREWPUBS

Artisan's Brewery & Italian Grill	8
Iron Hill Brewery & Restaurant	10
Tun Tavern	13

BEER BARS & RESTAURANTS

Blue Monkey Tavern	9
Brickwall Tavern & Dining Room	3
Firewaters	14
Geraghty's Pub	5
Goodnight Irene's Brew Pub	18
Irish Pub	15
Keg & Kitchen	11

N

Southern New Jersey & The Shore

Gone are the days of the countless traffic circles and dearth of decent beer venues in New Jersey. Even the typically pale, fizzy, macro-leaning Jersey Shore has been beefing up its beer menus with more diversity in recent years. Breweries, too, have been tapping into the southern New Jersey market.

For the sake of drawing a line, I am roughly using the east-west US-195 from Trenton to Belmar as the line of demarcation between the north and south. Most I discussed this with generally agreed. With recent changes in New Jersey laws, brewing establishments are now freer than ever to provide samples, sell full glasses of beer, and provide take-home sales.

New Jersey used to be thought of as a beer wasteland. That's no longer the case. First up, southern New Jersey and the Shore points.

Breweries

CAPE MAY BREWING COMPANY

1288 Hornet Rd., Rio Grande, NJ 08242; (609) 849-9933; capemaybrewery.com;
@CapeMayBrewCo
Founded: 2011 **Founders:** Ryan Krill, Chris Henke, and Robert Krill **Brewers:** Chris
Henke, Brian Hink, Paul Nease (Cellarman), Andrew Ewing (Cellarman) **Flagship Beer:**
Cape May IPA **Year-Round Beers:** Devil's Reach Belgian Ale; Cape May Honey Porter;
Coastal Evacuation Double IPA **Seasonals/Special Releases:** Staff Series and many
others **Tours:** Every day, 12 to 8 p.m. both guided and self-guided **Taproom:** Yes

If you stop here during the Shore's off-season, you'll find an atmosphere that
looks anything but off-season. The young Cape May Brewing Company certainly
has found a fan base in the summer travelers to New Jersey's most southern beach
towns of Cape May and Wildwood. But the off-season crowds prove that the locals
love them too. The reputation and resulting demand for the beer has grown so significantly in such a short period of time that the brewery, which is tucked away off
Route 9 at the site of the Cape May airport, is looking to expand in 2015.

The year-round **Coastal Evacuation Double IPA (formerly known as
Centennial IPA)** is featured as our Beer Lover's Pick and the brewery keeps around
an additional 15 beers on tap at all times in their laid-back tasting room. Outfitted

with communal-style picnic tables and oversized throw rugs, the tasting room provides a comfortable atmosphere to enjoy their takes on saisons, lagers, stouts, and Scottish ales.

The **Honey Porter** (5.2% ABV) is a standout in their regular lineup. This traditional porter has caramel and molasses sweetness and an extra touch of smoke as well as a smooth texture and sweetness from local Cape May honey. This is one of which you could easily put back a few.

An additional angle to the tap list at Cape May is the Staff Series. Each employee can develop a recipe of ingredients and flavor and aroma profiles from which a unique beer results and is named after the employee. Some employees join in the brewing process as well.

One such standout earlier in 2014 came from Maggie Clark. Her beer was called **Day Off Session IPA** and drank quite nicely at 5.4% ABV with a nice crisp and slightly floral and fruity presentation. Keep an eye open for this and other interesting employee-inspired/employee-brewed beers, as they may come around again from time to time.

When it comes time to leave, there are plenty of great take home "souvenir" options including various shapes of glassware, two different growler sizes (plus growler koozies), and all types of clothing and accessories including cycling jerseys.

Beer Lover's Pick

Coastal Evacuation
Style: Double IPA
ABV: 7.8%
Availability: Year-round; 12-ounce bottles
On the way to Cape May . . .

I've dated myself with this lyrical reference, but when on the way to Cape May, provided you are a self-proclaimed hophead, you will want to stop off at the brewery's tasting room and take along a growler of the Coastal Evacuation.

This beer has a lot of floral and grapefruit citrus going on both in the nose as well as the flavor. There's also a touch of earthiness and, at 7.8%, you might not be able to drink it all day, but come nighttime, down the shore everything's alright. There's another old Jersey Shore lyrical reference.

EAST COAST BEER COMPANY

801 Main St., Belmar, NJ 07719; (732) 202-7782; beachhausbeer.com; @BeachHausBeer
Founded: 2007 (current location: 2014) **Founders:** John Merklin and Brian Ciriaco
Brewer: Tom Przyborowski **Flagship Beer:** Beach Haus Classic American Pilsner **Year-Round Beers:** Beach Haus Cruiser IPA and Beach Haus Kick Back Ale **Tours:** Free
Taproom: Yes

East Coast has undergone a major transformation from being known as "the Beach Haus brewery"—the name behind its flagship pilsner—to having a full production brewery in downtown Belmar.

The 30-barrel brewhouse will allow them to expand distribution farther into their current markets of New Jersey and parts of Pennsylvania, New York, Connecticut, and North Carolina and open up the Virginia market. Once the move has been fully completed, all bottle and can packaging will be done at the new Belmar location. Until then, Rochester-based North American Breweries handles production, which according to owner John Merklin has been "one of the best decisions we have ever made."

At the time of this writing, construction on the new Belmar brewery was due to complete in the winter of 2014/2015 with a full opening to the public shortly thereafter.

East Coast is invested in its community through relationships with Brewer's Apprentice in Freehold, NJ and fundraising and sponsorships for local needs such as "Superstorm Sandy" relief.

Beer Lover's Pick

Beach Haus Classic
Style: American Pilsner
ABV: 5.3%
Availability: Year-round; 12-ounce bottles

Residents of Belmar will soon have fresh access to this pilsner that does exactly what it is meant to do: provide clean refreshment with a pleasant graininess and mild levels of sweetness, bitterness, and alcohol. A good beer year-round that stands out more so in the heat and humidity of a northeast summer.

FLYING FISH BREWING COMPANY

900 Kennedy Blvd., Somerdale, NJ 08083; (856) 504-3442; flyingfish.com; @JerseyFreshAle

Founded: 1995 **Founder:** Gene Muller **Brewers:** "Team Flying Fish" **Year-Round Beers:** Abbey Dubbel, Exit 4, Exit 16, Extra Pale Ale, HopFish IPA, RedFish **Seasonals/ Special Releases:** Farmhouse Summer Ale, Grand Cru Winter Reserve, OktoberFish **Tours:** Wed through Fri 3 to 8 p.m.; Sat. 12 to 6 p.m.; Sun. 12 to 4 p.m. Tours are free, samples pay-as-you-go. **Taproom:** Yes

Sustainable. It's a word that's thrown around quite a bit these days. It's what has driven Flying Fish for nearly 20 years. Back when both the Internet and sustainable were young ideas barely known to the masses, Gene Muller started the brewery on the Internet. No kickstarters and no social media. Just a desire to bring different beer to the people and . . . it worked.

In 2012, the brewery moved from its Cherry Hill location to a much larger space with plenty more room to grow almost three times over. And the theme is still sustainability. From using as much natural light and brewing during daylight hours to steam recapture, lessening the negative impact of brewing is front and center at Flying Fish.

Fortunately for fans of Flying Fish beer—99 percent of which is sold within a 100-mile radius of the brewery—the sustainability model is working and has allowed the brewery to continue expansion, adding 150-barrel fermenters into its 50-barrel brewhouse.

Of its core brands, **Extra Pale Ale** (5.2% ABV) is the oldest and has survived the test of time as a downright enjoyably tasty and easy-drinking beer with a pleasant, but not overwhelming hop presence. In more recent times, the **Forever Unloved (F.U.) Sandy** (6.3% ABV) was released as a benefit beer and brewed with donated experimental hop ADHA 483. This loosely described "wheat pale ale" was so successful in its release that the brewery was able to donate $75,000 of proceeds to rebuilding efforts in New Jersey in the wake of "Superstorm Sandy" in 2012.

No stranger to competitive acclaim, 2014 was a particularly good year for Flying Fish as the brewery collected a gold and a bronze medal at the Great American Beer Festival and World Beer Cup, respectively, for the HopFish and a silver medal for the RedFish.

<div align="center">~~~~~~~~~~~~~~~~~~ <strong>Beer Lover's Pick</strong> ~~~~~~~~~~~~~~~~~~</div>

Exit 4
Style: American Trippel
ABV: 9.5%
Availability: Year-round; 12-ounce bottles
Awards: Great American Beer Festival (Gold, 2009)
No Flying Fish beers have likely captured the imagination and interest of the beer-loving public more than those from the Exit Series. Exit 4 was the first to be released as a beer corresponding to an exit along the New Jersey Turnpike. Since then, seven other beers have been made in the series, incorporating anything from oysters to chestnuts to wild rice.

Exit 4 is a big-time Belgian-inspired tripel full of malt- and yeast-driven flavors and aromas including a warming sweetness, noticeable clove presence, mild fruitiness, and a pleasant hop kick in the finish.

It was so popular in its initial release that it was later added to the year-round lineup. While you should be sure to always grab it while it's fresh, it's a beer that holds up well with time.

KANE BREWING COMPANY

1750 Bloomsbury Ave., Ocean, NJ 07712; (732) 922-8600; kanebrewing.com; @KaneBrewing

Founded: 2011 **Founder:** Michael Kane **Flagship Beer:** Head High IPA **Year-Round Beers:** Overhead Imperial IPA **Seasonals/Special Releases:** Mysterioso Series, Tidal Series, Barrel-aged beers **Tours:** Free; Fri 5 to 8 p.m., Sat 12 to 5 p.m. **Taproom:** Yes

A fellow barstool squatter at Maloney's in Matawan upon learning of this book project said something to the effect of "You've got to get out of here and get to Kane. Go. Now. They are, without a doubt, the best brewery in New Jersey."

That's some mighty high praise I was anxious to check out firsthand. Arriving at Kane is rather uneventful in its low-rise industrial park neighborhood, just a stone's throw or two from the location of the long-ago Heavyweight Brewing Company. Furthermore, a quick left and right through the front doorways takes visitors into the small tasting room/retail shop after passing through what first feels like a doctor's office waiting room.

But, then one more doorway leads guests into the impressively large and photogenic brewery of boil kettles, fermenters, and wood barrels among which are scattered large picnic tables and an oversized tasting bar.

Night To End All Dawns [2014]
Style: Imperial stout
ABV: 12.4%
Availability: Occasional; 750-milliliter bottles
Awards: Great American Beer Festival (Gold, 2014)

The barrels. They can't be missed when visiting the brewery and they are not just for display. They have plenty of highly acclaimed beer inside. The barrel-aged beers are some of the brewery's fans most sought-after beers. A range of styles with an accompanying range of ingredients comes from the numerous barrels.

The Night To End All Dawns is a barrel-aged version of Silent Night, which itself is a nice, dry, bitter, and not-too-rich 9.2% imperial stout. When subjected to the bourbon barrels, the stout takes on a new life complete with rich aromas and flavors of bourbon, chocolate, raisins, vanilla, and coffee. An experience worth sharing with others.

Since opening in 2011, Kane has won fans over with beers such as the very drinkable **Belgian Blonde** (4.6% ABV), which has a touch of earthiness, a bit of sweet ripe fruit, and finishes with a slight tart edge.

Kane also gets major alpha acid points for its **Head High IPA** (6.5% ABV) and the **Overhead IPA** (8.2% ABV), the latter basically being an amped-up version of the relatively balanced former. Both present combinations of citrus and pine sure to please the most discriminating hophead's palate.

Port Omna (6.2% ABV) is wonderful as an American stout. It's limited in its release, so you must keep a careful eye open for it. Not too big on the alcohol, it takes on big flavors when subjected to recipe additions and tweaks (as it was more than 15 times through mid-2014, to the delight of many Kane fans). One of particular note was infused with mole and coffee and was a beautiful balance of spice, chocolate, and coffee.

Is Kane the best brewery in New Jersey? Ultimately, that's a personal decision for each to make, but with what Kane has put out there for consumption, it's understandable how some arrive at that decision.

RINN DUIN BREWING

1540 Rte. 37 W., Toms River, NJ 08755; (732) 569-3261; rinnduinbrewing.com; @rinnduinbeer

Founded: 2014 **Founders:** Chip Town and Jacqui Town **Brewer:** Ryan Michaels **Flagship and Year-round Beers:** St. John's Irish Red, Sandpiper English Brown, Trinity Scottish 70 **Seasonals/Special Releases:** Pota Caifé, The River Toms **Tours:** Every 30 minutes **Taproom:** Yes

When owner Chip Town said enough was enough with the banking industry, his homebrewing partner and daughter, Jacqui, agreed that it was finally time to give the commercial brewing project a try. Between the two of them, they have nearly 25 years of homebrewing experience, business acumen, and an Irish castle in the family.

Therein the beginnings of the young Rinn Duin Brewing were rooted, and they continue to gain accolades from both industry professionals and consumers.

Located along a fast and busy Route 37 just 10 miles from the beaches of Toms River and Seaside Heights, the brewery shares a large space with the Bacchus Winemaking School. Town envisions future barrel-sharing partnerships with Bacchus.

In the front tasting room, the UK theme is evident throughout. Family history and photographs line the walls. Across the draft list, "Irish," "Scottish," and "English" are all words used to describe the solidly made ales available for tastings and growler fills.

Beer Lover's Pick

The River Toms
Style: English IPA
ABV: 6.8%
Availability: Seasonal; draft only

Regardless of whether we call them Belgian, black, imperial, or white, IPAs are traditionally rooted in England, yes? So when you want to look to traditional IPAs and their much more balanced profile of malt and hops, you can look across the pond for some classic examples.

Now, you can also look to Toms River and the Rinn Duin homage to the IPA. Served via draft or as a handpumped cask-conditioned version, this beer shines with its delicious bready malt profile and pleasant dose of East Kent Golding, Challenger, and Sovereign hops.

Inside the brewery, the cavernous space comfortably houses a 25-barrel brewhouse and numerous 50-barrel fermenters. A bottling line fits in there too and could turn out 3,800 bottles an hour, but as Rinn Duin is just getting up to speed bottling its three primary beers, the current rate is 1,200 to 1,500 per hour.

The seasonal River Toms has been a big hit with customers (see Beer Lover's Pick) and due to overwhelming support, the brewery plans to do a year-round IPA with rotating variations on the theme, like an imperial red IPA.

RIVER HORSE BREWING COMPANY

2 Graphics Dr., Ewing, NJ 08628; (609) 883-0890; riverhorse.com; @RiverHorseBrew
Founded: 1996 **Current Owners:** Chris Walsh, Glenn Bernabeo **Brewers:** Chris Rakow (Head Brewer), Casey Cramer (Operations Manager), Joe Laluk, Mike Hilty, Matt Antinoro, and Brendan McClatchey **Flagship Beer:** Tripel Horse **Year-Round Beers:** Hop Hazard, Special Ale, Lager, Hop-A-Lot-Amus **Seasonals/Special Releases:** Summer Blonde, Hipp-O-Lantern, Belgian Freeze, Oatmeal Milk Stout **Tours:** Sat and Sun 12:15, 1:15, 2:15, 3:15, and 4:15 p.m.; $5 per person **Taproom:** Yes **Naming Inspiration:** River Horse = Hippopotamus. In Egyptian hieroglyphics, the hippo is typically found in illustrations of the brewing process and is said to symbolize sustenance and fertility.

The reputation of River Horse's beer in the past had been all over the place, depending upon who was asked. Since the ownership change in 2007, the response has been trending toward "great."

Part of the plan to get to "great" included a location move, one that was completed in 2013, relocating the brewery from a relatively cramped space in Lambertville to a cavernous space roughly 250 percent larger a bit more than 10 miles away in Ewing.

A few festivals make the brewery a destination each year in the fall (Oktoberfest), winter (cask ales), and spring (outdoor festival).

Inside the brewhouse, visitors are struck not only by the size but also by the collaborative graffiti. The Green Villain graffiti artists from Jersey City were commissioned to add some brand-inspired artwork that successfully gives the brewery a little something extra in the aesthetics department.

The new brewery is so large that they claim to have room to grow the production output by nearly 10 times what it was in 2013. Even the front tasting room is larger than some of the more typical tasting rooms. A tasting counter, merchandise racks, and a retail beer cooler surround the high tops, and there's space in which customers there to tour can mingle over a few beer samples.

River Horse is doing some level of production work in the brewhouse every day but Saturday as it pumps out fan favorites like Hop Hazard and Tripel Horse with ease for its local market, which it defines as New York City to Philadelphia.

The brewery, in its expansion, has also focused on more one-offs and seasonal beers to keep beer lovers coming back for more. Notable in recent months have been **Oatmeal Milk Stout** and **Hipp-O-Lantern Imperial Pumpkin**.

Beer Lover's Pick

Blonde
Style: American blonde ale
ABV: 4.5%
Availability: April through August; 12-ounce bottles
In a stable of beers that burst with flavors and higher alcohols, it's nice to see the brewery do a beer like the River Horse Blonde that is relatively lighter and more refreshing, yet with enough flavor of sweet orange citrus and a touch of earthiness to still be interesting. A great summer brew.

TUCKAHOE BREWING COMPANY

9 Stoney Ct., Ocean View, NJ 08230; (609) 827-5375; tuckahoebrewing.com; @TuckahoeCo

Founded: 2011 **Founders:** Tim Hanna, Matt McDevitt, Chris Konicki, and Jim McAfee
Brewers: Matt McDevitt, Chris Konicki, Amanda Cardinali **Flagship Beer:** Dennis Creek Pale Ale **Year-Round Beers:** Steelmantown Porter, Anglesea Irish Red Ale, and Reeds Bay IPA **Tours:** $5; Fri 5 to 8 p.m., Sat 12 to 5 p.m. **Taproom:** Yes **Naming Inspiration:** The town of Tuckahoe has ship-building roots and the three-masted schooner is in the brewery's logo

Tuckahoe Brewing is tucked away on the inland side of the Sea Isle City exit of the Garden State Parkway in a new building that is shared with Harry and Bean's Coffee Company. Which means, like Cape May Brewing 10 miles down the road, Tuckahoe is a great stop for vacationers looking to stock up their shore house with not only fresh and local beer but fresh-roasted coffee beans as well.

Three school teachers and an architect started the business, which has grown into a popular stop for a sampler flight of their beers on tap. Plus, during any given visit, there could be a pin of something special sitting on the bar top for a taste of cask-conditioned goodness.

Two beers that have turned into local favorites include the **Reed's Bay IPA** (6.1% ABV) and the **Steelmantown Porter** (6.5% ABV). The richly flavored American

Beer Lover's Pick

New Brighton Coffee Stout
Style: Coffee stout
ABV: 9.0%
Availability: Winter seasonal; draft only

The New Brighton has coffee from the neighboring Harry & Bean's packed into this wonderful stout that smells like a coffee, drinks like a stout, and then finishes with some hallmark burnt coffee roast.

The sentimental upside to this beer's story is that a portion of profits from the sale of this beer are donated to the Marine Mammal Stranding Center in Brigantine, in honor of longtime East Coast surfing icon George Gerlach, who passed away unexpectedly in 2011.

porter has a nice, dry touch of smoke and wood. The IPA is a hop-forward IPA giving off tropical fruity characteristics that is likewise not too overwhelming.

Growler fills, both half-size and full, are available to go, so light up the grill and pour yourself a taste of Tuckahoe.

VILLAGE IDIOT BREWING COMPANY

42 High St., Mount Holly, NJ 08060; (609) 975-9270; villageidiotbrewing.com; @VillageIdiotNJ

Founded: 2013 **Founders:** Vince Masciandaro and Rich Palmay **Brewers:** Vince Masciandaro and Rich Palmay **Flagship Beer:** Bridgetown Blonde **Year-Round Beers:** Mullin's Irish Red, Revolutionary Rye, Bike Rail Pale Ale, Dry Irish Stout, Oatmeal Chocolate Stout, Saison du Idiot, Teddy Hopper DIPA **Tours:** By video screen at the bar **Taproom:** Yes **Naming Inspiration:** Part of a longer story: After missing a bank appointment the owners—who wanted to create a village-like experience—dubbed themselves the "village idiots."

Billed as the first Main Street brewery in New Jersey since the passage of the 2012 law that enabled brewery establishments to sell beer both for consumption on site and to take home, Village Idiot is capitalizing off a fortuitous location in downtown Mount Holly. Not only are they within walking distance of the township's Mill Dam, Monroe Street, Ironworks recreational parks, and the curiously interesting Burlington County Prison Museum, they have been joined by an even newer brewing neighbor in the Mount Holly beer scene, Spellbound Brewing Company.

Stop by Village Idiot at almost any time of any day and the crowds will testify to the thirst for great beer in New Jersey that for too long had been too little satisfied.

Satisfying that thirst at Village Idiot are a crisp, refreshing, and slightly bitter **Bridgetown Blonde** (4.8% ABV) and **Oud Dublin** (4.2%), with great roasted coffee flavor.

It's no accident that Village Idiot is popular as not only another watering hole in town, but one that makes great beer. Co-owners Vince and Rich have over 30 years of combined home-brewing experience. Expect much more from these two to come as they plan to double their brewing to 3-barrel batches in 2015.

While New Jerseyans will still cross the river to the Philly side for great beer, Village Idiot, among others, is giving locals more tasty reasons to think twice before doing so.

Beer Lover's Pick

Thong Remover Tripel
Style: Belgian-style tripel
ABV: 9.5%
Availability: Year-round; draft only
The name may scream for attention but, after just a couple of sips, the wonderful balance of fruit sweetness and alcohol presence elevates this beer to one of the most pleasingly drink-able tripels around. This beer deserves the accolades that consumers are heaping on it.

PHOTO COURTESY OF VILLAGE IDIOT BREWING COMPANY

Brewpubs

ARTISAN'S BREWERY & ITALIAN GRILL

1171 Hooper Ave., Toms River, NJ 08753; (732) 244-7566; artisanstomsriver.com; @ArtisansTR

Founded: 2009 **Founders:** Peter and Petros Gregorakis **Brewer:** Dave Hoffmann **Year-Round Beers:** Lite Ale, Irish Red Ale, West Coast IPA **Seasonals/Special Releases:** Alt, Czech Pilsner, Hefeweizen, Double Chocolate Oatmeal Stout, and others

Upon visiting Artisan's, if the location across the parking lot of the Ocean County Mall feels familiar, it might be the ghost of Basil T's second location. The owners of Artisan's picked up the location in 2009 and currently has Dave Hoffmann of Climax Brewing Company brewing the standard house beers and a few specialties three or four times a month.

Hoffmann's pedigree as a commercial brewer suggests the beer should be up to snuff in the 15-barrel brewhouse at Artisan's, and it is. The **English-style IPA** does just as the name suggests it should and presents itself as a stereotypically malty English IPA followed with a dose of tropical hops peeking through.

In contrast, the **Double Chocolate Oatmeal Stout** (6.2% ABV) is a seasonal favorite on the menu and is full of rich, dark malt flavor that is further complemented

by a healthy dose of Tcho Chocolate. The smooth beer finishes up nicely with bitter hops and dry chocolate notes.

One particular dish that pairs up nicely with the brewery's winter seasonal **Alt** beer is the warm heirloom farro salad. This relatively light but flavorful dish of roasted butternut squash, walnuts, apple, spinach, bacon, and sherry vinaigrette goes perfectly with the balanced beer of smoke, roast, and bittersweet chocolate.

Live music is presented most weekend nights and, when it comes time to leave, growler fills of brewhouse favorites are available to go.

IRON HILL BREWERY & RESTAURANT

124 E. Kings Hwy., Maple Shade, NJ 08052; (856) 273-0300; ironhillbrewery.com/mapleshade; @IronHillMS
Founder and Owners: Kevin P. Finn (President), Kevin Davies (Director of Culinary Operations), Mark Edelson (Director of Brewing Operations) **Opened:** 2009 **Brewers:** Kevin Walter and Andrew Rubenstein **Brewing Output:** 10-bbl brewhouse; 1,500 barrels/year

13107 Town Center Blvd., Voorhees, NJ 08043; (856) 545-9009; ironhillbrewery.com/voorhees; @IronHillVH
Opened: 2013 **Brewers:** Kevin Walter and Andrew Harton **Brewing Output:** 8.5-bbl brewhouse; 1,200 barrels/year

Of Iron Hill's multiple locations, Maple Shade represents its first foray into New Jersey and Voorhees became the brewpub family's 10th overall as of summer 2014.

As described in the Delaware and Pennsylvania chapters, the Iron Hill group is remarkably consistent in the approach to everything from decor to food to beer. Or, at least the core beer menu. As previously mentioned, where Iron Hill shines—and the due respect and just rewards garnered in national and international competitions are testaments—is in the gathering of head brewer talent in each of its locations.

After his longtime service at the West Chester location, Chris LaPierre earned the opportunity to help the company open the New Jersey market and put his stamp on the Maple Shade location. LaPierre is widely praised and liked within the industry and by consumers and late in 2014 moved on to the company's Chestnut Hill spot. Locally, he worked with the Barley Legal homebrew club and that relationship continues under Rubenstein.

While the Maple Shade location is off a busy road, the Voorhees location is wrapped inside a mixed-use environment called Voorhees Town Center.

Kevin Walter made his Iron Hill circuit through three locations before being handed the keys to the new Voorhees location in 2014. In keeping with the Iron Hill standard, Walter is an extremely personable and friendly brewer willing to talk shop with anyone posing a question. Voorhees has given him the opportunity to showcase

a wide variety of beers that he personally enjoys, like various takes on Belgian-style beers. His **Bedotter**, a Belgian-style tripel, earned him a silver medal at the 2014 Great American Beer Festival.

Why You Buggin'?

Chris LaPierre's brewing résumé shows his brewing career criss-crossing the beer industry from Harpoon to Dock Street to Iron Hill, where he has been on the payroll since 2003.

His skills working with diverse styles are evident in his annual event—Barrels, Bourbon, and Bugs—for which he gathers up and presents some of his most sought-after beers. Fans of this event can track down these unusual beers at LaPierre's new post in Chestnut Hill (Philadelphia) and the event is likely to continue at the Maple Shade brewpub as well.

Making regular appearances on the event's list of beers are bourbon barrel–aged beers like the Bourbon Quadfather, a big burly 10%+ Belgian strong ale aged in bourbon barrels.

Other beers that have been known to show up regularly on the list of crowd-pleasing delights include the F.red, a bracingly sour Flemish red ale; the period is not a typo. F.red is brewed roughly every other year and is enough to satisfy the event as well as bottle sales for the coming year with a little leftover to occasionally appear on a vintage menu.

Late in 2014, when LaPierre moved to Chestnut Hill, Walter was named Senior Lead Brewer over both locations in New Jersey. These two locations likely will not be Iron Hill's last in New Jersey. But, they are very solid showings from the company's band of brewers.

TUN TAVERN

2 Convention Blvd., Atlantic City, NJ 08041; (609) 347-7800; tuntavern.com; @ACTunTavern
Founded: 1999 **Founder:** Montgomery Dahm **Brewer:** Tim Kelly **Flagship and Year-Round Beers:** Tun Light, Irish Red, IPA, Leatherneck Stout

Tun Tavern was a beer destination in Atlantic City long before beer became as popular as it is now. If you're taking the train from Philadelphia (or anywhere in between), Tun Tavern can either be the first stop upon arriving or the last stop before leaving as the train station is just across the street from the restaurant's doorstep.

Once located in a near wasteland of the city and counting the Convention Center (original home to the Miss America contest) as one of its few neighbors, Tun Tavern is now surrounded by a seemingly endless patchwork of outlet shops and chain restaurants, which makes the pub a perfect place when looking to escape the shopping strip.

Head brewer Tim Kelly has been pumping out the beers since 2007 and has built up a set of beers that make the bar a popular nightspot for locals and tourists alike.

Tun Tavern, the name, evokes the Colonial-era pub in Philadelphia where history books place the founding of the Marine Corps in 1775. The brewpub adopted the name and fittingly serves up beers with military and patriotic names.

Two of the brewery's more memorable beers include the **Wee Heavy** (6.5% ABV), full of rich maltiness and a touch of smoke, and the **Leatherneck Stout** (4.5% ABV), a medium-bodied stout, full of flavor but low in alcohol. It pairs up nicely with the Piled High and Deep on the menu, which consists of roasted turkey breast, cheddar, and honey mustard.

Beer in growlers and occasional bottles of special ones are available to go, which means the party can continue back in the hotel room.

Beer Bars & Restaurants

BLUE MONKEY TAVERN

2 S. Centre St., Merchantville, NJ 08109; (856) 661-8008; bluemonkeytavern.com;
@BluMonkeyTavern
Draft Beers: 40, plus 1 handpump **Bottled/Canned Beers:** 25+

The Blue Monkey Tavern resides inside a 120+-year-old building that originally served as an entertainment hall—Collins and Pancoast Hall—just a block off the center of town. The homey front porch suggests an inviting atmosphere inside, and that's what waits down a short hallway to the mahogany bar and restaurant seating area.

Monkeys show up both in the decor and the drinks menu where a dozen "monkey drinks" promote the theme of the restaurant. A significant list of single-malt whiskeys is available as well.

Flowing from the many taps are high quality beers, including some lesser-seen ones from breweries such as the local, small, and young Tuckahoe. The bottle list is equally impressive, with a few Trappist beers and an occasional Fifty-Fifty sighting.

The food menu offers a few interesting twists on the typical pub menu. Blue Monkey Drummers are chicken drumsticks wrapped in bacon and served with sour cherry chipotle and Gorgonzola sauce. Imagine that paired with the Bockor Cuvée des Jacobins Flemish sour which they have on tap from time to time.

Orecchiette carbonara with slab bacon is a great dish for solid carbs to go with the liquid carbs in a glass of a strong Belgian ale like Unibroue Maudite, which stands up nicely to the big pasta dish and supplies complementary flavors as well.

If brunch is on the docket, it's tough to go wrong with french toast made with baguettes and made even more perfect when consumed with an Andechser Doppelbock.

BRICKWALL TAVERN & DINING ROOM

522 Cookman Ave., Asbury Park, NJ 07712; (732) 774-1264; brickwalltavern.com;
@BrickwallTavern
Draft Beers: 24 **Bottled/Canned Beers:** 100+

Asbury Park has come alive in the last few years and the Brickwall Tavern has pulled its weight in support of restoring some of the beach-side city's former destination appeal. The restaurant is actually a part of a group of restaurants that includes other local favorites such as Goldie's, The Annex, and Porta Pizzeria, the latter of which is located just a block from the beach and the legendary Stone Pony music venue.

Brickwall serves up a creative menu of food in an energetic and fun atmosphere with playful artwork, televisions, and a beer menu that showcases nearly every style and strength of beer. The menu includes delectable bites like Cajun-seared shrimp with Parmesan grits and a hot-fried chicken salad to more substantial dishes such as half-rack bourbon chipotle St. Louis ribs and a 14-ounce pork chop. A full raw bar awaits those with a hunger for the nearby sea.

Late-night drinking, or weekend brunch drinking for that matter, may call for smaller plates of food and the "minis" certainly fit the bill. The pork roll and cheese mini and fried buffalo chicken mini are two favorites.

The full experience at Brickwall deserves a beer float, and the kitchen comes through with a number of varieties, including Jack Daniels and root beer with vanilla ice cream and Guinness with coffee ice cream.

FIREWATERS

2831 Boardwalk (at Tropicana Casino), Atlantic City, NJ 08401; (609) 344-6699;
firewatersbar.com; @FirewatersBar
Draft Beers: 50 **Bottled/Canned Beers:** 101

Las Vegas has a marketing strategy whereby they appeal to the broadest public base by not always focusing the gambling side of the city. In recent years, Atlantic City has been taking a cue from the western "oasis in the desert" by beefing up the promotion of diverse, non-casino entertainment available in the oft-maligned city.

Case in point: Firewaters has been in Atlantic City since 2003, inside the Tropicana at the southern end of the strip and boardwalk. The addition of The Quarter in 2004 has added even more retail, dining, and drinking options.

Firewaters is typically open until 3 or 4 a.m. on the weekend and sits across from Tony Luke's cheesesteak and sandwich restaurant in The Marketplace, which works out perfectly when looking for a beer and a cheesesteak.

This means that when strolling the boards or awaiting family or friends, Firewaters is open and ready to serve up everything from local beers (think Flying Fish RedFish) to great beers of the world such as Firestone Walker Union Jack and Franziskaner Weissbier.

Atlantic City offers more tasty options like Firewaters than ever before and gives non-gamblers a reason to go without ever stepping foot on a casino floor. Firewaters also has locations in Hackensack, NJ, Newark DE, and Concord, PA, delivering similar experiences, sans beach and casino.

GERAGHTY'S PUB

148 E. Broad St., Burlington, NJ 08016; (609) 386-1121; geraghtyspub.com; @GeraghtysPub
Draft Beers: 18, including 1 handpump **Bottled/Canned Beers:** 100+

Seeing the River Link complete is a great thing. Some call it a boondoggle, but what I see is more than one way to get to Geraghty's, a great neighborhood pub that serves up great beer and sports near the Burlington-Bristol Bridge at the PA-NJ state line.

Geraghty's is rather unassuming from the outside and deceptively larger inside. Five flat-screen televisions surround the U-shaped bar, which makes for a rollicking atmosphere come game time and a cordial neighborhood-type atmosphere when quieter.

Adding to the atmosphere is plenty of sports memorabilia and photographs lining the walls, including fighting (as in boxing) pictures and a Dr. J-Larry Bird fighting picture thrown in for good measure.

The beers flowing from the taps come primarily from the northeast and mid-Atlantic regions and at any given time could include the likes of Captain Lawrence (NY), Weyerbacher (PA), and Starr Hill (VA). Customers visiting around the late-winter/early-spring time of year might be treated to a cask-conditioned Innis & Gunn Irish Whiskey Stout on the handpump.

Coming from the kitchen are plenty of pub grub options to keep you going throughout the game. A half-dozen cheesesteak variations, sandwiches, burgers, fish-and-chips, and tons of apps will help keep your "session" going for hours.

All aboard; next stop Geraghty's.

GOODNIGHT IRENE'S BREW PUB

2708 Pacific Ave., Wildwood, NJ 08260; (609) 729-3861; goodnightirenes.com;
@GoodnightIrenes
Draft Beers: 38 **Bottled/Canned Beers:** 40+

Goodnight Irene's is not a brewpub as is frequently assumed but what they do, however, is serve up plenty of great brews and fun times in a pub atmosphere. They opened in 1973, and before just about anyone else at The Shore, they thought they could, or should, serve anything but tasteless, low-alcohol, mass-produced beer.

Goodnight Irene's continues to present guests with everything from the tastiest pilsner for the hot days, like Sly Fox Pikeland Pils, to the big and burly Avery Maharaja (10.2% ABV) for the cool nights.

A haven for die-hard sports fans (particularly Philadelphia and some New York teams), Goodnight Irene's has a kitchen that cranks out solid plates of food to accompany the stellar list of beers. Brick oven pizzas work perfectly on game day and some incorporate beer, like the Arrogant Bastard Buffalo Pie, where the beer has been blended into the buffalo sauce. Or, for a lighter bite during a break from the beach life, the Stone IPA chicken salad takes a West Coast hoppy favorite and marinates the chicken for extra flavor.

When drinking great beer at The Shore these days, Goodnight Irene's is still there to thank after all these years—where every day is a holiday and every night is a Saturday night. (Yet, another Shore musical reference.)

IRISH PUB

164 Saint James Pl., Atlantic City, NJ 08401; (609) 344-9063; theirishpub.com; @IrishPubAC1

What this original Atlantic City establishment (since 1972) might lack in beer-menu diversity is made up for in atmosphere, with vintage boxing photograph–adorned walls that look like they are just waiting to tell a few good stories from years past. Low ceilings, lots of woodwork, Tiffany lamps, small side dining rooms, and a horseshoe-shaped bar go a long way to create a comfortable environment.

Bartenders are down-to-earth and a mixed crowd of customers from all walks of life makes it the kind of bar that's easy to hang out in when the bright lights and high energy of the casino bars go on overload. For those with a strong aversion to smoking, be forewarned that it is still allowed here.

It's the Guinness, though, that you came for and it just seems fitting at this bar. So get one. Sit back. Sip. Savor. Soak in the atmosphere that will take you back a hundred years.

A standard pub grub food menu accompanied by classic Irish dishes and a liverwurst and onion sandwich that my father would approve of round out the experience at the Irish Pub. They are open until 6 a.m. Saturday and Sunday nights (or would that be Friday and Saturday nights?) and the remainder of the week are open "only" until 4 a.m.

KEG & KITCHEN
90 Haddon Ave., Westmont, NJ 08108; (856) 833-9800; kegnkitchen.com; @Keg_and_Kitchen
Draft Beers: 17 **Bottled/Canned Beers:** Around 100

Just a few blocks from the Westmont PATCO train station is a local favorite for beer and food. The food menu demonstrates creativity with dishes like asparagus fries with spicy aioli, spaetzel and brussels sprouts, and a short rib sandwich with garlic and spicy ricotta. Add to that a beef brisket *cemita*, flatbreads, Korean BBQ taco wrap, and a bunch of burgers, and it makes a full table for a group dining night out. The meat and cheese board changes daily based upon availability and can be built a la carte by the customer.

From the taps, a geographically diverse group of breweries can be found from around the region (Ommegang, Captain Lawrence, Neshaminy Creek, Tröegs, Brooklyn, Victory, and Dogfish Head to name a few) to much farther abroad (Firestone Walker, Lagunitas, Stone, Terrapin, and Schlafly, for example).

Keg & Kitchen routinely conducts beer events, many of them with a food pairing component, like the Beer School event that focuses on beer's history, science, and affinity to food.

From a beer, food, and service perspective—not to mention a side room that is often used for private parties and has brewery artwork on the ceiling done by a customer—Keg & Kitchen is a very comfortable neighborhood place to hang out.

Collingswood/Westmont—Pub Crawl

Trains are a critical component to life in the northeast. Not only do city and regional ones provide effective (and mostly efficient) transportation in and around big cities like Boston, New York, Philadelphia, Baltimore, and Washington, Amtrak links up these major Eastern Seaboard cities.

In New Jersey, there's the eastbound PATCO train line that Philadelphians can easily hop on and wind up at Tortilla Press, just 18 minutes after leaving any one of its three station stops in Center City Philadelphia.

TOTAL WALKING DISTANCE: 1.60 miles
PATCO TRAIN COST: $3 one-way from Philadelphia or $1.60 one-way between any two NJ stations

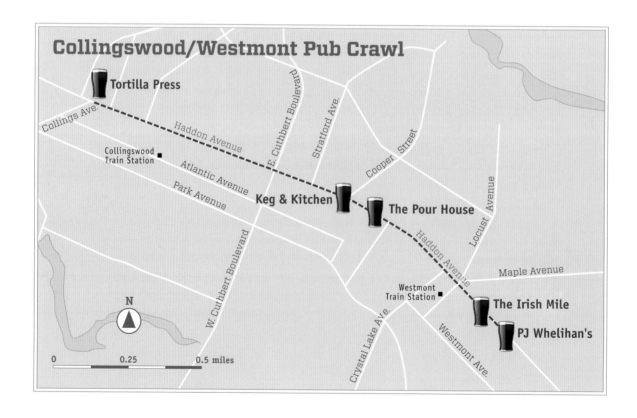

Directions: If taking the train, disembark at Collingswood, find your way to Haddon Avenue, and head west for roughly one-third mile to Tortilla Press. If driving, find a central parking spot on the street.

Tortilla Press, 703 Haddon Ave., Collingswood, NJ 08108; (856) 869-3345; thetortilla press.com; @TortillaPress

If you start off the South Jersey Pub Crawl on either a Saturday or Sunday at Tortilla Press, you'll be in for a treat. Now this may be the most atypical way to suggest starting a pub crawl, but bear with me here. Because as I've mentioned more than once, a good pub crawl should always start with a solid food base. And you can do it here at Tortilla Press, a BYOB.

Grab your favorite brunch bottle of beer and bring it with you to this excellent starting point for a pub crawl. I'm thinking maybe you'll take a bottle of Sly Fox Black Raspberry Reserve and order a plate of cinnamon cream cheese–stuffed french toast with a berry salsa whipped cream. Or how about a bottle of Flying Fish ESB and a chorizo breakfast burrito?

Give it a try; there's no corkage fee. I know this was a bit of a curveball and I promise there will be no other BYOs in the book, but I think you'll find it well worth the visit before embarking on the remainder of the stops listed here.

Directions: Make a left from the front door and walk east for nine-tenths of a mile, the longest walking stretch of this itinerary, to the next stop.

Keg & Kitchen, 90 Haddon Ave., Westmont, NJ 08108; (856) 833-9800; kegnkitchen .com; @Keg_and_Kitchen

Presuming you had brunch at Tortilla Press, you may not be inclined to eat at this point. Good thing there's beer. At Keg & Kitchen, if the weather is warm, you may find Yards Saison (6.5% ABV), Stoudts Pils (5.4% ABV) or Heifer-in-Wheat (5% ABV), or Gasthaus Berliner Weisse (3% ABV) to your liking. They keep a well-stocked and frequently rotating list of diverse drafts—a full bar of wine and cocktails too—so finding something for everyone should not be an issue.

If food is necessary, you've come to the right place as there are several shareable plates of food such as edamame, an Amish pretzel, Mediterranean olive mix, cheese and cured meat boards, and U-peel shrimp.

Admire the brewery-inspired art above the bar and then prepare to move on.

Directions: Turn right out the front door and challenge your pub-crawling mates to see who takes the fewest steps to go the barely one-tenth of a mile to the next stop.

The Pour House, 124 Haddon Ave., Westmont, NJ 08108; (856) 869-4600; pjspour house.com; @ThePourHouseNJ

The Pour House opened a second location in Exton, PA, in 2013 and has been doing to the western Philly suburbs what they did to southern New Jersey when they opened back in 2009: flowing great beer to the eager masses. The Westmont location has 20 taps (Exton has 30) and well over 100 bottle selections.

But you will only need a couple to get you through this stop of the tour. Again, I'll point you to some warmer weather beers like River Horse Blonde, Dogfish Head Festina Peche (both 4.5% ABV), or Kane Head High IPA (6.5% ABV). If the weather or your taste is suited for it, however, feel free to dive into a big stout like Southern Tier Mokah (10% ABV) or Stone Imperial Russian Stout (10.5% ABV).

For food, if needed, a sausage mushroom flatbread, the Pour House Deluxe Burger, fish tacos, and the short rib melt all come highly recommended. Be sure to balance the food; there are two more stops to make.

Directions: Hang a right out the front door and walk off a few of the beers that you've had thus far with a half-mile walk along Haddon Avenue.

The Irish Mile, 350 Haddon Ave., Haddon Township, NJ 08108; (856) 858-8500; theirishmile.com; @TheIrishMile

There are 66 draft lines of beer at The Irish Mile and most fall squarely in the "craft" camp. It's typical to find some New Jersey combination of Cape May, Carton, Kane, Tuckahoe, and River Horse. Then, there's this daily special that they run. All. The. Time. Flying Fish pints, all varieties, are always $3.50. Now that's what I call turning talk about "local love" into practice. As of this writing, Farmhouse, FU Sandy, and HopFish are on tap. Drink the locals!

Directions: Another short hop down Haddon Avenue, one-tenth of a mile, to the last stop.

PJ Whelihans's, 700 North Haddon Ave., Haddonfield, NJ 08033; (856) 427-7888; pjspub.com; @PJs_Pub

The forebearer to The Pour House, PJ Whelihan's dates back to 1983 and has a dozen locations, a "Wing Truck," and two arena locations in the family. This is the original location.

Here, you'll find a similar (though not quite as intense as at The Pour House) focus on great beer and food. That means instead of multiple Cape Mays, Cartons, Dogfish Heads, Flying Fishes, and Kanes, you might find one or two. Oh, are we not spoiled around these parts?

To wrap up your day on Haddon Avenue, if it's time for a meal to balance everything out, PJ's has you covered with lots of pub grub, of which the buffalo wings are a must, but so too are the eggplant fries with Bloody Mary dipping sauce, Alaskan amber fish-and-chips, and the Italian roast pork sandwich with long hots.

Now that you've wrapped up this tasty five-stop tour of Collingswood and Westmont, it's either a short walk back to your car or a much shorter walk to the Westmont PATCO train station, which is just a quarter-mile back in the direction from which you came.

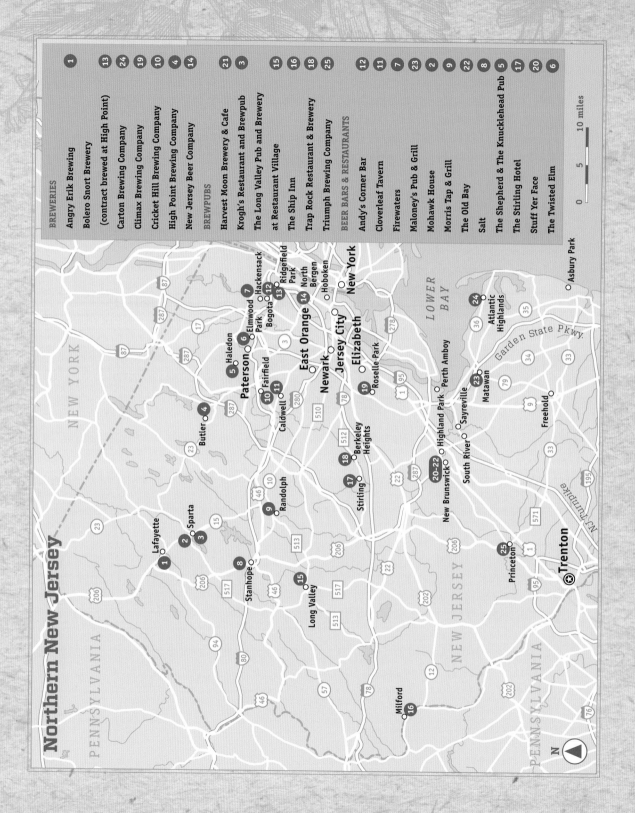

Northern New Jersey

BREWERIES

1 — Angry Erik Brewing
13 — Bolero Snort Brewery
24 — (contract brewed at High Point)
19 — Carton Brewing Company
10 — Climax Brewing Company
4 — Cricket Hill Brewing Company
14 — High Point Brewing Company
— New Jersey Beer Company

BREWPUBS

21 — Harvest Moon Brewery & Cafe
3 — Krogh's Restaurant and Brewpub
15 — The Long Valley Pub and Brewery
— at Restaurant Village
16 — The Ship Inn
18 — Trap Rock Restaurant & Brewery
25 — Triumph Brewing Company

BEER BARS & RESTAURANTS

12 — Andy's Corner Bar
11 — Cloverleaf Tavern
7 — Firewaters
23 — Maloney's Pub & Grill
2 — Mohawk House
9 — Morris Tap & Grill
22 — The Old Bay
8 — Salt
5 — The Shepherd & The Knucklehead Pub
17 — The Stirling Hotel
20 — Stuff Yer Face
6 — The Twisted Elm

0   5   10 miles

Northern New Jersey

This book covers several major metropolitan areas where the roadways and the congestion can be maddening. Then there is this chapter on northern New Jersey.

It's not difficult to see the frantic pace of driving ratchet up the farther north and closer to New York City you go. In a perfect world, you could do your beer exploration with a hired driver, or at least a trusted friend or family member as your designated driver, so that you could sit back and enjoy the ride without the stress of driving. Hurry up. Now. Faster. Go!

Breweries

ANGRY ERIK BREWING

10 Millpond Dr., Lafayette, NJ 07848; (862) 432-9003; angryerik.com
Founded: 2014 **Founders:** Erik and Heide Hassing **Brewer:** Heide Hassing **Seasonals/ Special Releases:** 3-Ball Porter, The Dainty Viking, Hoppy Heide Series **Tours:** Thurs through Sun **Taproom:** Yes

Head brewer and co-owner, Heide left her day job in 2014 and since then has been making whatever strikes a flavor chord; it's partly the beer lover in her and partly the chemist at work that is fascinated with flavor and aroma profiles.

And beer geeks have been taking notice. As of this printing, Angry Erik is the northwesternmost brewery in the Garden State, roughly equidistant from Poughkeepsie, Allentown, Scranton, and New York City. Beer lovers make the trek here for the rarely-brewed-twice beers. Though Heide will concede that as the brewery continues to find its path, certain beers, like the **3-Ball Porter** featured below, stand a better chance to be brewed somewhat regularly.

Beer geeks who share the same passion as Heide for beers that rarely dip below 6% ABV will find that to be yet another reason to seek out this brewery staking a claim in northwest New Jersey. During any given visit, you may find a nicely refreshing, crisp, and dry **Apricot Ale**, which smacks of the apricot peel as opposed to the sweet pulp of the fruit. The **Dainty Viking** (7.6% ABV) delivers just what

the description promises—that is, a big floral aroma—and matches up nicely with foods of similar nature, like a beet salad with an herbal dressing.

As many beer lovers are finding across the country, interesting breweries are no longer confined to major metropolitan markets. New breweries, like Angry Erik, are giving consumers a great chance to take that leisurely drive to explore an area and some beers that they'd previously not seen.

3-Ball Porter
Style: American Porter
ABV: 6%
Availability: Occasional; draft only

I'm inclined to say that this is one of the most interesting porters I've come across in quite some time. Nontraditional could be one way to describe it; delicious and food pairing–worthy would also be accurate.

Brewed in memory of the family dog—affectionately named for his tendency to pick up and carry three tennis balls at once in his mouth—this beer prominently features three key flavors: cardamom, orange, and chocolate. It immediately brings to mind roasted herb chicken or any number of Indian dishes where the flavors should match up perfectly to complement the beer.

BOLERO SNORT BREWERY

Contract-brewed at High Point Brewing Company in Butler, NJ
bolerosnort.com; @BoleroSnort
Founded: 2013 **Founders:** Robert Olson, Jr. and Andrew Maiorana **Brewer:** Andrew Maiorana **Year-Round Beers:** Ragin' Bull Amber Lager, Longhop Session IPA **Seasonals/ Special Releases:** Blackhorn American Black Lager, There's No Rye-ing in Basebull **Tours:** No **Taproom:** No **Naming Inspiration:** An anagram of owner's name

Bolero Snort is another brewery that goes on the "how-many-things-could-possibly-be-different-about-them-by-the-time-you-read-this" list. After successfully starting up under a contract relationship at High Point in Butler since February 2013, the team at Bolero Snort is on its way to brewing at a new facility of its own.

The brewery has no shortage of visibility, being found on tap at bars around northern New Jersey, at ShopRite Liquors in Westfield, NJ, and at festivals like Garden State Beer Fest, Big Brew Beer Fest, and Brew at the Zoo. Not bad for a self-distributed 2-year-old.

The expansion in 2015 will take Bolero Snort from doing approximately 60 barrels per month to a 10,000-square-foot facility that will allow them to do 30 barrels per batch and potentially enter select New York and Pennsylvania markets.

There's No Rye-ing in Basebull
Style: Rye Lager
ABV: 5%
Availability: April–October; 12-ounce bottles

The good news about this beer, aside from its crisp and refreshing flavor with a pleasantly not-over-whelming dose of rye spiciness, is that at 5% ABV, it's a beer begging to be drunk all game long.

This beer goes well with ballpark fare like pretzels and hot dogs or grilled items like vegetables and rotisserie chicken.

PHOTO COURTESY OF BOLERO SNORT BREWERY

This will be good news for fans of the brewery that have awarded Bolero Snort the People's Choice award at both the 2013 and the 2014 Atlantic City Beer Festival. Not only did the hand-filled, numbered, and wax-sealed **Happy Buck'n Anniversary** sell out at retail outlets in mere days in early 2014, it took a bronze medal home from the festival.

CARTON BREWING COMPANY

6 E. Washington Ave., Atlantic Highlands, NJ 07716; (732) 654-2337; cartonbrewing.com; @CartonBrewing
Founded: 2011 **Founders:** Augie Carton and Chris Carton **Brewers:** Pete Dixon, Jeremy Watts, Doug Phillips (Cellarman) **Year-Round Beers:** Boat Beer, 077XX, Carton of Milk, B.D.G., Red Rye Returning **Seasonals/Special Releases:** Coffee Stout, GORP, Harvest, Pumpkin Cream Ale **Tours:** Thurs and Fri 5 to 7:30 p.m., Sat and Sun 12 to 5 p.m.
Taproom: Yes

For your first visit, if you drive past Carton's location swearing that the GPS must have the location wrong, you can't be blamed. After all, no sign hangs out front and no gathering of beer geeks on a front patio give away that you have arrived at one of New Jersey's rising stars on the brewing scene.

Immediately impressive is the circa-1906 building that the brewery occupies and, later inside, the efficient use of first-floor space that fits a 15-barrel brewhouse

Beer Lover's Pick

Boat Beer
Style: Session ale
ABV: 4.2%
Availability: Year-round; 16-ounce cans

It's taken quite a few years from the early session rumblings to what is looking more like an actual "movement." Brewers and consumers who want to have the most flavorful and lowest-alcohol options available in the market now appear to be more on the same page than ever before.

Boat from Carton fits the bill on both counts. It's packed full of ripe fruit sweetness, citrus snappiness, and hop bitterness that make this a perfect quencher and an enjoyable beer to drink.

and a handful of 30- and 45-barrel fermenters. If taking a tour, don't forget to ask what's in "the Tippy."

The second floor is home to the modest-size tasting room, outfitted with a few comfortable sofas, area rug, and barstools to give the feeling of drinking at your buddy's converted living room. Typically there are eight beers on tap for tasting. To go, there is the option for growlers, half-growlers, and the recognizable bright-orange, 16-ounce cans of Boat Beer. An impressive lineup of glassware is available alongside brewery-emblazoned clothing and accessories.

A growing collection of wood barrels from Brinley Rum in St. Kitts is laid down in the cellar, aging beers like the **Honey Porter**. A few bourbon whiskey barrels that previously held Brooklyn Brewery's famed Black Ops might also be spotted down there.

Back upstairs, in addition to the Boat Beer (see Beer Lover's Pick), the **Carton of Milk** with its moderately roasty flavor and slight coffee aroma and **GORP** (trivia answer: GORP is short for Good Old Raisins and Peanuts), which uses chocolate and peanuts in the brew and raisins in fermentation, are ones to search out. The **077XX** has quickly become a local Double IPA favorite.

CLIMAX BREWING COMPANY

112 Valley Rd., Roselle Park, NJ 07204; (908) 620-9585; climaxbrewing.com
Founded: 1996 **Founders:** Dave Hoffmann and Kurt Hoffmann **Brewer:** Dave Hoffmann
Flagship and Year-Round Beers: India Pale Ale, Extra Special Bitter Ale, Nut Brown
Ale, Cream Ale, Helles Lager **Seasonals/Special Releases:** Oktoberfest, Doppel Bock,
Hefeweizen **Tours:** Yes **Taproom:** Yes

Climax has been doing its thing for a long time, so owner Dave Hoffmann and staff easily communicate their passion in lively conversation during and after tours of the brewery. The tour actually consists of standing between the tasting bar and the brewing operations and hearing about the process of making Climax's beer.

Operations continue to hum along after nearly 20 years with a very balanced **IPA** (6% ABV), a **Nut Brown Ale** (5.2% ABV) with a mild roast character, and a **Doppel Bock** (7.5% ABV) that is sure to impress the lovers of hearty, dark fruit–forward beers.

Hoffmann Helles Lager

Style: German helles lager

ABV: 4.6%–4.8%

Availability: Year-round, with a small break in December and January; 12-ounce bottles

This is a beauty of a lager, clean and crisp and so basic in nature and brewed under the Hoffmann line of Climax's lager beers. Three malts and one hop (the German Spalt "Noble" hop) make this one of owner Dave Hoffmann's favorite beers to make and drink.

Lucky for the consumer it is; Hoffmann says that throughout the year there's a tank of helles lager in play at any given time. Growlers and sixtels of it can be picked up at the brewery and bottles make it to all markets. This can work well, too, for beer drinkers crossing over to the craft segment.

By the time you read this, the front of the building space may have been built out to provide more of a true tasting-room experience. That will have to wait to be described here in the second edition. But if the past at Climax is any indication, this bit of growth will serve the brewery and its fans quite well in the near future.

CRICKET HILL BREWING COMPANY

24 Kulick Rd., Fairfield, NJ 07004; (973) 276-9415; crickethillbrewery.com; @CricketHillNJ

Founded: 2002 **Owners:** Rick Reed, Ed Gangi **Brewer:** Mark Tilley **Flagship and Year-Round Beers:** East Coast Lager, American Pale Ale, Hopnotic IPA, Colonel Blide's ESB **Seasonals/Special Releases:** Jersey Summer Breakfast Ale, Pumpkin Ale, Fall Festivus Ale, Nocturne Chocolate Ale **Tours:** Free; Thurs and Fri 4 to 7 p.m.; Sat 12 to 4 p.m. **Taproom:** Yes

Next in the alphabet comes Cricket Hill and, like Climax's Dave Hoffmann, owner Rick Reed is passionate about his beer. Reed is known for his Friday Night Rants. It's a spirited and opinionated message and one that not many take exception to. It's all about bolstering the case for non-macro, locally made, "real" beer.

The fun continues from the tour into the tasting room where typically six beers are on tap, which gives customers an idea of what makes Reed and his team so passionate.

Completing the northeast New Jersey triple play with Ramstein (next listing) and Climax, Cricket Hill also does a German helles very well with **East Coast Lager** (4.2% ABV), a high quality, warm weather refresher. Also impressive from the brewery is a biscuity English **Colonel Blide's ESB** (5.5% ABV) and malt-forward, tropically hopped **Jersey Devil Imperial Red Ale** (7.4% ABV, 66.6 IBU). All packaged products—including kegs, clothing, and accessories—are available to go for your later enjoyment.

Beer Lover's Pick

Hopnotic
Style: India pale ale
ABV: 6.5%
Availability: Year-round; 12-ounce bottles
This is an all-American IPA thanks to a blast of citrus and fruity hop presence and big hop aromas from dry-hopping. But the malt does its job in backing up the hops and creates a wonderful IPA that you can drink several of without palate fatigue. The balance reminds you it's from the East Coast and tips its malt bill to the original homeland of IPAs. A burger

with cheddar and guacamole would complement the Hopnotic quite well.

HIGH POINT BREWING COMPANY

22 Park Pl., Butler, NJ 07405; (973) 838-7400; ramsteinbeer.com
Founded: 1996 **Founder:** Greg Zaccardi **Brewer:** Greg Zaccardi **Flagship Beers:**
Ramstein Blonde, Ramstein Double Platinum Blonde, Ramstein Golden Lager, Ramstein
Imperial Pilsner **Seasonal/Specialty Beers:** Ramstein Winter Wheat, Ramstein Maibock,
Ramstein Oktoberfest, Ramstein Pale Ale **Contracted Beers:** Boaks, Bolero Snort, and
occasional others **Tours:** Free, informal **Taproom:** Yes

High Point makes a lot of beer in its 15-barrel (30-barrel fermenters) brewhouse.
Boaks and Bolero Snort are brewed here. But the beers most associated with
this converted rubber mill are ones from the home-turf brand Ramstein.

Brewed in the traditional German *Reinheitsgebot* manner (four ingredients only:
water, barley/wheat, hops, and yeast), the Ramstein line of beers is known for its
adherence to standards and for being a well-made, German-style product.

The tasting room is small and can get quite crowded at times. It's a popular
place for both beer tourists and locals. Late in the afternoon, folks returning home
from work stop for bottles and growler fill-ups and, of course, a few tastes.

Quality tastes include the **Hefeweizen** (5.5% ABV; traditional banana and clove
abound), the seasonal **Maibock** (7% ABV; big malt bill, slightly sweet caramel), and the
Double Platinum Blonde (7% ABV; very smooth and dangerously drinkable wheat).

Golden Lager

Style: German-style helles lager

ABV: 3.5%–4.0%

Availability: Year-round; 12-ounce bottles

Seems fitting, does it not, that a German *Reinheitsgebot* brewery has a beer like this lager, which stands out in a lineup of well-made beers? Turns out, as I decided to nominate this as my Beer Lover's Pick, owner Greg Zaccardi chimed in that it's his favorite as well.

There must be something in the water in north Jersey because, as at Climax, the Ramstein Helles Lager is also is a fantastically clean and crisp beer with just a touch of pleasing malt sweetness but never too much to be considered overwhelming. A great beer drinker's beer.

Brush up on your German because when you visit High Point, it would not be surprising to find German tourists critiquing the beers.

NEW JERSEY BEER COMPANY

4201 Tonnelle Ave., North Bergen, NJ 07047; (201) 758-8342; njbeerco.com; @NJBeerCo

Founded: 2010 **Chairman:** Paul Silverman **Brewers:** Brendan O'Neil and Dave Manka

Flagship and Year-Round Beers: LBIPA, 1787 Abbey Single Ale, Garden State Stout, Hudson Pale Ale **Tours:** Fri. 5 to 9 p.m., Sat. 1 to 6 p.m.; free, and includes 4-ounce samples of whatever draft beer is available at the time **Taproom:** Yes **Naming Inspiration:** An intense pride in the "honest and straightforward" nature of brewing and the State

New Jersey Beer Company is tucked in an industrial strip of busy North Bergen, just a stone's throw from Hoboken and less than a half-mile from the Tonnelle light rail station. The name doesn't suggest anything particular about what to expect other than a bunch of Jersey pride behind it.

The nice thing about the brewery's location is the ability to park, more or less, anywhere you'd like upon arrival. No parking lots, no valets, no parallel parking. Once inside, the impressively large space fits a 10-barrel brewhouse and numerous 20- and 40-barrel fermenters.

With a name that honors the year New Jersey joined the Union, this **1787 Abbey Single** (4.8% ABV) beer is refreshing with just enough flavor to remind you that it's a mild Belgian style. Great undercurrent of fruit and cleans up nicely to invite the next swig.

LBIPA (a bit of a New Jersey beer portmanteau, if you will; LBI stands for Long Beach Island) at 7% ABV is on the high end of a "regular" IPA and just on the south side of an imperial IPA. That means you'll get a great tasting IPA balancing a solid malt backbone with enough citrus and floral hops to get your attention in both the aroma and the flavor. It's got a slight bitterness to it and is not at all boozy for 7%. If you need another reason to drink this beer, a portion of its sales is donated to Alliance for a Living Ocean.

The brewery shows its involvement in their namesake community with an ongoing relationship at Thirsty Quaker homebrew shop in Jersey City, where they also sponsor events like the Hamilton Park BBQ and Newport 5k/10k races each year.

As growth in 2015 dictates, New Jersey Beer Company may find itself relocating elsewhere in Hudson County. You can bet, however, that you will still find the beer to your liking.

Garden State Stout
Style: American stout
ABV: 6.6%
Availability: Year-round; 12-ounce
    bottles

This is a chocolate beer balanced nicely with a mild roast and bitter character to keep things interesting. The dark chocolate notes, however, are prevalent and have you thinking dark chocolate mousse cake or chocolate pecan pie for a decadent dessert pairing. But since it's not an imperial stout, having more than one is not unreasonable.

Brewpubs

HARVEST MOON BREWERY & CAFE

392 George St., New Brunswick, NJ 08901; (732) 249-6666; harvestmoonbrewery.com; @NJMoonBrew

Founded: 1996 **Founder:** Neil Glass **Brewer:** Kyle McDonald **Year-Round Beers:** Moonlight Kölschbier, Jimmy D's Firehouse Red, Full Moon Pale Ale, Double IPA

In the heart of Rutgers country and just a couple of blocks from the banks of the Raritan River is where Harvest Moon calls home. The brewpub is usually bustling due in part to the college town, local businesses, and nearby residents. Being a couple of blocks from the northeast corridor's Amtrak and NJ Transit train station is also a plus.

But it's the beer, food, and environment that have kept people coming back for nearly 20 years. Being a small brewpub allows Harvest Moon to do many varieties of beer. One standout includes the year-round **Moonlight Kölschbier**. A 4.5% ABV pretty-close-to-authentic German kölsch wins this beer high marks with a beautiful balance of light fruitiness, dry crispness, and slight hop bitterness.

A **Belgian Witbier** (4.3% ABV) starts sweet with hints of apricot and ends clean, begging an immediate repeat sip. The **OQ Imperial Coffee Porter** (7.2% ABV) is brewed with coffee from the namesake shop in Highland Park and is exactly how a coffee porter should present itself, with noticeable dark chocolate balancing out the strong roasted coffee component. The **Simcoe Double IPA** (9.2% ABV) showcases tropical fruit and piney notes and is not overly slick like some amped-up IPAs.

From a food menu that changes with the seasons, lots of pub reliables are available, with beer-friendly standouts that include Onion Petals with smoked bacon aioli (**American Joe Schwarzbier**), spinach and goat cheese with strawberries and honey-balsamic vinaigrette (**Belgian Wit**), and buffalo mozzarella ravioli with hot soppressata (**Double IPA**).

The brewpub hosts the monthly meeting of Ferment the World homebrew club and a monthly cask night.

KROGH'S RESTAURANT AND BREWPUB

23 White Deer Plaza, Sparta Township, NJ 07871; (973) 729-8428; kroghs.com;
@KroghsBrew
Founded: 1999 (brewery); 1927 (restaurant) **Current Owners:** Robert & Barbara Fuchs
Brewers: Carl David Cooper and Victor Usinowicz **Flagship and Year-Round Beers:**
Krogh's Gold, Alpine Glow Red Ale, Brodgen Meadow Pale Ale, Old Krogh Oatmeal Stout,
Three Sisters Golden Wheat **Seasonals/Special Releases:** Madi's Maibock, Gruney's
Belgian Dubbel, IPA, Belgian Grand Cru, Blum's Belgian Wit, Beaulah's Pumpkin Ale
Naming Inspiration: The family name of the Dutch owners of the business from
1937–1973

The charming, alpine-like town of Sparta at the edge of Lake Mohawk provides a
scenic backdrop for the oldest brewpub in Sussex County. The name comes from
the Dutch family that owned the property from 1937 to 1973. The current owners,
Robert and Barbara Fuchs, have carried forward the history with a brewery installed
in 1999 that produces beers named after their community.

The 5-barrel brewhouse turns out enough beer to keep six draft lines, one handpump, and one rotating seasonal occupied. If all goes as planned in 2015, the construction of a 40-barrel brewhouse in Newton, New Jersey, to expand the reach with
self-distribution of their well-made beers will be under way.

The **Three Sisters Golden Wheat** (4% ABV) is the perfect place to begin with a soft balance of wheat and fruit. The **Log Cabin Nut Brown** (5.1% ABV) displays the hallmark flavors of a well-made, easy English brown in a beer that tips its cap to Lake Mohawk's developer and the wooden logs used to build the town around the lake. The **Old Krogh Oatmeal Stout** (4.5% ABV) is a great example of a low-alcohol dark beer that bursts with roasted, nutty flavors.

The food menu is filled with casual-dining appetizers, salads, burgers, pizzas, meats, fish, and even a substantial kids' menu, making it a great family place as well. After a visit to the pub, take a walk along the boardwalk on the lake and admire the surrounding natural beauty.

THE LONG VALLEY PUB AND BREWERY AT RESTAURANT VILLAGE

1 Fairmount Rd., Long Valley, NJ 07853; (908) 876-1122; restaurantvillageatlongvalley .com
Founded: 1995 **Current Owners:** Steven and Andrea Bussel **Brewer:** Joe Saia **Year-Round Beers:** American Pale Ale, Lazy Jake Porter, German Valley Amber, Hookerman's Light **Seasonals/Special Releases:** Typically two

Drive due west from Hoboken to Long Valley and find the charming "Village at Long Valley." This pub and brewery calls a 250-year-old barn home on a vast property that also has an Asian bistro, a wine cafe, and a stylish romantic restaurant.

Oktoberfest

The prevailing German theme at Long Valley Pub and Brewery suits it well come the fall season. The Oktoberfest beers, music, and *gemütlichkeit* are flowing for the afternoon in the parking lot surrounding the brewpub.

Long Valley makes for a relaxing stop, especially if the weather permits, to sit outside at the spacious bar or ample patio area. Inside, a two-floor restaurant dining room overlooks the brewing area on display for all to see.

The beers coming out of the 7-barrel brewhouse over the years have collected more medals than any other brewpub in New Jersey. The most award-winning is the **Lazy Jake Porter** (Great American Beer Festival gold medal, 2000 and 2005; silver medal, 2006 and 2009; and bronze medal, 1999). A taste of the porter reveals the roasted, slightly chocolate, medium-bodied reason why it has been so justly rewarded. There may be no better pairing for it on the food menu than with the traditional sauerbraten, whose meat falls apart at the touch of the fork and is served with red cabbage and roasted potatoes.

Also shining on the beer list is the **Nut Brown Ale**, which itself has a 2005 GABF gold medal and 2004 bronze medal to its name. It pairs up well with either the schnitzel and spaetzle entree or the simply roasted chicken and grilled vegetables on the dinner menu.

THE SHIP INN

61 Bridge St., Milford, NJ 08848; (908) 995-0188; shipinn.com
Founded: 1985; brewery installed in 1995 **Founders and Owner:** Ann and David Hall, founders; Timothy Hall, current 2nd generation owner **Brewer:** Lea Rumbolo **Flagship Beer:** Best Bitter **Year-Round Beers:** ESB and Golden Wheat **Seasonals/Special Releases:** IPA, Irish Stout, Scattergood Summer Wheat, Spring Honey Mild, Muddy Waters, and occasional others **Naming Inspiration:** As a former merchant seaman, founder David Hall thought the long and narrow building resembled a ship.

Along the Delaware River, as New Jersey's first brewpub opening since Prohibition, The Ship Inn has carried on for nearly 20 years, day in and day out serving up

a predominantly British food menu, cask-conditioned ales before many knew what they were, and an atmosphere absent of televisions. Longtime chef Lonnie Lippert has turned in recent years to locally sourced meats for burgers and sausage and the customers have been supportive.

From the 7-barrel brewhouse with a brick-jacketed kettle, Rumbolo turns out a handful of very good traditional English beers. The other half of her working life is as the owner Red Spoon Cooking School and Catering, so she understands how making beer is another form of cooking.

The **Golden Wheat** makes a nice, refreshing introduction to the brewery. The **Best Bitter** performs perfectly as the flagship beer and drinks extremely well, especially when served cask-conditioned. This allows the maltiness of the beer to shine with just a touch of a fruity sweetness behind it. Following with some food, this pairs nicely alongside a serving of shepherd's pie or a Scotch egg, both of which are expertly done by the kitchen.

If the Lancashire cheese and onion pie or a Galley Burger with cheddar should happen to be on the table in front of you, then the **Irish Stout** will be a sure bet.

A visit to The Ship Inn is certainly different (thankfully so) from many other brewpub visits. For the avid cyclists out there, The Ship Inn is reachable by bicycle as well, as a recreational trail along the canal on the Pennsylvania side of the river gets you within approximately one-half mile of the brewpub.

TRAP ROCK RESTAURANT & BREWERY

279 Springfield Ave., Berkeley Heights NJ, 07922; (908) 665-1755; traprockrestaurant
.net; @TrapRockBrewery

Founded: 1997 **Founder:** Harvest Restaurant Group **Brewer:** Charlie Schroeder **Year-Round Beers:** Ghost Pony Helles Lager, Hathor Red Lager, JP Pilsner, Kestrel IPA
Seasonals/Special Releases: Many

Trap Rock has been around longer than most other brewpubs in this chapter. Though it doesn't show. The tastefully designed and decorated dining rooms and outdoor patio have stood the test of time, offering a comfortable space in which to enjoy a stellar wine list and a wide variety of beers, which are produced in view of the dining room.

The 10 beers on tap range from the "safer" pilsners, wits, and lagers but can also include a couple different IPAs, a double IPA, a saison, and a Belgian-style tripel. All are available by the sampler, pint, and "jumbo" glass sizes as well as reasonably priced growler fills to go.

A flight of all the beers is a fine way to check out the wonderful lineup of solid beers including, for starters, the **JP Pilsner**. This 5.2% ABV falls right in line with Old World pilsners, clean and crisp with bit of Noble hop spicy character and a solid toasted malt presence.

The **Desperado IPA** (6.5% ABV) was a limited beer that may come around again and is a fun IPA with the Citra and Simcoe hops, which get a lot of attention these days. This is a juicy citrus fruit–hop beer—aromatic and flavorful from the generous hopping plus dry-hopping. You'll want to get a full glass.

The **Trickster's Tripel** (8.2% ABV) lives up to its name and is tricky in its hiding of the alcohol amid a sweetness contributed to by the use of Indian jaggery. Elsewhere on the menu, the **Polar Vortex Porter** and the **Ghost Pony Helles Lager** are both nicely done interpretations of their respective styles.

The kitchen is no slouch either, producing plates of food on a constantly changing menu that features foods of the season in addition to house-made charcuterie and locally sourced meats, cheeses, and produce.

TRIUMPH BREWING COMPANY

138 Nassau St., Princeton, NJ 08542; (609) 924-7855; triumphbrewing.com/princeton;
@triumphpton

Founded: 1995 **Founder:** Adam Rechnitz **Brewer:** Matt Lally **Year-Round Beers:**
Honey Blonde, Amber Ale, Bengal Gold IPA **Seasonals/Special Releases:** Seasonal
lager, seasonal ale/lager, seasonal stout/nitro tap, and a seasonal handpump

Triumph was at the leading edge of the craft ("micro") brewing boom of the '90s and is still around serving a lineup of beers to complement the wide-ranging menus from the kitchen.

The brewpub family currently has two locations and is looking forward in 2015 to adding a third in Red Bank, NJ. Both existing locations—the other in New Hope, PA, with a brewery headed up by Matthew Suydam—benefit from high foot traffic, the Princeton location being across from the university. Inside, they have striking multiple-level floor plans, open and airy with views of the brewing operations.

Beers not to miss on the diverse sampler flight include the **Honey Blonde** (5% ABV), **Oatmeal Stout** (5.2% ABV), and **Vienna Lager** (5.5% ABV). The company has a fondness for German beers as well, which have netted the brewers quite a few awards at each location through the years, including a bronze at the 2014 Great American Beer Festival for its Winterbock. Get a superb Triumph Burger or choose a couple plates from their menu of intriguing twists on pub grub to accompany the beers. When it comes time to leave, check to see if any of the specialty 750-milliliter bottles are available to purchase.

Beer Bars & Restaurants

ANDY'S CORNER BAR

257 Queen Anne Rd., Bogota, NJ 07603; (201)
342-9887; andyscornerbar.blogspot.com; @
AndysCornerBar
Draft Beers: 10, plus 2 handpumps **Bottled/
Canned Beers:** 50+

Andy's may no longer be on the corner, but they have all the markings of a favorite neighborhood corner bar. Long cited as a destination bar for locals, beer geeks, and locals who are beer geeks, Andy's offers up an unpretentious environment where all walks of life can comfortably gather to unwind in a classic bar setting.

The family-run bar often finds the owner, George Gray (his father, Andy, previously owned the bar), serving up drinks from behind the bar. The bar does not serve food but has an open policy for bringing in food and supplying take-out menus to call for local delivery.

Draft beers are served with a pretzel hooked around a wood stick in the beer, something I can't say I've previously seen but when served with a Tröegs Sunshine Pils, it seemed to be just the perfect accompaniment. Regulars who polish off a hundred beers in a year have their names honored on a Fraternal Order of Foam plaque hanging at the bar. This beer drinker's "club" was formed in 1993, when Andy's was down on the corner.

Continuing the helpful pronunciation guide to town names, it's pronounced Bo-GO-ta—as in pagoda but with a "b"—not like the Colombian capital Bogotá.

CLOVERLEAF TAVERN

395 Bloomfield Ave., Caldwell, NJ 07006; (973) 226-9812; cloverleaftavern.com;
@cloverleafinfo
Draft Beers: 24 **Bottled/Canned Beers:** 65+

The history is old at Cloverleaf, but the beers are very fresh and new. The tavern dates to the mid-1930s, when a 24-year-old George Dorchak Jr. borrowed money from his uncle to purchase the first post-Prohibition liquor license in Caldwell. There's much more history both in print and on the walls at the restaurant, so you'll just need to go and check it out for yourself.

Cloverleaf rolls out a monthly Beer Appreciation Night, a Burger of the Week special (e.g., the Fatburger, a 7-ounce beef patty topped with Taylor ham, Monterey cheese sticks, crispy fried onions, and chipotle mayo), and a beer list that covers a balance of locals and out-of-towners as well as a variety of styles and alcohol levels. There's a very popular all-you-can-eat Sunday brunch that often requires reservations.

When stopping in for a few beers and just a small bite to eat, it can be tough getting past the short rib fries with rich Guinness brown gravy, scallions, and feta. Maybe not so small of a bite, but definitely delicious and a good base for the beers. This is a job for something like a Flying Fish RedFish, a Dogfish Head 90 Minute IPA, or a bottle of Schlenkerla Rauchbier.

Now run by a third-generation Dorchak and made up of two properties that can seat well over 200 guests, the Cloverleaf continues to draw the locals and the beer-seekers to its classic tavern.

MALONEY'S PUB & GRILL

119 Main St., Matawan, NJ 07747; (732) 583-4040; maloneyspubnj.com; @MaloneysPubNJ
Draft Beers: 123

If you've no reason to find yourself in the crook of northern New Jersey where Matawan is located, then you may not be familiar with one of the most enticing beer bars in all of New Jersey.

Maloney's is located less than a mile from the Garden State Parkway, or a very short walk from the Matawan train station. With each beer, though, it becomes more difficult to leave.

They would kick you out first before you could get through the 123 taps (with the space to gradually move up to 160 lines in the future). Serving up this much draft beer is no mean feat, as while the dining room and bar areas are spacious enough to accommodate decent-sized crowds, the basement storage for all of the cold kegs is as cramped as a college dorm closet—if only college dorm closets contained kegs of beer.

The spacious L-shaped bar is situated around multiple TVs. But the real entertainment comes from the beer and food menus. Local breweries like Carton, Cricket Hill, Flying Fish, Kane, and River Horse are well represented among nearly 100 percent "craft-oriented" taps.

The food menu boasts a generally solid lineup of pub grub including nachos, wings, and fried mozzarella to tater tots and steak frites. But stealing the show is a local favorite, the Maloney Burger. Fairly basic in its presentation, this burger comes adorned with bacon, swiss cheese, and doused with a tasty horseradish mustard mayo. It's probably good on the English muffin; I recommend asking for the brioche bun instead.

Matawan certainly lucked out with Maloney's and its excellent beer selection and pub atmosphere.

MOHAWK HOUSE

3 S. Sparta Ave., Sparta, NJ 07871; (973) 729-6464; mohawkhouse.com; @Mohawk_House
Draft Beers: 50

Mohawk House was built from the ground up in 2004 with a lot of money and opened in 2005 with a lot of passion to deliver great food, beverages, and social experiences. Ten years later, the project appears to be a success even as they still continue to grow.

The extensive draft list gives proper respect to many locals (Angry Erik, Bolero Snort, Captain Lawrence, Carton, Kane, River Horse, and Sly Fox) as well as to "exotic" beers from farther afield (Allagash, Founders, Maine, Ommegang, and Stone). Regularly scheduled tap takeovers bring out the brewers and reps plus scores of brewery fans.

The food menu pulls its weight equally well and impresses with creative plates of "small" food, locally and ethically sourced. While it's impossible to run down the laundry list of appealing menu items, those that get well-deserved attention are the duck confit spring roll with hoisin glaze; bacon-wrapped scallops with cauliflower puree; a raw bar with lobster, shrimp, oysters, clams, and crab; Berkshire pork chop with bacon brussel sprouts; tuna tartare tacos; and stone-oven pizza seven different ways with optional whole-wheat beer crust.

The ample dining rooms sport four fireplaces and create a comfortable atmosphere. Recently, a new room was added to the rear of the building, perfect for facilitating parties, receptions, homebrew meetings, etc. For entertainment beyond the table and bar, bocce courts can be found behind the building and live music fills the bar area most weekends.

The experience at Mohawk House is rich in many ways. With Krogh's just down the street (see profile in the Brewpubs section earlier in this chapter), there's a nice little one-two punch of great times with great beer in Sparta.

MORRIS TAP & GRILL
500 Rte. 10 W., Randolph, NJ 07869; (973) 891-1776; morristapandgrill.com; @MorrisTapnGrill
Draft Beers: 24 **Bottled/Canned Beers:** nearly 50

Open since July 2011, Morris Tap & Grill has planted itself firmly on the radar of foodies and beer geeks. A winner of Food Network's Chopped competition, Chef Eric LeVine takes up residence in the kitchen and between GM Michael DeSimone and head bartender Craig Michaels, the great beer flowing from the taps is matched in quality by the plates of food coming out of LeVine's kitchen.

The integration of the kitchen and bar's beer offerings is apparent in the knowledgeable service and the recurring beer dinners. On a menu replete with meats of every variety, flatbreads, pastas, fish, and vegetarian and gluten-free options, several come to the forefront.

Asian-glazed pork sticks are full of delectable rib meat and go very well with Mischief from The Bruery. Get a Saison Dupont Cuvée Dry Hopping to ride shotgun with the Thai chicken flatbread. The grilled shrimp pairs perfectly with an Otter Creek

Fresh Slice White IPA. A superstar on the menu, the short rib pappardelle shines when chased by a bottle of Rochefort 8.

Morris Tap & Grill further demonstrates its support and promotion of great beer through tap takeovers, hosted homebrew meetings of the M.A.S.H club, special firkins and vintage beers, hosted Cicerone classes, and attention to proper pouring and glassware.

If Morris's concept sounds appealing, but you live closer to New York City, you're in luck—

September 2014 brought a new location, Paragon Tap & Table, to Clark, New Jersey, not far from Newark International Airport.

THE OLD BAY

61 Church St., New Brunswick, NJ 08901; (732) 246-3111; oldbayrest.com; @TheOldBay
Draft Beers: 24 **Bottled/Canned Beers:** 30+

The Old Bay exudes New Orleans at every turn, from decor to food to special events to its downright friendly and welcoming nature. Like a good Louisiana story, The Old Bay has a solid history in its building that dates to 1857, originally the National Bank of New Jersey. The bar, for example, is the old bank vault, made from old iron train rails to discourage bank robbers from using dynamite.

The beer happens to have a solid story as well. Anthony Tola and bar managers have been at the craft beer game since 1987, before it became fashionable. To match the quality selections from breweries that can include Abita (naturally), Carton, Chimay, Founders, Green Flash, Kane, Ommegang, Stone, Tröegs, and Victory, servers are well trained to communicate necessary information about the beer. This ensures that even on a busy and loud Saturday night, customers can expect to learn what they need to know to make informed beer selections.

The food side of the equation delivers unique offerings that you might expect from a Cajun/Creole type of establishment. Crawfish, catfish, po' boys, and andouille sausage are found a number of tantalizing ways on the menu.

In a college town like New Brunswick, the crowd and the pulse can change from day to day and night. But the beer remains and keeps up.

SALT

109 Hwy. 206, Stanhope, NJ 07874; (973) 347-7258; saltgastropub.com/saltgastropub .html; @SaltGastropub
Draft Beers: 10 **Bottled/Canned Beers:** 70

Salt refers to itself as a "roadhouse" because of its 1930s roots as such. While several modifications have been applied throughout the years, some of the original structure's exterior stone walls remain, though now as part of the interior design. Guests to the restaurant seem to appreciate the unique touches.

The creativity continues on the menu, where dishes that intrigue include goat croquettes with berry balsamic reduction, orecchiette with grilled chicken and spicy sausage, beet salad with mint vinaigrette, salmon cakes with a spicy peach salsa, and a tofu burger with sriracha aioli sauce.

As for the beers, the restaurant is a big fan of Angry Erik Brewing, which is approximately 20 minutes north. Lagunitas and Long Trail can frequently be found on tap or in bottles.

The support for the craft-brewing segment extends to the Salt Studio, a few miles away in nearby Andover, where they recently doubled the capacity to 80 guests who

can partake in the ongoing Beer Schools, which focus on specific breweries, beers, and styles.

Yet another reason to wind up at Salt—a trail head to Allamuch Mountain Park is at the back of the restaurant's parking lot, and the local Salt Shakers Trail Running Club (around 75 members strong, and sponsored fittingly by Long Trail) ends each run at Salt, where a free beer awaits (21+, of course). If running is not a good enough reason to visit, live music takes the stage most Friday and Saturday nights.

THE SHEPHERD & THE KNUCKLEHEAD PUB

529 Belmont Ave., Haledon, NJ 07508; (973) 942-8666; theshepnj.com; @TheShep_
Draft Beers: 90

The Shep shows up routinely on many lists of favorite and best bars, particularly in northern New Jersey. With a top-notch beer list and an atmosphere that somehow, despite being just feet from the intersection of two busy roads and down the street from William Paterson University, suggests a secret hideaway. People who know good beer have found this beer destination, which has been doing its thing since 1998. Those who live nearby are quite fortunate.

The short back story to the establishment is that it takes its name from the bar owner's first published work of the same name. His writing takes cues from famous "beatnik" writer Jack Kerouac, who has fictional ties to the area.

The bar consists of two rooms (plus an outdoor patio), a pool table, a jukebox with a solid lineup of '70s–'90s rock/hard rock/pop singalongs, and a kitchen that turns out satisfying foods like "Knucklehead-sized" wings, poutine with braised pork shoulder, paella, and a variety of sliders.

But it's the beer that brings it all together for the complete pub experience. They love the big out-of-town beers from Dogfish Head, Firestone Walker, and Founders. Plenty of support is given to the locals too like Beach Haus, Carton, Climax, Cricket Hill, Kane, Flying Fish, and River Horse. Drop a few selections on the jukebox, order a little food, shoot a little stick, grab a few beers, discuss the merits of Jack Kerouac's philosophies, and before you know it, you'll fit right in at The Shep and be returning for more.

THE STIRLING HOTEL

227 Main Ave., Stirling, NJ 07980; (908) 647-6919; thestirlinghotel.com; @StirlingHotel
Draft Beers: 17 **Bottled/Canned Beers:** 30+

The Stirling Hotel sits nestled in the middle of the I-87, I-78, and NJ-24 triangle on the edge of the Great Swamp National Wildlife Refuge and within a very short walk from the Stirling train station.

At first glance from the front street, the bar appears somewhat small and quaint. The inside bar and dining area of this 110+-year-old property is indeed more on the small side.

From the back parking lot, however, there's a different perspective. For all of the indoor cozy feel of being at a neighborhood pub, the outdoor seating during nice weather, naturally, is where most want to be sipping on their drinks. Like other bars

of their quality, the Stirling regularly schedules beer events like tap takeovers, and on a daily basis serves beers from nearby like Bolero Snort and from not-so-nearby like Schlafly and Chimay.

Sipping alfresco with beers from knowledgeable servers will have you staying longer than you intended before you know it.

STUFF YER FACE
49 Easton Ave., New Brunswick, NJ 08901; (732) 247-1727; stuffyerface.com; @StuffYerFaceNJ
Draft Beers: 14 **Bottled/Canned Beers:** Around 100

Remember days gone by of eating like there was no tomorrow? Gorge fests before or after a debaucherous night out?

Stuff Yer Face (or simply Stuff) is on the edge of the Rutgers campus in downtown New Brunswick and is a perfect hangout for college kids looking to stuff their faces before or after a night of partying. On the other hand, these same college kids might find it the perfect place to take mom and dad when they come to visit.

Not only can junior show off the excellent "bolis" that Stuff has become famous for—around three dozen varieties that even the popular food show *Man v. Food* has checked out—but the 'rents can chase the food with a great bottled beer list that includes the likes of Früh Kölsch, Uerige Alt, Schneider Weisse, Schlenkerla Rauchbier Märzen, a few Belgian Trappists and domestic favorites like Allagash White, Tröegs Nugget Nectar, and Stone Enjoy By.

It's easy to see that owner Bill Washawanny and general manager Matt Poznick (both Cicerone Server–certified) are passionate about a fun hangout with great food and a diverse lineup of great beer.

Hard time choosing? They've put together a beer book that makes it easier by organizing the available beers by styles and by brands. And for those who are planning multiple visits and want to try a variety of beers, the Beer Club tracks the list of unique beers consumed and has "payouts" at 15, 30, 50, and 75 beers consumed.

THE TWISTED ELM
435 River Drives, Elmwood Park, NJ 07407; (201) 791-3705; twistedelm.com; @Twisted_Elm
Draft Beers: 8 **Bottled/Canned Beers:** 7

The Twisted Elm didn't make it into these pages solely because of the beer list. It's a small list, yet a well maintained one. Local/regional beers from River Horse, Kane, Cricket Hill, Weyerbacher, Carton, and Sixpoint come onto—and off almost as quickly—the draft list among out-of-state interlopers like Port Brewing and Oskar Blues.

The food menu offers up plenty of possibilities sure to delight, like a high-quality basic Margherita pizza from the wood-burning oven, fried brie with orange-ginger chutney, a special blend burger (chuck, brisket, and short rib), and fresh pastas like cappellini, ravioli, and pappardelle. Fresh is the name of the game and Twisted Elm delivers both in the kitchen and on the taps.

Hoboken/Jersey City— Pub Crawl

Hoboken and Jersey City combined have roughly 300,000 residents. Around these two cities, you get the feeling—both in atmosphere and attitude—of being in New York City, which is visible from many points along these fine Hudson River cities.

Being that this is the greater NYC area, this 11-stop pub crawl is going to be just as big and in your face as life in the Big Apple and surrounding areas. If you appreciate numbers and want to lay claim to a full dozen stops on this epic pub crawl, then after stop number one, take the light rail all the way to Tonnelle Avenue for a short walk to New Jersey Beer Company, then backtrack on the train to stop number two.

Are you ready? Buckle up because this is going to be a wild ride.

Disclaimer: While I completed this so-called proof of concept all in one day, it's not for the faint (or sober) of heart. This pub crawl, perhaps for the saner type, could easily be broken into two days.

TOTAL WALKING DISTANCE: 5.60 miles
LIGHT RAIL COST: $2.10 x 2 one-way rides = $4.20

Directions: As you can see from the map, this pub crawl could begin almost anywhere and, using the light rail option, bring you back to where you began. This suggested route begins at the southern end of downtown Jersey City.

Light Horse Tavern, 199 Washington St., Jersey City, NJ 07302; (201) 946-2028; lighthorsetavern.com; @LightHorseTav

Here we go again, getting a pub crawl started with a brunch that both energizes and satisfies. Located in Jersey City, home of the St. Anthony high school powerhouse basketball program, the two-floor bar and restaurant has a basketball jersey hanging amid a tastefully decorated and light-filled room.

Brunch here can begin with blueberry and pecan pancakes or Light Horse Benedict with either lobster or house-smoked salmon along with Chimay Cinq Cents or Allagash Saison from a well-maintained draft and bottle list. Sitting inside the comfortable atmosphere or dining alfresco on a beautiful day can run the risk of setting you behind schedule before you reach your second stop. Enjoy, but don't delay; get to the light rail stop.

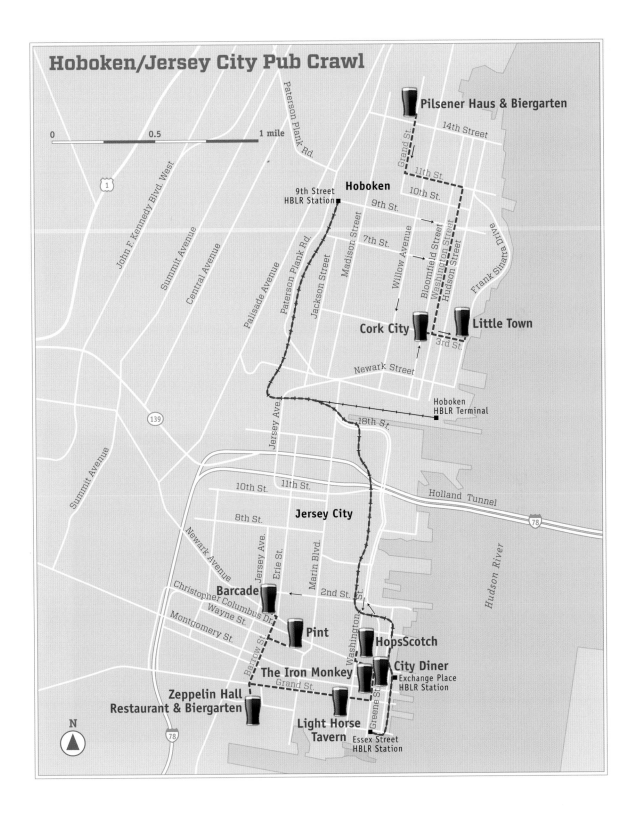

Directions: It's a quick two-block walk to the Essex Street stop on the Hudson-Bergen Light Rail line (HBLR). Buying tickets is easy; simply use the touch screen to buy a one-way ticket (to save time later, buy as many as you and your group need to complete the roundtrip) and be sure to use the "validater" machine to timestamp your ticket. Remember the train operates on the honor system. Then simply hop on the next northbound Tonnelle Avenue train to Hoboken's 9th Street stop. Walk approximately three-quarters of a mile—five blocks east to Grand and six blocks north to 15th Street.

Pilsener Haus & Biergarten, 1422 Grand St., Hoboken, NJ 07030; (201) 683-5465; pilsenerhaus.com; @Pilsenerhaus1

Hoboken's contribution to the world of beer gardens is the Pilsener Haus, opened in 2011 by one of the original owners behind Radegast Hall & Biergarten in Brooklyn.

The oversized space is perfect for large groups of friends meeting on the "uptown" side of Hoboken—the relatively genteel side of Hoboken compared to "downtown." The Pilsener Haus is a perfect place to grab a liter of beer (or two halves instead), choosing from a menu that boasts over 60 beers, including drafts of Weihenstephaner Hefe-Weissbier, Radeberger Pilsner, and Hacker-Pschorr Oktoberfest. There is a small supply of local beers from New Jersey as well.

The food menu has enough going on to provide quality options for your day ahead, like kielbasas and knockwurst. If you did not begin this excursion with some

food, since there's a good bit of walking ahead, a pretzel with liptauer cheese and house-made mustard or a light bite might be worth your time over your second half-liter before heading out.

Directions: It's a healthy 1.3-mile, but lovely, walk from Pilsener Haus in uptown Hoboken to the next stop, Cork City, in downtown. Head four blocks south to 11th Street and six blocks east to Washington. You may wish to stop here briefly at a historical marker that denotes the first baseball game and to remember the historic Helmers' Restaurant (see sidebar below). Then take a leisurely stroll along Washington Street. In three-quarters of a mile, after walking eight blocks south to 3rd Street and one block west to Bloomfield, you will arrive at Cork City.

Cork City, 239 Bloomfield St., Hoboken, NJ 07030; (201) 963-5512; corkcitypub .com; @CorkCityNJ

A bit of a breather from the hustle of Washington Street is a block off the main drag at Cork City. There's no food to get in the way of having a beer or two and throwing a game of darts. Though, in the walk from uptown Hoboken, it would not be held against you if the call of pizza from the legendary Benny Tudino's distracted you.

Cork City delivers a classic corner pub experience with a draft list of 26 beers that includes many of the requisite NJ breweries and other highly sought after ones from the region and the world. Dogs can usually be found hanging out with their human friends too.

Hoboken's History of Ball Fields and German Beer

On your way from Pilsener Haus in uptown Hoboken to Cork City in downtown, take a pause along the way to read this sidebar. It's being placed here not only for the historical marker at 11th and Washington Streets commemorating the generally accepted first baseball game ever, in 1846, between the Knickerbockers and the New Yorks at Elysian Fields, but also for the unfortunate lowering of the German flag at 1036 Washington Street. Since 1936, Helmers' Restaurant was a classic tavern meeting place with the authentic cuckoo clock, the locally made stained glass, the imported bar, and a rich neighborhood history. Citing an inevitable changing of the times, ownership closed for good on December 31, 2014, meaning a perfect Weisswurst plate with a Paulaner Weiss is just a tasty memory of the past.

If you really like Cork City's beer and pub experience, you might sign up for the Great American Beer Challenge, which gives access to special beer events and awards points as you drink through their beer menu. Ultimately the challenge results in a grand prize trip to the annual Great American Beer Festival in Denver. Drink up!

Directions: A short 5-minute walk to the next stop is simple by heading east to the Hudson River and turning left onto Sinatra Drive. There are reminders of Sinatra all around town and can serve as additional distraction if you care to seek them out.

Little Town, 310 Sinatra Dr., Hoboken, NJ 07030; (201) 716-7070; littletown.com/ Hoboken; @LittleTownNYNJ

Bringing focus to all things New Jersey on the beer menu, especially north Jersey, is not as difficult as it used to be. At Little Town, with 30 taps and 20 bottles, it's a veritable who's who of the New Jersey brewing scene.

The kitchen is no slouch either when it comes to putting out interesting food with a local twist. You'll be hard-pressed not to grab a bite to eat at this stop on the pub crawl. It could be the Little Town Rice Balls stuffed with Taylor ham and cheese that catches your eye. Fried "mutz" (mozzarella) with New Jersey tomato marinara sauce should whet your appetite. The "R U Ready" layers chicken fingers, fried mutz, french fries, and New Jersey tomato marinara sauce into a local Hoboken hoagie roll if you have a serious appetite.

You're barely halfway through this tour. It's time to head back to Jersey City on the train. As I mentioned early on, this could make a good breaking point if you chose to be a more reasonable person and make this a 2-day pub crawl. For those who want to go for it all, all aboard!

Directions: Have your picture taken with Manhattan as a backdrop before a leisurely stroll on the recreation path (watch out for cyclists and skaters) along the river for nearly half a mile to the Hoboken HBLR terminal. Using a ticket you've hopefully already purchased, get on board the southbound train to 8th Street. The trip should take barely 10 minutes to the Exchange Place station stop.

After arriving back in Jersey City at the Exchange Place station, walk west along Montgomery Street for six blocks, turn right on Grove, and walk two blocks north to Wayne Street.

Pint, 34 Wayne St., Jersey City, NJ 07302; (201) 367-1222; pintbar.com; @Pint_Bar

Your next stop is one of the oldest bar locations in Jersey City, dating back to 1911.

It has seen various ethnic bars and styles come and go. Now the building houses Pint, an LGBT-friendly bar and one that serves 16 draft lines and 36 bottles of craft beer.

All walks of life are welcome at Pint, where the beer selection is predominantly northeast-focused, with a near-permanent spot for local favorite NJ Beer Co. There's no food served, but they will serve up a bowl of popcorn when you arrive, and fun cocktail fishbowls, sangria (seasonal), and spiked green tea shots are also available.

Plus, at Pint, with the Rockbot app, customers control the music selections by "voting" for upcoming songs from a database of an advertised 7 million songs. Sounds like fun; get your vote in early because it will be time to move along before you know it.

Directions: For the shortest walk of the day, turn right out of Pint's front door, walk one block to Barrow Street, turn right, and walk two short blocks to arrive at Barcade for some fun 'n' games.

Barcade, 163 Newark Ave., Jersey City, NJ 07302; (201) 332-4555; barcadejerseycity .com; @barcadejersey

You'll see Barcade featured along Philadelphia's pub crawl too; both branches opened in 2011. The first location was in Brooklyn in 2004, but the theme remains the same at all three: great beer and fun times with vintage arcade games.

The Jersey City Barcade sits on a bustling corner and houses 25 draft lines of great beer, much of it from the northeast, including Captain Lawrence, Fisherman's, and Sixpoint, and nearly 50 vintage arcade games ranging from Asteroids to Zaxxon.

Sandwiches, small plates, and a daily selection of local sausages might tempt you and, when they are in season, you may be fortunate to find pickled hop shoots. Do not pass them up.

Directions: Walk south on Barrow for eight blocks to arrive at Zeppelin Hall & Biergarten. Note that at Grand Street, Barrow becomes Liberty View Drive. Why, you ask? Because with a keen eye, pause before entering Zeppelin and look off into the distance to spot the Statue of Liberty.

Zeppelin Hall Restaurant & Biergarten, 88 Liberty View Dr., Jersey City, NJ 07302; (201) 721-8888; zeppelinhall.com; @ZeppelinHall

Did you think Pilsener Haus earlier in the day was big? Zeppelin Hall is larger. How much exactly, I'm not certain. The sprawling German-themed complex includes multiple large indoor rooms, bars, and an oversized outdoor biergarten that alone is a reported 12,000 square feet with rows of traditional communal tables under trees and umbrellas.

The numerous bars pour nearly 50 beers, a good portion of them American and European lager-style beers, in liters, mugs, and flights.

If food is required at this point, various sausage platters, sandwiches, and traditional German plates of schnitzel, spaetzle, sauerbraten, and pretzels await. This could be an excellent last stop of the night but hang in there because the last three are worth the wait.

Directions: One more long walk before hitting up a couple last spots. Head north one block and turn right to walk along Grand Street for seven blocks, after which you will turn left on Greene Street. The Iron Monkey is one block ahead on the left at York Street.

The Iron Monkey, 99 Greene St., Jersey City, NJ 07302; (201) 435-5756; ironmonkey.com; @TheIronMonkey

The Iron Monkey has been pouring mighty fine beer and aging over 800 bottles since 1996. In the next couple of years, the owner intends to expand the size by nearly three times. Until then, the best part of the stop at The Iron Monkey is the beer and the rooftop deck; you haven't seen a rooftop deck along this pub crawl.

Provided the weather is on your side, sitting three stories above Jersey City as you near the end of the day is a pretty relaxing thing to do. Plus, you'll have 39 drafts from around the world to choose from including stellar brews like Anderson Valley Barney Flats, Delirium Tremens, Founders All Day IPA, St. Bernardus Abt 12, and Voodoo Love Child.

If you need something a bit more refreshing and lower in alcohol at this point, kicking back on the rooftop with an Allagash White or Oskar Blues Mama's Little Yella Pils might be in order. But don't get too comfy, as easy as that will be to do.

Directions: A short two-block walk to the north and one to the west will bring you to HopsScotch.

HopsScotch, 286 Washington St., Jersey City, NJ 07302; (201) 451-4677; hopsscotchjc.com; @HopsScotchBar

The owners at HopsScotch "aspire to be the best beer bar in the land," currently serving up 40 taps and 85+ bottles of very good beer, nearly 100 whiskies, plus board games and table shuffleboard. Their intentions are grand with an eye toward the future with multiple locations, possibly a brewpub setup, and doing a scotch barrel-aging as a tie-in to the beer-focused kitchen.

This could either be a great way to start the day (if you began the pub crawl in reverse order) or begin to wind it down. The borderline obsessive curation of a top-notch beer cellar has been a big hit with customers since opening in 2012. Beers that have graced the draft list at HopsScotch include Birrificio Del Ducato's Brett Peat Daydream, LoverBeer's Beer Bera, Andechs' Dopplebock, and Brouwerij Dilewyns' Vicaris Generaal.

In the side dining room, be sure to check out specific beer country–themed murals done by a local artist and see how many beer references you can find. Needless to say, when you stop by, there should be no problem finding a beer to your liking, particularly if you enjoy sleuthing a menu for something rare and exciting. With a motto like "where recess meets happy hour," you know you're in for something good.

Directions: In a day that saw you take a couple of light rail train rides and walk nearly 6 miles, your last stop is only one block to the east and one to the south.

City Diner, 31 Montgomery St., Jersey City, NJ 07302; (201) 721-5331; citydiner .com; @CityDinerNJ

Congratulations, you've made it. New Yorkers and New Jerseyans don't mess around. And neither did you on this pub crawl. City Diner serves its full menu (including breakfast) all day long so feel free to get a breakfast platter or a steak dinner. You may have room for food at this point, or you may be looking for that one last beer before calling it quits for the day.

This is fine place to make last call. City Diner is known for catching people both on their way into and back from Manhattan as well as Jersey City residents, tourists, and businesspeople.

City Diner has 12 taps, all of which should be pouring something to your liking at this, your finally final, last stop of the day. Left Hand Milk Stout on nitro would work well, an offering from Kane, or one last big beer from Stone or Avery could well send you off to a restful night's sleep.

If you finished this tour all in one day, I'd love to hear from you. Did you curse me or thank me along the way for crafting this 13-hour, 11-stop pub crawl searching out some of the best that Hoboken and Jersey City have to offer?

Pittsburgh & Western Pennsylvania

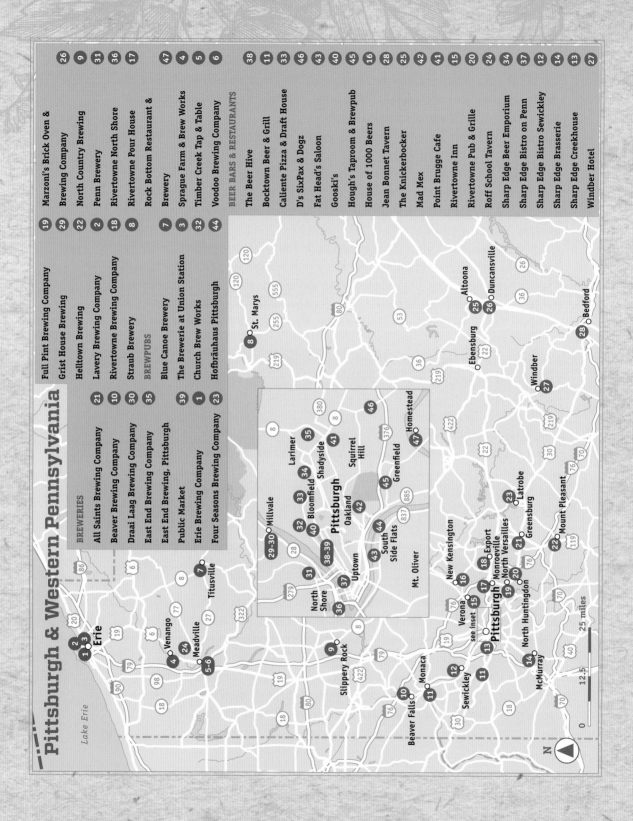

BREWERIES

㉑	All Saints Brewing Company
⑩	Beaver Brewing Company
㉚	Draai Laag Brewing Company
㉟	East End Brewing Company
㊴	East End Brewing, Pittsburgh Public Market
①	Erie Brewing Company
㉓	Four Seasons Brewing Company
㉖	Full Pint Brewing Company
⑨	Grist House Brewing
㉛	Helltown Brewing
㊱	Lavery Brewing Company
⑰	Rivertowne Brewing Company
	Straub Brewery

BREWPUBS

㊼	Blue Canoe Brewery
④	The Brewerie at Union Station
⑤	Church Brew Works
⑥	Hofbräuhaus Pittsburgh
⑲	Marzoni's Brick Oven & Brewing Company
㉙	North Country Brewing
㉒	Penn Brewery
②	Rivertowne North Shore
⑱	Rivertowne Pour House
⑧	Rock Bottom Restaurant & Brewery
⑦	Sprague Farm & Brew Works
③	Timber Creek Tap & Table
㉜	Voodoo Brewing Company

BEER BARS & RESTAURANTS

㊳	The Beer Hive
⑪	Bocktown Beer & Grill
㉝	Caliente Pizza & Draft House
㊻	D's SixPax & Dogz
㊸	Fat Head's Saloon
㊵	Gooski's
㊺	Hough's Taproom & Brewpub
⑯	House of 1000 Beers
㉘	Jean Bonnet Tavern
㉕	The Knickerbocker
㊷	Mad Mex
㊶	Point Brugge Cafe
⑮	Rivertowne Inn
⑳	Rivertowne Pub & Grille
㉔	Roff School Tavern
㉞	Sharp Edge Beer Emporium
㊲	Sharp Edge Bistro on Penn
⑫	Sharp Edge Bistro Sewickley
⑭	Sharp Edge Brasserie
⑬	Sharp Edge Creekhouse
㉗	Windber Hotel

Pittsburgh & Western Pennsylvania

Folks from the East Coast who have never been to Pittsburgh may think of the Steel City as the Midwest. Maybe it's the gateway to the Midwest, or maybe it's really more in the class of its East Coast brethren, even though perhaps neither would readily admit it.

Personalities aside, the western slice of Pennsylvania, particularly Pittsburgh, has a rich brewing history. It's been fairly strong in the micro/craft segment for nearly 30 years—Penn Brewery lagered its first beer in 1986, and things have been quickly getting to great in recent years with the help of newcomers both making the beer and selling it. For purposes of defining western Pennsylvania in this chapter, I've drawn a north-south line through Altoona.

Breweries

ALL SAINTS BREWING COMPANY

1602 Rte. 119, Greensburg, PA, 15601; (724) 396-4968; allsaintscraftbrewing.com; @AllSaintsCraft

Founded: 2011 **Founder:** Jeff Guidos **Brewer:** Jeff Guidos **Year-Round Beers:** Archangel Pale Ale, Crimson Halo, IPA **Seasonals/Special Releases:** Many **Tours:** Call ahead **Taproom:** Yes **Naming Inspiration:** Guidos's schooling at local St. Vincent College

Jeff Guidos, a chemist and technically astute brewer, came from the shuttered Red Star brewery and brought with him the equipment to open his first brewery. To the delight of longtime customers, he brought his recipes, which include a very well-made English Barleywine (10.2% ABV), full of big caramel malts and just a slight bitterness.

The long-term vision is slowly being developed within the building, which currently includes the brewing operations, a tasting area, and a pool table. Future plans could include an outdoor deck and a larger seating area in full view of the brewhouse.

For now, customers flock to the popular tasting room for samples, full pours, and growler fills. In addition to the barleywine, **Crimson Halo Amber** (5.3% ABV), **St. Timothy Rye** (5.5% ABV), **Voodoo's Child Dunkel** (5.2% ABV), and **Heavenly Hefe Weizen** (5.2% ABV) are all very well-calibrated representations of their styles and could make for perfect long day, or night, sessions.

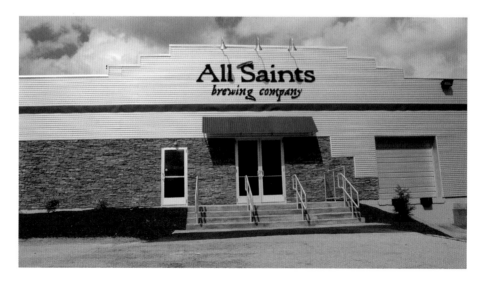

Beer Lover's Pick

IPA

Style: English-style India pale ale

ABV: 6.9%

Availability: Year-round; draft only

As malt-forward English-style IPAs go, this is one that makes the list with a pleasant citrus aroma and dialed-down bitterness—yet a reported 70 IBUs—wrapped up in a smooth grain bill of six malts.

With the brewery's saintly disposition, it made sense not long after opening that a collaborative spirit would ensue with neighboring Helltown Brewing Company—the most recent called **Dark Angel** for Pittsburgh Craft Beer Week.

BEAVER BREWING COMPANY

1820 7th Ave., Beaver Falls, PA, 15010; beaverbrewingcompany.com; @BeaverBrewing
Founded: 2010 **Founder:** Dan Woodske **Brewer:** Dan Woodske **Year-Round Beers:** I.Porter.A, Chamomile Wheat, Nelson Sauvin, Basil **Seasonals/Special Releases:** An ever-growing list **Tours:** Free; Sat 4:30 p.m. **Taproom:** Yes

Handcrafting is taken quite seriously here. From the tap handles to the small-batch (1.5-barrel) beer, owner Dan Woodske takes pride in crafting everything by hand. Furthermore, he has crafted several books covering topics like hops, making kvass, and a how-to for opening a nanobrewery.

Opening a nanobrewery appears to have gone well for him as around a dozen beers are available in the tasting room and typically include the porter/IPA mash-up **I.Porter.A.** (5.5% ABV) and the tropically hoppy **Nelson Sauvin Pale Ale** (6.5% ABV). For those with the concern, all Beaver beers are vegan. Woodske self-distributes his beers that can be found on limited basis around the hometown of Joe Namath and the greater Beaver County area.

The tasting room serves simple plates of meats and cheeses to accompany the beer tastings. Additionally, a few pinball games keep customers entertained and, if you enjoy Justin Bieber or Pamela Anderson, you'll wish to check out the restrooms.

Beer Lover's Pick

Chamomile Wheat
Style: American wheat ale
ABV: 4.4%
Availability: Year-round; draft only

This wheat beer is a well-executed example of fresh floral aromas packed into a light, refreshing beer without being overdone in a perfumy way. The beer can be a great summertime refresher or enjoyed any time of year with seafood and salads.

DRAAI LAAG BREWING COMPANY

501 E. Ohio St., Millvale, PA, 15209; (412) 821-1762;
draailaag.com; @DraaiLaag
Opened: 2011 **Founder:** Dennis Hock **Brewers:**
Anthony Zamperini, Nate Hoylman **Year-Round Beers:**
Aureus, Simon Girty, Gouden Brugge **Rotating Beers:**
Goedenacht, Geestelijke, Cru, La Pienture, Black Briar,
Red Briar, Blue Briar, Ragnarok, St. Angus, Haviken,
Yodeler, Choco-Lantern **Tours:** No **Taproom:** Yes

As the brewery prides itself on painting outside the lines, its beers can mostly be described as strong—in flavor and alcohol level—and rooted in creativity.

Draai Laag still operates on a small scale after a few years in business and that affords them the luxury of turning out many varieties of beer throughout the year. They are shooting for unique and small-batch beers made in an unassuming environment and thus far they've succeeded.

A couple of beers reflecting this mission are the **La Pienture** (8% ABV), a fruity sour/wild ale, and **Goedenacht** (9.5% ABV), a creatively successful melding of cider, mead, and wild ale flavors and fermented with Brettanomyces.

As of this writing, the hours at their Saints and Turncoats Public House tasting room are limited to Thursday, Friday, and Saturday; so a better bet for finding Draai Laag's beers may be to ask for them at a local Pittsburgh watering hole or bottle shop. In case you wondered, add this one to the pronunciation guide: You'll get by just fine if you say "dry lawg."

Beer Lover's Pick

Simon Girty
Style: Belgian strong ale
ABV: 8%
Availability: Year-round; draft only
Simon Girty was a controversial figure in colonial-era history. Simon Girty, the beer, is not quite as controversial as others where the brewery applies its creative license. This beer is a warming blend of dark fruit, chocolate, and mild bitter flavors to create a beer worthy of desserts like berry cheesecake or toffee crème brûlée.

EAST END BREWING COMPANY

147 Julius St., Pittsburgh, PA, 15206; (412) 537-2337; eastendbrewing.com;
@EastEndBrewing

Founded: 2004 **Founders:** Scott and Julie Smith **Brewers:** Scott Smith, Brendan
Benson, Nordy Siljander, Joe Green **Flagship Beer:** BigHop IPA **Year-Round Beers:**
Black Strap Stout, Fat Gary's Nut Brown Ale, Monkey Boy Hefeweizen **Seasonals/Special
Releases:** East End Witte, Joe Melt, Monkey Girl, Pedal Pale Ale, and too many other
recurring ones to list **Tours:** $25; every other Sat 1 p.m. **Taproom:** Yes

East End is about as local a brewing company as they come. Even after moving
into a much larger brewing and storage space at the end of 2012, the company's
adamant position is that they will not brew more than needed to satisfy the western
Pennsylvania market. The brewery currently has capacity to output approximately
4,000 barrels annually with a combination of a 20-barrel brewhouse and fermenters
up to 40 barrels in size.

Out of those tanks comes beer that the locals love in area bars. Standards like
the nearly perfect **Fat Gary's Brown** (3.8% ABV) is an example of a low-alcohol,
high-flavor beer that showcases the wonders
of an underappreciated style. The **Big Hop IPA**
(5.8% ABV) makes a beautiful delivery of just
what the name promises. **East End Witte** (5.2%
ABV) has a lovely bouquet of fruit and flowers
and, on the other end of the spectrum, **Gratitude
Barleywine** (11.4% ABV) brings a strong and
satisfying profile of rich malt, bitter hops, and
warming alcohol.

Even just to satisfy the western Pennsylvania
target market, the brewery embarked on a significant expansion throughout 2014 bringing a
1,000-gallon dairy tank on line devoted exclusively to sour beers. A 3,000-square-foot room
was built above the tasting room bar dedicated to
barrel-aging and the sour fermentation projects.

They began down the path of canning the
East End beers late in the year. The growler shop/
tasting stand is still in the Pittsburgh Public
Market, though that location was moved in 2013.
And, after years of saying that East End is not a

Eye Opener
Style: Coffee Porter
ABV: 5.6%
Availability: Occasionally
One of the best examples of a coffee-beer collaboration became even more logical—and convienent—when Commonplace opened a roasting facility and retail shop in the tasting room of East End Brewing's building. The blend, Cafe Vida Costa Rica, is a smooth, low-acid roast that works so nicely with the beer to create an excellent low-alcohol coffee beer that might work just as well for breakfast.

pub, East End now has a pub license to serve light fare as a complement to the beers brewed just feet away. Lots of exciting change over the past few years.

The annual Pedal Pale Ale Keg Ride gives bike-riding enthusiasts of East End beer a chance to ride along as owner Scott Smith delivers the first keg of the season to a selected retail account. Last year, 700 participated in the ride. You might also homebrew a session beer under 4.5% ABV and enter it into the local homebrew contest. If you win, your recipe will get scaled up and brewed at East End. Plenty of ways to enjoy a great local product with great people behind it.

ERIE BREWING COMPANY
1213 Veshecco Dr., Erie, PA, 16501; (814) 459-7741; eriebrewingco.com; @ErieBrewingCo
Founded: lineage to 1993, current ownership since 2012 **Owner:** Rob Lowther **Brewers:** Shawn Strickland, Matt Dever, Mike Stacy **Flagship Beer:** Railbender Ale **Year-Round Beers:** Mad Anthony's APA, Misery Bay IPA, Presque Isle Pilsner **Seasonals/Special Releases:** Drake's Crude Oatmeal Stout, Fallenbock, Golden Fleece Maibock, Heritage Alt, Johnny Rails Pumpkin Ale, Ol'Red Cease and Desist **Tours:** Wed through Fri 12 to 5 p.m., Sat 1 to 4 p.m. **Taproom:** Yes

The brewery as far northwest in the state as possible has been around in multiple forms for over 20 years. Current management has been breathing new life into the brand and its beers since taking over in 2012.

The **Railbender Ale** (6.8% ABV) is still around and still a wonderful malty Scottish-style beer. **Drake's Crude** (6.9% ABV) is a luxuriously smooth oatmeal stout with pronounced roasted and chocolate malts on full display.

When you visit the brewery, beer is available to go both in bottles as well as growler fill-ups. The tasting room also carries plenty of other beer accessories including beautiful brewery-branded stone coasters.

They are no longer alone on the lakefront brewing scene as new friends at The Brewerie and Lavery are in town giving beer tourists more to taste when visiting the Lake Erie region.

Beer Lover's Pick

Johnny Rails
Style: Pumpkin ale
ABV: 6.5%
Availability: Seasonal in
late summer, early fall;
12-ounce bottles

It was just a matter of which brewery would get the nod for their pumpkin beer as a Beer Lover's Pick. It won't happen again in these pages, so make a note that in a world

of pumpkin beers gone crazy with heavy-handed spices and alcohol, there's no doubt that Johnny Rails is a pumpkin beer. But, it strikes the right balance of being a beer first with a pleasant and passing current of clove, nutmeg, and cinnamon.

FOUR SEASONS BREWING COMPANY

745 Lloyd Ave. Ext., Latrobe, PA, 15650; (724) 520-4111; fsbrewing.com;
@FourSeasonsBrew
Founded: 2013 **Founders:** Mark Pavlik and Christian Simmons **Brewers:** Mark Pavlik,
Drew Bauer, Jason Bevan, Eamon McDonough **Year-Round Beers:** High Hopes IPA,
Bang Bang Double IPA, Darkside of the Pint Oatmeal Stout, Local American Pale Ale
Seasonals/Special Releases: 60° & Snowing Belgian Single, Das Boot Hefe-Weizen, Get
Down Brown Ale, Kickin' It Kölsch, Session 4.0 **Tours:** Call ahead **Taproom:** Yes

Latrobe used to be synonymous with Rolling Rock. Those years are long past and new breweries are dotting the area landscape. On the outskirts of town near St. Vincent College is one of the newest and smallest breweries in this chapter. Though that may not last for long.

Four Seasons, as a name, is a nod to the outdoor beauty of the region throughout the four seasons of the year. As a business concept, the brewery team looks to enmesh itself with the local community. They display local artwork on the brewery walls for sale where a portion of the sale price goes back to local causes.

The guys did roughly 400 barrels of beer in 2014 and are on track to do 600 barrels of beer in 2015 (a sixfold increase over 2013) and self-distribute to nearly 50 accounts within 100 miles of the brewery. Added fermenters in 2014 (with room for more) are helping get them there.

Dark Side of the Pint
Style: Oatmeal stout
ABV: 5.8%
Availability: Year-round; draft only
Awards: Great American Beer Festival (Silver, 2014)

A well-made oatmeal stout is not a common enough occurrence. This one makes the cut with a noticeable roasted and chocolate malt presence. The beer goes down smoothly and is clean and dry enough to invite sip after sip. A plate of grilled flank steak and mole sauce rounds out the experience quite nicely with this beer.

Beers like the floral hop, easy-drinking **High Hopes** IPA (6.9% ABV), a classically done clean and slightly fruity **Kickin' It Kölsch** (5.4% ABV), and the **60° & Snowing Belgian Single** (4.2% ABV) have been catching on quickly with locals.

FULL PINT BREWING COMPANY

1963 Lincoln Hwy., North Versailles, PA, 15137; (412) 467-6414; fullpintbrewing.com; @FullPintBrewing
Founded: 2010 **Founders:** Barrett Goddard, Mark Kegg, Sean Hallisey, and Jake Kristophel **Brewers:** Barrett Goddard, Sean Hallisey, Jake Kristophel, Mike Washil (Sr. Assistant Brewer/Cellarman) **Flagship Beer:** White Lightning Belgian White, Chinookie IPA **Year-Round Beers:** All In Amber, Hobnobber Session IPA, Gus IPA, Tri-PA, Little Brown Ale **Seasonals/Special Releases:** 3-2-1 Win, King Kölsch, Perc E Bust, Rye Rebellion, Wild Side Series (sour), and Nerd's Reserve Series **Tours:** Call ahead **Taproom:** Yes

Full Pint is a regional powerhouse in the making. At a capacity of 8,500 barrels and distribution in four states outside Pennsylvania, the brewery sits a half-hour outside of downtown Pittsburgh but can be found seemingly everywhere.

The brewery is set up with a tasting room attached and recently added a kitchen that creates a lineup of very interesting and satisfying pizzas using spent grain in the house-made dough. To play their conservation part, the kitchen replaces the water ingredient in the dough with the brewery's White Lightning Belgian beer. There's a "412" topped with mashed potatoes and pork lardons and an "Irish Breakfast" with

bangers, chips, and a sunny-side-up egg. But sometimes you're in the mood for a classic "plain" pizza (and it proves to be a good test of the kitchen too, if we're being honest) and with a well-made, hopped-up **King Kölsch** (6.2% ABV) Full Pint has you covered here on both accounts.

Also standing out on tap at the brewery are the **Rye Rebellion** (11% ABV), full of vanilla and whiskey character, and the **Gus IPA** (8% ABV), a smooth, earthy, and slightly bitter IPA in honor of their local bluesman.

Look for the new Full Pint Wild Side pub in Pittsburgh's Lawrenceville section. No brewing will take place there, but it serves as an extension of the brewery and provides some cellaring options.

Beer Lover's Pick

Chinookie IPA
Style: India Pale Ale
ABV: 7.1%
Availability: Year-round; 12-ounce bottles

The Chinookie is all about the Chinook hop with its mildly intense blast of piney and slightly bitter notes. The beer still comes across as fairly well-balanced, yet full-bodied. With its flavor and strength, the Chinookie goes down best with a full-flavored pizza like the sausage and mushroom that they serve in the tasting room.

GRIST HOUSE BREWING

10 E. Sherman St., Pittsburgh, PA, 15209; (412) 447-1442;
gristhousebrewing.com; @GristHouse
Founded: 2014 **Founders:** Brian Eaton and Kyle Mientkiewicz
Brewers: Brian Eaton, Kyle Mientkiewicz **Flagship Beers:**
Camp Slap Red **Year-round Beers:** Gristly Bear Brown,
Wheatin' for the Weekend, Gristful Thinking **Seasonal/
Specialty Beers:** Crouching Porter, Hidden Chocolate **Tours:**
By request **Taproom:** Yes

Located in a former slaughterhouse and honoring the gristmills that crush barley and wheat, Grist House brewery has an honest feel to it. The authenticity has been maintained in the decor which features the original hanging mechanical hooks that moved the animals through the slaughterhouse. Nice touch, but probably a wise marketing move to choose the name Grist House.

The brewery is tucked into a commercial sliver of a residential neighborhood and has a nice front deck and area for cornhole and visiting food trucks at the edge of Girty's Run (see also Simon Girty at Draai Laag for a cross-reference). Inside, the tasting room has a clear line of sight into the 15-barrel brewing operations, where solid beers like the easy-drinking and slightly malty-sweet **Gristly Bear Brown Ale** (4.6% ABV) and the floral **Gristful**

Beer Lover's Pick

Crouching Porter, Hidden Chocolate
Style: Chocolate Porter
ABV: 6.6%
Availability: Occasional; draft only
The danger of me sharing a beer here with you considered seasonal, or occasional, at such a new brewery is that the lineup shakeout can still be many months to come. But this porter impressed with a roasted malt profile of a solid porter and with a nice bitter chocolate line running through it and begged to be singled out here as a Beer Lover's Pick.

PHOTO COURTESY OF GRIST HOUSE BREWING

Thinking Session Pale Ale (4.8% ABV) are shaping up to be year-round favorites at this young and popular brewery.

HELLTOWN BREWING

13 Henry C. Frick St., Mount Pleasant, PA, 15666; (724) 542-4339; helltownbrewing.com; @HelltownBrewing

Founded: 2011 **Founders:** Shawn Gentry **Brewer:** Shawn Gentry **Year-round Beers:** Extra Sinful Bitter, Mischievous Brown, Rapture IPA **Specialty/Seasonal Beers:** Barleywine, Dranik, Idle Hands Imperial IPA, Perverse Stout, Reaper's Harvest, Spiteful Saison **Tours:** Yes **Taproom:** Yes **Naming Inspiration:** The rough-and-tumble nature of Mount Pleasant in centuries past

Helltown is another story of seasoned homebrewers stepping up to the next level. The brewery continues to grow and gather fans as the beer spreads in distribution across the state and more fans find them at the brewery.

Capturing the attention of beer lovers are the very hop-dominant **Rapture IPA** (7% ABV) and **Idle Hands Double IPA** (8% ABV). The **Mischievous Brown** (5.5% ABV) is another nod to the east—as with the barleywine featured below—and should be asked for immediately if spotted at your local watering hole. As common sense suggests, Helltown got together with All Saints during Pittsburgh Craft Beer Week and did a collaboration beer, which as you would imagine spawned fun parties.

Beer Lover's Pick

Barleywine
Style: English-style barleywine
ABV: 9.5%
Availability: Seasonal; 22-ounce bottles
There's something very nice about beers that give a nod to their country of origin. This barleywine from Helltown does a great job making its barleywine showcase the rich flavors of caramel, raisins, chocolate, and vanilla and downplay the hops. It was aged on maple for some added depth.

LAVERY BREWING COMPANY

128 W. 12th St., Erie, PA, 16501; (814) 454-0405; laverybrewing.com; @LaveryBrewing
Founded: 2009 **Founders/Owners:** Jason D. Lavery, Nicole L. Lavery, Jason U. Lynch
Brewers: Jason D. Lavery, Jason U. Lynch **Flagship Beer:** Dulachan IPA **Year-Round
Beers:** Imperial Red Ale, Liopard Oir Farmhouse Saison, Madra Allta IPA **Tours:** $5, Sat 4
p.m. **Taproom:** Yes

L et's begin with a pronunciation check: Lav-ree, not Lave-er-ee.
The **Liopard Oir** (4.5% ABV) was one of the first distributed Lavery beers
to catch widespread market attention across Pennsylvania. In 2013, it took home
a well-deserved gold medal from the Great American Beer Festival in the French &
Belgian-style Saison category. A dose of Brettanomyces yeast in the bottle means
that while it's a perfectly good beer to drink fresh, it will do some nice things over
time as well.

For a different approach, the **Dulachan** (5.6% ABV) brings the IPA concept front
and center with big geeky hops like Simcoe, Citra, Amarillo, and Columbus. With a
reported 70 IBUs, you might be thinking double IPA, but at 5.6% ABV, you'll think
more like three or four of these in a session.

The taproom at Lavery has room for these beers plus four others, along with a
local wine. In addition to the sampling, full pours, and growler fills, a small kitchen
creates a handful of tasty morsels to satisfy while sampling.

Beer Lover's Pick

Devil Bird Holiday Ale
Style: Imperial porter
ABV: 8.5%
Availability: Limited seasonal; 750-milliliter bottles
The bottle label has a wild back story behind the
naming of the beer, but what's inside is much more
straightforward. Not that the list of ingredients—big
malts, extra malts, significant bittering hops, bourbon barrels—yields anything but complex aromas
and flavors. Make the holidays go just a bit easier
with this dangerously drinkable imperial porter.

RIVERTOWNE BREWING COMPANY

5578 Old William Penn Hwy., Export, PA, 15632; (724) 519-2145; myrivertowne.com; @RivertownBrew

Founded: 2002 **Founder:** Christian Fyke **Brewer:** Andrew Maxwell **Year-Round Beers:** Babbling Blonde, Maxwell's Scottish Ale, Grateful White, RT Lager, Old Wylie's IPA, Hala Kahiki **Seasonals/Special Releases:** All Aboard Anniversary Stout, Hop Lace, OH-PA, Patrick's Poison, Rudolph's Red **Tours:** $8, Sat 2 p.m. **Taproom:** Yes

From the small, original Monroeville pub where its first beer was brewed, to four locations, a company-branded bar at the Pittsburgh Penguins arena, a large production facility, and distribution in six states, Rivertowne is more on the map than ever before.

The brewery tasting room is a comfortable getaway with television, popcorn, shuffleboard table, a retail shop, and beers to sample. Not a bad place to learn about Rivertowne and its beers. Try them all, but be sure to check out the malty and slightly smoky **Maxwell's Scottish** (5.1% ABV) and the pungently impressive **Old Wylie's IPA** (6.2% ABV). Maxwell's was bestowed a silver medal at the World Beer Cup in 2014.

Hala Kahiki Pineapple Ale
Style: Fruit beer
ABV: 4.8%
Availability: Seasonal; 12-ounce cans

As the only pineapple beer making it to a Beer Lover's Pick, it turns out to be a pretty good one. Not a fruit juice as some would think; you still can tell that there's a base beer behind it with noticeable pineapple sweetness and a touch of tartness. Mind you, it may not be an everyday beer but when the situation calls for a refreshing beer by the pool or a fruit beer to pair with dessert, a can of Hala Kahiki will work.

For a fuller experience, head back to the original pub in Monroeville (which has the largest selection of Rivertowne beers of the four locations) where you can drink from up to 18 of the brewery's beers, depending upon seasonal availability, along with a full menu of food to balance the equally long list of beers.

STRAUB BREWERY

303 Sorg St., St. Marys, PA, 15857; (814) 834-2875; straubbeer.com; @StraubBeer
Founded: 1872 **Founder:** Peter Straub **President/CEO:** William Brock (5th-generation family) **Brewers:** Vince Assetta (head), TJ Steele, Ray Frank, and Dave Baumgratz **Flagship and Year-Round Beers:** 1872 Lager, American Amber, American Lager, American Light, IPL **Seasonals/Special Releases:** Hefeweizen, Munich Lager, Pilsner, Straubator **Tours:** 12:30 p.m. Tues through Fri; by appointment Sat **Taproom:** Yes, the Eternal Tap

Straub is to western Pennsylvania as Yuengling is to eastern Pennsylvania. Somewhat like Yuengling, unless you live nearby, Straub too takes some driving determination to visit. A beautiful country drive, though, it certainly is.

Locals have their fierce loyalty to each of the breweries and at Straub the regulars still come to the drive-though for a pickup of their favorite liquid. The drive-up brewery store concept is quite something to see.

Inside the fascinating old-school brewery, it's a top-down process beginning on the top floor with grains in the mash tun. Gravity plays a starring role as beer traverses the old building and eventually winds up in the ground floor fermenters. In 2013, approximately 42,000 barrels of beer came out of this big brewery in a small town.

Tastes of the beer are free, which makes Straub's tasting room like many others. But, not exactly. The tasting room is setup with an "Eternal Tap." The process can be daunting for first-time visitors: 1) Walk in; 2) Take a clean glass; 3) Pour your own sample from among 4 to 6 taps, depending upon availability; 4) Rinse, sanitize, and return glass. What a simple concept!

From the longtime beers, the **Amber Lager** (4.1% ABV) holds up well as a solid example of a dependably malty lager. It's the new seasonals and a couple year-round beers that have helped shine Straub's star a bit brighter in recent years. In addition to a new focus on packaging and sales, the seasonal **Hefeweizen** and **Pilsner** (both 5.5% ABV) are true-to-style beers that have brought new fans to the brewery.

Straub is looking well positioned to remain an "American Legacy Brewery" into a seventh generation.

Beer Lover's Pick

Straub IPL
Style: India pale lager
ABV: 5.6%
Availability: Year-round; 12-ounce bottles
Take a smooth, solidly built lager. Mix in some biscuit malts. Add Bravo, Cascade, and Columbus hops and you've got an India Pale Lager. It's a fun twist that is getting attention from beer drinkers as one of the new favorites from this old brewery.

Brewpubs

BLUE CANOE BREWERY

113 S. Franklin St., Titusville, PA, 16354; (814) 827-7181; thebluecanoebrewery.com
Founded: 2008 **Founders:** Bill Zimmer and Jeremy Potocki **Brewer:** Justin Dudek **Year-Round Beers:** Class 5 APA, Flashlite Lager, Heavy Kevy, Titusville Gold Lager **Seasonals/Special Releases:** Burning Desire, Lumberjack Stout, Pearry Manilow, Wit-ney Houston

Titusville has been big into oil, iron, steel, and lumber through the last 150 years. The city was also home to the college football award namesake, John Heisman. As for beer, Blue Canoe has been a town favorite since opening in the space of a former brewpub in 2008.

From the year-round menu, the **Class 5 APA** (5.2% ABV) is a standout with its restrained tropical hop notes. The brewery shines with its seasonals like the **Pearry Manilow** (6% ABV) and its Belgian fruit flavor, which works well alongside the Harvest Salad with dried cranberries. Another seasonal, **Lumberjack Stout** (5% ABV), and its light smoky character matches up well with the pulled pork pizza or a plate of pierogies.

If the timing works in your favor, you might find both a jambalaya on the specials menu and a rotating specialty, the **Burning Desire Habañero IPA** (6.5% ABV), on the tap tower. A nice pairing and quite a treat indeed.

THE BREWERIE AT UNION STATION

123 W. 14th St., Erie, PA, 16501; (814) 454-2200; brewerie.com; @BrewErie
Founded: 2006 **Founder:** Chris Sirianni **Brewer:** Tate Warren **Flagship Beer:** Uncle Jackson's Blonde Ale and Apparition Amber **Year-Round Beers:** Hopness Monster IPA, Railway Hefe Weizen, Major McNair's Nut Brown **Seasonals/Special Releases:** Over 25 varieties

If you read this western Pennsylvania chapter in its entirety, you will notice that opportunities to drink great beer exist in venues that once served as a church, a slaughterhouse, a schoolhouse, a coffin manufacturer, a warehouse, a farm, a hotel, and a colonial-era inn and tavern. Brewerie adds to the list of unique experiences with its brewpub inside a grand former train station. There is no distribution of their beer so there are at least two reasons to visit this brewery in a train station.

Brewer's Cup Home Brew Fest

Each February at Brewerie, around 500 thirsty customers come to sample from, and award a "people's choice" to, over 50 beers entered into the annual competition hosted at the brewpub.

The beautiful building has been renovated, restored, and preserved throughout the years and retains marble and lighting fixtures from the train station's early days. An Amtrak train comes by once a day at the adjacent train stop, but the original building is now all about Brewerie and a few other business offices.

Dining in the rotunda with a view of the 3.5-barrel brewing operation is special. Sitting at the bar in the area where newsstands used to be takes you back in time. But sitting outside at the Trackside Beer Garden, complete with its own bar, a bocce court, and closeups of passing trains, is a highlight of visits to Brewerie.

Like at most brewpubs, getting a sampler flight of beer is a good way to get to know the spectrum of what a brewery produces. At Brewerie, be sure not to miss brewer Tate Warren's **Railway Hefe Weizen** (4.8% ABV lightly flavored wheat) along with an Old Cobb Salad and the roasty **Major McNair's Nut Brown** (5.6% ABV) with one of the many burgers on the menu or the bacon peanut chicken sandwich.

As is common with the supporting network of local brewers, the bar at Brewerie does its part by serving a decent bottle list from locals including Erie, Lavery, and Voodoo among many others.

CHURCH BREW WORKS

3525 Liberty Ave., Pittsburgh, PA, 15201; (412) 688-8200; churchbrew.com; @ChurchBrewWorks

Founded: 1996 **Founder:** Sean Casey **Brewer:** Justin Viale **Year-Round Beers:** Celestial Gold, Pipe Organ Pale Ale, Pious Monk Dunkel **Seasonals/Special Releases:** Blast Furnace Stout, Millenium Tripel, Oktoberfest, Quadzilla, Sleigh Wrecker, Thunderhop IPA, and many others

When talking about Pittsburgh and brewing, two topics seem to come up the most: Iron City and "that church brewery." The Lawrenceville neighborhood already had plenty of brewing history with Pittsburgh Brewing Company on the other side of Liberty Avenue. When Church Brew Works opened nearly 20 years ago in the former St. John the Baptist church, it bought into a different type of history that would draw both the beer lovers and the curious to see a brewery on the altar of a church.

The church, which through renovations retained many of its original features (pews, stained glass, pipe organ, lanterns, and even the confessional), lives on as an award-winning brewery and restaurant in the 21st century. In 2001, the property was designated a local historic property. As for beer recognition, all three of the year-round beers brought home medals in 2012 en route to winning the Large Brewpub of the Year honor at the Great American Beer Festival.

Folks come for the food and beer as much as they do to admire the beauty of the place, giggle at the idea of an altar brewery, and take pictures. Available year-round, the **Pious Monk Dunkel** and **Pipe Organ Pale Ale** are both very well done beers that can satisfy the beer geeks and newbies alike. With dinner, the pale ale with a bowl of mussels makes a lot of sense and the dunkel with a Pittsburgh pierogie pizza from the wood-fired brick oven is a slam dunk(el) winner.

From the beer menu that rolls out plenty of rotating seasonals and specialties, the **Thunderhop** is one of the most available and dependable throughout the year as a solid 6% IPA. When it comes time to leave, forgo the traditional growler and instead take a 5-liter mini keg of **Oktoberfest** or **Celestial Gold** and bottles of the **Millenium Trippel** and the **Cherry Quadzilla**.

HOFBRÄUHAUS PITTSBURGH

2705 S. Water St. Southside Works, Pittsburgh, PA, 15203; (412) 224-2328; hofbrauhauspittsburgh.com; @HofbrauhausPitt
Founded: 2009 **Founders:** Nick Ellison, Eric Haas, and Jay Lang **Brewers:** Shawn Setzenfand, Levi Rounsville, Kyle Klein **Year-Round Beers:** Light Lager, Premium Lager, Dunkel, Hefe Weizen **Seasonals/Special Releases:** One rotating seasonal per month

The brewing staff is highly trained here and delivers solid German beers to the masses that pass through the beer hall every day. All are made spectacularly well, with the Dunkel (5.5% ABV) and Hefe Weizen (5.4% ABV) as two excellent

representations of their styles. Liters of these can be consumed quite easily while relaxing with a view of the river, the tugboats, and the recreational path.

Brewer-led tours are available, by appointment, for $10, and conclude with a sampler tray of the available beers. To keep selection fresh and interesting, the brewery releases a monthly seasonal, which gets ceremoniously tapped the first Wednesday of every month.

The oversized facility is considered the largest restaurant in Pittsburgh and includes a large outdoor patio and biergarten in addition to the main dining room, where live German music fills the air most of each day and night. The crowds include recreational trail users, group parties, tourists, and families during the day and a younger set at night in this unique setting on the banks of the Monongahela River.

Those in Ohio may be interested to know that a fifth location opened in Columbus late in 2014.

MARZONI'S BRICK OVEN & BREWING COMPANY

164 Patchway Rd., Duncansville, PA, 16635; (814) 695-2931; marzonis.com
Founded: 2003 **Founder:** Bill Campbell **Brewers:** Bill Kroft and Alex Delozier **Year-Round Beers:** Locke Mt. Lager, Marzoni's Amber Lager, Highway 22 Wheat, Patchway Pale Ale, Avalance IPA, Stone Mason Stout **Seasonals/Special Releases:** Usually two rotating seasonals available

Marzoni's has been making beer in Duncansville for quite a few years and in 2012 added a second (non-brewing) location in Altoona. Recent expansion brought a third location in Selinsgrove in early 2015. They also brew two house beers for the historic Jean Bonnet Tavern in Bedford. All of the beer is made in Duncansville, which even with the expanded fermenting, conditioning, and storage room added behind the kitchen is no simple feat.

A visit to the brewpub brings a rewarding experience with both the pizza and the beer. The menu is full of sandwiches and pastas but really shines with the brick-oven pizza. Fortunately, the brewery serves up solid beers like the **Amber Lager** (5% ABV), the **IPA** (7.5% ABV), and the **Pale Ale** (5.5% ABV) that work really well with the wheat-crust pizzas.

Also check out Marzoni's in Altoona at the annual Pints for Pets fundraiser, for which they are a primary and proud sponsor.

NORTH COUNTRY BREWING COMPANY

141 S. Main St., Slippery Rock, PA, 16057; (724) 794-2337; northcountrybrewing.com; @NCBrewingCo

Founded: 2005 (production facility in 2013) **Founders:** Bob and Jodi McCafferty
Brewers: Sean McIntyre and Aaron Fries **Year-Round Beers:** Firehouse Red Ale, Paleo IPA, Slimy Pebble Pils, Buck Snort Stout **Seasonals/Special Releases:** Many including Devil's Waltz, Squirrel's Nut Brown, Slippery Rock Dew, and Stinkie Hippie Pale Ale
Naming Inspiration: The North Country Hiking Trail

Folks around western Pennsylvania have known North Country's unique hangout in Slippery Rock for quite some time. When they opened the production canning facility in 2013 minutes southwest of the pub, production capacity increased tenfold and the rest of Pennsylvania began catching on to not only where Slippery Rock is located but the beer that comes from there as well.

The brewpub operates on a property with a 200+-year history that served as home to a series of family-run businesses, including cabinet and coffin making, undertaking, and furniture dealing. When the McCaffertys purchased the property in the 1990s, they completed extensive renovations but kept original barn beams and significantly reused lumber left by the sellers.

A visit to North Country is one of the most unusual brewpub experiences in the state. The restaurant space winds its way from the front bar to side dining rooms, upstairs to additional dining rooms, and out to the back patio complete with firepit. The brewery somehow fits into the front corner of the restaurant.

The tap list is typically full, with a wide range of beer styles. Two exceptional year-round selections include the earthy **Paleo IPA** (6.3% ABV) and the solid **Station 33 Firehouse Red** (4.7% ABV), from which 5 percent of sales is donated to the Slippery Rock Fire Department.

On the rotating occasionals beer menu, you can't go wrong with the slightly hoppy **Squirrel's Nut Brown Ale** (5.1% ABV) or the **Devil's Waltz** porter (6.4% ABV) with a hint of smoke.

Many of North Country's beers are versatile and food-friendly, and the kitchen satisfies with just as diverse a menu as the brewery. The typical roundup of pub food is joined by the creative (e.g., frog's legs), the gluten-free, and the vegan. To complete the gastronomic experience, local wines from Narcisi, Volant, and Winfield are also available.

PENN BREWERY

800 Vinial St., Pittsburgh, PA, 15212; (412) 237-9400; pennbrew.com; @PennBrewery
Founded: 1986 **Founder:** Tom Pastorious (original); Sandy Cindrich, Corey Little, Linda Nyman (current owners) **Brewers:** Andy Rich, Nick Rosich, Steve Crist (cellarman) **Flagship Beer:** Penn Pilsner **Year-Round Beers:** Penn Dark, Penn Kaiser Pils, Allegheny Pale Ale, Penn Gold, Penn Weizen **Seasonals/Special Releases:** Oktoberfest, Penn Märzen, Penn Ginger Beer, St. Nikolaus Bock, Nut Roll Ale, Overlook IPA, Cool River Kölsch, Pumpkin Roll Ale

Pittsburgh has plenty of brewing history. Penn Brewery has its own that spans nearly 30 years, but its building's history goes back even longer. Following in the brewery boots of German brewers at Eberhardt & Ober in the city's North Side neighborhood, Penn continues to hold its place as the historic German brewery in a city that once had no shortage of them.

At Penn, beer and food can be enjoyed upstairs with a view into the brewery, downstairs in the Bierhalle, or outdoors in the Biergarten. **Kaiser Pils** (4.5% ABV) is an authentically wonderful way to begin a session at the brewery with an aromatic and spicy Noble hop pils. The **Penn Dark** (5% ABV) brings a bit more alcohol and a touch of roasted malt flavor. If the time of year is right, do not pass up the **St. Nikolaus Brewer's Reserve Doppelbock**. At 8.5% ABV, it's just warming enough for the cold winter months and delivers a wonderful classic doppelbock richness with chocolate malts and a small dose of bittering hops.

The kitchen carries through on the German theme as well, serving traditional potato pancakes, Hungarian goulash, a wiener schnitzel sandwich on pretzel bun, and hasenpfeffer with spaetzle dumplings, all of which come highly recommended.

Live music follows the dinner hour most Fridays and Saturdays and gives visitors a reason to stay and check out a few of the brewery's more limited offerings.

SPRAGUE FARM & BREW WORKS

22043 US 6, Venango, PA, 16440; (814) 398-2885; sleepingchainsaw.com/brew_works .htm; @SpragueFarmBrew

Founded: 2006 **Founders:** Brian and Minnie (Mary) Sprague **Brewers:** Brian Sprague, Minnie Sprague, Ira Gerhart **Flagship Beer:** Spraguer Logger **Year-Round Beers:** Rustbelt Amber Ale, Hellebender, Fighting Scotchtoberfest, I.B.U.D. 59, Ale Mary **Seasonals/Special Releases:** Lover's Lager, H.I.G.H. Pa., Spragueson Saison, Mug Tippin Stout, Cin-O-Sure, Spruce Lee, KickBock, and many others

A visit to the Sprague Farm is a comfortable and casual event, like going to a family picnic. Plus, it is just downright lots of fun. Start by parking around the brewery or in the field. Step up to the converted dairy barn's tasting-room bar amid oodles of breweriana and order from a bunch of creatively named and well-made beers. Take your beer and wander the property to check out the hops and the chainsaw art. Or take a tour that informally begins at no particular set time in the early afternoon. Sit in a comfortable chair overlooking the farm property. Listen to some live music, often coming from the stage in the same barn. Throw some games of cornhole or horseshoes into the mix.

The beer, the people, and the atmosphere play equally starring roles at Sprague. As for the beer from Sprague's 15-barrel brewhouse, the **Hellbender** rises quickly to the top as a big, roasty, chocolatey beer with notes of fruit and bitter hops. Yet this robust porter drinks quite easily and makes for a perfect porch-sitting companion as the sun sets over the field. The **Spraguer Logger** (6% ABV) is considered the flagship and is a solid märzen worth sampling. If the timing of a visit is right, you may find an estate beer—one of the few in the country by any unscientific count—like a H.I.G.H. PA made with barley and hops grown on the 66-acre Sprague Farms property, bounded to the west by French Creek. Friend and agronomist Joel Hunter is a driving force behind the Estate of Mind series of beers, of which HIGH PA (Hunter Indigenous Grained & Hopped Pennsylvania Ale) is one.

When it's all over, 32-ounce Crowlers™ of select beers are available to go and there's lodging available on the property as well to complete the experience at the farm.

TIMBER CREEK TAP & TABLE

11191 Highline Dr., Meadville, PA, 16335; (814) 807-1005; timbercreektapandtable.com; @TimberCreekTap

Founded: 2012 **Founders:** Devin Kelly and Dustin Kelly **Brewer:** Jacob Vorisek **Year-Round Beers:** Fresh Squeezed IPA, Black Bear Porter, Liberty Blonde, Werkzeug Stadt **Seasonals/Special Releases:** 2 rotating seasonal and 1 rotating Belgian-style

It's harder to stand out on the exploding craft-brewing and beer-bar landscape than ever before, even in northwestern Pennsylvania. Timber Creek is one of the newest entrants on the scene and they have quickly impressed.

The establishment is split between two buildings—one called Tap and one called Table—connected by a covered walkway and makeshift patio with a few tables and chairs. The bar sits above the brewing operations and has a clear view through the floor onto the 10-barrel system that pumps out enough beer to keep eight lines, including a root beer, flowing at the bar.

Worth the attention are three very different beers, including the **Black Bear Porter** (a 6% ABV that puts the robust in this tasty porter), **Werkzeug Stadt Lager** (a very crisp and clean 5.5% ABV German lager), and **Fresh-Squeezed IPA** (a 7.5% ABV hop-lover's delight), all for their own unique reasons. The brewer, Jake Vorisek, also rotates a couple of seasonals on the menu as time and space allow.

The kitchen puts out a menu that satisfies the hungry and curious beer traveler. The appetizer menu contains some tantalizing starters like lobster nachos, lamb lollipops, and Cajun filet tips that may make it difficult to get to the rest of the menu, which serves a wide array of sandwiches, salads, burgers, and entrees.

VOODOO BREWING COMPANY

215 Arch St., Meadville, PA, 16335; (814) 337-3676; voodoobrewery.com; @VoodooBrewery
Founded: 2006 (pub in 2012)
Founder: Matt Allyn **Brewer:** Curtis Rachocki **Flagship and Year-Round Beers:** Good Vibes, Gran Met, Hoodoo IPA, Pilzilla, Voodoo Love Child, White Magick of the Sun, Wynona's Big Brown Ale **Seasonals/Special Releases:** Big Black Voodoo Daddy, Cowbell, and the Barrel Room Collection series

Only a couple of years in the pub business, Voodoo has gone from bar to restaurant to live-entertainment venue. Their brewing star continues to shine brighter as the beers make it farther abroad into new markets. In turn, consumers are searching out the brewery's hometown of Meadville.

The pub is a comfortable atmosphere of sofas and communal tables at which to enjoy around a dozen or so of Voodoo's beers along with a small, but nicely built and constantly rotating, kitchen menu of things like tacos, spent-grain pizzas, pretzels, quesadillas, dips, and salads—all sporting some combination of local and organic ingredients.

At the bar, all of the usual suspects from Voodoo are available as expected, such as the **Big Black Voodoo Daddy Russian Imperial Stout** (12.5% ABV), which was a silver medal winner at the 2013 Great American Beer Festival. The **Voodoo Love Child Belgian Tripel** (9.5% ABV), aged on cherries, raspberries, and passion fruit, and the **Hoodoo IPA** (7.3% ABV) are just two more of the excellent Voodoo beers that fans eagerly seek out at the pub.

When in season, the **Gose** (4.2% ABV) is a wonderful summertime thirst quencher and the **Cowbell Imperial Oatmeal Milk Stout** (8.5% ABV) is a smooth and rich beer perfectly suited for cooler-weather months. The upstairs lounge has become a destination for lovers of both beer and music to converge for a fuller Voodoo experience.

THE BEER HIVE

2117 Penn Ave., Pittsburgh PA 15222; (412) 904-4502; thebeerhive.com; @TheBeerHive
Draft Beers: 12 Bottled/Canned Beers: 100+

The Strip District has long been a shopping and eating destination for both locals and tourists. Beer had never been a main part of the equation until The Beer Hive came along.

They've been recently joined by Milkman Brewing Company four blocks away on Penn Avenue, but The Beer Hive has been taking care of thirsts and serving sandwiches, tacos, fried appetizers, and wings 20 different ways in the Strip since 2011. The spot is a fun place to duck away from the occasional chaos of the shopping district and also a source for takeout growlers and bottles.

BOCKTOWN BEER & GRILL

690 Chauvet Dr., Pittsburgh, PA 15275; (412) 788-2333
500 Beaver Valley Mall Blvd., Monaca, PA 15061; (724) 728-7200
bocktown.com; @Bocktown
Draft Beers: 16 Bottled/Canned Beers: 400+

This chapter discusses some of the longtime beer establishments of western Pennsylvania, particularly of Pittsburgh. Others have come along in the past year or two, and then there are those like Bocktown that are part of the middle generation.

Better beer in the 'burbs is something that Bocktown helped pioneer around Pittsburgh. The original Bocktown Beer and Grill opened near the Pittsburgh airport in 2006 as the latest wave of popularity in the craft-brewing segment was gaining momentum. The model from the beginning—which continues at the second, much larger location in Monaca, opened in 2011—has been all about creating a casual, friendly environment in which to serve local produce, cheeses, and meats to accompany a lineup of great beer.

In addition to carefully maintaining a solid year-round beer program roughly split between locals and outsiders, both locations host weekly free samplings of spotlighted breweries where a brewer, rep, or distributor may show up to provide additional information and insights. The Beeried Treasures weekly event puts extra-special beers, some vintage, on the menu. Brewser the Infuser is also a weekly event where beers are doctored up with an infusion of other interesting flavors to imaginatively extend the possibilities of the base beer. The restaurant supports the homebrewing segment as well, with occasional meetups and tastings of the TRUB (Three Rivers Underground Brewers) hosted at Bocktown.

The kitchen turns out an interestingly wide spectrum of food, including lightly fried clam strips, a spicy buffalo chicken dip, a grilled portobello mushroom, a pulled-pork sandwich with house-made barbecue sauce, and a slew of savory local grass-fed beef burgers.

To continue our helpful pronunciation guide, when looking for the second location of Bocktown, be sure to say mo-NACK-ah and not, like the woman's name, Monica.

CALIENTE PIZZA & DRAFT HOUSE

4624 Liberty Ave., Pittsburgh, PA 15224; (412) 682-1414; calientepizza.com;
@CalientePDraftH
Draft Beers: 24 **Bottled/Canned Beers:** 100+

It took an off-chance drive through the city's Bloomfield section toward Church Brew Works to question what this pizza shop with craft-beer signs in the window was all about. It took one visit and conversation with owner, Nick Bogacz, to determine that Caliente (which fittingly translates to "hot") is a rising star in the Pittsburgh beer scene and deserves a mention in these pages. In the pizza business for roughly 9 years, Bogacz went down the craft beer road in 2012 and immediate success helped open a downstairs bar in 2014 that is dubbed Railsplitter Speakeasy and a second location in Hampton Township north of Pittsburgh.

Attention to detail on the beer menu is impeccable, bringing in the likes of locals All Saints, East End, Helltown, and a monthly "rare cask" from nearby Church Brew Works. Also featured are ciders from local Arsenal in the Lawrenceville neighborhood just down the street. From outside the region, Avery, Firestone Walker, Jolly Pumpkin, Stone, and the occasional Russian River find their way either onto the taps or into the coolers.

As the name suggests, there's plenty of pizza to go around at Caliente, not to mention calzones, wings, sandwiches, and burgers. A decent happy hour special each weekday brings out $5 pizzas and half-priced drafts of beer. Now that's Caliente.

D'S SIXPAX & DOGZ
1118 S. Braddock Ave., Pittsburgh, PA 15218; (412) 241-4666; ds6pax.com; @Ds6Pax
Draft Beers: 27 **Bottled/Canned Beers:** 1,000+

Hot dogs and beer. For over 15 years in the Regent Square neighborhood at the edge of Pittsburgh, D's has been selling plenty of great beer and hot dogs—to the tune these days of hot dogs a dozen different ways and a toppings list to make your eyesight blur. The kitchen is about wings, pizza, and sandwiches too, but yet it often comes back to the hot dogs and beer—served up like a local piece of art.

The growth in the food, the beer, and their popularity resulted in a 2007 expansion into the neighboring property. The selection of packaged retail beer in "The Beer Cave" has grown to well over a thousand different beers and has become a great source for locals as well as visitors on the way in or out of Pittsburgh.

FAT HEAD'S SALOON
1805 E. Carson St., Pittsburgh, PA 15203; (412) 431-7433; fatheadspittsburgh.com; @FatHeadsPgh
Draft Beers: 42 **Bottled/Canned Beers:** A handful

Fat Head's is getting to the point where it might be possible to write a short book on this legendary Pittsburgh beer destination. Since 1992, mention good beer in Pittsburgh and locals would likely point you to a handful of places, of which Fat Head's was typically near the top of the list. It still deservedly is, even as the options around town have grown more plentiful.

The sandwich platters are epic in size and in flavor and the beer list bursts with locals and internationals. Between 2009 and 2012, Fat Head's added a full production-sized brewery outside Cleveland that fills the distribution channels and a dozen taps at the original Pittsburgh pub with plenty of highly acclaimed and award-winning beer.

Rushing in and out of Fat Head's is not usually the best game plan since, to varying degrees, most days and nights are crowded at both the bar and restaurant. Plan to spend a couple of hours sampling some beers, a few orders of wings, a 3 Little Pigs plate (three meats, sauerkraut, and pierogies), and a Double D sandwich platter (tempting ingredient list much too long to print here—check it out for yourself). Spend a few more hours if there are local sporting events as the bar and dining rooms are great places in which to watch a game with friends.

GOOSKI'S

3117 Brereton St., Pittsburgh,
PA 15219; (412) 681-1658;
@Gooskis
Draft Beers: 12 **Bottled/
Canned Beers:** Nearly 200

Gooski's is nestled into the mostly residential Polish Hill neighborhood just down the street from the landmark Immaculate Heart of Mary Church. It's truly a neighborhood dive bar off the beaten path, serving as the perfect escape from whatever, or whomever, you're trying to escape. And it just so happens to serve some pretty decent beer.

Daunting from the approach and dimly lit on the inside, Gooski's is a fun hangout for friends to listen to great live music or punk rock jukebox music, smoke, play ping-pong or pool, eat pierogies (very limited menu), sit on vinyl stools, chat with one of the coolest bartenders around (that'd be Tim), use the graffiti-covered bathrooms, and drink the likes of East End, Full Pint, and Yuengling at some of the most reasonable beer prices in the city. Like all great dive bars, though, it should be kept a secret—please don't tell anyone.

HOUGH'S TAPROOM & BREWPUB

563 Greenfield Ave., Pittsburgh, PA 15207; (412) 586-5944; houghspgh.com;
@HoughsPGH
Draft Beers: 73 **Bottled/Canned Beers:** 200+

Is it possible that a beer heaven exists tucked away in the Greenfield section of Pittsburgh? If a high-quality neighborhood bar with one of the largest selections of beer, above-average pub grub, darts, shuffleboard, and televisions for sporting events sounds appealing, then the answer is probably yes.

But, if further convincing is needed, the family-run establishment has a connected brewpub/homebrew shop next door to provide customers the ability to make their own beer and come back a few weeks later when the beer is ready to package and take home.

The brew-on-premise operation is a comfortable atmosphere outfitted with everything needed to make the beer (plus, staff does the cleanup!) and local-themed decor that reminds you that you're in Pittsburgh. The bar and brewery are in full view of each other through windows and a large glass door, but the crossover doesn't end there. There are house-made beers that are served at the bar and, while brewing, customers are permitted to drink a beer from the bar in the brewery.

One of the newest additions at the bar is a twist on the growler fills to go. They rolled out a machine (actually, rather simple) behind the bar that seals a filled one-use 32-ounce can in seconds and is even more convenient than a glass growler.

HOUSE OF 1000 BEERS

357 Freeport St., New Kensington, PA 15068; (724) 337-7666; houseof1000beers.com; @Ho1kB
Draft Beers: 24 **Bottled/Canned Beers:** approximately 1,200

There may not be much craft beer to be found around this upriver town, so House of 1000 Beers has become a leading destination of sorts. Check them out during Pittsburgh Craft Beer Week and see the crush of beer fans who travel from hundreds of miles away for a Voodoo Brewery Tap Takeover. Or a sour beer–themed event.

This is a substantial retail shop and well-organized beer geek's delight of a retail shop at that. However, with 24 taps, a small kitchen that cooks up pubby appetizers, sliders, and pizzas, a couple of TVs, and seating (including a small patio) for 40 to 50 people, it qualifies for this list as a beer bar and is worth the excursion out of Pittsburgh.

JEAN BONNET TAVERN

6048 Lincoln Hwy., Bedford, PA 15522; (814) 623-2250; jeanbonnettavern.com
Draft Beers: 18

As an inn and tavern dating back to 1762, the Jean Bonnet Tavern has seen a lot of history come and go. The original tavern keeper is the restaurant's namesake. Protests of the Whiskey Tax occurred here, and George Washington had a militia base camp established nearby so it's safe to say that this is another place where Washington slept.

In current times, Shannon and Melissa Jacobs have owned the establishment since 1999 and persisted from the beginning in bringing some of the best and most different beer to Bedford County long before most others caught on. Longtime Chef Faye Blackburn has been part of the equation as well, pairing dessert with featured seasonal beer selections.

The draft tower is mostly focused on beers from Pennsylvania like East End, Erie, Lancaster, Tröegs, Victory, Weyerbacher, and Yards. Sly Fox O'Reilly's Stout is typically on tap because "you can't be a beer bar without a good stout." Two exclusive house beers are made by nearby Marzoni's. Weekly tappings of special new beers at discounted prices provide another way for customers to learn more about the industry.

The property oozes history at each fascinating turn, there's a gift shop on site to explore, and the herb garden is watched over by nearby goats, which can be fed with food dispensed from the gift shop. All serve as extra interesting layers to your visit.

After a meal that might include a satisfying bowl of Tavern Onion Soup, diver sea scallops or strip steak, and a triple-layer carrot cake, the Inn's quaint rooms upstairs have a place to lay your head. As in many 18th-century buildings, you may even "bump" into a former resident.

THE KNICKERBOCKER

3957 6th Ave., Altoona, PA 16602; (814) 942-0770; knickerbockertavern.com; @TheKnickTavern
Draft Beers: 18, including one handpump **Bottled/Canned Beers:** Several hundred

The Knickerbocker in Altoona is an historic property—like the Windber Hotel later in this chapter—that in modern times has become a local go-to spot. The Knick serves up great beer in an inviting atmosphere, particularly in their outdoor Kourtyard [sic]. The building dates to the early 1900s and the bar has been under the ownership of Terry and Lillan Reed since 1996. Their son Bjorn, as beer and wine director, has a persistent drive to provide the best beer selection.

He has developed a 46-page menu of bottle selections, including a special vintage section, that presents the inventory by style and origin. Special regional attention is paid to Dogfish Head, Elk Creek, Great Lakes, Otto's, Tröegs, and Yards.

The kitchen prides itself on using local meats, making sauces and dressings in-house, and creating from-scratch cole slaw and soups that have a loyal following. The Greek panini, avocado and brie sandwich, and Parmesan-battered zucchini all come strongly recommended.

The Knickerbocker has growth plans in its sights—both in terms of additional seating, crafting a house beer with a local brewery, and an additional 10 draft lines.

MAD MEX

370 Atwood St., Pittsburgh, PA 15213; (412) 681-5656; madmex.com/pittsburgh/oakland;
@MadMex_Oakland
Draft Beers: 14 **Bottled/Canned Beers:** 35+

Opened in 1993, Mad Mex, as with Fat Head's discussed earlier, has long been one of the leading venues for great beer in Pittsburgh. Located in the Oakland neighborhood adjacent to the University of Pittsburgh, the bar makes effective use of its relatively small space to serve up 14 taps of great beer, including locals like Fat Head's and Full Pint.

The relationship with Fat Head's actually goes a bit deeper as head brewer Matt Cole credits Mad Mex with the introduction to craft beer that set him down the road to becoming a brewer. He brewed a Fat Head's beer, Dos Decadas, for the bar's 20th anniversary in 2013.

The food menu carries on a southwestern theme with well-done quesadillas, burritos, and tacos. And, when beer is not on the evening's agenda, be sure to check out the 22-ounce Big Azz Margarita special. In addition to six other locations around the Pittsburgh region, Pennsylvanians can find the fun and delicious experience replicated in Philadelphia, State College, Willow Grove, and Wynnewood with still more locations on the horizon.

POINT BRUGGE CAFE

401 Hastings St., Pittsburgh, PA 15206; (412) 441-3334; pointbrugge.com; @PointBrugge
Draft Beers: 4 **Bottled/Canned Beers:** 75

The charmingly small restaurant is in the city's Point Breeze section, which has seen significant growth in recent years due in part to the success of nearby Bakery Square (formerly a Nabisco plant). From the front door, the entire bar and dining room are visible in a cozy environment with comfortably friendly service.

In a nod to the food and beer inspiration as well as the neighborhood it operates in, Point Brugge (get the name?) serves up a complete list of Belgian goldens, wits, dubbels, tripels, quadrupels, saisons, and lambics that complement the food menu.

While the kitchen does other things quite well, like the Point Burger with bacon, fontina, and shallots, and the Chaud Chevre Salad with asparagus and roasted red peppers, the Moules and Frites steal the limelight here as you might expect. Get a bottle of Orval and a bowl of mussels done up either in Classic style (with white wine, shallots, garlic, and light cream), Red Curry with coconut milk, or Chili Verde with tomatillos, and be transported across the ocean for a delightful lunch or dinner.

ROFF SCHOOL TAVERN

13388 Leslie Rd., Meadville, PA 16335; (814) 333-8641; roffschooltavern.com; @RoffSchoolBar
Draft Beers: 8 **Bottled/Canned Beers:** 250

Meadville has its beer producers (Timber Creek and Voodoo) and it has a bar that serves it very well. The location, at the eastern edge of the city, had a liquor license for almost three decades prior to Roff opening in 2008. The current owners took the building back to its roots, naming it after the original 1930s schoolhouse, and beefed up the beer selection. Underscoring their commitment to the community and, in a nod to the past, each year they award a scholarship to a graduating high school senior.

For those over 21, the Tavern has become a beer destination for those looking for great beer and a fun time. The "playground" outside the bar is fenced in and has plenty of recess activities like horseshoes, cornhole, picnic tables, and fire pits.

The bar serves a wide selection of beer and a combination of 20 creative burgers and pizzas and has a decent-sized bottle shop to supply your take-out needs. If you drink enough of their beer, they'll put you in their Beer Club, with benefits.

SHARP EDGE BISTRO

922 Penn Ave., Pittsburgh, PA 15222; (412) 338-2437; sharpedgebeer.com/bistro-on
-penn; @Sharp_Edge
Draft Beers: 30 **Bottled/Canned Beers:** Nearly 200

The Sharp Edge family goes back to 1990 and they celebrated the 20th year serving great beer in Pittsburgh by opening their fifth location, this one on Penn Avenue in the heart of the downtown cultural district. It makes for a great visit when staying at a nearby hotel or attending a meeting at the convention center. Plus, PNC Park is just a little more than a half-mile walk across the Clemente Bridge from Penn Avenue.

Beginning with the Beer Emporium as the original location, owners Jeffrey and Sherri Walewski have put great beer, with an emphasis on Belgian beer, front and center long before most others in the region. For his work, Walewski was knighted in 2003 by Belgian royalty.

The typical draft menu at the downtown location is roughly three-quarters Belgian, including near permanent residents Piraat, Gulden Draak, and the sweet, hop spicy, yeasty, and boozy Over the Edge (9.5% ABV Belgian IPA), brewed exclusively since 2007 for the Sharp Edge family of bars by Brouwerij Van Steenberge.

Sharp Edge has hosted the Great European Beer Festival for nearly 20 years, which is a showcase of Belgian and other European beers and grows in popularity each year. Finally, if further proof of the bar's standing in Pittsburgh's beer scene is needed, they have been recognized in the past as the Best Belgian Beer Bar in the USA by the *Petit Futé Guide to Belgian Beers*. As you read this, Sharp Edge is actively laying plans in Murrysville for its next southwestern Pennsylvania location.

WINDBER HOTEL
502 15th St., Windber, PA 15963; (814) 467-6999; thewindberhotel.com
Draft Beers: 15 **Bottled/Canned Beers:** 130

The Windber Hotel has a rich history, one that according to experts has sent ghosts to the present-day bar, which is serving some very good beer in a unique setting. The bar sports an authentically original look and feel while serving up beers from both the region (East End, Fat Head's, Full Pint, Happy Valley, Otto's, Penn, and Rivertowne to name a few) and elsewhere (Duck Rabbit, Great Divide, and Stone).

Brett Hollern and Charlie Clark have been largely responsible for bringing beers not typically found in the area to Windber. From the kitchen, expect to find a standard tavern menu that adequately covers a diversity of interests.

Housed in the former Hotel Leister, which dates back to 1897, the bar was purchased by owners Scott Penrod, Tom Piscitella, and Becky Piscitella and was gutted, renovated, and reopened in 2007 to the delight of locals. Many original features were retained in the renovation, including the original long bar. When you're settled in for a drink, ask the bartender to see newspaper clippings of the building's fascinating history.

Pittsburgh—Pub Crawl

The South Side has been the undisputed king of nightlife in The 'Burgh for quite some time. There are some up-and-coming neighborhoods—like Lawrenceville—that could qualify, but let's stick with the South Side for this go-round. Get your walking shoes on and join the local "Yinzers" for a pub crawl. This is going to be a good one.

TOTAL WALKING DISTANCE: 1.60 miles

Hofbräuhaus Pittsburgh, 2705 S. Water St. Southside Works, Pittsburgh, PA, 15203; (412) 224-2328; hofbrauhauspittsburgh.com; @HofbrauhausPitt

Many would rather start the day at Hofbräuhaus than end it here. Not that there's anything wrong with late night at this über German-themed beer hall. It's just a much different—relatively quieter—experience sitting by the Monongahela River with a liter of dunkel or hefeweizen on a beautiful afternoon. If it's raining, there's

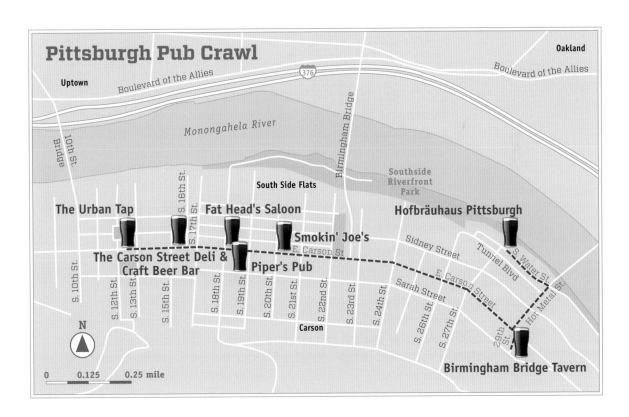

always the indoor beer hall with requisite rows of communal dining tables with the brewhouse as backdrop behind the bar. It's still a German beer hall so fear not, the atmosphere will be filled with lederhosen, dirndls, oompah music, and festive groups of tourists, sports fans, and some locals.

The beer is the same at night, but the party goes up another couple of notches and the table dancing never ends. Fun—in a different way.

Starting the pub crawl here makes sense too from a parking perspective, often a great challenge around the South Side, with the retail complex's parking garages.

Directions: Make a left out of Hofbräuhaus and walk toward the Hot Metal Bridge. Turn right, cross Carson Street on to 29th Street, and the next stop is on the left.

Birmingham Bridge Tavern, 2901 Sarah St., Pittsburgh, PA, 15203; (412) 381-2739; birminghambridgetavern.com; @BirmBridgeTavrn
Compared to other South Side bars, the Tavern feels like an out-of-the-way neighborhood bar. And, they like it like that. Not to say that crowds don't fill this cozy spot. But when the Carson Street strip gets too hectic, this provides a nice respite.

While here on the second leg of the South Side tour, be sure to check out the tap list, which may not be the geekiest in Pittsburgh, but when choosing on a warm day between Bell's Oberon, Smuttynose Bouncy House, and Victory Summer Love, life is good.

They also like to do monthly beer specials, spotlighting a particular brewery or importer/distributor, and give out swag and prizes to customers. If you need a bite to eat, the chicken wings come highly recommended amid a menu of fairly typical good pub grub, but be advised to pace yourself since several more very good food options are to come.

Directions: This will be your longest walk of the day between bars, roughly three-quarters of a mile along Carson Street. You'll pass plenty of other bars and shops on the way.

Smokin' Joe's Saloon, 2001 E. Carson St., Pittsburgh, PA, 15203; (412) 431-6757; smokinjoessaloon.com; @Smokin_Joes
The atmosphere at Smokin' Joe's used to be truly smoking; it hung thick in the air. But, that was years ago and you can now clearly see the stellar beer list. The beer selection has remained top-notch throughout the years—60 drafts and 350 bottles—and the pool table and dartboard have likewise remained making this a fun, and required, stop when pub tripping along Carson Street.

If you didn't get a pretzel at Hofbräuhaus or wings at Birmingham Bridge Tavern, you'll probably have a tough time resisting the smokehouse ribs at Smokin' Joe's. Served up along with a beer list that pays decent attention to the western part of the state (e.g., Erie, Full Pint, Lavery, Penn, Rivertowne can routinely be spotted), you might find it difficult to leave, but the pub crawl really gets fun and into full swing now.

Directions: Pub hoppin' along this stretch of Carson Street is fun when you can bounce across the street and down the block to finish off this stretch of the itinerary. Across the street and one block west is Piper's.

Piper's Pub, 1828 E. Carson St., Pittsburgh, PA, 15203; (412) 381-3977; piperspub .com; @PipersPub

There's just something about Piper's that has the potential to make it your favorite stop on a pub crawl already full of stellar stops. There's the welcoming feeling that you get from both sides of the bar that suggests the beer you just bought is more than just a simple transaction.

There's the soccer (football, if you prefer) that always seems to be on at least one of the televisions at the bar. There are the nearly 40 taps, including two hand-pumps, pouring a roughly 50-50 split between beers from Pennsylvania and beers from elsewhere.

There's the Scotch egg and a slew of UK-inspired dishes on the menu. Let's add it up: great beer (much local), solid menu of food from the kitchen, cask-conditioned beer, soccer, friendly service. See how long it takes for you to leave this leg of the tour.

Directions: Back across the street again and less than a block west, this time to Fat Head's.

Fat Head's Saloon, 1805 E. Carson St., Pittsburgh, PA, 15203; (412) 431-7433; fat headspittsburgh.com; @FatHeadsPgh
If the timing of your visit gets you to Fat Head's in the late afternoon hours, you may hit the sweet spot. Though predicting when this longtime Pittsburgh beer mecca (est. 1992) will not be busy is rarely a productive exercise.

Since opening the Fat Head's Brewery outside Cleveland several years ago, the already crowded draft board at Fat Head's now routinely sports around eight or more of its own. Since you may already be quite familiar with Green Flash, Helltown, and Avery, just to name a few frequent taps, take this opportunity to discover one of the beers that started it all for Fat Head's—the Head Hunter IPA (still winning awards and recognition)—or one of the many others like Sunshine Daydream (session IPA) or Bumbleberry (honey blueberry).

See earlier in this chapter where the food menu at Fat Head's is discussed. However, be advised of the portion sizes—the wrong selection could weigh you down and inhibit progress on the remainder of the pub crawl.

Directions: A little more than two blocks west and on the same side of Carson Street is the deli.

The Carson Street Deli & Craft Beer Bar, 1507 E. Carson St., Pittsburgh, PA, 15203; (412) 381-5335; carsonstreetdeliandcraftbeer.com; @BestBrewDeli
They love their creative sandwiches at the Carson Street Deli. But the addition to the name is just as important as they have around 20 taps—many of them local—plus two handpumps from which to choose. No other stop on the tour has 300+ bottles to choose from, to take home or back to your hotel room.

All Saints, Church Brew Works, East End, Fat Head's, Full Pint, Helltown, Hop Farm, Lavery, and Voodoo are all very local or regional beers that you will quite often find available to chase down a Balboa, Godfather, Cheesy Beefy, or a Schnickelheimer sandwich before hitting up the last stop of the night.

Directions: Three more blocks, still on the same side of Carson Street, and you'll arrive at your last stop.

The Urban Tap, 1209 E. Carson St., Pittsburgh, PA, 15203; (412) 586-7499; theurban tap.com; @TheUrbanTap

If this pub crawl began in the midday hours, chances are good that you will be witness to what Carson Street looks like at night. Typically a roving party of mostly young people and plenty of security keeping an eye on it all. A fun time for sure, but if you're looking to get one or two last beers at The Urban Tap, be aware that there could be a line outside the door and a crowd inside.

However, once you must choose from the six beers on the Founders draft tower, or from the 40 others that include hometown favorites East End, Full Pint, and Voodoo, all worries go away.

When you review the gastropub's menu, you may decide to turn this pub crawl on its head and begin at The Urban Tap for brunch and end at Hofbräuhaus for some *gemütlichkeit* and table dancing; your call.

Directions: If you left your car back near Hofbräuhaus, walking the nearly 1.25 miles may not be that big of a deal, but after a day eating, walking, and drinking, you may opt for a taxi instead. Be forewarned that taxicabs do not generally cruise the South Side for rides except during the busier late-night hours.

Central & Northeastern Pennsylvania

BREWERIES

8	Breaker Brewing Company
29	The Brewery at Hershey
36	Gunpowder Falls Brewing Co.
7	The Lion Brewery
2	Nimble Hill Brewing Company
21	ShawneeCraft Brewing Company
6	Susquehanna Brewing Company
28	Tröegs Brewing Company
19	Yuengling Brewery

BREWPUBS

24	Al's of Hampden (Pizza Boy Brewing)
25	Appalachian Brewing Company
20	Barley Creek Brewing Company
33	Battlefield Brew Works
18	Berwick Brewing Company
9	Bullfrog Brewery
14	Elk Creek Cafe and Aleworks
10	The Gamble Mill Rest. & Microbrewery
13	Happy Valley Brewing Company
31	JoBoy's Brew Pub
16	Old Forge Brewing Company
11	Otto's Pub & Brewery
15	Selin's Grove Brewing Company
32	Stoudts Brewing Company
17	Turkey Hill Brewing Company
34	Warehouse Gourmet Bistro & Brew Pub
1	Yorkholo Brewing Company

BEER BARS & RESTAURANTS

4	Backyard Ale House
22	Boxer's Cafe
30	Bulls Head Public House
23	Cafe Bruges
3	Exit 190 Beer Deli
27	Federal Taphouse
35	Holy Hound Taproom
5	Sabatini's Pizza
26	Shady McGrady's
12	Zeno's Pub

Central & Northeastern Pennsylvania

This chapter carves a large half-moon swath from lower-central Pennsylvania—in the areas of Lancaster, York, and "Amish Country"—through the middle of the state and State College, to the far northeastern reaches of the state around the Poconos and the "Coal Regions."

While Philadelphia and its close suburbs have long stolen much of the beer spotlight, the spectacular growth in beer production and beer sales in these areas no longer goes unnoticed.

Breweries

BREAKER BREWING COMPANY

787 E. Northampton St., Wilkes-Barre Township, PA 18702; (570) 392-9078; breakerbrewingcompany.com; @BreakerBrew

Founded: 2005 **Founders:** Chris Miller and Mark Lehman **Brewers:** Chris Miller and Mark Lehman **Year-Round Beers:** Lunch Pail Ale, I-Love-PA, Olde King Coal Stout, 5 Whistle Wheat **Seasonals/Special Releases:** Belsnickler Ale, Black Mariah, Laurel Line Lemongrass Ale, 16 Ton Double IPA **Tours:** No **Taproom:** Yes

Opening a brewery on a former church school property is no easy feat in any community; Breaker had a small but vocal opposition that was finally overcome in 2013 to the delight of those ready for a local small brewery.

In early 2014, they cleared another hurdle when they were legally permitted to serve more than just sample size beers in their tasting room. While you can still order flights of 5-ounce tasters, a full-size glass of any Breaker beer is a good way to go, and if you can't find a style to your liking, you might question whether you like beer.

Beer Lover's Pick

Coal Cracker ESB
Style: Extra-special bitter
ABV: 5%
Availability: Year-round; draft only
For a style that sees limited success in the States both in terms of quality and popularity, Breaker delivers a beer with roots in the UK that should leave beer lovers clamoring for more.

The ESB at this neighborhood brewpub has a strong and pleasing biscuit malt backbone and just a dose of hops to keep the beer dancing on the palate and inviting another sip.

Half growlers, always a welcome sight, are available at Breaker, but with the ESB clocking in at a very sessionable, and dare say drinkable, 5% ABV, a full 64-ounce growler to go is highly recommended.

For starters they have a great stateside representation of a German kölsch (4.5% ABV)—**Cöalsch**—with subtle fruit flavors and a slightly tart snap as well as an occasional **Lemongrass Ale** (4.5% ABV), which has a noticeably pleasing, but not overpowering, presence of the aromatic herb.

If you like a bit more punch in your glass, give one of their IPAs a try, like the **16 Ton Double IPA** (10.6% ABV), which sports a great fresh hop aroma and flavors of pine and citrus. The tasting room also supplies a nicely built list of paninis and small plates of food like soft pretzels (made with **Lunch Pail Ale**) and an antipasto platter.

THE BREWERY AT HERSHEY

598 Schoolhouse Rd., Middletown, PA, 17057; (717) 944-1569; vineyardathershey.com/the-brewery; @BreweryHershey
Founded: 2012 **Founders:** Jason Reimer, Doug Gellatly, Michael Wilson, L. Paul Vezzetti, Ryan DeLutis **Brewer:** Ryan DeLutis **Flagship and Year-Round Brands:** Chocolate MILF, Hip Hops Hooray IPA, Pond Jumper, Weize Guy Hefeweizen **Seasonals/Special Releases:** 2 to 3 per quarter **Tours:** By appointment **Taproom:** Yes

The Brewery at Hershey ranks near the top of the list of picturesque brewery settings, as its hilly 40 acres overlook a pond, hops, grapevines, and a fruit

Beer Lover's Pick

Pond Jumper
Style: American special bitter
ABV: 5.4%
Availability: Year-round; draft only
This may be only the second extra-special bitter in the book; that shows how rare it is to find well-made versions of the English classic. At Hershey, they present a well-balanced biscuit malt profile with an extra dose of hops to give it an American-

ized twist. It's light enough to be refreshing and beg additional glassfuls, substantial enough to be interesting, and yet it's not overwhelming.

and vegetable garden. The 10-barrel system in a new 12,000-square-foot facility has given the brewery a chance to increase its visibility, and its popularity has grown to the point where visitors coming to taste beer some days match, or outnumber, those looking for a wine tasting.

The attention is justified after sampling some regular suspects on tap, like the chocolatey **MILF Brown Ale** (5.2% ABV—Microbrew I'd Like to Finish, in case you were curious), the grapefruit-citrusy and bitter **Hip Hops Hooray IPA** (6.6% ABV), and the well-dosed **Maple Sap Sucker Porter** (5.5% ABV). Friday nights bring outdoor live music and a featured beer in what's been termed the **Special Ops Series**, which entails doing a little something interesting and different with a beer. The IPA, for example, has been known to undergo fermentation with local strawberries and then is dry hopped along with some melon thrown in for that little something extra.

Combining the two sides of the business, the brewery and winery throw a big party in September for the annual debut of its two popular fall seasonals: **Flash Gourd'n Pumpkin** beer and Merlot wine.

GUNPOWDER FALLS BREWING COMPANY

15556 Elm Dr., New Freedom, PA 17349; (717) 759-0330; gunpowderfallsbrewing.com; @GFBrewing
Founded: 2012 **Founder:** Martin Virga **Brewer:** Martin Virga **Flagship and Year-Round Beers:** Dunkel, Pilsner **Seasonals/Special Releases:** Export Hell, Märzen, Schwarzbier **Tours:** Ask in the tasting room **Taproom:** Yes

Pilsner

Style: German-style pilsner

ABV: 5%

Availability: Year-round; 12-ounce bottles

This German-style pilsner from Gunpowder Falls immediately fits right in with the regional brewing excellence of this style. Clean and crisp with a mild spicy hop kick, Virga's Pilsner should be a mainstay on all summertime picnic tables with freshly grilled meats and vegetables.

Trying to spot the brewery while speeding by on Interstate 83 is not the wisest idea. Pay more attention to the GPS as it winds you a couple of miles from the highway exit into a small industrial park and back to the embankment of the highway.

Virga found his way to Gunpowder Falls via Washington DC's Capitol City Brewing Company and Baltimore area's Ellicott Mills Brewing Company. His Bavarian training in German brewing has paid off with very well done German-style beers like the **Dunkel** (5% ABV), **Märzen** (5.4% ABV), and the **Pilsner** described in the Beer Lover's Pick. The tasting room is rather straightforward with a couple handfuls of seats, taps, wall hangings, and some small bites of food.

THE LION BREWERY

700 N. Pennsylvania Ave., Wilkes-Barre, PA 18705; (800) 295-2337; lionbrewery.com; @LionBrewery

Founded: 1905 **Current Owners:** Ron Hammond and Cliff Rissell **Brewer:** Leo Orlandini

Year-Round Brands: Lionshead, Stegmaier, and numerous contract relationships **Tours:** No **Taproom:** No

The Lion Brewery, over 100 years old, is one of the country's oldest operating breweries. History runs deep at The Lion, and Stegmaier has been an important part of it. The Lion picked up the Stegmaier brands in 1974 and both the Stegmaier and Lionshead names are quite familiar to locals, particularly around college campuses. Filling out the diverse lineup of beverages, The Lion also produces the Olde Philadelphia line of sodas. In recent years, the brewery has invested both in

infrastructure and brand development and marketing to help carry it into the future of new beer drinkers. Stegmaier's Pumpkin, a Belgian wheat, and Oktoberfest are a few such varieties.

Stegmaier IPA
Style: India pale ale
ABV: 6.7%
Availability: Year-round; 12-ounce bottles and 16-ounce cans

With the IPA, the Stegmaier name is being taken in a direction of the masses—and the masses should be pleased with this IPA. The opening presents a pleasing floral aroma that continues with tropical flavors of pineapple, grapefruit, and a mild bitter flavor that fades just quickly enough to beg another sip.

If hops aren't your thing, the Stegmaier name is also on a decent porter.

NIMBLE HILL BREWING COMPANY

3971 PA Rte. 6, Tunkhannock, PA 18657; (570) 836-9463; nimblehillbrewingcompany.com
Founded: 2012 **Founder:** Gary Toczko **Brewer:** Michael Simmons **Year-Round Beers:**
Flinke Hügel, Cluster Fuggle, Midnight Fuggle, Hop Bottom, Fuggle English **Seasonals/**
Special Releases: Midnight Flinke, Nim Wit, and occasional barrel-aging projects **Tours:**
No **Taproom:** Yes

Getting to Tunkhannock is an exercise in the perfect Sunday drive—they're not open Sunday, so let's just leave that as a figure of speech. As you come from the Scranton area, the drive includes winding roads along the picturesque Susquehanna River and a few turns.

All will be rewarded upon arrival at the combination wine and beer tasting room. The wine lovers in your group will enjoy their own tasting room while the beer lovers, on the other hand, will partake in free beer samples and the ability to choose from large-format bottles and growler fills of the dozen or so beers usually on tap.

In addition to their IPAs and double IPAs, Nimble Hill does both German and English well. Solid entries like the **Fuggle** (3.5% ABV) English mild and **Midnight Fuggle** (5.5%) robust porter showcase a knack for big flavors and low alcohol and are usually on the list of available beers. **Flinke Hügel** (5% ABV) expresses a Munich helles lager quite well.

Bonczek
Style: Double IPA
ABV: 9%
Availability: Occasionally; 22-ounce bottles

When a Double IPA such as the Bonczek presents itself on the tasting menu, the opportunity should not be passed up. These sorts of amped-up "imperial" beers, which contain more of something to "imperialize," still demand a level of balance to make them more than just novelty, one-off beers.

In the Bonczek, the blast of whole-leaf estate-grown Cascade and Centennial hops is tempered just enough by a smooth texture and malt backbone to invite a second taste, a third, and maybe even a fourth.

At 9% ABV, it likely can't be the session beer for the night, but you won't be blamed if you try and make it one.

The brewery has easy access to wine barrels, naturally, and does occasional barrel-aging. In 2014, after one year in oak wine and whiskey barrels, to celebrate the one-year anniversary of being the first beer brewed on the 15-barrel system, the resulting oak-aged IPA was blended, dry-hopped with their own grown hops, and called **Mysteria 3.0.** The beer was a balanced presentation of big hop and wood flavors and moderate alcohol (6% ABV) and had customers clamoring for more.

Distribution expanded in 2014—along with 12-ounce bottles of Flinke Hügel, Cluster Fuggle, Hop Bottom, and Nim Wit—to include south and central Pennsylvania.

SHAWNEECRAFT BREWING COMPANY

100 Shawnee Inn Dr., Shawnee Inn and Golf Resort, Shawnee on Delaware, PA 18356; (570) 213-5151; shawneecraftbrewingcompany.com; @SCBrewingCo
Founded: 2009 **Founders:** Pete Kirkwood and The Kirkwood Family **Brewers:** Ian Detrick (Lead Brewer) and David Miracle (Cellarman) **Year-Round Beers:** Apiarius, Biere Blanche, Double Pale, Session Porter **Seasonals/Special Releases:** Imperial Porter, Chestnut Braun, Saison, Tripel, and a list of barrel-aged Heirloom Beers **Tours:** Free, Thurs and Fri 4 p.m., Sat 12 p.m., meet at the Shawnee Inn **Taproom:** Yes

At the eastern edge of the Poconos and near the Shawnee ski resort, the ShawneeCraft brewery has formulated a philosophy that plays out in their beers. The philosophy incorporates the natural beauty from the nearby river, mountains, and forests and drives the brewers to create beers that reflect their surroundings. The concern with natural elements is evidenced throughout the brewery, even in the calculation of an "organic content" percentage in each beer.

In the past year, the brewery has added a couple of 20-barrel fermenters to help meet demand as they prepare to push into northern New Jersey and New York City. The beers are brewed by the bank of the Delaware River, which provides a picturesque backdrop for brewery favorites like the Apiarius and Session Porter. At this idyllic setting, brewery tours and tastings can easily lead to a full meal at The Gem & Keystone restaurant and even a night's stay at the Shawnee Inn, both also on the property.

There are approximately 25 beer hives on the property and honey from them is incorporated into the **Apiarius** (5.5% ABV), a refreshing pale ale, to give it a touch of honey sweetness and make it a very food-friendly beer, particularly with lighter fare. The **Session Porter** (5.12% ABV) delivers what its name suggests: a beer full of flavor that is easy on the alcohol. When the brewery barrel-ages its beers in the Heirloom series, the results are usually pretty good as in the **Bourbon Barrel Porter** and **Frambozenbier**.

ShawneeCraft supplies more ways to enjoy their beers including regularly scheduled concerts—Rhythm & Brews—in the brewhouse featuring local bands and the annual Bike 'n' Brew in the spring.

Beer Lover's Pick

Double Pale Ale
Style: India pale ale
ABV: 7.2%
Availability: Year-round; draft only
This hop-forward beer hits all the right marks with delightful floral aromas and easy-going bitter flavors. Put together a plate of strong cheeses, charcuterie, and spicy nuts or pair with a bowl of spicy chili or gazpacho and enjoy the ride.

SUSQUEHANNA BREWING COMPANY

635 S. Main St., Pittston, PA 18640; (570) 654-3557; sbcbeer.com; @SBCBeer
Founded: 2012 **Founders:** Ed Maier, Fred Maier, Mark Nobile **Brewers:** Guy Hagner, Mark Finnarelli **Year-Round Beers:** Goldencold Lager, HopFive IPA, 6th Generation Stock Ale, Pils-Noir, and SoWheat Ale **Seasonals/Special Releases:** Oktoberfest, Pumpkin Ale, Southern Rye IPA, Toboggan Chocolate Doppelbock **Tours:** Free, Sat 2 p.m. **Taproom:** No

If any brewery of northeastern Pennsylvania has the potential in its current footprint to significantly grow in the coming years, it is Susquehanna Brewing Company. Ideally located between Scranton and Wilkes-Barre, its oversized facility sits on 11 acres, with new fermenters filling in the cavernous space.

Beer Lover's Pick

Pils-Noir
Style: Black pilsner
ABV: 6%
Availability: Year-round; 12-ounce bottles
The Pils-Noir is one of those myth-busting dark beers that is a great example of a refreshing dark beer full of flavor and aroma while not feeling heavy on the palate or being overly high in alcohol. Sausages or a burger off the grill would make a great accompaniment.

The owners come from a long history of both brewing and the wholesale beer distribution business. Six generations of brewing, including Stegmaier, ran through the Maier family bloodline until the brands were sold to The Lion Brewery in 1974.

Brewmaster Guy Hagner brings his own long, varied brewing history to his current position here, which sees him brewing solid beers like Southern Rye IPA and Stock Ale.

The **Southern Rye IPA** (8.6% ABV) was done originally for Philly Beer Week 2013 and was put into regular rotation, including 22-ounce bombers, later in 2014. It boldly stands out as a beer that is full of dry hop citrus aroma and bitter hop flavor, yet it's easy to drink. The **Stock Ale** (5.5% ABV) is a wonderful balance of sweet malt and bitter hops.

The wealth of experience from both owners and brewer bodes well for Susquehanna's future. Currently, the beers are found in eastern Pennsylvania but if they stick to plans of reaching 30,000 barrels of annual production, it won't be long before Susquehanna is found across neighboring state borders.

TRÖEGS BREWING COMPANY

200 E. Hersheypark Dr., Hershey, PA 17033; (717) 534-1297; troegs.com; @TroegsBeer
Founded: 1996, current location in 2011 **Founders:** Chris Trogner and John Trogner
Brewers: John Trogner (Brew Master) and a team of 11 brewers **Flagship Beer:**
HopBack Amber Ale **Year-Round Beers:** DreamWeaver Wheat, JavaHead Stout, Perpetual IPA, Troegenator Double Bock, Tröegs Pale Ale, and LaGrave **Seasonals/Special Releases:** Flying Mouflan, Mad Elf, Naked Elf, Nugget Nectar, and the Scratch series of one-offs **Tours:** Free self-guided tours during all open hours; $5 for a guided tour at scheduled times **Taproom:** Yes

The kitchen at Tröegs has reached the point where it almost feels time to begin calling Tröegs a brewpub. After all, though the brewery pumps out enough beer to leave no doubt that it is first and foremost a full-fledged brewery, the restaurant operation has quickly grown to make Tröegs both a dining and beer destination. Many days, with the traffic-control cones and ropes, it nearly resembles nearby Hersheypark.

The move from Harrisburg and opening of the new brewery in 2011 gave yet another reason to make a visit to Hershey. A spa resort, gardens, minor league hockey, concert arena, automobile museum, chocolate factory, and amusement park can all be found within the confines of rural Pennsylvania farm country—and now a brewery. But, a brewery that you can take the family to for a decent meal to go along with your beers. Plus, the self-guided tours provide an educational way to introduce kids to the process of making beer and responsible beer consumption.

Beer Lover's Pick

Sunshine Pils

Style: German-style pilsner

ABV: 4.5%

Availability: Spring/summer seasonal; 12-ounce bottles

Awards: Great American Beer Festival (Gold, 2012; Silver, 2011, Bronze, 2013, 2009); World Beer Cup (Bronze, 2008)

This pick would not have been so difficult if the Perpetual IPA, Nugget Nectar, and Troegenator were not such beautifully made beers. But, German pilsners have a place in my heart—and on my palate—and this quite simply is one of the best in the US.

Low in alcohol, big on clean maltiness, spicy in hop flavor, and tantalizing in hop aroma, this beer captures summer in a bottle and goes extremely well on the picnic table next to a pile of crabs.

To supplement the freshly prepared and locally sourced plates of food coming out of the "snack bar" (seems a gross injustice to still call it a snack bar), the bar pours 15 drafts of year-round beers plus a handful of Scratch-series and one-off beers. The production beers come through the 100-barrel brewhouse while the relatively smaller Scratch series of beers come from the 15-barrel pilot brewery.

Tröegs has been justly rewarded through the years for its beers, most recently taking home three gold medals for **DreamWeaver Wheat**, **HopBack Amber**, and **Sunshine Pils** along with the Mid-size Brewery and Brewer of the Year from the 2012 Great American Beer Festival (GABF). During 2006–2014, the Sunshine Pils and **Troegenator** have won an astounding combined 16 medals between the GABF and World Beer Cup (7 gold, 3 silver, and 6 bronze).

As the brewery continues to grow its capacity (it recently installed eight 800-barrel fermenters), distribution will following accordingly in at least seven more states. Not bad for two brothers who like to brew beer.

YUENGLING BREWERY

501 Mahantongo St., Pottsville, PA 17901; (570) 628-4890; yuengling.com; @Yuengling _Beer
Founded: 1829 (Tampa in 1999 and Mill Creek/Pottsville in 2001) **Founders:** D.G. Yuengling (current owner: fifth generation, Dick Yuengling) **Brewers:** John Callahan (PA) and John Houseman (Tampa) **Flagship Beer:** Lager **Year-Round Beers:** Ale, Black & Tan, Light, Light Lager, Porter, Premium **Seasonals/Special Releases:** Bock, Oktoberfest **Tours:** Free, scheduled tours every day except Sun **Taproom:** No

Say the word "lager" at a bar in any of Yuengling's 16 eastern US states and most bartenders will reach for a bottle of Yuengling. That's what has become of the country's oldest brewery, family-run since 1829. And that's what makes a visit to Pottsville, PA, a special visit.

A 75 minute tour at the brewery pushed into the hills of Pottsville covers the history of Yuengling beer, which, considering Yuengling's age, pretty much covers the history of beer in the US. Even for those who have become numb to the "same old" brewery tour will find the story of Yuengling through the generations an endearing and educational one.

The tour gives guests the opportunity to marvel at the equipment and mechanization that have been built into the unique hillside space. If that is not enough, the portion of the tour in the caves should seal the deal as one of the most unusual brewery tours.

Yuengling was always a bit larger than life in the northeast/mid-Atlantic beer drinker's mind and a bit of a wonder to outsiders. With the significant expansion

into a former Stroh's brewery plant in Tampa, FL, and the opening of a massive plant in nearby Mill Creek, the brewery produced 2.5 million barrels of beer in 2013, with much capacity still to be filled. Take, for example, that as large as the downtown Pottsville facility is, the Mill Creek facility uses more than twice as much water (approximately 450,000 gallons) on a daily basis.

Those with a sweet tooth will appreciate that after a nearly 30 year hiatus, Yuengling is back making ice cream in 10 different flavors and is available in grocery store freezers.

Ownership only passes generations by way of purchase and Dick has four daughters who show an appreciation for the business that likely ensures that the brewery will be family-run well into a sixth generation and beyond.

Beer Lover's Pick

Porter
Style: Porter
ABV: 5%
Availability: Year-round; 12-ounce bottles
Awards: Great American Beer Festival (Bronze, 1987)
A Yuengling classic dating to its early years, this sweet and slightly roasty porter with hints of milk chocolate is a good example of a drinkable porter. It is a malt-forward beer without, however, being overwhelmingly sweet or heavy.

Brewpubs

AL'S OF HAMPDEN (PIZZA BOY BREWING COMPANY)

2240 Millennium Way, Enola, PA 17025; (717) 728-3840; alsofhampden.com;
@AlsOfHampden
Founded: 2002 (new location in 2013) **Founder:** Albert Kominski **Brewer:** Terry
Hawbaker **Beers:** Too many unique offerings to list

A small brewery operation inside a popular pizza business just outside of Harrisburg has become something of a phenomenon. Brewer Terry Hawbaker runs the Pizza Boy Brewing Company in plain view of the restaurant and fills around a quarter of the 100+ draft lines, including two handpumps. Pinning down Pizza Boy regulars is not so easy, but expect a diversity in styles to include pilsners, hefeweizens, wits, Berliner weisses, and grisettes to double IPAs, black sours, and American strong ales. Regional favorites like DuClaw, Tröegs, Victory, Weyerbacher, and Yards and newer guys like Free Will, Liquid Hero, Spring House, and The Brewery at Hershey occupy the remainder of the taps.

By moving around the corner into a low-rise business park in 2013, Al's has added a larger restaurant and bar facility to seat approximately 75, a kid-friendly game area, an outdoor patio, and the space for Hawbaker to grow the Pizza Boy brand. The move increased the brewing capacity by around four times. In mid-2014, distribution agreements were signed to get Pizza Boy beers—plus beers from the coveted and growing sour program—into the market.

Not only is the marketplace excited about the Pizza Boy beers, but judges at the World Beer Cup took notice in 2014, awarding the Hoptart a silver medal in the Experimental Beer category.

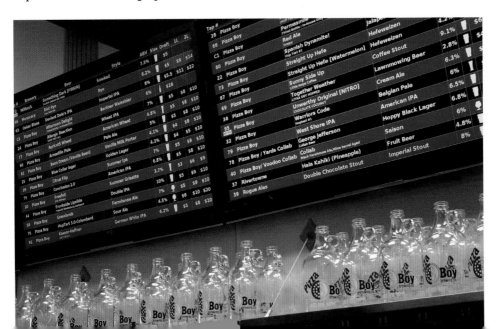

Back at the restaurant, trying to choose a perfect pizza and beer is nearly impossible given the overwhelming list of choices. A full kitchen menu of sandwiches, salads, wings, and fried appetizers provides plenty of distraction, but opt for a Porky Pizza, a buffalo chicken calzone, or white veggie pizza to go along with your order-by-number beers—with so many beers on tap, it's the most efficient way. When leaving, get in line for some growlered beer to go or choose from the many coolers of other commercial bottled beer.

APPALACHIAN BREWING COMPANY

50 N. Cameron St., Harrisburg, PA 17101; (717) 221-1080; abcbrew.com; @ABCBrew
Founded: 1997 **Founders:** Shawn Gallagher, Jack Sproch, Artie Tafoya **Brewers:** Artie Tafoya, Jay Kendig, Jason Simmons, and John Straitiff **Flagship and Year-Round Beers:** Water Gap Wheat Ale, Mountain Lager, Hoppy Trails IPA, "Jolly Scot" Scottish Style Ale, Purist Pale Ale, Trail Blaze Brown Ale, and Broad Street Barley Wine **Seasonals/Special Releases:** Monthly seasonals including Zoigl Star Lager, Kipona Fest, and Grinnin' Grizzly Spiced Ale, plus various others by location

Appalachian opened a new location for the third consecutive year in 2014. Harrisburg is the original and the largest; Mechanicsburg opened in 2014, adding another pub to the existing six locations but also adding a full production facility for the company's line of sodas that is due to come on line by early 2015.

Trekking the Appalachians

The main Harrisburg location of Appalachian Brewing Company may serve as the largest of the seven and as the main production facility, but the following all serve to bring a taste of the Appalachians to a Pennsylvania community near you.

Gettysburg Battlefield, opened 2003—401 Buford Ave.

Camp Hill, opened 2006—3721 Market St.

Collegeville, opened 2010—50 W. Third Ave.

Lititz, opened 2012—55 N.Water St.

Gettysburg Gateway, opened 2013—70 Presidential Circle

Mechanicsburg, opened 2014—6462 Carlisle Pike

The beers run the style gamut at Appalachian with the slightly hoppy **Purist** (5.5% ABV) pale ale, the easy-drinking fall favorite **Kipona Fest** (5.2% ABV), and the minimum 8-month vintage **Broad Street** (10.9% ABV) barleywine drawing the most attention.

Each of the locations does its own seasonals and occasional one-offs to complement the food menus that cover the spectrum of pub grub to burgers to full platters of chicken, steak, and fish. The Harrisburg location hosts two of the company's most anticipated events of the year: the Capital City Invitational Beer Festival in September and the multiweek Oktoberfest celebration.

Complimentary tours of the Harrisburg location are available each Saturday at 1 p.m. and shorter tours are available by appointment only at each of the other brewpub locations.

BARLEY CREEK BREWING COMPANY

1774 Sullivan Trail, Tannersville, PA 18372; (570) 629-9399; barleycreek.com; @BarleyCreekBrew

Founded: 1995 **Founders:** Trip and Eileen Ruvane **Brewers:** Matthew Doughty, Dylan Transue, and Matt Daniels **Flagship and Year-Round Beers:** Antler Brown Ale, Rescue India Pale Ale, Navigator Golden Ale, Angler Black Lager, CB50, and Iron Arm Belgian Wheat **Seasonals/Special Releases:** Mountaineer Mai Bock, Summerfest Lager, Traveler Foreign Stout

Barley Creek continues to bring back both locals and the scores of winter seasonal tourists that pass through the area each year. The brewpub offers around

10 of its own beers at any given time but also demonstrates its support for the brewing industry by including at least a half-dozen mostly local beers. The establishment does much for the community in general and was awarded the Outstanding Corporation Award at the National Philanthropy Awards Dinner in 2011 for its work with numerous events and charities.

On a menu that covers golden ales and Belgian wheats to black lagers and Irish reds, two stand out. The longevity of the **Antler Brown Ale** (4.8% ABV) is a testament to its solid quality and popularity. It bears resemblance to a well-made English brown, replete with its toasted bread and low-hopped profile. It's a versatile beer that also makes its way into the beer cheese soup.

The **Rescue IPA** (5.6% ABV) has a pleasantly restrained hop bitterness in the presence of a firm malty component. Both the traditional hot and the sesame ginger sauce versions of the chicken wings work well with the IPA, which provides the perfect palate cleanse between wings and blue cheese dipping.

The rest of the menu features numerous sandwiches, around a dozen creatively built burgers, and fuller-sized entree dishes. One noteworthy sandwich is the mouthwatering Highlander. It's full of thinly sliced slow-roasted beef, sautéed onions and peppers, and horseradish chive sauce.

If that's not enough flavor, consider chasing it with one of their seasonal stouts like the **Foreign Export Stout,** which has enough complementary roasty flavors

at a moderate level of alcohol (6% ABV) to make it part of a perfect post–ski run meal and drinking session. And, if you weren't already having enough fun at Barley Creek, check out their official whiffleball stadium called Pint Size Park and, according to Barley Creek, the world's first firkin curling club.

BATTLEFIELD BREW WORKS

248 Hunterstown Rd., Gettysburg, PA 17325; (717) 398-2907; battlefieldbrewworks.com
Founded: 2013 **Owners:** Daniel Kulick, Paul Lemley, and Eric Beaudoin **Brewer:** Dan Kulick **Year-Round Beers:** Extreme Hop Artillery Imperial IPA, Red Circle Ale, Lincoln Lager **Seasonals/Special Releases:** Mandarina Pale Ale, PA Dutch Style Smoked Porter, Peach Wheatfield

The historic Monfort farmhouse is the striking setting for the modern-day Battlefield Brew Works. It served as one of the largest Confederate hospitals during the Civil War and today carries much of the history forward through the preservation of the property and the interior decor.

The restaurant side of the business serves a bounty of meats including chicken, pork, beef, elk, buffalo, and boar. A platter with sides like homemade coleslaw or potato salad goes the extra yard to satisfy any remaining hunger.

Leave plenty of room for beer, which Kulick is doing quite well. The three standout beers could not be much more different from one another. The **Lincoln**

Lager (4.6% ABV) is a true-to-form, deliciously refreshing malty lager and not over-done with hops, with which some tend to abuse the style. Speaking of hops, they were saved for a full assault of Nugget, Cascade, and Centennial in the excellent **Extreme Hop Artillery Imperial IPA** (9.5% ABV), which shines quite well from the firkin. Finally, some delicate local farm peach flavor is highlighted in the **Peach Wheatfield** (4.5% ABV) and makes for a perfect summertime refresher.

BERWICK BREWING COMPANY

328 W. Front St., Berwick, PA 18603; (570) 752-4313; berwickbrewing.com
Founded: 2008 **Founder:** Tom Clark **Brewers:** Steven Zourides, Kyle Kalanick, Joseph Slavick **Year-Round Beers:** Berwick IPA, Front Street Wheat, Grumpy Bill's Porter, Red Bank Dark Lager, Hondo Keller, Zwickel Pils **Seasonals/Special Releases:** Enough to always keep at least 18 house-made beers on tap

In the heart of Berwick and at the edge of the mighty Susquehanna River sits Berwick Brewing Company in a massive building that previously housed a bakery. It has established itself as a vital part of the community complete with excellent pizza (try the Curd and Jager, the Hunky, or the plain and simply good Margherita), an outdoor beer garden with a river view, and, naturally, well-made beer. Owner Tom Clark is a former owner/brewer at the Red Bank Brewery in New Jersey and draws much brewing inspiration from time spent living in England and Germany.

Playing to a predominantly European geographic slice of Pennsylvania, the **Zwickel Pils** and **Hondo Keller Bier** are two excellently clean and crisp German-style beers that can take you through happy hour, a couple of pizzas, and into the late night hours. The **Grumpy Bill's Porter** is a delightfully sweet and mildly roasty homage to Clark's father, who coincidentally painted the beautiful Rhine River wall mural in the pub.

The restaurant interior stretches from the front bar through a couple of comfortable gathering rooms until the far back exit where, rain or shine, *gemütlichkeit* and beers can be enjoyed in the biergarten. Continuing the pronunciation guide that I've been fond of providing, you'll note that Berwick sounds more like a cross between Burke and Burrick, than Ber-wick.

BULLFROG BREWERY

229 W. 4th St., Williamsport, PA 17701; (570) 326-4700; bullfrogbrewery.com; @BullfrogBrewery

Founded: 1996 **Founder:** Steve Koch **Brewer:** Nate Saar **Beers:** After the immensely popular and regularly seen Edgar IPA, too many unique offerings to list

Bullfrog has grown from a decent size brewpub (10-barrel system) in upstate Pennsylvania that captured the attention of beer-seekers across the state—particularly with its sour beers in the last 5 to 10 years—into a brewing establishment with a production facility (50-barrel fermenters) distributing its product across the state.

As at Al's of Hampden (Pizza Boy) earlier in the Brewpubs section—and it makes perfect sense given Pizza Boy brewer Terry Hawbaker's roots at Bullfrog—diversity rules the Bullfrog taps, with a particular fondness for sour beers. After the **Edgar IPA** (7.5% ABV), a big and clean citrus hop-forward double IPA, eyes quickly turn to the **Old Gold**, **Oud 15**, **Mise en Garde**, **Vous et Moi**, **Le Roar Grrrz**, or whatever other interesting wild yeast–fermented beers may pop onto the menu.

For as much as the Frog is about the beer, it's also about the food, the social aspect, and the live music. Much of the menu teems with local beef, pork, and produce products, and the corkscrew mac and cheese and abundant brunch menu are not to be missed.

Live music adds to the rollicking atmosphere of good times at Bullfrog with a variety of music nearly every night and a Jazz Brunch Workshop on Sunday. For the combination of food, beer, music, and a vibrant social scene, Bullfrog continues to be one of the best around.

ELK CREEK CAFE AND ALEWORKS

100 W. Main St., Millheim, PA 16854; (814) 349-8850; elkcreekcafe.net
Founded: 2007 **Founder:** Tim Bowser **Brewer:** Tim Yarrington **Year-Round Beers:**
Brookie Brown, Double Rainbow IPA, Elk Creek Copper Ale, Great Blue Heron Pale Ale, Poe
Paddy Porter, Winkleblink Ale **Seasonals/Special Releases:** Elton's ESB, Hairy John's
IPA, and many others

Amid state forests, near Penn's Cave, and situated roughly equidistant from State College, Bellefonte, and Lock Haven, the
town of Millheim is seemingly in the middle of nowhere. But it's in
the middle of a beautiful nowhere that Elk Creek serves as an oasis of
food, beer, and music to an appreciative local crowd.

Well-traveled brewer Tim Yarrington has found himself a home at
Elk Creek after numerous stops around the brewing industry, including the second incarnation of the Times Square Brewery, Ruddy Duck
(see Maryland chapter), and Long Valley (turn to the northern New
Jersey chapter). He pumps around 1,200 barrels of beer annually
through the modest brewhouse behind the restaurant.

Deserved attention is paid to the **Poe Paddy Porter** (5.8%
ABV)—it's probably no coincidence that the porter at Long Valley was also a noteworthy favorite of mine—and the **Hairy John's IPA** (9% ABV). The Porter is a downright solid roasty porter with just a touch of hop flavor to make it interesting and
is named after a local state park. Hairy John's is a dangerously drinkable double
IPA that is named for the legend of a local hermit in the early 1800s from nearby
Roundtop Mountain.

Elk Creek is another one of those places with a constant eye toward doing the
right things. Being a place of social lubrication (e.g., no televisions), supporting
the local arts and providers (e.g., plenty of featured live local musicians and farm-
sourced produce, meats, and cheeses), working toward being a zero-waste operation
(e.g., concerning itself with reducing its environmental impact as much as possible),
and serving great food and beer and in a family-friendly environment makes Elk
Creek a natural beer destination for all beer lovers.

THE GAMBLE MILL RESTAURANT & MICROBREWERY

160 Dunlap St., Bellefonte, PA 16823; (814) 355-7764; gamblemill.com; @GambleMill
Founded: 2010 **Founders:** David Fonash and Paul Kendeffy **Brewer:** Mike Smith **Year-
Round Beers:** HB-48 Session Ale, Bush House Brown Ale, Victorian Secret Raspberry
Wheat, J. Rose Pale Ale, Pig Iron IPA **Seasonals/Special Releases:** Many

Brewer Mike Smith came to Gamble Mill with a résumé that included Ithaca Beer and Dogfish Head. That bodes well for this brewery housed in a former grist mill that has an eye toward opening a production facility from which to distribute its product throughout the state.

Until then, most of his beer from the 7-barrel fermenters can only be found at the brewpub, select restaurants in the State College-Bellefonte area, and festivals such as Pints for Pets in Altoona, Hops Vines and Wines in Selinsgrove, and the State College Brew Expo.

Keep an eye open for the rich **Bush House Brown Ale** (5.75% ABV), the silky sweet **Curtin Abbey Ale** (8.6% ABV), and the smooth and roasty **DiNallo and James Coffee Stout** (7.4% ABV). A diverse and moderately-sized menu packs a lot of flavor into selections that cover most animals (turkey, fish, pork, beef, and duck) some vegetarian, and carry courteous labels of "gluten-free," "dairy-free," and "nut-free."

Things you too might learn while visiting the Centre County seat: it is referred to as Central Pennsylvania's Victorian Secret and seven governors (five of Pennsylvania) have called Bellefonte home, including Andrew Curtin, for whom the Curtin Abbey Ale is named.

HAPPY VALLEY BREWING COMPANY

137 Elmwood St., State College, PA 16801; (814) 234-4406; happyvalleybeer.com;
@HVBCBeer
Founded: 2013 **Founders:** Scott Lucchesi, Greg Somers **Brewer:** Josh Davies **Year-Round Beers:** Barnstormer IPA, Craftsman Brown, LeMonster Imperial IPA, Phyrst Family Stout, Stratus Loftbier, Tailgater Pale **Seasonals/Special Releases:** Many

A few miles outside of downtown State College, one of the area's newest brewpubs is located inside a large former barn. It's been converted to a brewery with a two-floor bar and restaurant. Upstairs the atmosphere is casual, yet more dining room-like with tasteful decor and plenty of sunshine flooding through the large windows. Downstairs is much darker and more pub-like with an oversized rectangular bar, fitting for a boisterous late-night crowd.

Beers hitting their stride early coming out the brewery have included the **Phyrst Family Oatmeal Stout** (5% ABV), which becomes a smooth treat when served on nitrogen along with a chocolate pudding pot for dessert. Fried ribs (take my word for it) are a must-try and with the **LeMonster Imperial IPA** (8.2% ABV) could be a contender for pairing of the year.

JOBOY'S BREW PUB

27-31 E. Main St., Lititz, PA 17543; (717) 568-8330; joboysbrewpub.com;
@JoBoyBrewPub
Founded: 2010 (current location 2014) **Founders:** Jeff and Jo Harless **Brewers:** Jeff Harless and Kevin Shaw **Beers:** Too many unique offerings to list

The beauty of a small, kitchen-based nanobrewery is the ability to make whatever you want as much as you want. That's why it's fruitless to list beers above in the profile header as is standard with most other brewing establishments.

At JoBoy's, you can always count on plenty of ale and occasional lager selections. Light and dark colored. Low alcohol and high. Brewed with the addition of coffee, fruit, spices, and the like. Plenty of hop profile and some with close to none at all. The adage if you think you don't like beer, maybe it's because you haven't found one yet that you like could not be more appropriate than here in Lititz. At JoBoy's there's a very good chance of finding that one to like.

The traditions started at the old location in Manheim are immediately noticeable on the menu. Plenty of low and slow smoked meats (beef, chicken, and pork) along with appropriate side dishes like beans, slaw, hush puppies, and greens will ensure you do not leave hungry.

In this book, there are plenty of places serving up a barbecued meats section of the menu, but none other focuses almost exclusively on it as well as making their own beer. Now residing in the quaint and beer-bustling Lititz, JoBoy's is nicely positioned as a beer destination more than ever before.

OLD FORGE BREWING COMPANY

298 Mill St., Danville, PA 17821; (570) 275-8151; oldforgebrewingcompany.com; @Old_Forge_Brew
Founded: 2008 (production brewery in 2012) **Founders:** Damien and Maria Malfara
Brewers: Damien Malfara, Darren Stonecypher **Year-Round Beers:** T-Rail Pale Ale, Overbite IPA, Paradise Pils **Seasonals/Special Releases:** Many

The last couple of years have seen tremendous growth for Old Forge. First, a huge 20-barrel production facility just a short walk/shorter drive away, and then a new pub on Mill Street. The growth has helped the brewery expand its available

16-ounce canned selections to more than eight from the original Endless Sun Ale and T-Rail Pale Ale.

The owner's love for creatively handcrafted items doesn't begin or end with beer. Throughout the brewpub, local artisanal work is evident in the artwork and design. The mug rack above the bar is one such striking object that hoists Pub Club member glassware on a rotating wheel within easy grab for the bartender.

In the glassware go very good beers like the **Overbite IPA** (7.5% ABV), which works well with the incredible Barnyard Burger (8 ounces of beef covered with mozzarella cheese atop both bacon and pulled pork on a pretzel roll). The German-style Pilsner, **Paradise Pils** (4.5% ABV), is no slouch either. Order this versatile and well-made beer at the bar, or in the 16-ounce can for home consumption, with hummus, a crab-stuffed jalapeño, grilled turkey and pesto sandwich, or bangers and mash.

OTTO'S PUB & BREWERY
2235 N. Atherton St., State College, PA 16803; (814) 867-6886; ottospubandbrewery.com; @OttosPub
Founded: 2002 **Founders:** Roger Garthwaite and Charlie Schnable **Brewers:** Charlie Schnable and Chris Brugger **Year-Round Beers:** Apricot Wheat, Double D IPA, Mt. Nittany Pale Ale, Red Mo Ale, Slab Cabin IPA **Seasonals/Special Releases:** Many

Imagine heading to State College for a football game or some other activity and there are no hotel rooms downtown near campus. Think all is lost? Think again. Otto's is just a few miles from downtown and has a hotel just across the parking lot from it. Plus, while you could drive downtown, there is also a bus line that stops on North Atherton Street just across from the brewery and hotel to make life even more convenient. Finally, if you want beer to take home with you, there is the brewery's retail shop in addition to a Wegmans grocery store behind the hotel to satisfy those needs.

Back at the brewpub, the atmosphere is inviting, with a focus on brewing history and much breweriana lining the walls and glass cabinets. The food menu is sourced largely from local farmers and bakers and has a wide variety of pizzas, sandwiches, burgers, and pubby appetizers. They go out of their way to mark up the menu with notations for the significant amount of vegetarian and vegan offerings.

From the taps, Otto's is typically pouring 12 of its own beers plus 2 on the handpump, in addition to one guest tap. Not-to-miss beers include the big malty **Maibock Lager** (6.4% ABV) and both the **Slab Cabin IPA** (6.3% ABV) and its even bigger stepbrother **Double D IPA** (9.2% ABV), both very good takes on the Americanized styles.

As mentioned, the retail shop has plenty of beer to go, but other accessories as well, including soap, clothing, glassware, and dog biscuits made from the brewery's spent grain.

SELIN'S GROVE BREWING COMPANY

121 N. Market St., Selinsgrove, PA 17870; (570) 374-7308; selinsgrovebrewing.com
Founded: 1996 **Founders:** Steve Leason and Heather McNabb **Brewers:** Steve Leason and Heather McNabb **Most-of-the-time Beers:** Captain Selin's Cream Ale, IPA, Stealth Tripel, Two Penny Scottish Ale, Wit, a Pale Ale, a fruit beer, and a Stout **Seasonals/ Special Releases:** St. Fillian's Wee Heavy and many others

Selin's Grove has a fascinating history of cobbling together their brewing operations that is matched by an equally fascinating and unique experience of eating and drinking in their basement floor pub inside the nearly 200-year-old mansion property of Pennsylvania's third governor.

I've lost track in this book of how many brewing establishments and good beer bars are within spitting distance of the mighty Susquehanna River—both in Pennsylvania and Maryland. Selin's Grove is yet another. In Selinsgrove, the funky college town has a bit of everything to offer including the brewpub that does a wide variety of beers without much of a schedule.

That means the IPA, stout, or wit that you recently enjoyed might be back again next week or month, or maybe not again until next year. A few beers that do show themselves with some regularity and garner much well-deserved praise include the spicy and bitter **IPA** (7.5% ABV) and the dark-roasted Irish **Snake Drive Stout** (5.5% ABV), each of which could nicely accompany one of the many delectable sandwiches on the menu.

If dessert is on the agenda during your visit, the cherry-popping sweet/tart and not-a-lambic **Kriek** (~6.5% ABV) could do the trick quite nicely. But also look for the sweetly complex **Stealth Tripel** (~9% ABV) to complement a cinnamon and sugar hot pretzel with caramel dipping sauce.

STOUDTS BREWING COMPANY

2800 N. Reading Rd., Adamstown, PA, 19501; (717) 484-4386; stoudts.com; @StoudtsBrewery
Founded: 1987 **Founders:** Ed and Carol Stoudt **Brewers:** Brett Kintzer, Justin Lee
Flagship Beer: American Pale Ale, Scarlet Lady ESB, Gold Lager, Pils **Year-Round Beers:** Fourplay IPA, Fat Dog Stout, Double IPA, Triple **Seasonals/Special Releases:** Blonde Double Maibock, Heifer In Wheat, Karnival Kölsch, Old Abominable, Smooth Hoperator, and more

Not only has Stoudts been brewing great beer in rural Pennsylvania for nearly 30 years, they were one of the first to help the region stake a claim to some of the best brewed German-style beers, particularly pilsners, in the country.

Stoudts Pils (5.4% ABV) has racked up more awards than any of their other beers and they are proudest of one of the most recent. In 2014, their Pils came back from the World Beer Cup with a bronze medal, placing third in 71 entries behind two German breweries.

Oktoberfest in Lancaster County

Stoudts hosts many events throughout the year—like its popular Microfest—but none seems more geographically appropriate than the German-themed Oktoberfest at the über German-themed brewery. For five weekends each September and October, Stoudts rolls out a barrel full of family-friendly good times with plenty of live German music, fun 'n' games, and foods and beers befitting the annual celebration.

In other beer news at Stoudts, the longtime **Fat Dog Stout** (8% ABV) continues to be a crowd favorite with its big, full-bodied flavors of chocolate, coffee, and mild hop bitterness. Newer beers and fan favorites in Stoudts portfolio include the well-made **Triple**, **Heifer in Wheat**, and **Double IPA**, which help keep Stoudts in beer lovers' minds in the rapidly changing beer landscape.

Visitors to the landmark brewery along a fast rural road in Lancaster County typically get much more than they bargained for. Complementing the brewery operations is the bar and restaurant of the Black Angus Pub. The menu overflows with a sumptuous offering of steaks, lobster, raw bar, Black Angus burgers and beef tip sandwiches, and German-influenced dishes like *Jägerschnitzel* and local sausage platters with red cabbage and sauerkraut.

Also on the sprawling Stoudts property is the Wonderful Good Market, from which you can take home cheeses, meats, and steaks among other kitchen delicacies.

A perfect visit to Stoudts may include a well-planned overnight stay at the neighboring motel just across the parking lot. It's a bargain for sure and gives the opportunity to wake the next day, explore the area, and wander into Stoudts to do it all again.

TURKEY HILL BREWING COMPANY

991 Central Rd., Bloomsburg, PA 17815; (570) 387-8422; turkeyhillbrewing.com
Founded: 2011 **Founder:** Andrew B. Pruden **Brewers:** Donny Abraczinskas, Jim Coulter
Flagship and Year-Round Beers: Barn Dance Blonde, Journeyman IPA, Revelation Pale Ale **Seasonals/Special Releases:** Many, including a Sour & Wild Series of barrel-aged beers

Turkey Hill proves that you can be a stone's throw from a major interstate (I-80 to be exact) and feel as relaxed as if in the middle of nowhere. Sitting on what is known as Turkey Hill Ridge, the brewpub operation is joined by a fine dining

restaurant and a couple dozen nicely appointed rooms for overnight stays on the mid-1800s family farm property.

The brewpub is still relatively small, outputting approximately 600 barrels in 2013 from its combination of open and closed 7-barrel fermenters. Abraczinskas and Coulter have been brewing up a storm since getting the brewery up to speed in 2012. It's fair to say they haven't met a style that they didn't like or do well. However, the **Journeyman IPA** (7.3% ABV) and **Penelope Pilsner** (5.2% ABV) are two standouts on the menu of 10 taps and 2 handpumps. A full menu ranging from satisfying burgers to creative entrees provide sustenance through a tasting of the beer menu.

Tuesday nights are a good time to visit as a chosen beer is paired with special cheese, meats, nuts, and other accompaniments. Thursdays, Saturdays, and Sundays often feature live music.

Lovers of barrel-aged experiments should be looking forward to 2015 and 2016 as oak wine barrels currently hold the **Farmhouse Kölsch** (ready in summer 2015), **Saison** (fall 2015), and **Revelation Pale Ale** (spring 2016). Each underwent a secondary fermentation with a strain of Brettanomyces yeast. Fun times ahead for Turkey Hill.

Eat, Drink, Relax

Make the trip to Turkey Hill extra special by booking a room at the inn, which contains a variety of rooms and a generous pet policy. Guests are treated to a resort-like experience of relaxation and access to a stellar experience of food, wine, and beer.

WAREHOUSE GOURMET BISTRO & BREW PUB

7 Pennsylvania Ave., Hanover, PA 17331; (717) 451-9898; warehousegourmet.net; @WarehouseG

Founded: 2012 **Founders:** Keith Stambaugh and Melinda Stambaugh **Brewer:** Warren Hendrickson **Flagship Beer:** Passive Aggressive Pale Ale **Year-Round Beers:** Hop Knocker IPA, Small Town Brown Ale, Leggy Blonde Imperial Blonde Ale, Unkle Joe's Funky Unkle Dunkleweiss **Seasonals/Special Releases:** Many

Warehouse Gourmet exists as a great example of building reuse. The 100+-year-old building formerly housed a cigar factory, a ribbon factory, and numerous other businesses. Owner Keith Stambaugh has used it for his art studio. The bi-level space now holds a cozy, neighborhood-like restaurant and small bar with eight beers on tap and a food menu to impress as well. The pub won't be quite so cozy much longer as an extra 17 seats are being added as well as a second-floor restroom. The brewery is seeing its own expansion with a separate mill room and larger walk-in cooler.

The **Small Town Brown** (5.3% ABV) is a fun local reference and solid brown ale and the **Passive Aggressive Pale Ale** (5.6% ABV) lives up to its name with a beautiful hop aroma and restrained hop flavor. They both play extremely well with a constantly changing menu that could include pairworthy items such as, respectively, braised short ribs and tarragon chicken salad sandwich (with cranberries, walnuts, and honey balsamic vinaigrette).

YORKHOLO BREWING COMPANY

19 N. Main St., Mansfield, PA 16933; (570) 662-0241; yorkholobrewing.com;
@Yorkholo_Brewer

Founded: 2011 **Founders:** Jarrod York and Ashley Rodgers **Brewer:** Jarrod York **Year-Round Beers:** Bungy Blonde Ale, Mountaineer Pale Ale, PA Grand Canyon Vanilla Porter, Jam Session Saison, Coal Miner's Black IPA, Pine Creek Raspberry Wit **Seasonals/Special Releases:** Many

Before landing on Main Street with a place to call his own, York built up his credentials in brewing school and in real life at Ithaca Beer in New York. Yorkholo, the brewpub name, came about as a nod to his family and its York Hollow (or later, Yorkholo) Dairy Farm. With farming and brewing in the background, a brewpub should work well—and it does.

It may be familiar to see "many" listed in the Seasonals/Special notation of the brewery profiles. Many small establishments these days, however, are afforded the luxury of making many styles and batches due to their size. At Yorkholo, with its 3-barrel system, the bar keeps a handful of regulars on tap along with a constantly rotating selection of others.

Exceptional standouts on the beer list include the surprisingly balanced **PA Grand Canyon Vanilla Porter** (6.5% ABV) and bone-dry **Jam Session Saison** (5.3% ABV). The food menu is eye-catchingly well done with a full array of small bites to big plates to satisfy both the carnivore and the vegetarian. It bursts with words like natural, grass-fed, organic, and locally sourced, all to suggest that the kitchen and ownership are keenly aware of their role in caring for the rest of the planet and its inhabitants.

To that end, the grass-based Yorkholo Brewpub Burger from a local farm could be one of the best you've had in some time. Monday nights are not to be missed for Pizza Nights with pizza chef Dan "Wildhorse" Hollister, who creates impressively unique spent grain-based pizzas each week.

In case you're not familiar with the Pennsylvania Grand Canyon reference above, Tioga County is teeming with natural beauty and is home to what is referred to as the PA Grand Canyon—a 45-mile stretch of trails, gorges, waterfalls, and quarter-mile depths. A slow drive through the area, or even a vacation, is highly recommended. Plus, it would give you more than one opportunity to stop at Yorkholo.

Central & Northeastern Pennsylvania

BACKYARD ALE HOUSE

523 Linden St., Scranton, PA, 18503; (570) 955-0192; backyardalehouse.com;
@BackyardAleHous
Draft Beers: 28 **Bottled/Canned Beers:** Around 400

With the recent addition of the bottle shop, Backyard Ale House cemented its significant role in the Scranton beer scene. The Ale House opened in 2008 across from Courthouse Square and, true to its name, has a backyard that in the wintertime is tented and heated.

Backyard has consistently offered up some of the most recognizable beers from the region and beyond, as well as some of the smaller, newer guys on the block (think 3 Guys and a Beer'd and ShawneeCraft). When it comes time to leave, the adjoining bottle shop has your takeout needs covered with a growler station and a large selection of bottles.

Televisions are spread around the bar area and make the atmosphere conducive to watching everything from college basketball tournaments to auto racing. It follows that if you're going to be spending a few hours at Backyard, you'll need some food. They've got you covered there as well.

In addition to the long list of standard "pub grub," enticing menu entries include the Breakfast Bomb Scotch Egg, Franzi(skaner) Fishwich, and the daily special One Night Stand Burger. The Bucket of Balls is a fun presentation of a variety of meatballs served by the bucketful. Demonstrating their love for beer at Backyard, each menu item is listed with a suggested beer pairing.

BOXER'S CAFE

410 Penn St., Huntingdon, PA 16652; (814) 643-5013; sites.google.com/site/410penn
Draft Beers: 10

In the bustling town of Huntingdon, home to Juniata College, it's all about the beer at Boxer's but yet it's all about everything else. To call Boxer's, and its owner Tony Seguin, eco-friendly would be a big understatement.

The restaurant and bar seat nearly 50 people amid a cafe full of reuse and recycling. Cardboard backs of checkbooks serve as coasters. Table scraps never get thrown in the trash but rather into a bucket that goes off to feed local pigs. Even Seguin's car runs on recycled vegetable oil from the kitchen.

And the beer? Check. It too plays a small part in Boxer's world of no-waste. The first pours off each keg that at most bars get dumped down the drain go to the kitchen for beer battering of menu items like fried fish fillets. Then, the lines are pouring the likes of Elk Creek, Stone, Victory, Weyerbacher, and Yuengling. The menu also lists several good-looking vegetarian and vegan options.

BULLS HEAD PUBLIC HOUSE
14 E. Main St., Lititz, PA, 17543; (717) 626-2115; generalsutterinn.com/bullsheadph; @BullsHeadLititz
Draft Beers: 16, plus 2 handpumps **Bottled/Canned Beers:** Around 70

If you're looking for a bar without television, without a juke box, without table service, where sharing tables and conversations are encouraged, and where the draft beer is great and the cask-conditioned beer even better, then Bulls Head is the place for you.

The town of Lititz has had plenty of accolades heaped upon it for its quality of life. It would be faulty logic to think that having a British-style pub like Bulls Head doesn't factor into that quality of life. Walk the streets, browse the shops, check out a chocolate factory, lounge in the park by the creek, and feel a bit of the more genteel nature of this pleasant town. Then, go and have a couple beers at the pub.

Thanks in part to co-owners Paul Pendyck and Gary Simon, the pub has become a destination for those seeking this type of bar experience. They also host twice-yearly cask festivals to present some of the best "real ale" available, served by an

industry expert (Pendyck runs an equipment and supplies importing business for the cask segment of the beer industry) and Cicerone Certified Beer Servers. If further legitimacy is called for, like Standard Tap in Philly, Bulls Head is one of the small number of Cask Marque–accredited bars in the country.

Not to worry, though, for those unsure about UK beers, the draft lines pour plenty of American, Belgian, and German beers. From the kitchen, expect a full lineup of standard American tavern food in addition to the expected and excellent Scotch egg, chicken and leek pie, curries, and fish-and-chips.

CAFE BRUGES
16 N. Pitt St., Carlisle, PA 17013; (717) 960-0223; cafebruges.com; @CafeBruges
Draft Beers: 10 **Bottled/Canned Beers:** Around 100

Cafe Bruges has been serving excellent food and Belgian beers in a comfortably casual environment since 2009. Located in historic downtown Carlisle, the restaurant provides a unique experience not commonly found in the region.

Visit Cafe Bruges for a dinner that could include a Stoemp Saucisse platter of sausage and mashed potatoes; mussels any one of five ways, such as the perfectly done Provençal; stewed rabbit fricassee; and capped off with a Brussels-style waffle with fruit compote, whipped cream, and dark chocolate.

Beer-wise you'll easily find some of Belgium's finest, including a handful of Trappist ales, lambics like the Hanssen's Oude Gueuze, and a laundry list of other tempting Belgian liquid delights from Alvinne, Chouffe, De Dolle, and Landtsheer (Malheur).

Walking off the dinner to a downtown B&B, such as the Carlisle House, might make you feel as if you're walking through Bruges, minus the canals and bridges.

EXIT 190 BEER DELI

316 Main St., Dickson City, PA, 18519; (570) 382-3446; exit190beerdeli.com
Draft Beers: 20 **Bottled/Canned Beers:** 600+

Perfectly named, Exit 190 will not allow customers to easily forget that they are located just a stone's throw from Exit 190 off I-81. Perfectly executed, Exit 190 serves up a satisfying menu of sandwiches/wraps/paninis at its spacious bar, which is connected to its bottle shop that overflows with highly sought-after beers from across the region and world.

In addition to stocking the bar with a wide variety of tasty beers (no domestic "macros"), there are monthly samplings that serve to educate the customer and potentially open minds and palates to new breweries and their beers.

FEDERAL TAPHOUSE

234 N. 2nd St., Harrisburg, PA 17101; (717) 525-8077; federaltaphouse.com; @FedTapHBG
Draft Beers: 100

Similar to the Federal Taphouse's second location described below in the Lancaster Pub Crawl section, Harrisburg's Federal Taphouse is spacious, serves a hundred draft lines of very good beer, and has the added benefit of live music.

Lancaster's has live music as well but in Harrisburg there's a 500-person second-floor venue called Fed Live! that showcases a constant stream of touring acts. With plenty of downtown options, this presents a full night out under one roof to be able to first grab dinner and a few beers followed by a concert and more beers upstairs.

At the bar, the choices are near limitless from the well-organized and well-maintained beer list. Regular events featuring brewery spotlights and pairing dinners bring even greater attention to the push behind craft beer at Federal Taphouse.

HOLY HOUND TAPROOM

57 W. Market St., York, PA 17401; (717) 855-2410; holyhoundtaproom.com;
@HolyHoundTaps
Draft Beers: 30 **Bottled/Canned Beers:** 50+

York's craft beer scene took a big step up in 2012 when Holy Hound opened inside The National House, a landmark building that dates back to 1828 and has a storied history as a hotel and a department store.

In modern times the Taproom serves as a casual meeting place mostly for those seeking out great beer, though some wines and whiskeys are also available. The beer list is presented by a bar staff of Certified Beer Servers (under the Cicerone certifica-

tion program) and shows off roughly 30 percent regional representation among a bevy of out-of-town geek-worthy breweries like Firestone Walker, Founders, Lost Abbey, and Port Brewing.

The food concept is a unique one at Holy Hound, where small plates of food and a few more substantial platters like brats, brisket, and mac and cheese are prepared by local vendors and sold at the Taproom. Live music takes the stage most Fridays and Saturdays and adds to the good times at this downtown York beer destination.

SABATINI'S PIZZA

1925 Wyoming Ave., Exeter, PA 18643; (570) 693-2270; sabatinis.com
Draft Beers: 12, plus two handpumps **Bottled/Canned Beers:** Hundreds

Equal parts pizza joint and take-out beer shop, Sabatini's (est. 1958) serves both with a style unique to the area. In addition to the third-generation pizza, meatball sandwiches, chicken wings, and pasta bowls round out a full menu at this local family-run institution.

Over the years, Sabatini's has turned itself into a beer mecca, stocking the shelves with hard-to-find beers. They also conduct regular events including tap takeovers complete with brewery/distributor reps and a special, featured pizza.

SHADY MCGRADY'S

204 Verbeke St., Harrisburg, PA 17102; (717) 234-4070; @ShadyMcGradys
Draft Beers: 48 **Bottled/Canned Beers:** around 150

There's a pool table, an inviting angular bar, and great beer at this off-the-beaten-path dive bar in the city's Historic Midtown District. Be forewarned that smoking is still allowed. But if that's not an issue, you'll find plenty of great beer options both on draft and in the numerous coolers lining the barroom. Locals such as Sly Fox and Weyerbacher can be found next to out-of-state interlopers like 21st Amendment and Ballast Point. For the largely domestic craft lineup, just a few foreigners including Guinness and Huyghe get in on the act.

ZENO'S PUB

100 W. College Ave., State College, PA 16801; (814) 237-4350; zenospub.com; @ZenosPub
Draft Beers: 30 **Bottled/Canned Beers:** 80+

Closing out the chapter here with two dive bars suggests that bar owners in the center of the state know what they're up to, serving great beer in down-to-earth, no-frills locations.

Here in the heart of State College across from Penn State University's Old Main, Zeno's has been serving up good times for college kids, faculty, and locals since 1972. Squirreled away down a streetside flight of stairs beneath the Allen Street Grill, Zeno's small bunker-like space is all about Elk Creek, Tröegs, Voodoo, and many others on tap and live music on a regular basis.

Bar-top firkins and "Kitchen Sink Beerfests" comprise the special events held at Zeno's. There's no food served, but the restaurant above will send food down if needed.

Lancaster—Pub Crawl

The charming borough of nearby Lititz is a very close second behind Lancaster in terms of a beer lover's pub crawl. I'm going with Lancaster for its sheer volume and diversity of venues for building the perfect day- and night-long pub crawl. It also has the distinction of being a one-day capital of the United States.

To add a little something extra to your pub-crawl mix, you might consider including a minor league baseball game which you could take in either before heading off to Iron Hill early in the afternoon or later in the day depending upon game time.

TOTAL WALKING DISTANCE: If walking a roundtrip circuit from the Amtrak station, it's a hefty 5.3-mile circuit. It's only 1.9 miles if walking after getting a ride between the first three stops.

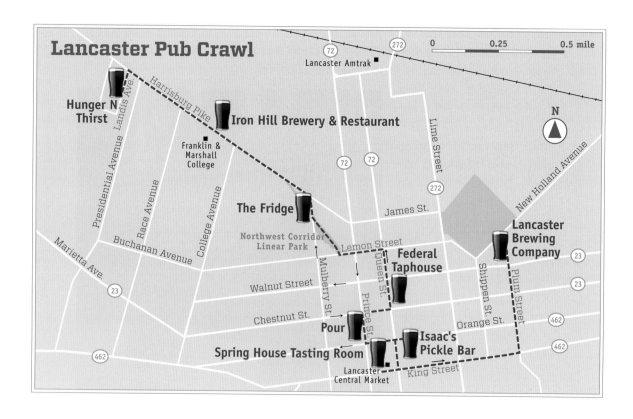

Directions: This pub crawl begins near Franklin & Marshall College at Hunger N Thirst just off Harrisburg Pike. If arriving by train, the Amtrak station is just over a mile by way of the recently completed pedestrian bridge.

Hunger N Thirst, 920 Landis Ave., Lancaster, PA, 17603; (717) 208-3808; hungern thirst.com; @HungernThirst

It's not exactly accidental that I begin this pub crawl for you at Hunger N Thirst, an extensively renovated former car dealership. As mentioned numerous times in this book, each pub crawl should begin with at least a small bit of food. They have you covered here with both great beer and food.

You might start with a pork banh mi, a Pig and Fig sandwich, a pâté plate, or a meat board; it will be difficult to decide. The beer list doesn't get much easier with a set of 24 well-regarded beers on tap and a couple hundred bottles from which to choose in the bottle shop.

Stopping here any other time would allow you to take home some beer, meats, cheeses, and assorted other morsels of food from the Marketplace shop.

Directions: Return to Harrisburg Pike, turn right and in less than a half-mile, Iron Hill will be on your left.

Iron Hill Brewery & Restaurant, 781 Harrisburg Pike, Lancaster, PA, 17603; (717) 291-9800; ironhillbrewery.com/Lancaster; @IronHillLanc

The Lancaster location of Iron Hill was the company's seventh installment of the continually growing giant on the regional brewpub scene. Once inside, veterans will recognize the decor and the format of the beer and food menus in keeping with the company's fairly consistent approach to brand delivery and quality service.

If you skipped food at Hunger N Thirst, great options here could include the Asian lettuce wraps, the stuffed piquillo peppers, or the beef brisket flatbread.

Choose either a year-round standard beer like the Pig Iron Porter or one of brewmaster Chad Rieker's specialty offerings like the Diplomat Dunkel brewed as an honorary beer for the graduating class across the street.

Directions: Turn left out of Iron Hill and walk toward downtown along Harrisburg Pike. After a half-mile, you will arrive at The Fridge.

The Fridge, 534 N. Mulberry St., Lancaster, PA, 17603; (717) 490-6825; beerfridge lancaster.com; @BeerFridgeLanc

The Fridge keeps it simple with pizza, beer, and a few other light bites. The fried Lebanon bologna sandwich is a standout on the menu in addition to the several well-made pizzas.

But your stop here on the crawl is for the beer and The Fridge boasts one of the larger selections of takeout beer in the area with 10 taps and more than 500 bottles from which to choose. Grab a bottle or draft and gaze at all the beautiful bottles. On a nice day, an outdoor table is the way to go.

Directions: Turn right down Mulberry Street and, at the next intersection, pick up the pathway through Northwest Corridor Linear Park and exit at Lemon Street. Turn left and walk three blocks to Queen Street. Turn right and after two more blocks your next stop is on the left.

Federal Taphouse, 201 N. Queen St., Lancaster, PA, 17603; (717) 490-6932; federal taphouselanc.com

This is the second location to the one in downtown Harrisburg near the Capitol building. This Federal Taphouse is equally spacious and hosts occasional live music.

With a hundred taps and frequent special events and tap takeovers, there is bound to be something to your liking on the menu, from the newest local like Funk Brewing to the rarer breweries from overseas like De Molen. Even for a large beer menu, it's segmented nicely by style with all the appropriate information—size, origin, price, and description—to make the right decision.

If you need a small bite to eat, Devils on Horseback or poutine would fit your savory needs, while sweet ricotta crepes would take good care of your sweet tooth.

Directions: Now you're in for a couple of well-deserved short walks. From Federal Taphouse, it's one block west and not even one block south to your next stop.

Pour, 114 N. Prince St., Lancaster, PA, 17603; (717) 290-8080; pouronprince.com; @POUR_Lancaster

Pour has a bit of something for everyone and does each of them very well. A stop here will net you a decent beer or two from their 10 drafts or nearly 50 bottles, a well-chosen wine, and an eye-catching menu of fresh and creative food from the kitchen.

Their European bottles are quite nicely chosen and tend to include ones like Saison Dupont, Orval, Schneider Aventinus, and Hanssens Oude Gueuze. The food menu changes with the seasons and delivers a flavor-popping watermelon gazpacho and ricotta herb dumplings with goat cheese and asparagus in the spring and summer to provide perfect accompaniment to the equally flavorful beers.

If whiskey and cigars are your thing, the comfortable off-street outdoor courtyard seating hosts a monthly cigar and whiskey tasting event.

Directions: One block east and a half-block south to the next stop make for another very short walk.

Isaac's Pickle Bar, 25 N. Queen St., Lancaster, PA, 17603; (717) 394-5544; isaacs picklebar.com; @PickleBar

Many around the area know Isaac's as a deli, a very good one that has been around for roughly 30 years with 18 locations.

What many may not know is that the original location, this one in downtown Lancaster a block from the historic Central Market and the Soldiers and Sailors War Memorial in Penn Square, is the only one to hold a liquor license.

With the license, the Pickle Bar has eight taps, roughly 15 bottles of interesting beers, and concocts a unique Bloody Mary with pickle juice. To further their craft-beer cred, they conduct monthlong brewery-focused events consisting of tap takeovers, food pairing, and brewery guests to help educate customers. Definitely include the Pickle Bar at Isaac's for one of the more unusual spots in Lancaster.

Directions: Just around the corner from the Pickle Bar is your next stop.

Spring House Tasting Room, 25 W. King St., Lancaster, PA, 17603; (717) 399-4009; springhousebeer.com; @SpringHouseBeer

The next best thing to visiting the brewing home of Spring House (south of downtown and closed to the public) is stopping at their downtown tasting room. A full variety of beers from their usual suspects to special releases is available alongside a nice menu of food items, many of which are sourced from the neighboring historic Central Market. Share a small plate of food like the meatball sliders if you wish, but leave room for dinner at your last stop.

Sit at the open and inviting square bar, which promotes conversation, and order the flagship Seven Gates Pale Ale or Diabolical Doctor Wit if you're looking for a more "standard" offering, or a Lil' Gruesome Peanut Butter and Jelly Stout, which always raises eyebrows but eventually turns doubters into fans.

Directions: Turn left out of Spring House and head east along King Street to Plum Street. Turn left and walk six blocks to Walnut Street for your last stop of the day.

Lancaster Brewing Company, 302 N. Plum St., Lancaster, PA, 17602; (717) 391-6258; lancasterbrewing.com; @LancasterBrew

There's a newer location 45 minutes away off the busy I-83/I-283/PA-322 jackpot in Harrisburg, but the last stop on this Lancaster-based pub crawl should be at one of the area's oldest brewpubs. It makes a great stop for the last meal of the day as well.

If you walked this entire pub crawl, you've earned a meal and it should begin with the Hop Hog IPA, which stands up nicely with the strong flavors of either the wings or the shrimp egg rolls. For a main course while in the Pennsylvania Dutch heartland, *Jägerschnitzel* with German potato salad, red cabbage, and a pint of milk stout makes perfect sense. Get the beer served on nitrogen for maximum enjoyment.

Directions: From Lancaster Brewing, it's a roughly half-mile walk along Walnut Street back downtown to find your hotel, or a bit more than a mile to the Amtrak station to catch your train.

Southeastern Pennsylvania

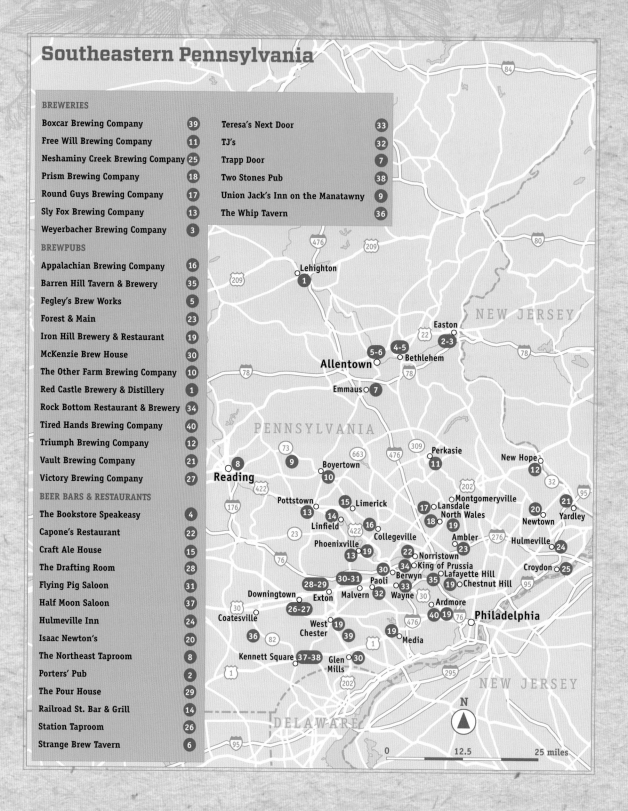

BREWERIES

Boxcar Brewing Company	39
Free Will Brewing Company	11
Neshaminy Creek Brewing Company	25
Prism Brewing Company	18
Round Guys Brewing Company	17
Sly Fox Brewing Company	13
Weyerbacher Brewing Company	3

Teresa's Next Door	33
TJ's	32
Trapp Door	7
Two Stones Pub	38
Union Jack's Inn on the Manatawny	9
The Whip Tavern	36

BREWPUBS

Appalachian Brewing Company	16
Barren Hill Tavern & Brewery	35
Fegley's Brew Works	5
Forest & Main	23
Iron Hill Brewery & Restaurant	19
McKenzie Brew House	30
The Other Farm Brewing Company	10
Red Castle Brewery & Distillery	1
Rock Bottom Restaurant & Brewery	34
Tired Hands Brewing Company	40
Triumph Brewing Company	12
Vault Brewing Company	21
Victory Brewing Company	27

BEER BARS & RESTAURANTS

The Bookstore Speakeasy	4
Capone's Restaurant	22
Craft Ale House	15
The Drafting Room	28
Flying Pig Saloon	31
Half Moon Saloon	37
Hulmeville Inn	24
Isaac Newton's	20
The Northeast Taproom	8
Porters' Pub	2
The Pour House	29
Railroad St. Bar & Grill	14
Station Taproom	26
Strange Brew Tavern	6

0   12.5   25 miles

Southeastern Pennsylvania (Not Philly)

Not content to let Philadelphia steal all the beer glory, Pennsylvania breweries and bars east of Reading and south of Easton will be the general focus of this chapter. Keeping pace with the big guy in the room—Philly (yes, outsiders, you can call it Philly just as we do)—is no easy task, but let's stop wasting words and get right to the evidence of the good beers flowing from the suburbs and exurbs of Philadelphia.

Breweries

BOXCAR BREWING COMPANY

306 Westtown Rd., West Chester, PA 19382; (484) 887-0538; boxcarbrewingcompany.com; @boxcarbrewery

Opened: 2010 (brewpub in 2015) **Owners:** James and Kymberly Robinson **Brewers:** Tom Connors and James Robinson **Year-Round Beers:** 1492 American Pale Ale, Boomer Brown Ale, Mango Ginger IPA, Passenger Pale Ale **Seasonals/Special Releases:** Belgian Tripel and others **Tours:** Upon request **Taproom:** No

The small 10-barrel brewery located just outside of downtown West Chester in a low-rise industrial park continues to grow. Over 600 barrels of beer went out the door in 2014, and 2015 looked to be even brighter as they opened a pub on Market Street barely a mile away from the brewery.

Examples of well-made Boxcar beers include the nutty, malty English-style **Boomer Brown** (5% ABV) and **Mango Ginger IPA** (7% ABV), which carries more pronounced mango than ginger.

Boxcar beer is distributed throughout Delaware, New Jersey, and approximately half of Pennsylvania. A more unusual way to enjoy the brewery's beers, however, is by joining them on the annual Ride the Rails event aboard the West Chester Railroad in 1930s-era train cars from West Chester to the Glen Mills Picnic Park, where plenty of food, live music, and naturally Boxcar beers awaits as part of the festive event.

Beer Lover's Pick

Passenger Ale
Style: English-style mild
ABV: 4.7%
Availability: Year-round; 12-ounce cans
This very clean and pale golden beer benefits from a nice balance of caramel and bready flavors tempered with a bit of earthy hop flavor. It's light in body and alcohol, so there's plenty of room for multiple pours of this tasty beer.

FREE WILL BREWING COMPANY

410 E. Walnut St., Perkasie, PA 18944; (267) 354-0813; freewillbrewing.com;
@FreewillBrewing

Founded: 2012 **Founders:** Dominic Capece and John Stemler **Brewers:** John Stemler
and Ethan Buckman **Year-Round Beers:** Techno IPA, Destiny's Wit, Community Kölsch,
Lowercase IPA, C.O.B., Pale Stout, 10w Porter, Danae **Seasonals/Special Releases:**
Many including the Sputnik Series **Tours:** Free, Sat 1 and 3 p.m. **Taproom:** Yes

Free Will had already made its presence known in the Philadelphia region during
the first couple years of brewing. They took the big step in 2014 getting out of
their not-too-small downstairs space into a much bigger brewing operation upstairs
that will allow them to grow comfortably in the foreseeable future. The existing
brewery will then be dedicated to sour beer production for the delight of the brewery's many fans.

Fronting the new brewery with 100-barrel fermenters, a catwalk system, and a
high ceiling is a tasting room with full view into the operations. Stemler came from
Keystone Homebrew and is a great example of homebrewers who apply themselves

Beer Lover's Pick

Free Will I. Am. Fergie Black Eyed Stout
Style: Dry Irish stout
ABV: 4.3%
Availability: Limited; 12-ounce bottles

This highly drinkable, pitch-black beer packs a bunch of
roasted coffee, chocolate notes, and hop bitterness into a
light-bodied beer that you could drink all afternoon. Bigger
than the beer's flavor and aroma profile is the back story.
As a one-time pro-am collaboration brew and with entirely
too many details to list here, the thumbnail sketch shows
Michael Lawrence (Philly Beer Geek 2013), Fergie Carey (Philadelphia Bar owner), both fathers of Lawrence and Carey,

and of course Free Will all contributing naming inspiration for the beer. If the beer
is brewed again—as all good Beer Lover's Picks should be—word has it that it may
simply be named William.

seriously to the craft and take it to the next level—a much bigger next level. Plus, with his biology and chemistry schooling, it's obvious in conversation with him that he knows what's happening at every stage of the process from boiling to bottling.

Many beers come and go on seasonal or limited status at Free Will, like the wonderful balance of wood, wine, and IPAs in **Two Brothers IPA White** (Chardonnay oak barrels) and **Two Brothers IPA Red** (Pinot Noir red Burgundy oak barrels). Also worthy of your palate's attention is the very nice and not overly tart **Kriek Lambic** (4.9% ABV) and beers from the **Sputnik Series** of one-offs like the Sputnik 31 **Smoked Porter** and its burnt roasted coffee flavor and hints of smoked bacon.

The **Saison de Rose** (5.6% ABV) was a charity beer done with pink peppercorns, pink grapefruits, ginger, and hibiscus flowers. Proceeds benefited the Rena Rowan Breast Center and was brewed in conjunction with noteworthy local females in the beer industry Tara Nurin, Marnie Old, Carolyn Smagalski, and Erin Wallace. Free Will hopes to expand this project in the future.

One of the most anticipated beers, however, is the **C.O.B.**—Coffee Oatmeal Brown, an imperial English-style brown ale at 8.3% ABV—complete with its sweet caramel and biscuit malt flavors and aged on ground coffee beans. Check the BYOB: Brew Your Own Beer section for a clone recipe from Keystone Homebrew Supply.

NESHAMINY CREEK BREWING COMPANY

909 Ray Ave., Croydon, PA 19021; (215) 458-7081; neshaminycreekbrewing.com; @NCBCBeer

Opened: 2012 **Founders:** Steve Capelli, Rob Jahn, Jeremy Myers **Brewers:** Jeremy Myers, Jake Howell, Jason Ranck, and Steve Capelli (production manager) **Year-Round Beers:** Churchville Lager, County Line IPA, Croydon Cream Ale, Trauger Pilsner, Tribute Tripel **Seasonals/Special Releases:** Blitzkrieg Hops Double IPA, Leon Russian Imperial Stout, and others from the Flood Water Seasonal Series **Tours:** Self-guided or call ahead to schedule **Taproom:** Yes

Neshaminy Creek is part of the next wave of Philadelphia-area breweries, and they captivated the beer scene right out of the gates after opening less then 3 years ago. The first beer to gain significant attention was the Trauger described in the Beer Lover's Pick. Gaining attention with a pilsner in the Philadelphia area is no small feat and the accolades continued from there.

Other year-rounds like the smooth and easy-drinking **Tribute Tripel** (9.3% ABV) and **County Line IPA** (6.6% ABV) brought in the faithful along with seasonals such as the big bad chocolatey **Leon Russian Imperial Stout** (11.3% ABV), brewed with graham crackers and house-made marshmallow fluff.

The crisp and easy-drinking traditional **Churchville Lager** (4.9% ABV) also caught the attention of judges at the 2013 Great American Beer Festival, where it was awarded a gold medal among 30 entries in the Vienna-style lager category.

Beer Lover's Pick

Trauger Pilsner
Style: German-style pilsner
ABV: 4.8%
Availability: Year-round; 12-ounce cans

Though the Churchville Lager was the first Neshaminy Creek beer with a major award, the Trauger was racking up accolades from beer writers and fans alike from the moment the pilsner rolled out the door in the brewery's early days. It's the beer that put the brewery on the map and its strong traditional Noble hop presence makes for an easy-drinking crisp beer that will be bringing home awards in due time.

Neshaminy Creek's brewing space in Croydon, just blocks from the Neshaminy Creek and the Croydon SEPTA train station, is ample with enough space to add numerous fermenters up to 60 barrels in size. With most beer names carrying strong ties to the local community and a popularity that continues to soar, chances are very good that they will be there for quite some time.

PRISM BREWING COMPANY

810 Dickerson Rd., North Wales, PA 19454; (267) 613-8572; prismbeer.com; @PrismBeer
Founded: 2010 **Founder:** Rob DeMaria **Brewer:** Matt Mihalovich **Year-Round Beers:** Bitto Honey, ParTea Pale Ale, Felony IPA **Seasonals/Special Releases:** Summer of '69, Shady Blonde, Red Zone, Insana Stout, Funk Zone, Love is evoL, and the Naked Series
Tours: $5, Sun at 3 p.m. **Taproom:** Yes

"Tucked away" might be a fine way to describe where Prism is located—off a main road, around the backside of building, and within a keg toss of the SEPTA regional rail line to Doylestown. Once you find the brewery and slide up to the bar, the next steps are an adventure in some of the most creatively interesting beers and their ingredients in the area.

Beer Lover's Pick

ParTea
Style: Pale ale
ABV: 5.5%
Availability: Year-round; 12-ounce bottles
Take a solid pale ale, add Orange Pekoe whole tea leaves and, if done right as at Prism, the result is an extremely refreshing and drinkable mild tea-like beer with a dry finish.

All "real food" ingredients are used in many of Prism's beers. Jalapeños and strawberries in **Love is evoL** (5.5% ABV) turn out to be pleasant and not overpowering. The pronounced hop bitterness in the **Bitto Honey** (6.7% ABV) is countered with soft and sweet local honey. The **Felony IPA** (10% ABV) is rather basic—a double IPA—compared to the other exotically built beers, yet accounts for nearly 30 percent of brewery sales. **Red Zone** (6.6% ABV) has a handful of spices along with local maple syrup. **Shady Blonde** has its blood oranges.

Furthering the intersection of beer and food, local Bespoke Bacon uses Prism beer in their bacon jam, Prism uses the bacon in their **Insana Stout** (7.9% ABV), and Bacon Wednesdays celebrate it all together. Speaking of food, there is a small, but satisfying, menu of perfect bar room nibbles headlined by a list of "gourmet hot dogs."

ROUND GUYS BREWING COMPANY

324 W. Main St., Lansdale, PA 19446; (215) 368-2640; roundguysbrewery.com; @roundguysbrewer

Founded: 2012 **Founder:** Scott Rudich **Brewer:** Scott Rudich **Year-Round Beers:** BerlinerWeister Berlinerweiss, Kiss Off IPA, Fear of a Brett Planet IPA, Sundown Saison **Seasonals/Special Releases:** Many **Tours:** Upon request **Taproom:** Yes

Round Guys is yet another suburban Philadelphia brewery of the "new generation" that appears to be set up with a long future ahead of it. The tasting room is a popular place for locals looking to sample from the brewery's short list of regular beers and longer list of ever-changing seasonal and one-off beers. Local wines and meads are also served.

Fear of a Brett Planet IPA (5.4% ABV) is neither big on the funky Brett component nor the bitter hops, making it a nicely balanced beer of fruit and hops flavor—one that took a third-place award at the Philly .com Brewvitational Awards in 2014. The tart and the sour, however, can be found in the **BerlinerWeisster** (3.7% ABV). For a

Original Slacker
Style: Brown ale
ABV: 4%
Availability: Occasionally; 12-ounce cans

By my account, finding well-made brown ales that are not overly "Americanized" with multiple aggressive hop additions is not so easy. This low alcohol, grainy and nutty one passes the test and presents an easy-drinking flavorful beer. It also makes a great base beer to do other things with, such as in a firkin with added coconut, caramel, and chocolate as the brewery has done in the past for Friday the Firkinteenth at Grey Lodge.

brown with an added twist, try **Adam's Psychedelic Breakfast Maple Brown Ale** (4.9% ABV) and its maple syrup and vanilla bean characteristics.

SLY FOX BREWING COMPANY

520 Kimberton Rd. (PA-113), Phoenixville, PA 19460; (610) 935-4540; 331 Circle of Progress Dr., Pottstown, PA 19464; (484) 524-8210; slyfoxbeer.com; @SlyFoxBeer
Founded: 1995 (production facility in 2012) **Founders:** The Giannopoulos family
Brewers: Brian O'Reilly (Brewmaster), Steve Jacoby, Tim Ohst (Production Manager)
Flagship Beers: Pikeland Pils, Phoenix Pale Ale, Rt. 113 IPA, Helles Golden Lager **Year-Round Beers:** 360 IPA, Saison Vos, Incubus Tripel, Ichor Quadrupel, Black Raspberry Reserve **Seasonals/Special Releases:** Christmas Ale, Dunkel Lager, Gang Aft Agley, Grisette, Odyssey Imperial IPA, Oktoberfest, and many others **Naming Inspiration:** The long history of fox hunting in local Chester County, Pa.

Play a little beer word association with someone and say the name Sly Fox. Chances are good that the first response will be: goat races. The Philadelphia beer region's event calendar on the first Sunday of each May is anchored by the Bock Fest & Goat Races at Sly Fox's brewery in Pottstown. See the Major Beer Events section later in this book for more details about this fun, family-friendly gathering of bocks, brats, goat racing, and live music.

Throughout the year, Sly Fox keeps the good times flowing with a long list of events, including a Robbie Burns Night in January, a St. Patrick's Day celebration in March—both at the Phoenixville brewpub location—and an afternoon of Kan Jam games and live music at the brewery in September. The tie-in is natural given that Sly Fox has been a leading brewery for canned offerings longer than others in the region.

The oft-decorated brewery most recently brought silver and bronze medals back from the annual Great American Beer Festival in 2013 for its **Grisette** (5.6% ABV, Belgian pale ale) and **Oktoberfest** (5.8% ABV, smooth and traditional lager), respectively. For an encore, the Grisette returned from Denver in 2014 with a gold medal.

When tasting from the long lineup of beers typically available at the Phoenixville pub (or the Tastin' Room in Pottstown), the year-round **Pikeland Pils** (4.9% ABV) is a great place to begin with its clean and crisp Noble hop profile.

Beer Lover's Pick

Saison Vos
Style: Belgian-style Farmhouse ale
ABV: 6.9%
Availability: Year-round; 750-milliliter bottles
This classic beer delivers a light-bodied, dry, and pleasantly crisp balance of pepper spice, mild citrus, and tempting hop aroma. Saison Vos is a joy to drink on its own and goes well all the same with a plate of strong mushroom brie cheese or seared pepper ahi tuna.

The flavors ramp up quickly with the year-round, hop-forward **Route 113 IPA** (7% ABV) and the raspberry-juicy and slightly tart **Black Raspberry Reserve** (8% ABV). In the winter months, if your timing is fortuitous at the pub, enjoy an **Oatmeal Stout** (5.2% ABV), which makes a very limited run as a super smooth, slightly bitter stout that is a nice and slightly bigger alternative to the classic **O'Reilly's Irish Dry Stout** (3.6% ABV).

The large brewery continues to grow into its cavernous space and brews for The Brewer's Art and Mikkeller even as it opens up the North Carolina market in 2015. Behind-the-scene tours are offered on weekends at no cost. Across the street from the airport-adjacent brewery is a new business with part ownership involvement from the Giannopoulos family, Manatawny Still Works, which offers its own weekend tours, tastings, food trucks, and occasional live music.

WEYERBACHER BREWING COMPANY

905 Line St., Suite G, Easton, PA 18042; (610) 559-5561; weyerbacher.com; @Weyerbacher

Founded: 1995 (current location 2001) **Founder:** Dan Weirback **Brewers:** Chris Wilson, Scott Bicksler, Chris Reilly, Chris Lampe (production manager) **Flagship Beer:** Merry Monks **Year-Round Beers:** Blithering Idiot, Last Chance IPA, Verboten, Double Simcoe IPA, Old Heathen, Tiny **Seasonals/Special Releases:** AutumnFest, Heresy, Imperial Pumpkin Ale, Insanity, Quad, Riserva, Winter Ale **Tours:** Free, Fri and Sat **Taproom:** Yes

Weyerbacher has grown its business slowly and steadily from the early years of being in downtown Easton—with an attached brewpub for a few years—to a full production brewery on the outskirts of town turning out nearly 20,000 barrels of hotly sought-after beer available in most East Coast and a few Midwest states.

Those using the nearby D&L Canal towpath along the Lehigh River will find Weyerbacher a convenient place to visit after a run or bike ride. But watch out, because many of the beers lean in the bigger direction—like the Tiny. Small beer you think? Not so much so.

Tiny packs a big punch of deliciously smooth and rich chocolate flavors and 11.8% ABV. **Double Simcoe** (9% ABV) goes in the other direction with a big blast of citrus hop flavor and aroma and created a crowd-pleasing hit in their portfolio when it was unveiled in early 2006. It was also a grand champion in the imperial IPA/red ale category at the 2014 US Beer Tasting Championship.

On the lighter side of alcohol, **Verboten** clocks in at 5.9% ABV and gives drinkers a chance to have several of this fruit-forward beer with just a pinch of hop bitterness. The **Imperial Pumpkin** (8% ABV) was one of the original amped-up pumpkin beers on the market and is still quite popular as one of the brewery's most anticipated seasonal and limited releases. But that title now likely falls to the **Riserva**, one of the most beautifully complex beers available with its array of sweet, sour, tart, woodsy, and fruity aromas and flavors. The recipe varies

a bit from year-to-year but is always aged on raspberries and comes in around 12% ABV—a beer to seek out for sure.

A free tour of the brewery comes with six samplings of beer at the 2013-renovated tasting bar, where the adjacent retail shop provides take-home beer and all its accompaniments for purchase.

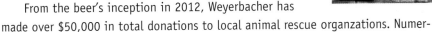

Beer Lover's Pick

Last Chance IPA
Style: India pale ale
ABV: 5.9%
Availability: Year-round; 12-ounce bottles
Better than all the citrus and pine hop flavor bursting out of this surprisingly well-balanced IPA (62 IBUs) is the story behind the beer. A portion of proceeds from this beer's sales goes toward a monthly donation to a local animal rescue of brewery employees' choosing.

From the beer's inception in 2012, Weyerbacher has made over $50,000 in total donations to local animal rescue organzations. Numerous other pieces of Last Chance–related merchandise—like leashes, bowls, and keychains—are also for sale in the online and in-person retail stores, and these sales contribute to the cause.

Brewpubs

BARREN HILL TAVERN AND BREWERY

646 Germantown Pike, Lafayette Hill, PA 19444; (484) 344-5438; barrenhilltavern.com;
@BarrenHillTav

Founded: 2013 **Founder:** Erin Wallace **Brewer:** David Wood **Beers:** Too many unique offerings to list

Barren Hill opened in 2013 in the former General Lafayette Inn & Brewery and takes its name from a Revolutionary War battle fought near the brewery site. Brewer Scott Morrison (aka "The Dude") got the brewery up and running through most of 2014 before handing over the mash paddle to David Wood, formerly of Free Will Brewing. Morrison is no stranger to award-winning beers (from his time at Dock Street and McKenzie Brew House), so it may come as little surprise that Barren Hill's Bière de Extra under his watch took a bronze medal at both the 2014 World Beer Cup and 2014 Great American Beer Festival.

Owner Erin Wallace's bar and restaurant teeth were cut for many years at Old Eagle Tavern and Devil's Den, both in Philadelphia. At Barren Hill, the bar's 30 taps are roughly divided in half between Barren Hill's house beers and guest taps from around the region. The bottle list is also extensive and contains quite a few sour beers. Early favorites from the brewery include a crisp and spicy **Grisette** (5.2% ABV), the citrusy **Mandraina Bavaria Belgian IPA** (6.8% ABV), the snappy **Berliner** (2.8% ABV), and the earthy **Rye Saison** (3.8% ABV). The 7-barrel brewhouse has

the potential to put out 900 barrels per year and, given the size of the menu and the brewhouse schedule, that estimate seems likely to be met.

Chef Paul Trowbridge adds to the equation as well, continuing to work with Wallace at Devil's Den and bringing his acclaimed work in the kitchen that dates back to his early days at Dock Street. Popular items on the menu include a smoked salmon sandwich, duck confit fries, beer-battered fish, and Aventinus mussels.

FEGLEY'S BREW WORKS

Allentown Brew Works at 812 W. Hamilton St., Allentown, PA 18101; (610) 433-7777
Bethlehem Brew Works at 569 Main St., Bethlehem, PA 18018; (610) 882-1300;
thebrewworks.com; @thebrewworks

Founded: 1998 (Bethlehem), 2007 (Allentown) **Founder:** Rich Fegley **Brewers:** Beau
Baden (brewmaster, both locations), Mike Wieboldt (Allentown), Josh Bushey (Bethlehem)
Flagship and Year-Round Beers: Always Sunny Pale Ale, Fegley's Amber Lager,
Fegley's ESB, Hop Explosion, Hop'solutely, Knuckleball, Pawnshop Porter, Steelgaarden
Wit, Steelworkers' Oatmeal Stout, Valley Golden Ale **Seasonals/Special Releases:** Arctic
Alchemy, Bagpiper's Scotch Ale, Blueberry Belch, Bourbon Barrel Insidious Imperial Stout,
Devious Imperial Pumpkin, Monkey Wrench, Rude Elf's Reserve, Space Monkey Raspberry
Saison, Pumpkin Ale, and more

Nearly 10 years after debuting Bethlehem Brew Works, the Fegley family opened the Allentown location with a much larger five-story space for both brewers and customers. The production facility at the Allentown brewpub location produces approximately five times as much as the Bethlehem location to help satisfy the distribution market.

Fegley's has been sensitive to environmental concerns as they have grown and striven to use alternative energy sources, "upcycle" their spent grain to farmers who in turn sell their beef back to the brewery, and compost table scraps and other biodegradable waste.

Fegley's plays its part in the community as well by conducting monthly Charity Cask Nights where a percentage of sales goes to a local charity, Doggie Yappy Hours, and by hosting knitting clubs, running clubs, and homebrewing clubs.

From the brewery, two year-round favorites include **Hop'solutely** (11.5% ABV), a triple IPA stuffed with seven floral and bitter hops, and the **Steelworkers' Oatmeal Stout** (5.3% ABV), a smooth and easy drinking blend of roast, chocolate, and bitter hops. The seasonal list of beers overflows with a wide variety of popular choices like the unfiltered very **Blueberry**

Belch (4.2% ABV and packed with 150 pounds of blueberries per batch), the boozy **Bourbon Barrel Insidious Imperial Stout** (9% ABV), **Devious Imperial Pumpkin** (9% ABV), and the dry and spicy **Monkey Wrench** (7% ABV).

The style diversity in the brewhouse is evident year-round and the 2014 Great American Beer Festival proved the point when Fegley's brought home a gold medal for the Arctic Alchemy in the old/strong ale category and a bronze for the Berliner Weiss in the German-style sour category.

As many kitchens do around the Lehigh Valley, both Allentown and Bethlehem Brew Works' kitchens play to the region's large Eastern European heritage and serve a handful of staples like Pork-n-Kraut, bratwurst, schnitzel, Bavarian pretzels, and pierogies. That's in addition to a litany of sandwiches, appetizers, salads, steaks, and seafood with a little something to please everyone.

Be on the lookout for potential future expansion of the family business into a larger production facility.

FOREST & MAIN

61 N. Main St., Ambler, PA 19002; (215) 542-1776; forestandmain.com; @ForestandMain
Founded: 2012 **Founders:** Daniel Endicott and Gerard Olson **Brewers:** Daniel Endicott and Gerard Olson **A few of the more regularly seen beers:** Kinch, Palomino, Poor Yorick, Solaire, Tiny Tim **Seasonals/Special Releases:** Many

One of the area's most unusual brewpub concepts has taken hold of Ambler at the intersection of Forest and Main Streets. Not that they needed to name the establishment after the crossroads—common sense says that fans of great beer would be able to find Daniel Endicott's and Gerard Olson's pride and joy no matter where it was located.

The brewer-owner team took a hundred-year-old Victorian house in Ambler and masterfully turned it into one of the area's homiest spots to enjoy a beer. Just like visiting a friend in the neighborhood, you can sit at a picnic table on the front porch among the hop bines, dine in one of two rooms, go up the creaky stairs to a group dining table, or hang out in yet another room that houses the bar, a few seats, and a dartboard.

The duo's beers primarily express their takes on British and Belgian favorites like porters, pale ales, bitters, IPAs, and saisons. The **Solaire** (4.5% ABV) is a light and refreshing saison—third place saison winner in the Philly.com 2014 Brewvitational—full of grainy malt and spicy yeastiness and makes for a wonderfully tasty session beer. The **Kinch** (6% ABV), on the other side of the spectrum, puts on a juicy display of hops.

While many of the beers that show up on draft at the pub appear to be one-offs, the beauty of a small operation is that there's rarely a time when never means never. So while **Three Tuns Ale** (4.2% ABV) may have looked like a one-off, do keep your eye open for this chocolate and fruity light English stout. Also keep the radar up for occasional special bottle releases, many of them barrel-aged.

On the topic of the group dining room, getting in on a monthly Sunday Night Dinner event or reserving the room for a private group dinner are a couple more ways to enjoy the charm of this suburban Philadelphia gem.

IRON HILL BREWERY & RESTAURANT
30 E. State St., Media, PA 19063; (610) 627-9000; ironhillbrewery.com/media; @IronHillMedia
Founder and Owners: Kevin P. Finn (President), Kevin Davies (Director of Culinary Operations), Mark Edelson (Director of Brewing Operations) **Opened:** 2000 **Brewer:** Bob Barrar **Brewing Output:** 8.5-bbl brewhouse; 1,200 barrels/year

Iron Hill and its 1,000+ employees have been profiled in the Northern Delaware and Southern New Jersey chapters as well as the previous chapter's pub crawl for its Lancaster location. The point has been made repeatedly that the standard Iron Hill corporate brand is stamped all over each location, from its decor to the several house beers, including the fantastic ol' standby, Pig Iron Porter, all the while giving each local head brewer and assistant the latitude to show off their skills on the second half of the menu.

Director of Brewing Operations, Mark Edelson, and Regional Brewer Head, Larry Horwitz, have their work made a bit easier by overseeing so much brewhouse talent. At the Media location, head brewer Bob Barrar has put his own skills on display and stamped the menu with the company's most award-winning beer—his **Russian Imperial Stout** (9.5% ABV).

Since 2003, at the Great American Beer Festival it has accumulated three gold, two silver, and one bronze medals and at the World Beer Cup it has garnered an

More Iron Hills to Climb

The Iron Hill family continues to grow with its 11th location, which opened in December 2014 in Ardmore, PA, and a 12th on its way. Paul Rutherford took the helm, moving over from the Chestnut Hill brewpub. The "family" has taken home the Large Brewpub of the Year award in 2005 at the Great American Beer Festival and in 2010 at the World Beer Cup. On its own, the Media location earned the nod as Small Brewpub of the Year in both 2012 and 2014 at the World Beer Cup. In addition to the Media location described above, Iron Hill is also well represented in Philadelphia and its suburbs at:

North Wales: Doug Marchakitus, head brewer in an 8.5-barrel brewhouse putting out approx. 1,200 barrels/year; opened in 2004

Philadelphia (Chestnut Hill): Chris LaPierre, head brewer in an 8.5-barrel brewhouse putting out approx. 1,200 barrels/year; opened in 2012

Phoenixville: Tim Stumpf, head brewer in a 5-barrel brewhouse putting out approx. 800 barrels/year; opened in 2006

West Chester: Andrew Johnston, head brewer in an 8.5-barrel brewhouse putting out approx. 1,400 barrels/year; opened in 1999

additional four gold and one bronze medals. The fresh and the vintage versions each deliver a fantastic expression of big and rich dark-roasted malts cut by a generous dosing of hop flavor. The Russian Imperial Stout, like at least a dozen other specialty Iron Hill beers, is available by the 750-milliliter bottle to take home and age or drink.

Outside of tasting Iron Hill's beer at the bar or over a meal, the Media location hosts one of the region's favorite festivals each May—Brandywine Valley Craft Brewers Festival—to benefit the Media Youth Center. The West Chester location plays host and title sponsor for the annual Iron Hill Twilight Criterium bike race through the city streets.

MCKENZIE BREW HOUSE

451 Wilmington Pike, Glen Mills, PA 19342; (610) 361-9800; Opened in 2001 with a 12-bbl brewhouse; 240 Lancaster Avenue, Malvern, PA 19355; (610) 296-2222; Opened in 2006 with a 15-bbl brewhouse; 324 W. Swedesford Rd., Berwyn, PA 19312; (610) 407-4300; mckenziebrewhouse.com; @mckenziebrew; Opened in 2011 with a 10-bbl brewhouse

Founders: William Mangan Sr. and William Mangan Jr. **Brewers:** Rob Pine and Nate Walter **Flagship and Year-Round Beers:** McKenzie Light, Brandywine Wit, Route 202 Pale Ale, Saison Vautour, and a constantly changing Brewers Choice IPA **Seasonals/ Special Releases:** Up to five rotating seasonals

The brewpub has been on the map for over 10 years, winning major awards for its beers under former brewers Scott Morrison, Gerard Olson (at Forest & Main), and Ryan Michaels (at Rinn Duin in New Jersey). The current brewers are carrying on the level of excellence found in beers like the **Saison Vautour** (6.5% ABV), which, over a 4-year span, took home an astounding three gold medals in the French and Belgian Saison category (2007, 2009, 2010) at the Great American Beer Festival.

The excellently dry and spicy Vautour occupies a coveted space on an otherwise standard lineup of house beers. It works quite well on the dinner table with a long list of entree salads at McKenzie's.

Saisons and twists on them are actually something that can be found with regularity on either the draft or the bottle beer menu at any of the three locations. A **Saison Brune** is a darker version and **Drizella** a sour barrel-aged one.

Not to think that Saison/Farmhouse beers are the only options at McKenzie's, the **Route 202 Pale Ale** (5% ABV) is a very good straight-ahead approach to an American Pale Ale, with just enough of an earthy hop presence to get attention. And, for dessert, the **Dark and Stormy Night** is a wonderfully big and rich barrel-aged quadrupel that won a silver medal at the 2013 Great American Beer Festival. The rotation of limited seasonals and one-offs is so frequent that you're guaranteed a new find at each visit.

Also coming from the kitchen and playing nicely with the beers are flatbreads and pizzas from the wood-fired oven, street tacos, sliders, comfort food like meat loaf and potpie, and a Santorini Sampler of tzatziki, hummus, and roasted artichoke Parmesan dip.

Each of the brewpub locations has a little something for every interest, from a pool table in Glen Mills to a comfortable lounge at Berwyn to outdoor fireside dining in Malvern. Live music, karaoke, bingo, and quizzo on various nights of the week are yet more ways that people find their way to great beer at McKenzie's.

THE OTHER FARM BREWING COMPANY

128 E. Philadelphia Ave., Boyertown, PA 19512; (610) 367-1788; theotherfarmbrewingcompany.com; @TheOtherFarm
Founded: 2013 **Founder:** Hank Frecon **Brewer:** Bryan McDonald **Flagship Beer:** Saisonner, Old McDonald Rye **Year-Round Beers:** Renart's Triple, Bahr Hill Estate IPA
Seasonals/Special Releases: Many

Take a coffee shop/cafe, add a concert stage, stick a Saturday-morning farmers' market in the back, and open a brewery owned by a local apple cider company, and you've got an image of what The Other Farm Brewing Company looks like.

In the brewery, they've capitalized on their sister company, 70-year-old Frecon Farms of Boyertown. The brewery uses hops from the Frecon Farms second farm (aka the "other farm") in several beers, as well as apple butter and other local botanicals. The masterpiece, though, comes in the **Renart's Triple** (10% ABV), which is a very nice, clean, and dry tripel with the extra flavor component coming in the form of residual sweetness from Frecon's apple cider, used in secondary fermentation, which nicely balances out the booziness.

Other Farm is a brewery to watch as it grows through distribution and continues to impress with its creative beers like the **Saisonner** (5.7% ABV), which changes with the seasons incorporating cherries, apricots, blueberries, peaches, raspberries, and blackberries from the family farm.

RED CASTLE BREWERY & DISTILLERY

80 E. Bridge St., Lehighton, PA 18325; (570) 732-0020; redcastlebrewery.com; @CastleGrill

Opened: 2013 **Founders:** Frank Potoczak, Anthony Serafino **Brewer:** Anthony Serafino
Flagship Beers: Dragon's Breath **Year-Round Beers:** Dark Dungeon, Queen's Guard

The former Castle Grill has morphed into Red Castle Brewery & Distillery and has taken on a more brewpub-like feel and cannot be missed while driving through the area with its distinctively high and pointed red roof. The bar seats around 15 people and additional table seating is available both indoors and outside.

In what is most likely the only brewing establishment in this book to have been launched at a nudist resort, Potoczak and Serafino hatched the brewpub plan while at a cigar event at nearby Sunny Rest a few years back. On an interesting side note, Sunny Rest conducted its second annual beer festival in 2014 to a record crowd of 700 attendees.

They have turned the idea into reality with Serafino—using his background as a chef and DuPont chemist—manning the mash paddle and Potoczak's family recipes providing excellent Eastern European/Polish potato pancakes, kielbasa, *haluski,* and *halupki*.

To wash down the satisfyingly excellent plates of food, the brewery serves eight taps of their own beer plus a handful of local wines also on tap in their effort to reduce environmental impact. Gaining worthy attention early on from the brewery

are the well-balanced **Dragon's Breath** (6.8% ABV) smoked rye IPA, the not-too-agressive **Dark Dungeon** (7.2% ABV) bourbon coffee stout, and the **Golden Scepter** (7.5% ABV) Belgian strong ale. **Lancer's Lager** (5.5% ABV) and **Queen's Guard** (6.2% ABV) American pale ale are two well-done standard style approaches that go over well with newcomers to the craft-brewing world.

The tidy 3.5-barrel system behind and beneath the restaurant may someday be joined by a 20-barrel system across the river. But until then Serafino is turning out beers that are gaining attention in an underserved area from locals and vacationers gathering beer for their Pocono retreat.

ROCK BOTTOM RESTAURANT & BREWERY

1001 King of Prussia Plaza, King of Prussia, PA 19406; (610) 230-2739; rockbottom.com/locations/king-of-prussia; @RockBottom; 171 Bridge St., Homestead, PA 15120; (412) 462-2739; rockbottom.com/locations/pittsburgh; @RockBottom

Founded: 1991 **Founder:** Frank Day **Brewers:** Brian McConnell and Tony Cunha (at King of Prussia); Brandon McCarthy (at Homestead) **Flagship and Year-Round Beers:** Kölsch, White, Red, IPA **Seasonals/Special Releases:** A rotating dark beer and a few Brewmaster's Choices, plus one handpump

It may not be well known that the Rock Bottom name was inspired by the first Rock Bottom's ground-floor location in the downtown Denver Prudential building.

As with the Rock Bottom in Bethesda, MD, the award-winning brewers at these two celebrated Pennsylvania locations of the chain of brewpubs have the latitude to do great things with the beer list outside of the family of regular house beers.

During a visit in mid-2014 to his brewpub just outside Pittsburgh, McCarthy was showing off (and showing it well) **My Boy Blue** (4.5% ABV) blueberry ale that folks from Maine would appreciate, a cask-conditioned **BBQ Brown with Roasted Habañeros** (4.2% ABV), and a **Fleeceflower Saison** (7.3 % ABV) using locally foraged Japanese knotwood to create a dry and herbal-like saison.

Don't be scared off by the location of McConnell's 15-barrel Rock Bottom brewpub, as easy as it may be to steer clear of the King of Prussia Mall. You need not step foot inside the mall as there's somewhat of a secret entrance from an adjacent parking garage (though during holiday season all bets are off).

Once inside, don't miss the floral **Prussia's Pride IPA** (6% ABV), the smooth **Oatmeal Stout** (5.4% ABV), or the seasonally perfect **Summer Honey Ale** (5.5% ABV). Since 2011, McConnell has brought home a gold and silver medal (2012 and 2013, respectively) from the Great American Beer Festival for his **Hammer Baltic Porter** and a silver medal in 2011 for the **Nevermore Lager/Schwarzbier**. One last beer with a local tie-in is the **Fire Chief Ale,** from which proceeds benefit the King of Prussia fire department.

TIRED HANDS BREWING COMPANY

16 Ardmore Ave., Ardmore, PA 19003; (610) 896-7621; tiredhands.com; @TiredHandsBeer
Founded: 2012 **Founders:** Jean Broillet IV and Julie Foster **Brewers:** Jean Broillet IV, Colin McFadden **Year-Round Beers:** HopHands, SaisonHands **Seasonals/Special Releases:** Too many unique offerings to list

To watch Tired Hands come to life as a beer destination in the small Main Line community of Ardmore is to understand the path of a young man coming of age in the craft-brewing industry. Owner Jean Broillet began his professional path to Ardmore as a cellarman at Weyerbacher approximately 1 hour north of Ardmore. His brewing career subsequently took off at the venerable Iron Hill family of brewpubs.

Throughout his journey, his plan to launch the Tired Hands concept became more real. After searching parts of Philly, he landed in 2012 with his 7-barrel brewhouse just across the city line in the town of Ardmore. The beer geeks have certainly found him and his wonderful execution of flavorful beers, small satisfying plates of big flavor, and comfortable atmosphere. His beers have been in such demand (evidenced by the long lines on special release days and the distance that people will drive for the Tired Hands experience) that work is nearing completion on a 20-barrel production facility not far from his original spot on Ardmore Avenue. When up and fully running, the 13,000-square-foot building will house the main brewhouse, a canning line, and a kitchen that focuses on tacos and crudo.

Back at the former dual-purpose office building, Broillet and team have delivered a beautiful space for enjoying some of the most interesting—not to mention most interestingly named—beers. To generalize would be foolish, but the best attempt would be to say that Tired Hands puts out beers with excellent attention to detail that fall into either a tart/sour/funky camp (think: saisons/farmhouse ales, Berliner weisses, goses, and assorted wild ales) or a hop-forward camp of pale ales, IPAs, double IPAs, and the like.

The **SaisonHands** (4.8% ABV) is one of the most regularly scheduled beers available on the pub's draft list and is a great example of a relatively low alcohol beer full of malt (barley, oats, rye, and wheat), a touch of earthiness, and refreshingly snappy citrus flavors.

Talking wth brewers and sampling their products, it becomes obvious fairly quickly who truly understands what happens with grains in a kettle of hot water, and later in the fermenter. Broillet, who has collaborated with talented brewers around the world, is clearly one who does. Plus, he understands the value of his business's role in the local community stating, "localization guides everything we do, from sourcing raw ingredients and materials, to employing area talent" and that his driving objective is to strike "a successful balance between giving back to our community and personal profit."

All Aboard the Train to Great Beer

Tired Hands sits at one end of the unofficial R-5 Pub Crawl. The lineup of great beer destinations includes those that can be reached within a very easy walk of a station stop along SEPTA's Paoli/Thorndale regional rail line, formerly known as the R-5.

The crawl has been done in both directions and after Tired Hands includes, in order to the west, Teresa's Next Door, TJ's, Flying Pig Saloon, and Station Taproom. In the Beer Is Going Places section, I describe how one of the longest-running great train station beer bars can be found at Bridgewater's Pub inside the 30th Street Station, reachable by this same train approximately 20 minutes to the east.

If you're a visitor to Philadelphia, grab a train schedule to review over a beer at Bridgewater's, then jump on board and head west. Next stop, great beer.

For fun with names, check out just a few of the most unusual (and longest) beer names in the industry that have graced the draft board at Tired Hands: The Light That Spills Out of the Hole in Your Head, We Are All Infinite Energy Vibrating at the Same Frequency, We Are 138, Stare at Yourself in the Mirror Until You Feel a Burning Sensation, Screeching Loud Thrashing Death Metal Offensive Song, Mrs. Pigman, and Communication Is the Key Lime Pie Coconut Cream Pie.

VAULT BREWING COMPANY

10 S. Main St., Yardley, PA 19067; (267) 573-4291; vaultbrewing.com; @VaultBrewingCo
Founded: 2012 **Founders:** James Cain, Jim Cain, John Cain **Brewers:** Mark Thomas, Jason Macias, Richard Bolster **Seasonals/Special Releases:** All beers are rotating seasonals with the Sweet Potato Ale, Breakfast Stout, Russian Imperial Stout (barrel-aged), Aussie IPA (in various forms), Chinook IPA, and Vault IPA returning the most frequently

Vault Brewing is one of the most aesthetically pleasing new brewpubs to hit the Philly area scene in the past couple of years. It could be the reuse of some of the old bank's (circa 1889) design. It could be the open-air kitchen. Maybe it's the use of the bank's original vault for conditioning and serving cask beers. Or it could be the sight of the brewing operation mere feet away from the barstools.

Put it all together with decent beers backed up by a solid kitchen menu and the recipe for brewing success in this Delaware River town is in place. The brewery saw output increase by around 200 barrels in 2014 and celebrated its 100th batch with only the second bottling effort—a very smooth and fruit-forward **Belgian-style Golden Ale** (9.2% ABV) that used labels to mimic bank notes that were found during the renovation and development of the brewpub. The actual bank notes can be found hanging as artwork in the vault dining room.

Since no beer has been brewed more than a handful of times in the 2 years of existence, it's a bit difficult to give recommendations that you can directly use. However, do be on the lookout for a dry and smoky **Rye Stout** (5% ABV), a citrusy and piney **Simarillo IPA** (6.1% ABV), and a biscuit malty **East Kent ESB** (5.2% ABV).

The kitchen does its thing the fresh way; there's no freezer. The wide variety of beer styles works well with the diverse menu, which includes well-done and popular dishes like pad thai popcorn, tomato bisque, and buffalo cauliflower, lightly breaded and served with blue cheese and hot sauce. Flatbreads from the wood-fired oven wow the guests with brown sugar buffalo, wild mushroom (with garlic truffle), and duck confit and apple (with bacon, blue cheese, and honey). For dessert, Hand Pie (strawberry, rhubarb, fig, berry reduction) and Wood-fired S'more (beer marshmallow, Belgian chocolate) take the beer pairing possibilities right through to the end of dinner.

VICTORY BREWING COMPANY

420 Acorn Ln., Downingtown, PA 19335; (610) 873-0881; victorybeer.com; @VictoryBeer
Founded: 1996 **Founders:** Ron Barchet and Bill Covaleski **Brewers:** Barchet, Covaleski, Scott Dietrich (VP of Brewing Operations), Adam Bartles (Director of Brewing Operations), and a team of many others **Year-Round Beers:** Braumeister Pils, DirtWolf, Donnybrook Stout, Golden Monkey, Headwaters Pale Ale, Helios, HopDevil, Prima Pils, Storm King Stout, Victory Lager, V-12 **Seasonals/Special Releases:** Old Horizontal Barleywine, St. Boisterous, Swing Session Saison, Summer Love, Yakima Glory, and many others

With breweries popping up seemingly every week around every corner, the back story of two buddies from childhood going into the beer business sounds more common than ever.

There could be others that go back further, but Barchet and Covaleski own that oft-quoted story. As Victory's history is told, it dates to the school bus in 1973 on the way to fifth grade. A lot of time and individual brewing and schooling took place on their way to 1996 and bringing their career paths together in Downingtown, approximately 35 miles west of Philadelphia.

Victory has continued to pour millions of dollars into their growth; the last major renovation came in 2008 when they replaced the long bar and relatively simple restaurant that was in a brewery with a bona-fide family restaurant that just so happens to have a connected top-notch brewery. The kitchen sports a full menu of appetizers, cheese, charcuterie, other small plates, and a hearty list of sandwiches and hearth-baked pizzas. Each menu item comes with a recommended beer selection, like a perfectly paired **HopDevil IPA** (6.7% ABV) with the Chester County pork shoulder sandwich and a Kennett pizza chock full of mushrooms to go with the crisp and earthy **Spalt Select Braumeister Pils** (~5% ABV).

Though, some days, the award-winning, perfect **Prima Pils** (5.3% ABV) seems to go with just about anything. Visitors to Victory from outside the region will find the choices at the pub staggering—23 taps and 3 handpumps of beer, a handful of which are typically exclusive to the Victory restaurant and bar.

Look for special events at the brewery throughout the year, from yoga to vertical tastings of Old Horizontal and dinners with their German hop farmers to chili cook-offs. Also be sure to ask if any special beers from the barrel-aging projects that the brewery undertakes from time to time are available. Oak Horizontal (**Old Horizontal** base beer), White Monkey (**Golden Monkey**), and Red Thunder (**Baltic Thunder**) are three that have spent time in wine or bourbon barrels.

The retail shop has all your Victory beer, accessories, and swag needs covered. I'll suggest one more that falls into the category of take-home, food, and beer all wrapped up in one container: Victory Ice Cream. The **Triple Monkey** version (**Storm Drop** and **Hopped-Up Devil** are two other mighty fine ones) could be the best thing to happen to ice cream in quite some time. It's Golden Monkey wort with bananas and pecans and it brings out the essence of walking through a brewhouse blended into rich ice cream. Doubters of beer and ice cream need only grab a **Golden Monkey** (9.5% ABV), a gold medal recipient at the 2014 Great American Beer Festival by the way, for a natural pairing (a **Sunrise Weiss** could work as well) with a couple of scoops of ice cream to cap off a perfect night.

More Hometown Victories

Victory Brewing Company was already a formidable establishment in the ranks of the country's largest and most significant breweries. In 2014, they unveiled the next big piece of the puzzle in Parkesburg, Pa., which is approximately twenty miles west of its original location. The potential to brew at least two to three times more Victory will be a huge win for fans of great beer worldwide when they near full production later in 2016.

Not to leave any stone unturned, to supplement growth plans, Victory also opened a brewpub called Victory at Magnolia. It is located on the edge of downtown Kennett Square, naturally delivering a full lineup of Victory beers, and featuring a 7-barrel brewing system from which "test batch" beers will emerge. Plans are also in place to bring a Victory brewpub to Leesburg, VA, in 2016.

Beer Bars & Restaurants

THE BOOKSTORE SPEAKEASY

336 Adams St., Bethlehem, PA 18015; (610) 867-1100; bookstorespeakeasy.com; @BstoreSpeakeasy

Draft Beers: 6 **Bottled/Canned Beers:** Around 50

One of many rules for a speakeasy is to always speak easy. A restrained rumble is the extent of the noise at this somewhat hidden gem in the Southside of Bethlehem. Not far from Lehigh University and the former Bethlehem Steel Plant, which is slowly transforming into an entertainment destination, The Bookstore Speakeasy is a dimly candlelit bright spot on the local food and beverage scene.

Opened in 2010, but with a building history that reportedly includes time served as an authentic speakeasy during Prohibition, the bar's emphasis on well-made and creative cocktails persists. Their focus on beer has picked up in the past couple of years and resident bartender Michael Claypool and his depth of knowledge are a part of the reason for its success. A careful list of six drafts and a longer bottle list categorized by geography and flavor profiles provide the liquid basis for a good night at The Bookstore, and the kitchen turns out supporting small plates of meats, cheeses, and delectable treats like escargots, cucumber and watermelon salad, and spiced chickpea popcorn.

Apart from speaking at respectable levels, other fun house rules printed in the menu include, among others: "Texting while in the company of others is impolite . . ."; "No standing at the bar . . ."; "Long Island is a place, not a drink . . ."; "Gentlemen, if in doubt, think 'What would Dean Martin do' . . ."; "Ladies, if in

doubt, think 'What would Audrey Hepburn do' . . ."; and "Exit the Bookstore quickly and quietly. We don't want the neighbors to know what we've been up to this evening."

CAPONE'S

224 W. Germantown Pike, Norristown, PA 19401; (610) 279-4748; thebottleshop.biz
Draft Beers: 30 **Bottled/Canned Beers:** 400

Capone's, the restaurant, was opened in 1974 and the bottle shop later in 1983. Matt Capone, second generation owner, raised the craft-beer cred at Capone's in the early '80s when he stepped up the selections to include six-packs of Sierra Nevada and later in the decade with Dock Street and Stoudts. He took it to yet another level when a customer made the analogy to wine drinkers and suggested that he could sell larger-format bottles.

Beer hunters now trek from around the region looking to procure bottles of rare beer for themselves or to use in online trades. Capone personally invests a lot of time and energy establishing relationships with distributors and brewers to match their supply with consumer demand.

Capone's hosts events of all stripes throughout the year—tap takeovers by brewery and by style are a particular strength—but the one that seems to capture the enthusiasm of the beer-loving geekerie the most is the Black Friday event. Beginning when legally allowed to serve alcohol—7 a.m. on weekdays—Capone's opens the day after Thanksgiving for a different kind of shopping. Many coveted beers are served on Black Friday and have been known to include Russian Rivers, Firestone Walkers, and Cantillons just to name only a few among the many drool-worthy beers that customers line up for in the pre-dawn hours.

Food-wise, the menu is filled with plenty of great tavern standards but the one most raved about item is the Bee Sting Wings. Offered as a special on Monday evening and late night Tuesday through Thursday, a dozen of these sweet and spicy wings pair up perfectly with a good porter or stout on tap such as the Stone Smoked Porter, Lancaster Milk Stout, or Heavy Seas Peg Leg Imperial Stout.

CRAFT ALE HOUSE

708 W. Ridge Pike, Limerick, PA 19468; (484) 932-8180; craftalehouse.com;
@CraftAleHouse
Draft Beers: 16 **Bottled/Canned Beers:** 375 to 400

An unofficial study might suggest that Craft Ale House is the closest high-quality beer bar to a nuclear power plant, the Limerick Generating Station. Craft opened in 2008 to give locals a wider variety of great beer than had previously been available. A few other establishments have come on board in recent years, but this cornerstone bar of Suburban Beer Week is still the top choice for many.

In addition to the Suburban Beer Week each April, the bar routinely has brewery spotlights throughout the year—like the annual Tröegs extravaganza each December and frequent bar-top firkins. The bar has a corner of beer coolers stocking many popular take-out options and live music regularly fills the air on Friday and Saturday nights.

The always-fresh kitchen (no walk-in freezer) consistently puts out a menu of satisfying and beer-friendly food such as a roasted pork sandwich, Funky Farmhouse Mussels, spinach and goat cheese salad, and shrimp and bacon mac 'n' cheese. Further tying in beer to the local cause, Craft makes their beer bread from Sly Fox Brewery's spent grain and sources many other menu items from local farmers and growers.

THE DRAFTING ROOM

635 N. Pottstown Pike, Exton, PA 19341; (610) 363-0521; draftingroom.com;
@Draftingoom
Draft Beers: 12, plus 1 handpump **Bottled/Canned Beers:** Around 100

The western suburbs of Philadelphia historically have been a bit ahead of the regional beer curve. Long before most of the newer competition came along, The Drafting Room (TDR) was on the scene beginning in 1994.

Through the years, TDR has seen more than its share of tap takeovers (before they were referred to as such), dinners, and annual anniversary parties. Sierra Nevada, Victory, Bell's, and Tröegs have near permanence on TDR's draft tower. Tröegs, in fact, has helped commemorate each of TDR's last 10 anniversaries with an exclusively brewed beer.

Behind the push for great beer and food at TDR is owner Howard Weintraub, manager Keith Bufford, and bartenders Heather Higgins and Caitlin Bailey. Through the years, TDR has been a launching pad for Patrick Mullin (director of sales at Sly Fox Brewery), Sean McGettigan (proprietor of Station Taproom), and Steven Hayden (Champps Americana).

TDR regularly stages eagerly anticipated events like animal-rescue fundraisers, the annual Hop Fest, Barrel-aged Stout Takeover, and Wet Hop Harvest promotion. In addition, locals return regularly for a customer loyalty program, a growler tracking program, and a well-regarded kitchen that puts out one of the area's best Sunday brunch values.

FLYING PIG SALOON

121 E. King St., Malvern, PA 19355; (610) 578-9208
Draft Beers: 18, plus 1 handpump **Bottled/ Canned Beers:** 150+

The Flying Pig Saloon sports the markings of any town's perfect neighborhood pub. Saturday nights of debauchery followed by Sunday's after-church crowd sitting next to rabid football fans—the kind of environment where anything can happen and all are welcome. From a beer perspective, it can be difficult to tell which is more coveted, the constantly rotating set of draft beers or the cellared vintage bottle collection, carefully maintained by co-owner Steve Iacobucci.

Located just off the train tracks and a short walk from the station, The Pig is often included on many "R-5 Pub Crawls," where beer lovers hook up a half-dozen of their favorite beer destinations near train stations of the former Pennsylvania railroad line that today carries SEPTA and Amtrak trains. (See "All Aboard . . ." sidebar).

HALF MOON SALOON

108 W. State St., Kennett Square, PA 19348; (610) 444-7232; halfmoonrestaurant.com; @HalfMoonKennett
Draft Beers: 20, plus 3 handpumps **Bottled/Canned Beers:** 50+

In Kennett Square, menus are expected to feature some of the local product that has made the area famous as the Mushroom Capital of the World. At Half Moon, what may come as a pleasant surprise is the wide variety of wild game on the menu in addition to a decently varied beer menu.

A visit to Half Moon is enjoyable enough spent at the throwback saloon bar at street level. In nicer weather, though, opt for the long climb (optional elevator) to the rooftop deck and its 360-degree views of the area. Windows can enclose the dining area during inclement weather.

A full list of draft and bottle beers—including an impressive three handpumps—will keep you busy enough, particularly with the serious attention given to the Belgian and Belgian-style beers on the menu.

It's the food, however, that will truly beg for your attention. For years, Half Moon has been known as the go-to place in the area for its dedication to wild game. Selections have included alligator, buffalo, camel, elk, kangaroo, pheasant, quail, rabbit, venison, and wild boar and prepared as steaks, tacos, sausages, and burgers.

HULMEVILLE INN

4 Trenton Rd., Hulmeville, PA 19047; (215) 750-6893; hulmevilleinn.com; @HulmevilleInn

Draft Beers: 19, plus 1 handpump **Bottled/Canned Beers:** 75–100

Just up the creek a bit from Neshaminy Creek Brewing Company in nearby Croydon is the Hulmeville Inn. There must be something special in the water that flows through it since just as the brewery makes top-notch beers, The Hulmeville has propped up three consecutive Philly Beer Geeks: in 2010 (Steve Hawk), 2011 (Natalie DeChico), and 2012 (Steve Mashington).

Hulmeville Inn is a fertile breeding ground for beer geeks with its year-round selection of stellar beers in a down-to-earth atmosphere where customers know their pilsners from their porters. Contestants in the annual competition that culminates during Philly Beer Week with a bounty of cash and beer-related prizes must first have passed a prequalifying round at a sponsor bar. They then must navigate a grueling process of surviving a semi-final and final round.

The beer education at the 200-plus-year-old historic former roadside hotel between Philadelphia and Trenton is year-round. The bar hosts numerous events including tap takeovers, special firkins, and the meeting of the local ALEiens Homebrew Club. Darts, pool, and recently going smoke-free provide yet more reasons to visit this Bucks County treasure.

ISAAC NEWTON'S

18 S. State St., Newtown, PA 18940; (215) 860-5100; isaacnewtons.com; @IsaacNewtons
Draft Beers: 22, plus 1 handpump **Bottled/Canned Beers:** 150 to 200

Isaac Newton's is nearing 25 years in a 200+-year-old barn building in the heart of this lower Bucks County town. The scientist's study of gravitational force must explain how the bar continues to put great beer out in droves and the beer faithful are attracted.

Beers like Delirium Tremens, Founders All Day IPA, Left Hand Sawtooth, and something from Yards and Allagash are nearly permanent on the draft lines. A well-planned list of IPAs, sours, wheats, and Belgians is dependably available on a regular basis, for weekly specialty tappings of something special and/or rare, and at monthly massive tap takeovers.

From the kitchen, a wide variety of flatbreads, Caesar salads, and burgers provides plenty of options to serve with great beers and fill a dinner table. Enjoy the beer and food in the comfortable inside space or, in nice weather, angle for an outdoor backyard patio table.

THE NORTHEAST TAPROOM

1101 N. 12th St., Reading, PA 19604; (610) 685-0102; northeasttaproom.com
Draft Beers: 12, plus 1 handpump **Bottled/Canned Beers:** around 70

Everyone defines "dive bar" a bit differently, but The Northeast Taproom probably turns up on most locals' list as one—one that's been serving "different" beer since 1983. Out-of-towners likely won't find themselves in this neighborhood, even if at nearby Albright College, Reading Liederkranz, an arena event downtown, or on a drive up to the scenic Pagoda and overlook.

But, if you know about this bar with its brewery swag, Elvis and kitschy collections of miscellany on the walls, lots of live music, the bathroom sink outside the restrooms, no food menu, Phillies games on the television, and tough-to-find parking, then you have found one of the favorite dive bars around.

From a beer perspective, they pay attention to proper spelling, like putting the umlaut in Tröegs, have fun with phonetic spelling of Ying-Ling, rarely pour a beer over $5, and host the occasional tap takeover.

PORTERS' PUB

700 Northampton St., Easton, PA 18042; (610) 250-6561; porterspubeaston.com
Draft Beers: 12 **Bottled/Canned Beers:** around 130

The Porter brothers saved the 1830s-era building by restoring and opening it 1990 as Porters' Pub, preserving some of the original stonework along the way. They've been satisfying Easton locals with food and beer ever since. The barroom and adjoining dining room strike the appropriate cozy neighborhood feel to encourage friendly banter among customers and with bar staff.

The well-trained staff serves a varied list of draft beers, an even more impressive bottle list, and a spectacular Bloody Mary with a German rauchbier and kitchen-made garlic mash mixed in for a truly unique experience. A Sunday morning beer or Bloody Mary works perfectly at Porters' with a brunch menu that includes a unique Mediterranean Benedict and Porters' Hash, with smoked salmon, bacon, and potatoes.

A few tables line the front sidewalk and live music ranges from open mic to jazz to Irish each week to provide additional entertainment. Inside, local artwork is scattered across the walls, further tying them to their neighborhood. If the Porters sound like fun to party with, the ownership plans annual trips around the world, such as the one they recently returned from in Belgium.

RAILROAD ST. BAR & GRILL

36 Railroad St., Linfield, PA 19468; (610) 495-7043; railroadstreet.com; @RailroadStreet
Draft Beers: 34, plus 1 handpump **Bottled/Canned Beers:** 100+

Remember that so-called unofficial study mentioned in the Craft Ale House list-ing a few pages earlier? The folks at The Rail might have something to say about that. Located not even two miles as the ol' crow flies from the Limerick nuclear power plant, the bar serves up local, geeky, drool-inducing Pizza Boy beers alongside equally geeky beers from Belgium's Struise brewery.

Housed in a 165-year-old former hotel, the bar's casual atmosphere is a perfect place to enjoy local burgers and sausage, tacos, and a host of delectable grilled cheese sandwiches such as the lobster grilled cheese. There's even a wall of pinball machines for additional entertainment.

STATION TAPROOM

207 W. Lancaster Ave., Downingtown, PA 19335; (484) 593-0560; stationtaproom.com; @StationTaproom
Draft Beers: 12, plus 1 handpump **Bottled/Canned Beers:** Around 30

Station Taproom is often the first (or last) stop along the R-5 Pub Crawl (see "All Aboard . . ." sidebar). The bar is located directly across from the Downingtown train station, which ervices both Amtrak and SEPTA trains.

Inside the cozy neighborhood tavern, owner Sean McGettigan's chalkboard beer list and well-built menu from a small kitchen do a great job at serving some of the area's most interesting food and beer in an easygoing atmosphere. Resounding favorites on the food menu include beet salad with feta, truffle fries with sea salt, fish-and-chips, Thai red curry, and green tomato Benedict.

Plenty of standouts on the bottle menu from Allagash, Chimay, Orval, Russian River, and Weyerbacher give the draft list a run for its money, which itself boasts a strong year-round diver-sity in varying flavors, colors, and alco-hol strengths.

STRANGE BREW TAVERN

1996 S. 5th St., Allentown, PA 18103; (610) 841-3610; strangebrewtavern.co;
@StrangeBrew610
Draft Beers: 20 **Bottled/Canned Beers:** 100+

Over the last couple of years, Strange Brew has built a following on the south side of Allentown with its large bar and dining area, a pool table, and an inviting oblong bar.

The taps are pouring typically at least 75 percent craft beers, and frequent guests join the Century Mug Club to track the pre-selected beers on the list and, upon completion, earn a special Strange Brew mug.

In addition to being another hangout at which to enjoy local sports, great beer, and company, there's weekly live music, events during Lehigh Valley Beer Week, and great bar food options. Boom Boom Shrimp, pierogies, chicken wings, and a long list of sandwiches are menu standouts to get you through an evening of beer.

TERESA'S NEXT DOOR

126 N. Wayne Ave., Wayne, PA 19087; (610) 293-9909; teresas-cafe.com;
@TeresasNextDoor
Draft Beers: 24, plus 2 handpumps **Bottled/Canned Beers:** Around 200

This is the fourth entry on the suburban Philadelphia list of high-quality bars that fall along the unofficial R-5 Pub Crawl rail route (see "All Aboard . . ." sidebar). Co-owner Andy Dickerson, beverage director Chris Peters, and the well-trained Teresa's Next Door team provide perfectly executed food and beer menus, with glassware and service befitting one of the top beer destinations in Philly's western suburbs.

Teresa's quickly began opening minds and palates in 2007 on Philadelphia's famed Main Line with the use and hand-drying of appropriate glassware that bordered on a near obsession. The beer menu selection has a strong Belgian focus but also contains other hard-to-find beers that also served as an eye-opener for many.

Hotly sought-after beers from breweries like Cantillon, De Dolle, De La Senne, Drie Fonteinen, Hof Ten Dormaal, Jolly Pumpkin, Malheur, Russian River, Struise, Tilquin, and all the Trappist breweries but Westvleteren can routinely be found either on the draft or bottle list. A special treat is a glass of the highly-regarded De Garre Tripel, an experience that is rarely replicated outside of Bruges.

The kitchen leaves nothing to chance with mussels and tacos, each done a half-dozen different ways, an assortment of wild game, and a special-events menu that elevates the concept of food and beer pairing to a higher level. Half-priced cheese makes Sunday a perfect day to visit.

TJ'S
35 Paoli Plaza, Paoli, PA 19301; (610) 725-0100; tjsbeer.com; @TJsBeer
Draft Beers: 26 **Bottled/Canned Beers:** Around 50

The third bar mentioned in this chapter near a rail station (see "All Aboard . . ." sidebar) is TJ's, which recently celebrated its 11th anniversary. After 2 years in, they began introducing customers to a more interesting and varied lineup of beer than they'd previously been accustomed to at TJ's predecessors. They also went smoke-free before the state required it by law. All steps to providing one of the most beer-friendly atmospheres in the area.

Over the years, as competition around them increased, TJ's continued to find ways to keep up with, and stay ahead of, the game. Special events and tastings, weekly theme nights, and keg kicker happy hour specials draw attention to the steady rotation of beer.

The dining room has its own digital draft boards hanging, but families come to TJ's as much for the food menu as beer geeks do for the beer. And as the beer menu has kept pace with the frantic geekerie surrounding the industry, so too has the kitchen's menu to match the beer. The menu is updated a few times throughout the year and is tightly focused on delivering high-quality and interesting food. The mac and cheese section, Korean boneless wings, nachos, and a long list of creative salads, sandwiches, and burgers are not to be missed.

But for all the great food and beer being served at TJ's, the recently updated atmosphere and standard-issue personalized and educated service make each visit memorable. Owners Terri Villante and Jeff Miller constantly give credit to the team of longtime staff members Amy Flather (assistant GM), Jon Reynders (kitchen manager), Scott Blain (head bartender), Sam Harrington (assistant kitchen manager), Joe Alway, Staci Klostas, Laurie DiMidio, Kevin Neill, and Colleen Fitzpatrick.

TRAPP DOOR

4226 Chestnut St., Emmaus, PA 18049; (610) 965-5225; thetrappdoorgastropub.com; @TheTrappDoor
Draft Beers: 6, plus 3 handpumps **Bottled/Canned Beers:** 175+

The roadside pub sneaks up on travelers zipping along Route 29 (Chestnut Street). But once parked in the ample parking lot and inside, guests are ensconced in comfortable surroundings shut off from the busy road and free to enjoy beers from a small but well-selected list of drafts (including an attention-grabbing three handpumps) and an extensive menu of bottles covering American, Belgian, English, and German.

The dining room holds around 40 people and the bar an additional 15 to 20; an outdoor patio provides alfresco dining and drinking on nice-weather days. From the menu, expect to find a frequently changing menu in response to local meats, cheeses, and produce favored by the kitchen. If the short rib pierogies are available, do order them and find a beer like a handpumped Oskar Blues Old Chub. Spring onion chicken sausage, pastrami-crusted pork belly sandwich, and pan-seared walleye are just a few other eye-catching selections.

Trapp Door also provides featured food and beer pairings such as a recent spot-on example of flank steak and eggplant with a Penn Bock from Pittsburgh. Live music is usually provided a few nights a week and creates a lively atmosphere.

UNION JACK'S INN ON THE MANATAWNY

546 Manatawny Rd., Boyertown, PA 19512; (610) 689-0189; unionjacksmanatawny.com; @UJsManatawny
Draft Beers: 17 **Bottled/Canned Beers:** 400+

Union Jack's has a handful of locations around the Philadelphia region, none perhaps more serene than the one tucked away behind cornfields and along a creek between Boyertown and Oley.

Though the charming pub provides a perfect place to enjoy a meal and a few glasses of beer—the list is roughly one-third local—the outdoor multilevel stone patio in pleasant weather is the place to be. The bank of the babbling Manatawny Creek holds the outdoor concert stage, which wakes up the bucolic scene a couple of times a week. Union Jack's takes care of the local beer geeks a few times a year with special events. Hopfest is one of the more popular ones and occurs the day before Easter each year to showcase some of the country's most hop-filled delights.

To complement the well-maintained year-round beer list, the kitchen does its part by turning out a menu full of standard, satisfying tavern fare, including chicken wings more than a dozen ways, La Fin du Monde–seasoned mussels, and English-themed shepherd's pie and bangers and mash befitting the cozy English-like pub atmosphere.

THE WHIP TAVERN

1383 N. Chatham Rd., Coatesville, PA 19320; (610) 383-0600; thewhiptavern.com; @TheWhipTavern
Draft Beers: 10, plus 1 handpump **Bottled/Canned Beers:** Around 100

The Whip has been serving up an English pub environment, horse country-style, in Chester County since 2005. As riders on horseback and foxhounds traverse the hilly countryside, diners at The Whip, which is roughly halfway between Coatesville and Kennett Square, relax either inside by the fireplace with around 50 seats or creekside by the babbling Doe Run.

Cyclists, too, find The Whip to be a pleasant place to stop while navigating the country roads, if not for the food and beverage then for the generously installed water bottle–filling faucet outside the kitchen entrance.

From the bar, the usual standbys include Guinness and Old Speckled Hen mixed in among drafts from locals like Spring House, Philadelphia Brewing, and Tröegs. The bottle list overflows with plenty of American and UK bottles ranging from Adnams, Belhaven, Fuller's, Thornbridge, Theakston, Samuel Smith, Wells, and Young's to Crabbie's Ginger Beer and BrewDog. They likewise stock quite a few ciders, including a house cider created by Phoenixville's Blue Marble.

Out of the kitchen, expect plenty of UK favorites like Welsh rarebit (even tastier at half price on Monday), bubble and squeak, toad in the hole, and curry specials executed quite well and served in the cozy atmosphere of this rural Chester County gem.

Ambler—Pub Crawl

Of course it makes perfect sense to have a pub crawl in a town named Ambler. It's the perfect kind of town to go ambling for a beer. Plus, the town is easily accessed by a regional rail line that runs through Center City Philadelphia.

If you come by car, this pub crawl can begin at the historic Broad Axe Tavern, but after that the keys can be put away as you stroll the streets of the charming, barely 1-square-mile town of Ambler. Perhaps no other pub crawl in this book comes with as many different ways to enjoy our favorite beverage as this one does—history, sports bar, barbecue, brewpub, dive bar. There are even a couple of very good BYOs (El Limon and Saffron) if you have some bottles in tow from Amber Beverage Exchange beer distributor. Test it for yourself to see if you agree.

TOTAL WALKING DISTANCE: 0.7 mile

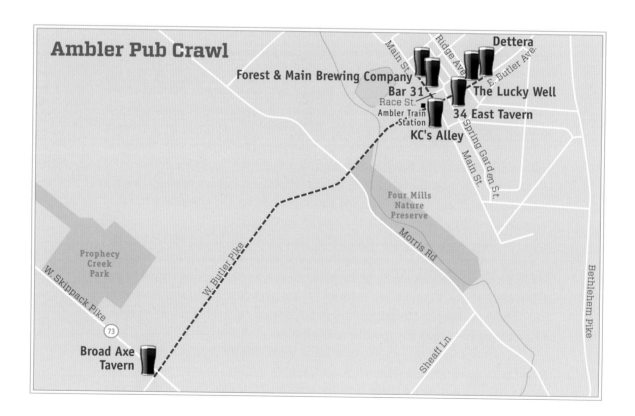

Ambler Pub Crawl

Forest & Main Brewing Company

Dettera

Bar 31

The Lucky Well

Race St.

Ambler Train Station

34 East Tavern

KC's Alley

Four Mills Nature Preserve

Prophecy Creek Park

Broad Axe Tavern

Main St.

Ridge Ave.

E. Butler Ave.

Spring Garden St.

Main St.

Morris Rd

W. Skippack Pike

W. Butler Pike

Bethlehem Pike

Sheaff Ln

73

Broad Axe Tavern, 901 Butler Pike, Ambler, PA 19002; (215) 643-6300; thebroadaxe
tavern.com; @BroadAxeTavern

History could be the only thing to overshadow the beers at Broad Axe Tavern, which
has been around since 1681 and has concentrated on a much-improved beer program
over the last several years. The reported ghosts might cast a shadow as well, but the
24 taps shine with beers that represent the local scene in addition to a very good
and lengthy bottle menu that features several Trappist ales.

As always, I recommend getting a good bite or two in at the beginning of each
pub crawl and here in Ambler is no different. Check out the Broad Axe's excellent
duck potstickers and cheesesteak spring rolls along wth a Westmalle Dubbel and
then head into downtown Ambler.

*Directions: From the Broad Axe Tavern, the next stop in the heart of Ambler is 1.5 miles
north on Butler Pike.*

KC's Alley, 10 W. Butler Pike, Ambler, PA 19002; (215) 628-3300; kc-alley.com

KC's Alley has everything a small-town tavern should have: cozy/warm atmosphere;
friendly bartenders; reasonably priced food; and of course a great list of 14 drafts.
Pop into KC's—"The House That Joe D Built"—for a beer or two from Michigan's New
Holland or Bell's. While it may not help you for a weekend pub crawl, the Monday
late-night and weekday happy hour specials are rather remarkable.

The kitchen puts out some nice offerings including small plates of crab wontons,
fries a half-dozen ways, and tavern-style French onion soup, which can help keep
your vitals in check as you move along this tour of Ambler.

*Directions: Turn right out of KC's Alley, cross Butler Pike, and walk three blocks to your
next stop.*

The Lucky Well, 111 E. Butler Ave., Ambler, PA 19002; (215) 646-4242; thelucky
well.com; @TheLuckyWell

Amber is full of good eats and The Lucky Well is in the class at the top of the
list. Beer and barbecue are a delight to behold (and consume, of course), so grab
a bowl of Texas poutine (i.e., with brisket) or a plate of BBQ deviled eggs and a
bottle of something like Dogfish Head's 90 Minute. If the timing is right for a bit
of whiskey, you've come to the right place and are in luck with a long list from
which to choose.

The aromas wafting through the air from the smoker will make it difficult to resist a full meal. Make a note to come back for a full dinner of brisket, ribs, and catfish.

Directions: Cross to the other side of Butler Pike, turn right, and walk two blocks to 34 East on East Butler Avenue.

34 East, 34 E. Butler Ave., Ambler, PA 19002; (267) 460-8269; 34easttavern.com; @34EastTavern

If you began watching a game at KC's Alley, this stop at 34 East will give you a great environment to continue watching it. There are draft lines of 24 beers, many falling into the sessionable range, perfect for lengthy pub crawls and watching games. Grab a Yards Brawler or Penn Dark Lager and enjoy the game and the social scene around the large square bar.

Directions: Back to the other side of Butler Pike once again to Dettera, which is only two blocks away and just a few doors from Lucky Well.

Dettera, 129 E. Butler Ave., Ambler, PA 19002; (215) 643-0111; dettera.com; @Dettera

Dettera is another stop in foodie-friendly Amber. No doubt wine is a serious focus here. For the sake of this beer tour, it's a good thing they bring the beer game to play too. Nine taps give you enough diversity in the beer list and the nearly forty bottles of beer provide even more interesting choices.

Whether it's local mushrooms (Kennett Square), oysters (Cape May), or tomatoes for gazpacho, they like local sourcing at Dettera and the Victory and DogFish Head breweries do their part in that role as well. Grab a Victory Golden Monkey and a sampler board of oysters, steak tartare, pork rillettes, and olives to satisfy any hunger pangs, but keep in mind that a meal is upcoming at Forest & Main.

Directions: For the longest walk of the crawl, ⅓ mile, turn right out of Deterra, walk four short blocks, turn right on Main Street and Forest & Main will be three blocks ahead on the right.

Forest & Main, 61 N. Main St., Ambler, PA 19002; (215) 542-1776; forestandmain.com

Daniel Endicott and Gerard Olson charged onto the regional brewing scene when they opened Forest & Main in 2012. It has turned into the perfect neighborhood getaway for a family dinner or a stop along the way on a night out with the crew.

At your second to last stop, grab a table or stool at the bar and soak up the attractively homey atmosphere. Plates of cauliflower lasagna, flatiron steak, fish-and-chips, or an F&M Burger with bacon mayonnaise for dinner should leave you quite content. Accompanying dinner should be a couple glasses of the beautiful Solaire saison (4.5% ABV) and, if you have time, an occasional release like the Wojtek strong porter (6.5% ABV).

Directions: On your walk along Main Street to Forest & Main, you passed your last stop, Bar 31.

Bar 31, 31 N. Main St., Ambler, PA 19002; (215) 646-0440; bar31.net
Dive bars have found their way into this book perhaps more so than might originally have been imagined. They're catching on. And even if the bar still allows smoking, as is the case at Bar 31, the beer list is top-notch. Bar 31 is an easy place to close out the night with a few more beers in its dimly lit throwback environment, complete with small windows, "guys" and "dolls" restrooms, and typical neighborhood dive-bar antics. Depending on the timing of your visit, you may have the pleasure of hearing some tales of the past from old-time bartender Gamby.

Directions: If you took the train to Ambler, you're a hop, skip, and a jump (hopefully no stumble) from the station. There's a shortcut through, Race Street, if that helps.

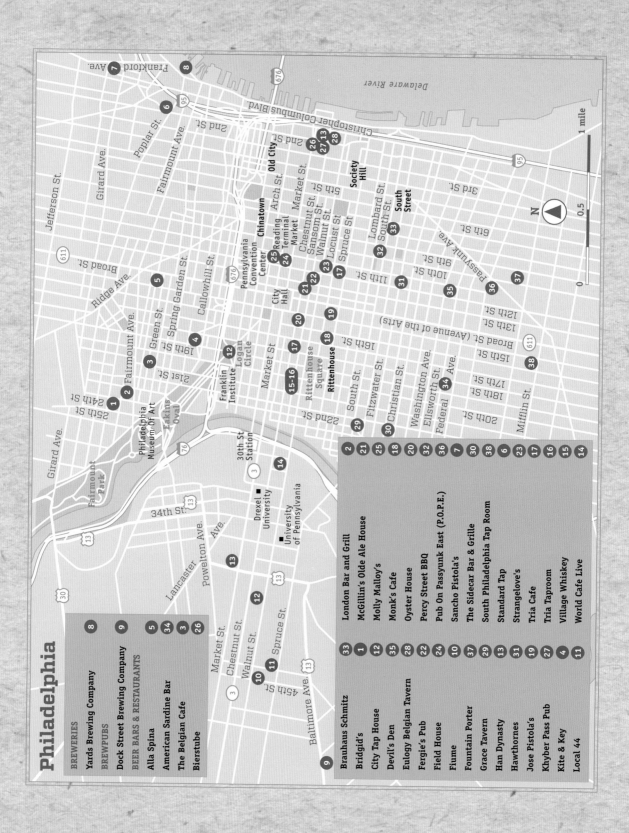

Philadelphia

BREWERIES

Yards Brewing Company — 8

BREWPUBS

Dock Street Brewing Company — 9

BEER BARS & RESTAURANTS

Alla Spina — 5
American Sardine Bar — 34
The Belgian Cafe — 3
Bierstube — 26

Brauhaus Schmitz — 33
Bridgid's — 1
City Tap House — 12
Devil's Den — 35
Eulogy Belgian Tavern — 28
Fergie's Pub — 22
Field House — 24
Fiume — 10
Fountain Porter — 37
Grace Tavern — 29
Han Dynasty — 13
Hawthornes — 31
Jose Pistola's — 19
Khyber Pass Pub — 27
Kite & Key — 4
Local 44 — 11

London Bar and Grill — 2
McGillin's Olde Ale House — 21
Molly Malloy's — 25
Monk's Cafe — 18
Oyster House — 20
Percy Street BBQ — 32
Pub On Passyunk East (P.O.P.E.) — 36
Sancho Pistola's — 7
The Sidecar Bar & Grille — 30
South Philadelphia Tap Room — 38
Standard Tap — 6
Strangelove's — 23
Tria Cafe — 17
Tria Taproom — 16
Village Whiskey — 15
World Cafe Live — 14

Philadelphia

Then there is Philadelphia. It cannot be avoided any longer. This book has gone to some pretty incredible destinations for beer at the brewery and beer at the bar. But for its history, the focus, and simply the sheer critical mass—which is both critical and massive—there's no beating Philadelphia's beer scene. Much of it, as you'll read, is in the long tradition of its pub-centric neighborhoods where residents and passers-through alike can easily sit and bend ears and elbows at the bar. Before you dismiss me as a homer, hear me out. Well, this isn't an audio book, so read all about it instead.

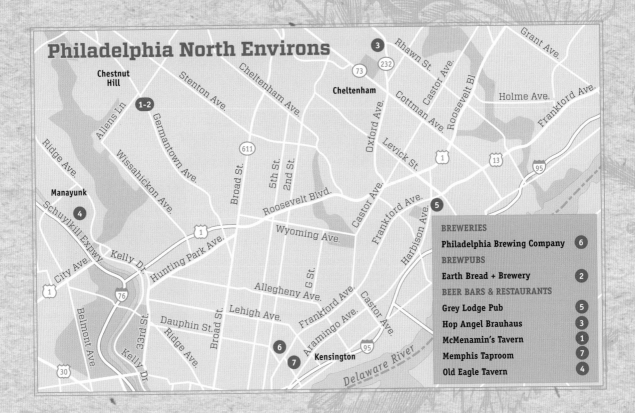

Philadelphia North Environs

BREWERIES
Philadelphia Brewing Company — 6
BREWPUBS
Earth Bread + Brewery — 2
BEER BARS & RESTAURANTS
Grey Lodge Pub — 5
Hop Angel Brauhaus — 3
McMenamin's Tavern — 1
Memphis Taproom — 7
Old Eagle Tavern — 4

PHILADELPHIA BREWING COMPANY

2440 Frankford Ave., Philadelphia, PA 19125; (215) 427-2739; philadelphiabrewing.com; @PhillyBrewing

Opened: 2008 **Founders:** Nancy Barton, William Barton, James McBride **Brewers:** Benjamin Schamberg and Joshua Ervine **Flagship Beer:** Kenzinger Beer **Year-Round Beers:** Walt Wit, Pennsylvania Pale Ale, Newbold IPA, Schwarzinger Black Lager **Seasonals/Special Releases:** Fleur De Lehigh, Harvest From The Hood, Joe Coffee Porter, Shackamaximum **Tours:** Free, Sat 12 to 3 p.m. **Taproom:** Open only during tour hours

The Philadelphia Brewing Company (PBC) could not be more aptly named. Formed in 2007 in the original Weisbrod & Hess brewery, PBC is hyper-focused in its community approach to representing itself and selling its beer in the local market. The brewery turns out a handful of year-round beers and a few extra seasonal ones to keep things interesting.

PBC is producing enough to keep the local markets around Philadelphia awash in their beer but still with an eye toward very carefully controlling growth into new markets like Pittsburgh. In the last couple of years, the brewery has purchased additional tanks, a centrifuge, and the property across the street.

From its core brands, the refreshing **Kenzinger** (4.5% ABV) and hop-flavorful **Pennsylvania Pale Ale** (5.25% ABV) are the ones that catch the quickest attention from beer lovers looking for a taste of the city's namesake brewery. The **Joe**

Beer Lover's Pick

Fleur De Lehigh
Style: Golden ale
ABV: 4.75%
Availability: Seasonal in spring and summer; 12-ounce bottles

Put this beer on the dinner table with plates of Thai food—like Tom Ka Gai, Vegetable Spring Roll, and Pad Kee Mao—and have your mind changed about the excellence of a beer when brewed with ginger root, lemongrass, rose hips, rhubarb, and cardamom.

Coffee Porter (5.5% ABV) combines roasted malts and roasted coffee in a wonderful beer, and the **Shackamaximum** (8% ABV) takes it to another level with a richly delicious imperial stout.

There are weekly tours, and the annual Open House after Thanksgiving offers the ability to taste the beer as close to the source as possible. The Atlantis Bar across the street from the brewery— it's a bit understated in its exterior appearance— gives beer lovers a chance not only to drink of the local brewery but also to soak up some the local community. You might even bump into an off-duty brewer.

YARDS BREWING COMPANY

901 N. Delaware Ave., Philadelphia, PA 19123; (215) 634-2600; yardsbrewing.com; @YardsBrew

Founded: 1994, in current location since 2008 **Founder:** Tom Kehoe **Brewers:** Tim Roberts (head brewer and production manager) and Mitch Albach (lead brewer) plus five shift brewers **Year-Round Beers:** Philadelphia Pale Ale, Extra Special Ale, India Pale Ale, Brawler, Love Stout, Thomas Jefferson Tavern Ale, George Washington Tavern Porter, and Poor Richard's Tavern Spruce **Seasonals/Special Releases:** Cape of Good Hope, Pynk, Rye, Saison **Tours:** Free, Sat and Sun **Taproom:** Yes **Naming Inspiration:** A loose British reference, not a yard of beer

Since moving the brewery in 2008 from the building where Philadelphia Brewing Company subsequently took shape, Yards has taken off and hit new levels in terms of both production output and regional visibility across five states. Where once it was a much smaller brewery in Kensington, Yards has been adding fermenters (up to 200 barrels in size) and longer brewing hours that produced 38,500 barrels in 2014.

Like many small startup breweries in recent years, Yards got its very nano-esque start in a Roxborough garage way back in 1994–95. It didn't take long for seekers of different beer to find the **Extra Special Ale (ESA)** on the down draft system at Bridgid's near the Philadelphia Museum of Art and other select accounts around the city. ESA is still one of Yards' most popular beers—a malt-forward brew with just a touch of hop bitterness for today's beer palates.

Yards is also well known for the **Ales of the Revolution** series, which can be found not only on retail shelves but at appropriately themed restaurants like City Tavern in Philadelphia and Jessop's Tavern in New Castle, Delaware. In the series, the **Poor Richard's Tavern Spruce** (5% ABV) is a food-friendly beer thanks

Philadelphia

to the blue spruce tips and molasses in the recipe. It holds up quite well with the rack of lamb at the City Tavern. The **Jefferson Tavern Ale** (8% ABV) is a dangerously smooth and easy-drinking beer. The **George Washington Porter** (7% ABV) presents big flavors of dark-roasted malts and goes great with a chunk of chocolate coffee almond brittle.

In recent awards news, the Tavern Spruce (bronze) and Brawler (silver) each took home medals in their respective categories from the 2013 Great American Beer Festival and the ESA a bronze in 2012. The Spruce repeated in 2014 with another bronze for its medal wall.

With the city and its Ben Franklin Bridge as scenic backdrop, Yards puts on two of the year's most eagerly anticipated beer events. The Real Ale Invitational is just as it sounds: some of the best cask-conditioned beer assembled by area brewers, plus a few from overseas. Smoke 'Em If Yous Got 'Em aims at a different cross-section of beer geekdom: those who love smoked beer and a barbecue competition with smoking-hot live music.

Beer Lover's Pick

Saison
Style: Saison
ABV: 6.5%
Availability: April through July; 12-ounce bottles
The style has a lot of latitude and Yards' Saison comes straight down the middle with a highly drinkable, pleasantly bitter, and slightly peppery profile. The beer is released in the warmer months, so think grilled chicken kebabs, spicy crab gazpacho, and shrimp ceviche as perfect companions on the dinner table.

Brewpubs

DOCK STREET BREWING COMPANY

701 S. 50th St., Philadelphia, PA 19143; (215) 726-2337; dockstreetbeer.com;
@DockStreetBeer
Opened: 1985 for bottling, 1989 on 18th Street, 2007 in current location **Founder:**
Rosemarie Certo **VP:** Marilyn Candeloro **Brewer:** Vince Desrosiers **Year-Round Beers:**
Rye IPA, Man Full of Trouble Porter, Summer Session, Royal Bohemian Pilsner **Seasonals/
Special Releases:** Dock Street Amber Ale and many others **Naming Inspiration:** Dock
Street, the road, passes over the old Dock Creek in Old City Philadelphia

Dock Street Brewing Company has a rich history and not just because they are
the oldest brewing establishment on this Philadelphia list. Dock Street's beers
served as the gateway for many discovering better beer around Philadelphia in the
late '80s and early '90s. Beer names like Bohemian Pilsner and Amber Ale should jog
some memories.

Dock Street fell off the scene for a few years around the turn of this century, but
when original owner Rosemarie Certo found herself again in ownership of the Dock
Street name, the brewery and restaurant took on a completely different focus from
its first time around. The first version of Dock Street was in the hustle and bustle of
downtown Philadelphia and in the shadow of the Four Seasons Hotel—as you can
imagine, a distinctively different atmosphere from today's incarnation.

Dock Street, today, lives at 50th and Baltimore in a converted firehouse. Easily
reached by the trolley, which deposits the thirsty beer traveler directly in front of
Dock Street's front door, or a healthy walk from University City and 30th Street
Station, Dock Street finds itself to
be a solid and integral member of
the local community. The brew-
ery actively and proudly supports
Philadelphia Film Society Film
Festival, ICA gallery openings, and
Women Against Abuse's Dish It Up.

At the table, the Trio Fries are
a must on the small bites menu
and give old-timers a throwback to
the original location. Order a basket with the **Rye IPA** (6.8% ABV)

and see what the fuss is about. A glass of **Bubbly Wit** (7.5% ABV) is a dangerously refreshing way to begin a visit to Dock Street, particularly on a hot summer day.

All of the beers from the 10-barrel brewhouse can find a pairing home on the menu, which draws the most attention for the exotically crafted pies coming out of the wood-fired pizza oven. The *Flammenkuche* with its gruyère, bacon, and crème fraîche matches up so well with the roasty and rich **Man Full of Trouble** porter (5% ABV). The Fig Jam bursts with sweet fig and savory bacon flavor and can be matched up with the strong flavor of the **Prince Myshkin Stout** (9.5% ABV) or contrasted with the light and crisp **Royal Bohemian Pilsner** (5% ABV), an original and still remarkable beer.

EARTH BREAD + BREWERY

7136 Germantown Ave., Philadelphia, PA 19119; (215) 242-6666; earthbreadbrewery.com; @EarthBreadBrew
Founded: 2008 **Founders:** Tom Baker and Peggy Zwerver **Brewer:** Tom Baker

Say "Tom and Peggy" to many beer lovers in the area and they know exactly where to send you. After leaving the beer geek destination—Heavyweight Brewing Company—behind in Ocean Township, NJ, Tom and Peggy opened what has become a widely appreciated destination for more than just beer geeks. Their establishment holds the name, Earth, in high regard as they practice everything from locally- and ethically-sourcing meats, cheeses, and produce to reducing their "true garbage" to four cans per week. Needless to say, the brewing equipment came from Heavyweight.

The brewpub sits on a corner of the historically rich and residential Mt. Airy and draws families as much as it does beer hunters. Baker hand-built the flat-

bread oven that sits in the corner of the restaurant and this oven turns out at least a dozen unique breads on any given day. The dough and mozzarella are freshly made daily at Earth and each flatbread is assembled upon ordering. "The Seed" (pine nuts, pumpkin seeds, and sesame seeds) and "The Caveman" (turkey sausage, chicken, and pepperoni) are two excellent versions to check out.

Fresh and unique is a mantra, likewise, in the 7-barrel brewery. Names of beers could not be listed above because Baker has rarely been known to brew the same beer twice in more than 6 years since opening. Neither can he be pinned to a style category as he brews what he feels or likes, including well-regarded Gruits, instead of by guidelines. It's another aspect of the brewpub that keeps local devotees returning on a regular basis. One beer, though, that Baker has done again is one that helped put him on the map back at Heavyweight Brewing—the Perkuno's Hammer. So he brews it again in 2014 and what happens? It wins a gold medal at the Great American Beer Festival against 41 other Baltic-style porters.

If Baker sounds like the kind of guy you'd like to brew with, Earth co-hosts an annual homebrew competition with The Malt House homebrew shop where the winner gets to brew their beer at the brewpub.

NODDING HEAD BREWERY AND RESTAURANT

noddinghead.com; @NoddingHeadBrew
Opened: 1999 **Owner:** Curt Decker **Brewer:** Gordon Grubb **Year-Round Beers:** 60 Schilling; 700 Level; All Night Ale; Bill Payer Ale; George's Fault, Grog; Ich Bin Ein Berlinerweisse; IPA; Monkey Knife Fight **Seasonals/Special Releases:** Many including variety of Phunk barrel-aged beers

The brewing history on the second floor at 1516 Sansom Street was begun by the Sam Adams Brewpub (malt extract brewing) in the '90s. Nodding Head converted it to an all-grain brew house and opened in 2000, turning out approximately 700 to 750 barrels per year. But the time came in 2014 for Nodding Head to move on to its next chapter, written in a south Philadephia neighborhood in the vicinity of Newbold. The signature bobbleheads (see below) will come along in the move and so will the beers that put the brewpub on the map. Check the website for details about their new location, which had not been confirmed at press time.

As customers reached the top of the long flight of stairs leading up from street level at the old Sansom Street location, they were greeted with a tall glass case filled with rows of bobbleheads. They wobbled slightly, hundreds of them, as if to acknowledge your arrival. One of owner Curt Decker's favorite bobblehead stories involves the beloved 2001 Philadelphia 76ers' improbable almost-championship season. During the finals, the brewpub auctioned off (for charity) the chance for a lucky patron to smash the Kobe Bryant bobblehead with a brewer's paddle. The remains will again be on display at the new bar among the 500+ fully assembled ones.

Ich Bin Ein Berliner Weisse (3.5% ABV) was one of the first, and arguably the largest produced, of its style to be made in the States. Long a low-alcohol, refreshing

Philadelphia

beer of German descent, the Berliner Weisse became a tart fan favorite at Nodding Head long before sours became all the rage. Be sure to try both with and without the flavored syrups.

After the Berliner Weisse, fans also flock to the brewpub for the superbly done English Brown **Grog** (5.25% ABV), crisp American Pale Ale **BPA** (5% ABV), the **Monkey Knife Fight** (4.5% ABV) lemongrass and ginger delight, and a slew of specialties, a growing number of which come from barrels stored at the back of the restaurant. These beers often, in proper Philadelphia Phorm, change Fs to PHs—as in **Phunky Tears**, a barrel-aged version of the popular **Crosby Tears**.

Rumblin', Stumblin', Bumblin'

The Royal Stumble has left many in its wake. This debaucherous event pits costumed brewers and reps against each other to see whose beer kicks first. It's a fairly frenzied and brash few hours and not necessarily for the faint of heart or liver. Great beers from local brewers come at attendees like rapid fire all in an attempt for the brewer/rep to be named the champion. If it were pretty, it wouldn't be any fun. Whether this continues at Nodding Head's new location remains to be seen.

ALLA SPINA

1410 Mount Vernon St., Philadelphia, PA 19130; (215) 600-0017; allaspinaphilly.com;
@AllaSpinaPhilly
Draft Beers: 20, including 2 handpumps **Bottled/Canned Beers:** 75+

With Alla Spina a member of the lauded Marc Vetri family of restaurants, the expectations for a high-quality kitchen and creative food menu should be obvious. A salumi plate, roasted bone marrow, poutine, and a carbonara burger are slam dunks on the dinner menu. Brunch is a great way to start the weekend with selections like pork belly biscuits, asparagus rotolo, and chocolate strawberry french toast.

They happen to deliver on the beer side of the equation as well. A steady flow of well-chosen Americans, Belgians, and Italians flow from the tap, can, and bottle list, fitting every pairing need, and served by a staff that is well trained to provide guidance.

In pleasant weather the doors open wide, and sidewalk dining just off Broad Street shows off the continuing turnaround of North Broad Street.

Philadelphia

BRAUHAUS SCHMITZ

718 South St., Philadelphia, PA 19147;
(267) 909-8814; brauhausschmitz.com;
@BrauhausSchmitz
Draft Beers: 30 **Bottled/Canned Beers:**
100+

In the '60s, all the hippies met on South Street, or so the song proclaimed. These days, it's lovers of soccer, German beer and food, and good times who flock to this destination that has helped the revitalization efforts of South Street. Owners Doug Hager and Kelly Hager (née Schmitz) have extensive German industry experience and heritage. They joined forces with Beate Green's deep knowledge and brewery relationships to create a unique atmosphere with great beers, some exclusive, from the likes of Andechs, Andorfer, Hacklberg, and Traunstein.

Chef Jeremy Nolen's kitchen upholds its end of the deal by putting out a menu that accentuates the authenticity of a German restaurant. Dishes like *Paprikash, Rouladen, Schweinshaxe,* and a *Wurst Brett* sampler are not to be missed.

The Brauhaus Schmitz team further demonstrates their appreciation for German beer and food with major festivals—Maifest and Oktoberfest—that they are driving forces behind, and a second spot called Wursthaus Schmitz in the historic Reading Terminal Market.

BRIDGID'S

726 N. 24th St., Philadelphia, PA 19130; (215) 232-3232; bridgids.com; @BridgidsPhilly
Draft Beers: 10, including two gravity taps **Bottled/Canned Beers:** Around 40

The ESA from Yards discussed earlier in their profile has been at Bridgid's on the down draft since the brewery's earliest days. Belgian beer? There was a focus on it here in the early '90s long before most others followed suit, and the beer menu still shows off a respectable number of Belgian selections mixed with a good dose of domestic craft beers.

Bridgid's quietly continues to exist as one of the city's neighborhood gems. Tucked neatly into a highly residential neighborhood near the Art Museum, the warmth exuded from the cozy bar scene and dining rooms make you feel as if you've walked around the corner to a friend's house for dinner. The updated kitchen serves fresh pasta dishes, mussels, and a delicious arancini plate with Humboldt Fog goat cheese. The separate bar menu and a late-night $5 "Shut Up 'n' Eat" are popular options as well.

CITY TAP HOUSE
3925 Walnut St., Philadelphia, PA 19104; (215) 662-0105; citytaphouse.com; @TapHouseUCity
Draft Beers: 60, including one handpump

The faculty and of-age college kids in University City had seen no comparable beer selection when City Tap House opened its doors in 2010.
The 12,000-square-foot establishment overlooking Walnut Street houses a large rectangular bar and a bilevel patio that has its own ample seating area around green gardens and five fire pits.

Andy Farrell is the recognizable face as managing partner at City Tap House and together with a well-trained staff puts out a year-round intense focus on beer with a wide offering of beers, education, and fun events. In 2014, they collaborated

with Yards on a house Belgian Brown called Just Off Walnut. Other breweries with frequent representation at City Tap House include Allagash, Bell's, Founders, Left Hand, Sierra Nevada, Sly Fox, and Victory.

The kitchen and its menu work well with the bar to present a dining experience where they complement each other. Exceptional menu items to seriously consider are the tartufo pizza with guanciale, the free-range PA turkey burger, and a bowl of the Pancho Spicy Chorizo Mussels.

City Tap House is part of the "family" that includes Pennsylvania 6, Field House, and a growing number of City Tap Houses, including a second City Tap House (Logan Circle) in Philadelphia and one in Washington, DC that opened in late 2013.

DEVIL'S DEN
1148 S. 11th St., Philadelphia, PA 19147; (215) 339-0855; devilsdenphilly.com; @DevilsDenPhilly
Draft Beers: 17 **Bottled/Canned Beers:** nearly 200

Nearing the magical seventh anniversary, it's difficult to recall when this space was the former beloved Felicia's restaurant. Devil's Den has become beloved in its own right as one of the first to create a beer destination south of Washington Avenue. Owner Erin Wallace also claims Old Eagle Tavern in the city's Manayunk section and Barren Hill Tavern & Brewery just across the city line in Lafayette Hill.

Taking its name from a hill in the Gettysburg Battlefield, Devil's Den serves as something of a bunker overlooking 11th Street. The cozy atmosphere, particularly with the fireplace aglow in the winter season, is the perfect place to hunker down with a bowl of Provençal mussels and a glass of Ommegang Witte or the duck confit fries with a Barren Hill Czech Pilsner. Executive Chef Paul Trowbridge's kitchen stocks

a menu full of favorites that also includes a salmon BLT and bacon-wrapped dates.

Devil's Den keeps customers coming back throughout the year with events that range from the annual lighting of the fireplace, to numerous featured brewery days, to Tour de France specials and giveaways. None, perhaps, is more popular than the Pucker Up Sour Fest in August, which has grown into a full week of rotating sour beers from both the US and abroad.

EULOGY BELGIAN TAVERN

136 Chestnut St., Philadelphia, PA 19106; (215) 413-1918; eulogybar.com; @ EulogyBar
Draft Beers: 28 **Bottled/Canned Beers:** 400

Philadelphia has Belgian beer covered. It's been doing it on a grander scale for a longer time than any other city in the States. Eulogy owner Michael Naessens, along with longtime veterans Chris Topham (beverage manager) and Theo Atkinson (executive chef), are a part of the reason. Topham's roots in Philly should serve him well as he has since gone off to Denver to open his own craft beer bar, Asbury Provisions.

The bar sits at the property where the renowned Bailey Banks & Biddle jewelry store was founded in 1832. These days it's the renowned Eulogy, which is serving Belgian beer cared for and presented with a near obsession to ensure the best experience for guests. The selection, the storage, the glassware, the staff education, and the serving are all part of the equation. For his efforts through the years, Naessens is one of a select group of Americans to have been knighted (in 2008) by the Chevalier du Fourquet des Brasseurs in Belgium and his establishment is consistently recognized as one of the top Belgian beer bars and restaurants of the area and the country.

When visiting Eulogy, be sure to check out the upstairs coffin room inspired by the bar Le Cercueil near the Grand Place in Brussels. From the menu, don't miss the exclusive Eulogy Busty Blonde Belgian Pale Ale, Belgian meatballs, Belgian rib eye, asparagus Ardennes (when in season), and naturally a bowl of moules and frites.

Naessens is also responsible for the growing lager scene at his Bierstube German Tavern just around the corner at 2nd and Market Streets.

FERGIE'S PUB

1214 Sansom St., Philadelphia, PA 19107; (215) 928-8118; fergies.com; @FergiesPhilly
Draft Beers: 10, plus 1 handpump **Bottled/Canned Beers:** around 30

Philadelphia's bar scene has quite a few recognizable people and places that come to mind, perhaps none more so than the inimitable Fergus Carey, aka simply Fergie. At the bar or walking the street, Fergie draws attention from anyone

Philadelphia

who has ever tipped back a glass in one of his bars. Fergie's Pub just hit its 20th anniversary and he also has ownership interests in Monk's Cafe, Grace Tavern, and The Belgian Cafe.

A visit to Fergie's delivers the Irish pub experience. There's typically Guinness and Belhaven on tap, along with something handpump-worthy, and a good representation of local beers. From the food menu, fish-and-chips, battered and fried in Yards Philadelphia Pale Ale, and shepherd's pie are sure bets. Traditional live Irish music from a group in the corner seals the deal.

During Philly Beer Week, Fergie's is one of a couple handfuls of dependable places putting on an event of some magnitude each day of the week, not the least of which is the unofficial ending to the 10-day week of debauchery: Totally Unnecessary Drink, affectionately referred to as The TUD.

FIUME
229 S. 45th St., Philadelphia, PA 19104
Bottled/Canned Beers: 120+

If a dive bar with no signage, website, or phone number located above an Ethiopian restaurant in West Philly sounds like a red flag, consider the great beer, creative cocktails and whiskey list, and live music nights to see if your mind is changed.

For nearly 14 years, Fiume has been the place to go that you want to tell everyone about while somehow not telling too many people. Chances are you'll see Kevin

or Brian behind the bar with their vast knowledge of beer, spirits, music, and the local scene. They love their Yards, Dogfish Head, and other locals as much as they love their Belgians, Germans, English, and West Coast friends at Green Flash, Lagunitas, and North Coast. It's small, it's different, and some live music nights it's downright crowded and frenzied, but that's what makes most dive bars cool. That's just between you and me.

FOUNTAIN PORTER

1601 S. 10th St., Philadelphia, PA 19148; (267) 324-3910; fountainporter.com;
@FountainPorter
Draft Beers: 20

Fountain Porter keeps it simple and simply does it well. The tastes, however, are much more complex in the diverse list of beers and the plates of meats, cheeses, pickles, olives, and cheeseburgers. Located in the vicinity of Passyunk Square—and drawing a naming reference from the nearby Singing Fountain—a stop at Fountain Porter makes for a nice one-two punch with the Pub On Passyunk East in the ever-growing quality beer scene of South Philadelphia.

GREY LODGE PUB

6235 Frankford Ave., Philadelphia, PA 19135; (215) 856-3591; greylodge.com;
@GreyLodge
Draft Beers: 10, plus 1 handpump **Bottled/Canned Beers:** 40

The general rule of thumb has typically been that the farther away from Center City to the northeast you go, the bleaker the beer landscape becomes. That rule has changed little throughout the years, but Grey Lodge as been doing its thing since 1996 in the Mayfair/Wissanoming section of the city. The bar, run by the incomparable Mike "Scoats" Scotese, draws inspiration for its name from the television show *Twin Peaks*. Like many Philadelphians, Scoats says that it all started with a Yards ESA in 1996 and that, along with similarly young breweries of that time, Grey Lodge has continued to grow with them.

Scoats, Chris Dominski (bar manager), and a team of bartenders (many with over 10 years of employment) conduct unique events throughout the year that often have a creative beer-date connection. Think Jan 20 (Dogfish 120 Minute IPA), Feb 2 (Groundhog Day festivities), Apr 4 (Quad Day), Apr 20 (Stone beer day), and Election Night (Yards Ales of the Revolution) as just a small sampling of the fun ways to enjoy great beer in Northeast Philly. Since 1998 all Friday the Thirteenths have become Friday the Firkinteenth, a daylong celebration of regional cask-conditioned beer served atop the bar.

Scoats (along with business partner Patrick McGinley) is also responsible for Hop Angel Brauhaus, which sits just inside the city's border in the Fox Chase section and focuses on locally made German-style beers.

Perhaps the best way to close out this entry on Grey Lodge is with a quote directly from Scoats: "Beer should bring people together, creating good cheer and good times. It should not divide people, which is why you can still buy a Miller Lite at the Grey Lodge if you so desire. But you can also get a Dogfish Head Bitches Brew too. Drinking beer should be fun. Going to a beer bar shouldn't be like going to beer church."

HAN DYNASTY
3711 Market St., Philadelphia, PA 19104; (215) 222-3711; handynasty.net;
@HanDynastyPhila
Draft Beers: 8 **Bottled/Canned Beers:** Around 40

You don't find many Chinese restaurants trying their hands at incorporating great beer on their menus. Han Dynasty, one of the Philadelphia region's most celebrated Szechuan-style Chinese restaurants, has taken up the cause of pairing the bold and sometimes intense flavors of the cuisine with the bold flavors from beers like Stone, Oskar Blues, Allagash, Russian River, and Sixpoint.

They've explored the craft segment of the beer list by hosting five-course pairing dinners with the breweries and matching the kitchen's spicy, flavorful dishes with equally big IPAs, stouts, and porters. The University City and Old City restaurants are the only two of the six Philadelphia area locations with a liquor license. Dining at Han Dynasty is a communal affair, so order some beers and try the spicy crispy cucumber, dumplings in chili oil, dan dan noodles, eggplant with garlic sauce, and dry pot style with pork to see if you agree that flavorful beers and Chinese food go quite well together.

HAWTHORNES
738 S. 11th St., Philadelphia, PA 19147; (215) 627-3012; hawthornecafe.com;
@HawthorneCafe

Hawthornes reopened in early 2015 after a long closure as a result of a devastating fire in February 2014. The spot that had been overwhelmingly popular for its bottled and growlered takeout beer as much as it has been for a satisfyingly solid weekend brunch promised to "be back, better than ever" and returned with more than just beer—a full liquor license and a beer delivery service. Fans of the restaurant made do in the meantime with the sister establishment, The Cambridge, at Broad and South, for its weekend brunch and equally strong list of 22 draft beers and a dozen extremely well-selected bottles.

JOSE PISTOLA'S

263 S. 15th St., Philadelphia, PA 19102; (215) 545-4101; josepistolas.com;
@JosePistolas
Draft Beers: 12 **Bottled/Canned Beers:** 60+

Jose Pistola's is another in a handful of Philly bars that delivers great beer, an impressive food menu, and fun times throughout the year and turns it up another notch during Philly Beer Week (PBW). During PBW, co-owners Joe Gunn (Pistola, Jose, get it?) and Casey Parker create an environment of special daytime beer sightings and nighttime antics that make it a must stop for most PBW revelers.

Pistola's is around the corner from just about everything in Center City—trains, theaters, several other high quality beer bars and restaurants—and provides the perfect ability to slip in for a plate of food from the menu with highlights like spicy tuna guacamole, shrimp ceviche, Korean rib tacos, carnitas steamed buns, and hearty burritos.

The beer plays its part as well with a typically diverse lineup that includes hop-centric American IPAs, malt-forward Germans, and Belgian sours. Pistola's is often a stop for brewers coming through the area to showcase their beers.

The upstairs getaway bar is where you want to be for the late-night antics as well as the regularly scheduled live music that, like the beer, spans a wide-ranging spectrum from rock and blues to funk and jazz. Sunday brunch is an even more sure bet with bottomless bloodies, margaritas, and mimosas.

Philadelphia

KHYBER PASS PUB

56 S. 2nd St., Philadelphia, PA 19106;
(215) 238-5888; thekhyber.com;
@KhyberPassPub
Draft Beers: 20, plus 2 handpumps
Bottled/Canned Beers: 50+

The Khyber's longevity is matched by its greatness as an old school tavern-slash-not quite dive bar with a solid-as-ever draft list. There's plenty of history behind the venue that dates to 1970 and was a long-time home to the region's indie rock scene, and live music may or may not be part of the bar's future.

The kitchen serves up a menu of Southern cooking with barbecue and Cajun influences. Boudin balls with creole mustard, fried green tomato BLT, and North Carolina–style pulled pork are all winners. Vegans too are quite content at Khyber Pass with vegan chicken, sausage, and pulled pork options.

In addition to an impeccable year-round beer list, the Khyber does a handful of events, the most eagerly anticipated likely being the Tsarpower, which each winter rolls out a tap takeover with nothing but big, burly Russian imperial stouts.

KITE & KEY

1836 Callowhill St., Philadelphia, PA 19130; (215) 568-1818; thekiteandkey.com;
@KitenKey
Draft Beers: 16, plus 1 handpump **Bottled/Canned Beers:** Around 40

Kite & Key is nestled between the cultural district of the Ben Franklin Parkway and the dense residential Fairmount and Spring Garden neighborhoods. It's an enviable location to draw professionals, families, and tourists.

The bar and restaurant opened in 2008, coinciding with the first year of Philly Beer Week (PBW). Since then, the bar has been a major player in PBW both in terms of events and co-owner Jim Kirk's involvement on the PBW board of directors.

Throughout the year, Kite & Key hosts events like significant tap takeovers and Savage Sixtel Sundays, at which an undisclosed set of new kegs is brought on line to a crowd that has come to expect some of the geekiest finds on a Sunday evening. To whet your whistle ever so slightly, lists in the past have included recognizable names

like Pliny the Elder, Oracle, Supplication, Consecration, Nugget Nectar, 120 Minute, and Cafe Racer 15.

During Philly Beer Week, its Throwndown in Franklintown has taken on something of a legendary element with breweries pitted against breweries for bragging rights. Their leg of the Hammer of Glory route that kicks off Philly Beer Week also brings out a level of both creative genius and madness.

To help soak up all the great beer that's found at Kite & Key on a daily basis, the kitchen matches the beer with popular selections such as the fried pickles, flatbreads, fish tacos, and a pulled pork sandwich.

LONDON BAR AND GRILL

2301 Fairmount Ave., Philadelphia, PA 19130; (215) 978-4545; londongrill.com; @LondonGrill
Draft Beers: 14, plus 1 handpump **Bottled/ Canned Beers:** around 40

Not far from Kite & Key on the other side of historic Eastern State Penitentiary is the well regarded London Bar and Grill. The former prison actually plays a part in the bar's history as co-owner Terry Berch McNally participates in the annual Bastille Day party where, amid an afternoon of other related antics, she plays the part of Marie Antoinette and throws Tastykakes from atop the prison wall to the masses below.

Back at the bar on more civil days, Berch McNally presides over a restaurant and beer program that have been a popular neighborhood fixture since she and co-owner and Chef Michael McNally took over in 1991. The building goes all the way back, in fact, to 1843, and the mahogany bar and tin ceiling originals are still there to prove it.

London Grill was leading the charge into better beer diversity in the mid-1990s and continues today. Typically, more than half of the draft list is dedicated to locals, including the Stoudts-brewed house beer named Willie Sutton Lager, after the infamous resident—and attempted escapee—of the penitentiary.

The food menu at London Grill dazzles with its *foie gras* pierogies, swordfish BLT, Korean fried chicken, and Szechuan duck spring rolls. Monday Night Meatballs and late-night menus until 12 a.m. are two more ways to enjoy London's kitchen while knocking back a few beers at the bar.

As mentioned in the Pub Crawl section that closes out this chapter, so many Philadelphia neighborhoods could serve as the walking map for a decent pub crawl and Fairmount is no exeption. Together with London Grill and Kite & Key, Bridgid's, The Belgian Cafe, and a handful of others would make for an enjoyable and beer-soaked adventure in the shadow of the Art Museum and Penitentiary.

MCGILLIN'S OLDE ALE HOUSE
1310 Drury Ln., Philadelphia, PA 19107; (215) 735-5562; mcgillins.com; @McGillins
Draft Beers: 30

McGillin's opened in 1860, the year in which Abraham Lincoln was elected president. We should pause and reflect upon that for a moment. It was originally called The Bell in Hand and was run by "Pa" and "Ma" McGillin. The McGillins were the first of only two sets of families to own the establishment to date. It's impossible to document a fuller historical account of McGillin's than what these few lines can hold. But beer travelers to Philadelphia eventually find their way to McGillin's to see and feel the history firsthand and drink some fine local beers. The collection of local memorabilia decorating the walls also tells a form of local history.

A first-timer's visit to McGillin's could be filled with a wrong turn or two, plus a bit of disbelief that this classic Philadelphia bar is hidden away down what amounts to almost an alley. You can imagine it wasn't quite so hidden many decades ago before the tall buidlings shot up around Drury Lane.

McGillin's, as a local landmark and the longest continuously operated tavern in Philadelphia, has been plugged into supporting the local beer scene for quite a number of years. On any given day, you can expect to see at least one of the owners—along with longtime bartenders John Doyle and Cassie Gaffney who each in nearly 40 years have worked for three generations of owners—serving some of the oldest regional beer such as Yuengling to the youngest like Boxcar, Spring House, and Twin Lakes.

The bar has a special relationship with Stoudts, having served their beers since the early days of Scarlet Lady ESB and sharing some of the same family-run business characteristics. In 2010, Stoudts brewed an unfiltered anniversary beer, 1860 IPA, which is routinely found on tap in addition to the house McGillin's Real Ale and McGillin's Genuine Lager, also from Stoudts.

A stop at McGillin's at any time of year can be special; however, visiting when the fireplace is crackling and the garland is hung from the low ceiling beams is the highlight for many during the winter holidays.

MCMENAMIN'S

7170 Germantown Ave., Philadelphia, PA 19119; (215) 247-9920
Draft Beers: 15, plus 1 handpump **Bottled/Canned Beers:** around 50

If the word quintessential has appeared in these pages more than a dozen times, it's only because cities like Baltimore and Philadelphia have neighborhood pubs that are so tightly woven into the daily fabric of life. McMenamin's is one of those places in the city's northwest community of Mt. Airy.

Reflecting its history as a diverse residential community, McMenamin's sits along the retail corridor of busy Germantown Avenue—and just a few doors west of Earth Bread + Brewery—and provides the perfect pub gathering place for all walks of life. Game days for local sports are particularly popular with the locals who come to cheer on the Eagles and Phillies and debate their playoff chances.

Classic tavern fare of sandwiches, pastas, fried appetizers, and an excellent Irish stew make for the perfect visit along with a draft list that fittingly features local brews.

MEMPHIS TAPROOM

2331 E. Cumberland St., Philadelphia, PA 19125; (215) 425-4460; memphistaproom.com; @MemphisTaproom1
Draft Beers: 10, plus 2 handpumps **Bottled/Canned Beers:** Around 100

With room here for only one of the high-quality beer-focused joints run by Brendan Hartranft and Leigh Maida, the oldest gets the nod. The others are certainly no slouches and fit well into each of their distinct neighborhoods of Washington Square West (Strangelove's) and Spruce Hill (both Local 44 and the very new Clarkville, which is due in spring 2015).

At Memphis Taproom in the Kensington neighborhood, Brendan and Leigh teamed up with Chef Jesse Kimball to create a neighborhood pub experience unlike any the neighborhood had seen. It didn't take long to learn after opening in early

2008 that the model would work. Hartranft brought with him a résumé that included bolstering Khyber Pass's beer reputation in the '90s and managing the Nodding Head Brewpub.

Kimball's kitchen is regarded for its fish-and-chips, smoked coconut club, slow roast pork sandwich, Port Richmond kielbasa platter, and chicken fried chicken. See his contribution to In The Kitchen, the chapter of food recipes later in the book.

The seasonal outdoor beer garden adds another element to the year-round list of beer events that include education, tap takeovers, and homebrewing.

Behind the bar, they are fervent supporters of craft stalwarts like Allagash White, Sierra Nevada Pale Ale, and Victory Prima Pils as much as they are seekers of the less common like Alvinne, Boon, Coniston, J.W. Lees, Struise, and Theakston. And their customers appreciate the efforts by continuing to flock back to this destination beer bar in an off-the-beaten-path neighborhood.

MOLLY MALLOY'S

1136 Arch St. (Reading Terminal Market), Philadelphia, PA 19107; (267) 525-1001;
mollymalloysphilly.com; @MollyMalloysRTM
Draft Beers: 24

There wasn't much to talk about in terms of local and/or high-quality beer in the city's historic Reading Terminal Market until Molly Malloy's came along in 2011. Under the same ownership as the neighboring Iovine Brothers Produce stand, much of Molly Malloy's kitchen is sourced from a handful of proprietors in the market. Be sure to give the spicy potato bacon hash and Angry Ralph's Lobster Mac & Cheese a try.

Keeping with the local theme—which shows well not just for city residents but also for the scores of tourists and conventioneers that pass through the market—the beer list is stocked with roughly ⅔ local representation of the ones you've come to expect around Philadelphia. The open-air restaurant and bar fit quite nicely as a perfect shopping break and open at 8 a.m. for breakfast (9 a.m. on Sunday) giving those heading from the train station a chance to grab a quick bite, if not a beer, on the way to work.

MONK'S CAFE

264 S. 16th St., Philadelphia, PA 19102; (215) 545-7005; monkscafe.com; @PhilliBeer
Draft Beers: 20 **Bottled/Canned Beers:** Around 300

Quite possibly the most frequent question after introducing yourself as a Philadelphian to an out-of-towner: "So I guess you've been to Monk's, right?"

The location's history was interesting long before Tom Peters and Fergus Carey opened Monk's in January 1997. Today the first-floor bar and restaurant take up the space formerly consisting of the turn-of-the-20th-century Royal Oak Hotel's lounge, kitchen, and restaurant, the service alley for which doubled as a whiskey drop during the Prohibition years.

Peters's own history, particularly as it intersects with Belgian beer, goes back to the mid-1980s managing the Copa Too! bar a couple blocks away. He was selling bottles of Chimay long before many knew there was good beer in Belgium. His introduction of Kwak was reportedly the first Belgian beer available on draft in the States. A beer festival (a small one at that, by today's standards) in 1995 and the enthusiastic response it got quickened the pace toward Monk's.

The history and accolades are too lengthy for these short pages: the brewer friends from around the world that he maintains; the collaboration beers that he has brewed, including at the famed Cantillon, De Molen, Firestone Walker, and Russian River to name but a few; the rare beers he procures; being a James Beard semifinalist

in 2013 and 2014; carrying the distinction of the first American to be knighted into the Chevalier du Fourquet des Brasseurs in Belgium in 2004 and also an Ambassadeur Orval since 2009. But the major takeaway is that particularly in the early days, and certainly still continuing, when the success of Belgian beer in the US market is discussed, most in the industry concur that Tom Peters is the man to thank.

The success of Monk's doesn't stop with Peters, who is quick to point out that this profile cannot be written without due credit given to longtime day and night managers, Jodi McCormack and Bernadette Roe, respectively. He gives credit as well to Bill Toner, who cleans and maintains the draft system on a daily basis. And there's Hannah, who comes in on Monday and Tuesday to provide professional massages for staff members.

All of this has been said so far to describe Monk's Cafe with barely a word written about the beer and food. While it's probably evident that Monk's has earned its place in the country's fantastic beer scene because of the selection, places like this would be nowhere without an equally strong ownership and staff and it doesn't happen merely by accident.

If you'd like some words about the beer, however, with the special relationships Monk's has established with top-notch breweries around the world, they put on a special event with Russian River Brewing Company each year as a charity fundraiser for Alex's Lemonade Stand. Consider that Philadelphia is one of the very few markets outside of this brewery's home turf of northern California that gets a regular supply of some of the coveted beers.

For this event, Peters and the crew are able to procure and save up at least a half-dozen, including the beer-geek drool-inducing Pliny the Younger. With 100 percent of sales from the Russian River beers as well as a complementary remaining set of rarely seen stellar beers from other breweries on tap, plus funds from raffled gift baskets, in 2014 Monk's was able to make its largest donation ever of $25,000 simply from this one-day event.

If the scene is a bit too frenzied at Monk's for your liking, try the sister establishment, The Belgian Cafe, across town near the Art Museum for the same dedication to great beer but on a slightly smaller and quieter scale.

OYSTER HOUSE

1516 Sansom St., Philadelphia, PA 19102; (215) 567-7683; oysterhousephilly.com; @PHLOysterHouse
Draft Beers: 6, plus 1 handpump **Bottled/Canned Beers:** Around 10

How to follow up an epic entry on Monk's Cafe here at the nearly 40-year-old Oyster House (5 years in its current incarnation)? How about with some of the best seafood in the city and a well-stocked raw bar, which might be the only thing that rotates more often than the beer.

The beer selection is nicely varied typically to include pale ales, ambers, saisons, and stouts. Yards Love Stout makes frequent appearances both on traditional draft and handpump and makes one of the most perfect food-beer combinations when served with a plate of oysters.

PERCY STREET BBQ

900 South St., Philadelphia, PA 19147; (215) 625-8510; percystreet.com; @PercyStreet
Draft Beers: 6 **Bottled/Canned Beers:** 110+ cans

Barbecue and lots of great canned beer. And, at past Philly Beer Weeks, a mechanical bull. The menu and the atmosphere scream Texas and customers have been flocking to South Street in search of it since Percy Street Barbecue opened in 2009. They are big on cans with over 110 offerings that cover the craft segment across the country and the style spectrum.

Sumptuous smoked brisket (with burnt ends of course) or a pork belly sandwich with sides, like jalapeño skillet cornbread and collard greens, and a beer like Brewer's Art Resurrection makes for a perfect meal. If the Sly Fox Rauchbier is on tap, opt for this well-made local smoke beer as an even more fitting partner in the glass. Skipping dessert at Percy Street is not an option. Ask for a piece of pecan pie and either a Cigar City Maduro Brown or Oskar Blues Ten Fidy to wash it down.

PUB ON PASSYUNK EAST (P.O.P.E.)

1501 E. Passyunk Ave., Philadelphia, PA 19147; (215) 755-5125; pubonpassyunkeast.com;
@POPE1501
Draft Beers: 15 **Bottled/Canned Beers:** 80+

Refer to this Passyunk Avenue fixture as The P.O.P.E. and you'll have no problem fitting in at this dimly lit South Philly neighborhood favorite. Since 2006, owner Dennis Hewlett, a native Philadelphian, has established ties to the neighborhood and the brewing community. Beers from locals Philadelphia Brewing and Sly Fox are often found on draft here and, from the other side of the brewing world, The P.O.P.E. became the first bar in the US to install an authentic La Chouffe tower to complement a respectable list of Belgian and German beers on the menu.

The atmosphere is cozy with knowledgeable and friendly service from an attentive staff. Renovations in the past year created "the conclave" room, which looks out to Passyunk Avenue through open windows. In addition to a beer list that never disappoints, the food menu sports satisfying plates such as pierogies, meat loaf, and a French dip (with au jus, naturally). Vegans are taken care of as well with seitan cheesesteaks, seitan fingers, and fries with vegan cheese.

SOUTH PHILADELPHIA TAP ROOM

1509 Mifflin St., Philadelphia, PA 19145; (215) 271-7787; southphiladelphiataproom.com;
@SPTaproom
Draft Beers: 13, plus 1 handpump **Bottled/Canned Beers:** Around 100

South Philadelphia Tap Room (SPTR) broke new territory over 10 years ago when it opened in the Newbold section of South Philly. To say this was taking a chance is an understatement, but not so much so for the studied real estate guy,

John Longacre, who is responsible for bringing a great beer scene this far into South Philly. American Sardine is now part of the SPTR family and is doing quite well on a similar trajectory in the neighborhood of Point Breeze.

At SPTR, the tag of neighborhood pub certainly fits, and this has been the theme for many featured in this Philadelphia chapter. Through the years, the bar has been a popular gathering spot, particularly for local sporting events, given its proximity to the professional sports complex.

The kitchen serves up favorites such as wild boar tacos, tomato and chickpea soup, and grass-fed burgers with meat sourced from nearby Lancaster County. You can usually find a spicy Belgian tripel, hop-solid double IPA, or a crisp, well-made local pilsner on the draft list to go perfectly with this type of meal. The brunch menu at SPTR is equally satisfying with entries like fritattas (look for a saison here) and cornmeal pancakes (seek out a refreshing, fruit-forward wheat beer) providing a great start to the weekend.

The bar has become a beer-geek destination for those fond of beers from Founders, with whom SPTR has developed a special relationship and from which one sees plenty of unique beers. Events during Philly Beer Week centered on this Michigan brewery typically border on epic and rarely leave leftovers.

STANDARD TAP
901 N. 2nd St., Philadelphia, PA, 19123; (215) 238-0630; standardtap.com; @StandardTap
Draft Beers: 20, plus 2 handpumps

Standard Tap began the idea of focusing on locally sourced beer and food long before almost anyone else gave it serious thought. In late 1999, locals flocked

to this Northern Liberties gem and soon the media followed, lavishing just praise on the bar for its focus on the food and beer of the region. In 2003, owners William Reed and Paul Kimport took the concept to Fishtown by opening Johnny Brenda's and added what has become one of the city's best live music venues.

Back at Standard Tap's historic building, circa 1810, you'd be hard-pressed to find a distributing brewery from eastern Pennsylvania, New Jersey, or Delaware that hasn't found its way on to the taps at some point. Philadelphia Brewing, Victory, and Yards flow most frequently. Reed, a former brewer himself at the long-ago-shuttered Sam Adams, has done multiple collaborations with local breweries Dock Street and Sly Fox. For the beauty of properly maintained and served cask-conditioned beer, Standard Tap was one of the first in Philadelphia, and very few in the country, to be Cask Marque–certified by the UK-based accreditation organization.

From the kitchen, first time visitors should head immediately to the pulled pork sandwich. Long a menu favorite, the meat is sourced from a local farm—as expected—and braised for 5 hours. Served with roasted long hots and garlic and bathed in its braising juices, the heaping pile of savory seasoned pork makes the perfect lunch or late-night meal. The kitchen goes off the straight and narrow a bit with successful dishes that incorporate sweetbreads, smelts, whole fish, and wild game.

Standard Tap does its part to serve great food and beer and also endeavors to do it while reducing its environmental impact. Solar panels on the roof and a kitchen oil recycling program are two ways that the bar makes you feel even better about a visit to this Philadelphia landmark restaurant.

TRIA TAPROOM
2005 Walnut St., Philadelphia, PA 19103; (215) 557-8277; triacafe.com/taproom; @TriaPhilly
Draft Beers: 24

Jon Myerow and Michael McCaulley opened Tria Cafe at the Rittenhouse Square location in 2004 and the Washington Square West location in 2007 with the intention of bringing beer, cheese, and wine together on a level playing field. They succeeded and later started up the Tria Fermentation School to bring industry luminaries in to help with the teaching and tasting of some of the best beers in the world.

In 2013, they opened Tria Taproom to be even more beer-focused than the cafes. The front-of-the-house staff is extensively trained in beer at hiring and in ongoing weekly 90-minute training sessions. This, in turn, helps Tria inform customers who are seeking new beers.

The well-maintained and seasonal beer list (draft only, as are the wine selections) typically features house favorites like Allagash White and Victory Braumeister Pils. The remainder of the taps span the globe, with wide-ranging styles and alcohol levels, in an effort to present the best options for a well-paired food experience. In keeping up with technology, not only do the iPad beer menus stay constantly in sync with reality, but they also show the customer the keg's percentage remaining level.

Both the Cafe and Taproom kitchens turn out delectable plates of small food and a wide range of cheese. Additionally, the kitchen at the Taproom delivers excellent flatbreads like the Philly roast pork, duck, burrata, and Kennett Square mushrooms, each of which provides much beer-pairing potential, with a depth and richness of flavors.

A fourth location, though more wine-focused, is expected to open in the spring of 2015.

VILLAGE WHISKEY

118 S. 20th St., Philadelphia, PA 19103; (215) 665-1088; villagewhiskey.com; @VillageWhiskPHL **Draft Beers:** 6, plus 1 handpump **Bottled/Canned Beers:** 10 to 15

Closing out the Philadelphia bar chapter with a place called Village Whiskey? Well, it's true that great beer can be enjoyed at many different types of establishments in the city and sometimes friends you're with are looking for one of the best whiskey selections around. You'll recommend Village Whiskey. You do this because you know that at this restaurant, from celebrated award-winning chef and owner Jose Garces, you'll be able to find some mighty fine beer to get you through the visit.

Locals like Flying Fish, Philadelphia Brewing, Sly Fox, Victory, Weyerbacher, and Yards are routinely available as are non-local favorites like Allagash, Firestone Walker, Founders, Left Hand, and Smuttynose. The relatively small list of beers is carefully built and substantial enough to provide plenty of options to go along with the much-celebrated burger menu (Whiskey King, if you're feeling decadent), duck fries with short rib and cheddar, truffled cauliflower, and turnips and black kale. A warm chocolate chip cookie with vanilla ice cream and a robust porter seems like a good way to close out this chapter.

Philadelphia—Pub Crawl

This pub crawl recommendation is purposely meant to be the pub crawl to end all pub crawls. Other pub crawls will whither in the immensity of the Philadelphia Pub Crawl. Truth be told, a pub crawl could be held in just about any of Philadelphia's numerous interesting and unique neighborhoods. Think of the great beer that could be drunk along a pub crawl in the city areas of Fairmount/Art Museum, South Street/Graduate Hospital, Passyunk Avenue, Germantown Avenue, and University City/West Philly.

This epic pub crawl, complete with all 11 of its stops along the way, must start early if you have any chance of pulling it off. Of course, a saner person would likely make a weekend of it and split the endeavor between Saturday and Sunday. However you attack it, enjoy some of the best that Philly has to offer.

TOTAL WALKING DISTANCE: 3.1 miles

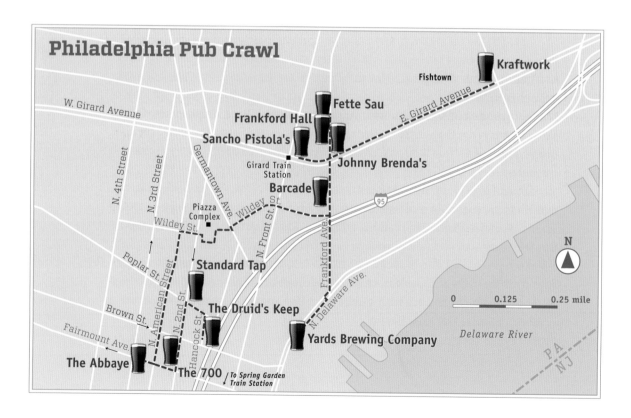

Directions: Begin your pub crawl by either taking the Market-Frankford El to the Spring Garden station or stashing your car in the general vicinity of 2nd and Poplar Streets and walk to Yards.

Yards Brewing Company, 901 N. Delaware Ave., Philadelphia, PA, 19123; (215) 634-2600; yardsbrewing.com; @YardsBrew

As discussed earlier in this chapter, Yards has come a long way. Its phenomenal growth has transformed it into a major regional brewery player situated in the shadow of the Ben Franklin Bridge along Delaware Avenue. They have a U-shaped bar perfect for bar chit-chat and with a view into the brewing operations.

In addition to the wide selection of beers available at their tasting room, you can also start your Philly-based pub crawl with a brewery tour and a bite to eat from their limited menu of soups, salads, and sandwiches. But, as I mentioned in the intro, get here early when the brewery opens at 12 p.m. in order to keep your pub crawl on track, at least early on.

Directions: From Yards, you'll embark on the longest walking stretch of this pub crawl. Head into the Fishtown neighborhood by crossing Delaware Avenue and walking north on Frankford Avenue to Girard Avenue. Turn right and walk four blocks to Kraftwork.

Kraftwork, 541 E. Girard Ave., Philadelphia, PA, 19125; (215) 739-1700; kraftwork bar.com; @KraftworkBar

Kraftwork is the younger sister establishment to Sidecar Bar & Grille located across town. Like every good neighborhood bar in a city like Philly, Kraftwork has its own unique identity.

Outfitted with a distinctly industrial decor reflective of this river ward's background, Kraftwork will keep your pub crawl moving with a well-conceived beer list that is at least a quarter regional in nature along with a handful of Europeans. Enjoy them around another square bar, which invites more socializing and less staring at phone screens.

Directions: You'll double-back down Girard Avenue to Frankford Avenue and turn right, resisting the urge to stop at Johnny Brenda's quite yet, on your way to Fette Sau.

Fette Sau, 1208 Frankford Ave., Philadelphia, PA, 19125; (215) 391-4888; fettesau philly.com; @StarrRestaurant

Many quality beer stops in Philadelphia also have kitchens of high repute, turning out tasty, quality food befitting the perfect pub crawl.

At Fette Sau, you'll find a lineup of beers perfect for the highly regarded barbecue coming off the spits and roasters. A robust porter with the Berkshire pulled pork or a saison with the FreeBird organic chicken are two can't-miss recommendations. Or pick from a long list of whiskeys if you prefer. These will be your decisions but you can't go wrong any way you choose.

The partial open-air space provides a spacious and comfortable environment in which to enjoy the meaty and beery delights.

Directions: You'll barely need to set foot on the front sidewalk when you turn left out of Fette Sau and in approximately 17 steps enter Frankford Hall.

Frankford Hall, 1210 Frankford Ave., Philadelphia, PA, 19125; (215) 634-3338; frankfordhall.com; @StarrRestaurant
If you found Fette Sau's partially open-air environment appealing, wait until you pull up a bench at Frankford Hall under the open-sky courtyard and wash down your Riesenpretzel with a liter or half-liter of dunkel or pils straight from Germany or one of the fine local breweries turning out award-winning German-style beers.

Frankford Hall is very much a communal experience. Ping-pong tables, card games, and picnic-table open seating will have you making new friends in no time at all.

If it's raining, fear not, there is a small indoor area, but hopefully when you stop by it will (mostly) be sunny in Philadelphia.

Directions: Now you may walk south a half block back to the corner of Frankford and Girard where Johnny Brenda's prominently sits.

Johnny Brenda's, 1201 Frankford Ave., Philadelphia, PA, 19125; (215) 739-9684; johnnybrendas.com; @JohnnyBrendas
Here's another example of a great beer bar married with a kitchen turning out creatively interesting food. The ownership is the same as Standard Tap, so if you are new to Johnny Brenda's, it will be of little surprise that the kitchen is deserving of the praise it gets for everything from weekend brunch (which lasts until 3:30 p.m.) to nightly dinners and special beer-pairing events.

Along with a beer or two from the many local breweries that they are proud to support on 12 taps and 2 handpumps, fresh oysters, pork and grits, or a banh mi give you an opportunity to get a taste of the good things going on here during this stop of your tour. Johnny Brenda's often does special events on weekends that include a good mix of food, beer, and music. Bocks and Brats, Kenzinger Clambake,

Trouble with Trippels, and Firkin Riot are four such examples that you could encounter while passing through.

Be sure to grab a bag of JB's on-premise roasted coffee as well; you'll thank me the next morning for it. As an added distraction to potentially take you off track from your pub crawl itinerary, the bar has a pool table where the action can get pretty hot if you've got the right playing partners.

Before leaving, check out upcoming shows and make a note to come back another night for some of the city's best live music on the second floor.

Directions: One block west on Girard Avenue from Johnny Brenda's, you'll find Sancho Pistola's.

Sancho Pistola's, 19 W. Girard Ave., Philadelphia, PA, 19123; (267) 324-3530; sancho pistolas.com; @Sancho_Pistolas

Do you know Sancho's older brother, José, across town in Center City? See the big brother's profile earlier in this chapter. Sancho Pistola's just passed its first anniversary in the Fishtown section of the city.

Joe Gunn (Pistola) and Casey Parker are known for their distinctively engaging personalities and for hosting rollicking gatherings over great beer, particularly during Philly Beer Week. The tradition continues across town here just steps from the Girard Avenue station of the Market-Frankford El.

Ten very good taps are supported by an even better bottle list. The long list of tacos on the menu will have you reconsidering your lack of hunger at this point. Think fish or pork tacos with a saison or double IPA. Or carnitas steamed buns with a doppelbock.

Directions: Turn left back east toward Johnny Brenda's to turn right on Frankford Avenue and walk an oversized block to Barcade.

Barcade, 1114 Frankford Ave., Philadelphia, PA, 19125; (215) 634-4400; barcade philadelphia.com; @BarcadePhilly

Order a beer from the dozens of taps at Barcade and slip some dollars into the change machine and relive your past. That is, if your past consisted of '80s-era video games.

As with Barcade's locations in Brooklyn and Jersey City, nearly 50 vintage stand-up arcade games line the walls here and allow you to test your recall of the tricks you once knew all for the vintage price of one quarter. Many talented players who seemingly haven't put down the joystick in 30 years have continued their mastery at Barcade.

Barcade routinely hosts massive tap takeovers featuring breweries from both near and far, which merely supplement the year-round list of great beer that they offer in addition to a food menu of hot and cold sandwiches and lighter bites.

Directions: The second part of this crawl takes you from Fishtown to the Northern Liberties neighborhood. It's nearly a three-quarter-mile walk from Barcade to The Abbaye by turning right out of Barcade's front door and heading west on Wildey Street. Zig your way through or zag around The Piazza complex, crossing 2nd Street to American Street and make a left. Head south for three blocks, make a right on Fairmount Avenue. It's less complicated than it sounds.

The Abbaye, 637 N. 3rd St., Philadelphia, PA, 19123; (215) 627-6711; theabbaye .net; @TheAbbaye

A quick stop at The Abbaye will give you enough time to split a large bottle of La Chouffe or Chimay with an order of traditional mussels or wings. The wings also come in vegan format and are one of several vegan/vegetarian options to choose from on the menu.

Directions: Head east from 3rd Street to 2nd Street on Fairmount where you'll find The 700.

The 700, 700 N. 2nd St., Philadelphia, PA, 19123; (215) 413-3181; the700.org; @The700Philly

If you've arrived too late at night, you must be behind schedule and not likely to complete the full circuit proposed here. That also means that depending upon the day you're embarking on this pub crawl, you'll either encounter DJ music at the bar or on the second-story dancefloor.

You can get your dance on along with a couple of beers from area locals like Sly Fox, Victory, Philadelphia Brewing, and Yards. Or "international" beers from across the pond like Samuel Smith, Young's, or Belhaven might go nicely if there's soccer being shown on the televisions, which is a popular pastime as well at this reputable neighborhood hangout. Twelve taps and 80+ bottles, as well as a high-quality selection of whiskeys, tequilas, and absinthes, will give anyone in your group something tasty to keep the night going strong.

If, on the other hand, the music is not your thing, head next door to The Blind Pig, where you can choose from over 60 cans of beer.

Directions: Head north on 2nd Street two blocks to Poplar Street, where if you can't see Standard Tap looming large over the corner, perhaps your day's work is already complete.

Standard Tap, 901 N. 2nd St., Philadelphia, PA, 19123; (215) 238-0630; standardtap.com; @StandardTap

Hopefully, inserting a high-quality standard-bearer for the Philadelphia pub scene this late into a daylong pub crawl is not a mistake. This is one place you certainly want to soak up and appreciate.

If the weather is nice, angle for a seat on the second-floor outdoor patio overlooking the street scene. Otherwise grab a seat inside where the prototypical neighborhood bar scene plays out on both sides of the tap handles.

If you've planned for another bite to eat at this point of the epic crawl, then you will not have made a mistake. Though to guarantee your table, you may want to lock in a reservation along the way to ensure a table when you arrive. On any given day, whole fish, wild game, or daily specials may grace the menu along side old standbys like the otherworldly pulled pork sandwich with meat from Lancaster County, which might go quite nicely with something, say, like a Stoudts Fat Dog Stout. A perfect example of local supporting local.

Directions: One last short walk for you before you can call it a night. Turn left out the front door of Standard Tap, go one block, and turn right on Hancock Street. At the end of the block, Druid's Keep is on the left.

The Druid's Keep, 149 Brown St., Philadelphia, PA, 19123; (215) 413-0455

Those who know The Druid's Keep would probably like to keep the place to themselves. If more than 10 people buy this book, I may not be helping that cause. After many years, this bar still somehow falls into the category of one of the city's best kept secrets.

Make this your last stop because it will be one of the most relaxing. Grab a beer from Yards to complete the day that began at Yards' brewery, drop a few dollars on the jukebox, shoot a game of pool if you're up for it, and chill in the backyard before calling it a night. You've earned it.

Beer Is Going Places

It's only been in very recent years that airports, train stations, etc. have caught on that people who travel like a variety of beers from which to choose. Shouldn't we expect that if gift stores in the airport are selling replica Liberty Bells in Philadelphia and fuzzy crab hats in Baltimore that we should also be able to get a Dock Street Rye IPA and a DuClaw Sweet Baby Jesus! porter at the airport bars?

Following are some of the ways you can track down a good beer when you're on the run.

Philadelphia (PHL)

JET ROCK BAR & GRILL
Terminals B & D, (215) 492-4800

Jet Rock has the market cornered at PHL. Locals who fly out of Philly know to head to Jet Rock for a good beer. Time permitting, many have been known to traverse terminals to get to one with a Jet Rock.

The recipe for success at Jet Rock is pretty simple: 40 of 48 taps of interesting craft beer; standard pub grub; and lively music to keep things rocking. Yards, Tröegs, and Great Lakes are common sightings and serve as great relaxants prior to boarding the plane, where you can usually expect a much less diverse selection of beers.

LOCAL TAVERN
Terminal F

Local Tavern comes from the same management team as Jet Rock, so the idea that a wide variety of interesting beer being served should come as little surprise. The emphasis here, as the name leads you to expect, is even more local in nature from the decor to the food.

Just as at Jet Rock, you'll find the Dock Streets, the Stoudts, and the Victorys. The food shines just as brightly with a locally-sourced menu drawn up by a local favorite, Iron Chef José Garces, and gives at least one really good reason for arriving at the airport much earlier than your scheduled flight.

At both Jet Rock and Local, if your timing is fortuitous you may pass by while they are doing a complimentary beer sampling. Local has the additional perks of serving taster-size flights of beers and doing tie-in promotions and giveaways with the local sport teams.

BRIDGEWATER'S PUB AT 30TH STREET STATION

2955 Market St., (215) 387-4787; thepubin30thstreetstation.com; @PubintheStation

There's plenty of fun to be had at train stations too, if you just know where to look. In Philadelphia, the 30th Street Station has been home to one of the best train station beer bars since it began turning away from some of the macro brands in 2002.

Named after the early 1800s Bridgewater Street, which 30th Street Station was built over, the bar maintains a well-balanced list of local beers, other American beers, and ones from Germany and Belgium that routinely fill the chalkboard and bottle list. Think: Innstadt, Ayinger, Schneider, a few Belgian Trappists, and a good representation of locals.

A creatively satisfying menu with items like pork roulade with Boursin, penne with short rib and wild boar, and a beef brisket sandwich with fennel-onion marmalade make for the perfect pre-boarding meal. Rocky Mountain oysters have even been spotted at Bridgewater's. Apparently understanding that the location is one based upon schedules and motion, the staff is effective at moving beers and food and completing transactions to keep you on the move to meet your schedule.

All regional SEPTA train lines, the westbound and Northeast Corridor Amtrak lines, the NJ Transit line to Atlantic City, city trolleys and subway, and many buses converge on 30th Street Station. At Bridgewater's, with all the good taste coming across the bar, it's a good thing the wall clock is kept running 10 minutes ahead of actual time.

Newark (EWR)

GARDEN STATE DINER

Terminal C, (973) 648-6791; gardenstatedinernj.com

They have but eight taps and they make the most of them here in the mostly United Airlines terminal. Amid a diner-ish type of menu, complete with milk shakes, this is the place to stop in when looking for beers in the ballpark of Allagash White, Dogfish Punkin, Kane Head High, or Sixpoint The Crisp. The carefully chosen beers are of little surprise to those who know the sister establishment in Jersey City, NJ—City Diner.

Pittsburgh (PIT)

BAR SYMON

AirMall Center Core, (412) 472-5067

There's an Iron Chef in the Pittsburgh airport and he serves up a stellar beer list alongside his highly acclaimed kitchen fare in an attempt "to combine high quality ingredients with a Midwestern sensibility." Opened in 2012, it quickly became a favorite for beer lovers passing through the airport who could count on 9 high-quality craft beers, often including Bell's, East End, Fat Head's, Great Lakes, Rogue, and Tröegs.

The menu overflows with tempting options. Try a Lola Burger (fried egg and thick bacon on challah) with an East End Fat Gary Brown Ale or a Pittsburgher sandwich (pierogi, kielbasa, and sauerkraut on sourdough) and Parmesan Rosemary Lola Fries with a Fat Head's Head Hunter IPA to see if it isn't one of the best airport meals you've had in some time.

Lehigh Valley (ABE)

PA PUB CAFE & SPIRITS
Wiley Departure Terminal

Lehigh Valley International Airport might be small—how small? How about 17 gates small? But at this sole ABE airport pub, you can count on finding beers from nearby Weyerbacher and a few other relative locals like Yuengling and Yards.

Baltimore (BWI)

DUCLAW BREWING COMPANY
Main Hall pre-security near Terminal B, (410) 850-4846

Sweet Baby Jesus! might be exclaimed for more than one reason outside security at BWI. It could be to welcome home a loved one who just walked through security. Or it could be for the chocolate peanut butter porter that just arrived from the bar.

Opened in 2010, DuClaw at the airport has served as a chance for departing travelers to grab a last taste of home and those awaiting incoming flights the ability to make time pass a bit more easily.

Major Beer Events

If unscientific reviews mean anything, it seems that the mid-Atlantic serves up more ways to enjoy a great glass of beer than anywhere else in the US. Simple samplings. Fun 'n' games. Charity. Sit-down beer dinners. Full-throttle traditional beer festivals.

The brewers, proprietors, and distributors of the mid-Atlantic are beer lovers themselves and show plenty of creativity in the events that they create for shared enjoyment of our favorite beverage. Here is a monthly review of some the best and most interesting that can be found on each year's calendar.

January
BELGIUM COMES TO WEST CHESTER AT IRON HILL
West Chester, PA; ironhillbrewery.com

There's a good reason why beer fans have fought blizzard conditions to attend this mid-winter festival. Actually, there are around 30 reasons and they can all be found in the glassware at this well-run and immensely popular event that showcases the best Belgian beers (many sour styles) that the Iron Hill family and at least a dozen other regional breweries have to offer.

February
BELGIAN BEER FEST AT MAX'S
Baltimore, MD; maxs.com

This highly regarded festival offers the best representation of Belgian and Belgian-style beers in the country. Over the course of 3 days, usually around President's Day, some 500 people line up beginning at 6 a.m. to get into this Fell's Point institution. The event has become so successful and the beers so numerous in their variety that the last day of the festival weekend is now dedicated to sours.

March
THE BREWERS PLATE AT THE KIMMEL CENTER
Philadelphia, PA; brewersplate.com

This event has gone through stages of growth in its 10 years of existence that has taken it from a few hundred customers at the city's historic Reading Terminal Market to the Kimmel Center—home to the Philadelphia Orchestra—in 2014 when it hosted just over 1,200 attendees. One thing, though, has never changed and that is the commitment to the natural wonder of pairing great beer with great food. The event has a hyper-local flair to it so expect to see many foods and beers that simply cannot be available in other parts of the country.

April
ATLANTIC CITY BEER AND MUSIC FESTIVAL
Atlantic City, NJ; acbeerfest.com

Lots of music and lots of beer in Atlantic City equals a rollicking good time. At least 20 bands, 100 breweries, 100 vendors, and a dozen restaurants spell it out. If you don't live in Atlantic City or very close by, reserving a hotel room ahead of time makes all the sense in the world. You could stay at one of the big casino hotels, or you could stay at the host convention center's neighboring Sheraton.

May
BOCK FEST & GOAT RACES AT SLY FOX BREWERY
Pottstown, PA; slyfoxbeer.com

More goats. More bocks. More food. More music. More family-friendly. Each year, Sly Fox promises more of what makes the German-based festival one of the most talked about in the region. There are goats racing in multiple heats in order to carry the honor of having the current year's maibock named after him or her. You will also find families with children, and some with dogs, relaxing and enjoying themselves in a very safe and fun atmosphere for all ages and backgrounds. By the way, there is plenty of great beer—much of it leaning more toward the "sessionable" end of the spectrum—that just happens to be another important component of the event.

June
PHILLY BEER WEEK
at hundreds of establishments in Philadelphia, PA; phillybeerweek.org

Anything written here in the next few sentences will pale in comparison to the hundreds upon many thousands of paragraphs already written about the one that started it all. The concept of a 10-day Beer Week, that is. The first go-round was in 2008 with a mere few hundred events. And the world took notice. San Francisco launched its version the following year and many other cities/states/regions joined in quickly thereafter. Philadelphia's consists of nearly 1,000 events each year held at over 200 locations that range from shenanigans to serious reflection upon the beer subject at hand. If you don't live in the city, this is best experienced with a driver and a hotel room at the ready.

BEER, BOURBON, AND BBQ
The Waterfront & Piers at National Harbor, MD; beerandbourbon.com

There's an installment of this 2-day festival in March at the Timonium Fairgrounds. This one in June outside of Washington, DC brings together what many beer lovers feel is the best plated companion for their beer—barbecue. The number of gustatory delights available to festival-goers is staggering after first counting the beer, the food, the music, and, oh yes, the bourbons. Plenty to do at this 5-hour sensory overload.

July
HOPS, VINES, AND WINES
Downtown Selinsgrove, PA; selinsgrovebrewfest.com

Each year, the middle of Pennsylvania comes alive for a mere four hours in downtown Selinsgrove (home to the praised Selin's Grove Brewing Company) as 50 breweries and wineries pour their liquid creations in the picturesque Susquehanna River town.

August
STATE COLLEGE BREW EXPO AT TUSSEY MOUNTAIN SKI RESORT
Boalsburg, PA; statecollegebrewexpo.com

Here's another popular central Pennsylvania beer festival. This one is near State College—home of Penn State University—and the forests, rolling hills, and mountains of the region provide a beautiful backdrop. The festival showcases a few dozen breweries—many small and medium-size ones from Pennsylvania as well—live music, food vendors, and seminars. Penn State's well-known Coaches vs. Cancer has been a longtime beneficiary of this well-run festival. Make a weekend of it in the area and explore the burgeoning brewing scene.

September
SMOKE EM IF YOUS GOT EM AT YARDS BREWING COMPANY
Philadelphia, PA; yardsbrewing.com

An event with a fun title but a serious mission—present smoke-style beers during an intense competition of both professional and amateur chefs in the world of barbecue. The event is no joke as it has opened minds and palates to smoke beers during the event's 5 years of existence and has shown off some of the best barbecue available in the region. It's all presented with Yards' fermenters and brew kettles as a backdrop and local live music as the soundtrack for one of the city's most anticipated annual events.

STEEL CITY BIG POUR AT CONSTRUCTION JUNCTION
Pittsburgh, PA; steelcitybigpour.com

The Big Pour continues to get bigger even after its 8th year in 2014. The festival showcases nearly 50 breweries and a couple dozen other beverage and food providers. With a mission statement that supports reusing, recycling, and sustainability, the organizing committee—Construction Junction—works to invite breweries that are similarly minded. Tickets for both sessions quickly sell out.

October
BEER BARONS TO HOMEBREWERS AT WEST LAUREL HILL CEMETERY
Bala Cynwyd, PA; forever-care.com

At one of the more unusual beer events, homebrewers put their beer on display for attendees to sample (and eventually award prizes) and the gravesites of significant beer people are visited in order to learn more about the Philadelphia region's significant beer history. The homebrew competition results in three winners of category prizes and the honor of saying that they served their beer among some of the country's richest brewing families.

KENNETT BREWFEST
Downtown Kennett Square, PA; kennettbrewfest.com

Coming off its 17th year of celebrating great beer in downtown Kennett Square, this festival has served as a model to many other regional ones around Philadelphia. According to chairman Jeff Norman, it was "one of the first large-format beer festivals that benefitted a nonprofit in the mid-Atlantic region." Another festival standard these days but once an original idea, the Connoisseur Session was an early success now going on its 12th year.

November
AUTOS AND ALES AT ANTIQUE AUTOMOBILE CLUB OF AMERICA
Hershey, PA; aacamuseum.org

Cars and drinking are not typically promoted together in the same sentence, unless it's a beer festival with antique cars, trucks, and motorcycles on display while attendees sip on beers from a couple dozen breweries and enjoy food and live music. Growing each year in popularity, Autos and Ales just came off its fifth anniversary and is another great reason to visit The Sweetest Place on Earth.

BYOB: Brew Your Own Beer

As homebrewing goes, so goes professional brewing. Or, is it as professional brewing goes, so goes the popularity of homebrewing? Actually, it goes both ways and history shows that the earliest professional craft brewers were homebrewers, just as we see many of today's upstart breweries run by homebrewers aspiring to a professional life of brewing on a much larger scale.

Following are only a handful of local homebrew shops that play a significant role in their homebrew communities across the four states covered in this book. I've noted where an introduction to the subsequent recipe has been written by a staff member of the establishment.

HOME SWEET HOMEBREW

2008 Sansom St., Philadelphia, PA 19103; (215) 569-9469; homesweethomebrew.com; @HomeSwtHomeBrew

Since 1986, George Hummel and Nancy Rigberg have counseled countless homebrewers and would-be professional brewers beginning their careers. They are an original homebrew authority in Philadelphia and continue to operate out of their modest Sansom Street shop near a thriving downtown bar scene. Hummel has done collaboration brewing with Nodding Head that resulted in two medals at the Great American Beer Festival and written the comprehensive *The Complete Homebrew Beer Book*. The following recipe is an unpublished recipe with an inspired back story.

George Hummel, co-owner, Home Sweet Homebrew: "In 1978 I found myself in San Francisco for the final concert at the Winterland Ballroom by the Grateful Dead. During this visit I had a pivotal beer, my first Anchor Steam. A few years later I returned to the Bay Area and had my first Sierra Nevada Pale Ale. These beers were a revelation. They were made in America; they were most definitely not fizzy and yellow. They were also quite different from imports.

"I quickly developed a taste for these flavorful West Coast beers, but upon returning home, there were no such beers to buy. Philly's first craft brewery had yet to open.

"This is an old-school 1980s homebrew recipe. Back in the day I'd have to drive to DC to get Sierra Nevada Celebration Ale. It was a long drive and the beer was not available year-round so I decided to brew up my own version inspired by the original. Although a 'pretty normal' IPA recipe in the 21st century, it was pretty wild stuff back in the day. Also, it is the first recipe for which I won a competition ribbon.

"Modern homebrewers now find themselves awash in a veritable sea of quality craft brews. They practice the art as an extension of their love of beer and not out of need. Thousands of products crowd the shelves. There are sources and social groups throughout the region. It's a good time to be a homebrewer. It's a good time to love beer. Cheers!"

HOMEBREW RECIPE: JACK O'ROE

YIELD: 5 GALLONS

Grains

1 pound Victory malt or similar toasted malt

8 ounces 30–40L Crystal malt

Malt Extract

8 pounds Alexander's Sun Country Pale or any extra-light malt extract

Hops Schedule

12–14 AAU (weight x alpha acid %) Chinook hops

0.5 ounce Chinook + 0.5 ounce Cascade boil for 45 minutes

0.5 ounce Chinook + 0.5 ounce Cascade boil for 30 minutes

0.5 ounce Chinook + 0.5 ounce Cascade boil for 15 minutes

0.5 ounce Chinook + 0.5 ounce Cascade add at the end of 60-minute boil

0.5 ounce Chinook + 0.5 ounce Cascade, add as dry hop during secondary ferment

Additives

1 Campden tablet (add to brewing water)

2 teaspoons yeast nutrient (last 15 minutes)

1 teaspoon Irish moss (last 15 minutes)

5 ounces dextrose (for bottling)

Yeast

Wyeast 1056 (either in starter or pitch 2 packs)

OG: 1.050 FG: 1.014 ABV: 5.5% IBU: 98 SRM: 7

Brewing Instructions

Heat 6 gallons of water to 170° F. Dissolve one Campden tablet in the water.

Coarsely crack malts and suspend in a cheesecloth bag in the brew kettle. Hold for 30 minutes at 150–160°F. Remove the grain bag and discard.

Heat to a boil; dissolve the malt extract and the hops. Return to a boil and boil for 45 minutes. Add yeast nutrient and Irish moss. Boil 15 more minutes. Add aroma hops.

Prime with 5 ounces of dextrose or keg and force carbonate.

COURTESY OF GEORGE HUMMEL FROM HOME SWEET HOMEBREW IN PHILADELPHIA, PA.

KEYSTONE HOMEBREW SUPPLY

435 Doylestown Rd., Montgomeryville, PA 18936; (215) 855-0100; 128 E. Third St., Bethlehem, PA 18015; (610) 997-0911; keystonehomebrew.com; @KeystoneHB

Keystone Homebrew plays a prominent role in the brewing world around Philadelphia's suburbs. They've grown up from a small one-store operation in 1992 to almost 25 years later with a 24,000-square-foot flagship store in Montgomeryville. In 2008, owner Jason Harris and beer writer Carolyn Smagalski founded the annual Philly Beer Geek competition, which rewards superior beer knowledge and elevates the understanding and appreciation of beer beyond his store walls.

The store has every need of brewers, winemakers, and mead- and cider-makers anticipated with a near endless supply of ingredients and equipment, regularly scheduled classes, and a well-educated staff. Countless homebrewers have passed through the doors over the years and quite a few have taken their brewing to a professional level at places like Conshohocken, Fegley's, Forest & Main, HiJinx, Iron Hill, Naked, Prism, Round Guys, and Tired Hands.

John Stemler has worked at Keystone Homebrew and now mans the mash paddle for Free Will Brewing Company in Perkasie, PA. The brewery's C.O.B. is available as a homebrew clone kit at his former place of employment and he and Harris pass it along here for your experimentation. They describe it as "an imperial southern English brown ale with fresh roasted coffee added after fermentation. It is a strong, luscious, malt-forward ale with notes of caramel, brown sugar, graham cracker, and coffee shop aromas."

CLONE BEER RECIPE: C.O.B. (COFFEE OATMEAL BROWN)

YIELD: 6 GALLONS

Grains

2 pounds Briess Carabrown*
2 pounds flaked oats*
0.5 pound Thomas Fawcett brown malt*
0.25 pound Thomas Fawcett pale chocolate malt*
0.25 pound Thomas Fawcett Crystal 45*

Malt Extract

9 pounds Briess Golden Light DME

Hops Schedule
   1 ounce UK Pilgrim Pellets (bittering) with 60 minutes left in the boil
   1 ounce UK Pilgrim Pellets (flavoring) with 15 minutes left in the boil
Yeast
   Wyeast #1318 London III (2 packs)
Other
   *8 ounces ground coffee (NOT INCLUDED. Note: Free Will uses Speakeasy Colombia
      Valle de Cauca but try it with Backyard Beans, fresh and local!)*
   5 ounces priming sugar for bottling
   ½ teaspoon of Irish moss or 1 Whirlfloc tablet (optional)

OG: 1.084 FG: 1.020 ABV: 8.3% IBU: 55 SRM: 21

Brewing Instructions

A few hours before you begin to brew, prepare your liquid yeast according to the package instructions.

Divide the cracked grains into muslin bags (no more than ½ pound per bag) and add them to your brew kettle along with 2 gallons of cold water. Heat slowly.

Steep the grains in hot water (about 145°F–160°F) to extract flavor and color—do not allow to boil. After about 30 minutes remove the grain bags and then bring water to a boil. Remove the pot from the heat and add the 3 bags of malt extract. Keep the kettle off the burner and stir until the malt extract is completely dissolved.

Put the pot back on the burner and bring it to a boil. Once boiling, place the bittering hops into a muslin bag, add them to the pot, and set your timer to boil for 1 hour. Keep an eye on the pot to avoid boil-overs.

After 45 minutes of boiling, add the flavoring hops (in a muslin bag). You may add ½ teaspoon of Irish moss or 1 Whirlfloc tablet to help clarify your beer (optional). After 60 minutes of boiling turn off the heat. Put a lid on your pot and cool it in an ice batch (use your sink) for about 30 minutes. Remove the hop bags from the kettle.

Pour 2 gallons of cold water into your sanitized fermenter, add the cooled wort (the stuff in your pot), and top up with additional water to 5 gallons. Aerate the wort with vigorous stirring, rocking the fermenter, etc.

Using a hydrometer, confirm completion of fermentation. When verified, add 8 ounces of course ground freshly roasted coffee in a muslin bag (don't forget to sanitize the muslin bag!) for 24 hours (no longer!). After 24 hours, bottle as normal.

When ready to bottle, siphon beer into your sanitized bottling bucket, leaving sediment behind. Boil priming sugar in 1–2 cups of water for a few minutes, gently stir into the beer, and bottle as usual.

COURTESY OF JASON HARRIS FROM KEYSTONE HOMEBREW SUPPLY IN MONTGOMERYVILLE, PA, AND JOHN STEMLER FROM FREE WILL BREWING CO. IN PERKASIE, PA.

THE BREWER'S APPRENTICE

865 Rte. 33 West (Park Avenue) Freehold, NJ 07728; (732) 863-9411; brewapp.com; @TheBrewersApp

The Brewer's Apprentice is a brew-on-premise operation with spacious digs and a lot going on under one roof. In business since 1996, The Brewer's Apprentice is fully stocked with a wide array of beer, wine, mead kits, and plenty of accessories alongside an educational space and an ample brewing facility. Reservations fill quickly for brewing time at this integral northern New Jersey homebrewing scene.

Jason Meehan, general manager, contributed this recipe that invokes the lore of the ominous Jersey Devil. "Out from the dark and haunted woods of the Pine Barrens comes a beer that packs a truly evil punch! A 'quad' is a traditional Belgian style that has quadruple the strength of a regular beer . . . this recipe is either the beer of your dreams, or it'll give you nightmares!"

HOMEBREW RECIPE: THE JERSEY DEVIL

YIELD: 5 GALLONS

Grains

15 ounces Melanoiden

12 ounces Munich

7 ounces Aromatic Malt

7 ounces Cara-Pils

3 ounces Crystal 20L

3 ounces Special B

2 ounces Chocolate

2 ounces Honey Malt

Malt Extracts

1.33 quarts Pale

1.33 quarts Amber

1 quart Adjunct

1 pound Extra Light DME

Add AFTER boil

1.25 pounds dark candi sugar

1 pound clear candi sugar

0.5 quart honey

Hops, Spices, Special Ingredients

Bittering Hop

1.15 ounces Magnum

Mid-Addition Hops

1 ounce Perle

Spices (last 5 minutes)

0.5 teaspoon Grains of Paradise

Flame Out Hops

0.1 ounce Opal

0.1 ounce Saaz

Finishing Hops

0.2 ounce Opal

Special Ingredients

1 scoop Fermax yeast nutrient

1 tab or 1 scoop Whirlfloc or Irish moss

Yeast

Trappist (2 vials!) starter recommended!

Description: Fruity, vinous with a hint of plums

OG: 1.100-1.105 FG: 1.018-1.020 ABV: 11% IBU: 21 SRM: 13.5

Brewing Instructions

Make sure your kettle is between 160°–170°F. Place all crushed grains into a grain sock and steep in the pot for 30 minutes, making sure to maintain the temperature indicated. After grains have steeped, drain and discard sock.

Raise the heat under your pot. When the temperature is approaching 200°, add all of your extracts and sugars (except the priming sugar!). Stir well. Wait for the pot to reach a boil. NEVER LEAVE YOUR POT FROM THIS POINT ON!

When kettle reaches a boil, temporarily turn the heat off and add your bittering hops. Immediately return to a heavy, rolling boil for 60 minutes. Make sure to stir your wort regularly throughout the brewing process so it doesn't scorch.

When there are 15 minutes left in the boil, temporarily turn off your heat again and add your finishing hops. Return to a light boil. Any spices or special ingredients are added with five minutes remaining in the boil.

After last 15 minutes of boiling, turn heat off and chill wort. When wort is around 70°–90°, pour into a fermenter and pitch yeast. That's it! Refer to more detailed brewing and bottling instructions if needed (available upon request).

Recipe will yield approximately 2 cases of 22-ounce or 12-ounce bottles. Brewing, fermenting, and conditioning times may vary depending on recipe, yeast, temperatures, and brewing experience.

COURTESY OF JO ELLEN FORD AND JASON MEEHAN FROM THE BREWER'S APPRENTICE IN FREEHOLD, NJ.

XTREME BREWING
11307 Trussum Pond Rd., Laurel, DE 19956; (302) 280-6181; 18501 Stamper Dr., Lewes, DE 19958; (302) 684-8936; 24608 Wiley Branch Rd., Millsboro, DE 19966; (302) 934-8588; XtremeBrewing.com

Doug Griffith has seen a lot over the last 20 years. From the early days of Sam Calagione opening the first brewpub establishment in Delaware to his current business, which includes three locations, Griffith has been a part of the booming landscape of brewing in The Small Wonder—Delaware. In fact, in Calagione's book *Brewing Up a Business*, the off-centered owner of Dogfish Head referred to Griffith as "a guardian angel for Dogfish Head."

Part of Xtreme Brewing's contribution to the brewing industry has been professional brewers who have started as either employees or customers of the homebrew shop. Jerry Franklin of 3rd Wave Brewing Company in Delmar, DE, is one of those employees; turns out the co-owner of 3rd Wave, Lori Clough, was a regular customer.

When exploring southern Delaware, I first found 3rd Wave and their lineup of very well-made beers—the Dawn Patrol Coffee and Cream Stout being one of them—and it led me back to Xtreme Brewing. They agreed to pass along this clone recipe originally created by Franklin as an employee and available at Xtreme Brewing to try at home.

CLONE BEER RECIPE: COFFEE AND CREAM STOUT

YIELD: 5 GALLONS

Ingredients and Supplies

Note: Time notations beside items indicate the length of time they are in the boil or when they are used during the boil or the day that item is added or used.

Amount	Ingredient	Time
4½ gallons	cool water	Pre-boil tea
4 ounces	black patent malt, crushed	Pre-boil tea
4 ounces	roasted barley, crushed	Pre-boil tea
4 ounces	Debittered Black	Pre-boil tea
1	grain bag	Pre-boil tea
7 pounds	dark dry malt extract	65 min.
½ ounce	Warrior pellet hops (bittering)	60 min.
¼ ounce	Warrior pellet hops (bittering)	30 min.
¾ ounce	Centennial pellet hops	10 min.
1 teaspoon	Irish moss	20 min.
1 pound	Lactose	End of boil
1	WLP002 English Ale Yeast or Safale S04	at 68–72°F fermentation
8 ounces	coffee cold steep	5th day of fermentation
1	grain bag for straining coffee	
5 ounces	priming sugar (about 1 cup)	Bottling
	caps	Bottling
2 packets	sanitizer	

OG: 1.072 FG: 1.016 ABV: 7%

Brewing Instructions

Fill the brewpot with 4½ gallons of cool water.

Fill grain bag with the crushed black patent malt, the crushed roasted barley, and the crushed Debittered Black. Tie off the top and place the bag in your brewpot.

Heat the pot and stir the water and grain bags every 5 minutes. Just as the water reaches 170°, pull out the grain bags using a large stirring spoon. Hold the bags above the brewpot for a minute allowing most of liquid to drain into the pot. Do not squeeze the grain bag.

As the water is beginning to boil, remove pot from heat. Add the dry malt extract. Stir to prevent clumping and scorching on the bottom of the pot. Return pot to heat.

Allow the wort to come up to a boil. After pre-boiling for 5 minutes add the Warrior hop pellets (bittering) and stir. Start timing the 1-hour boil at the point that you make this hop addition.

30 minutes before the end of the 1-hour boil, add the next Warrior hop pellets and stir for 1 minute.

20 minutes before the end of the boil, add the Irish moss. Stir for 1 minute.

10 minutes before the end of the boil, add the Centennial hop pellets and stir for 1 minute.

At the 60 minute mark, turn off heat source and add the lactose. Stir wort clockwise for 2 minutes as you build up a whirlpool effect. Stop stirring and allow wort to sit for 10 minutes.

Chill wort in cold-water bath until it is under 75°F. Transfer wort into fermenter or car-boy, aerate (rock the baby) for 1 minute. Pitch yeast into carboy and aerate for another minute. Top up the carboy to the 5-gallon mark with cool water.

In about 5 days, crush coffee, put in jar, cover with cold water. Steep cold for 12 to 24 hours. Strain with bag. Add liquid to fermenter.

In about 5 days, your beer should be ready to package. Before bottling, clean and sanitize bottles and caps and create a priming solution of 1 cup boiling water and priming sugar. Siphon the beer into a sterilized bottling bucket, add the water-diluted priming solution, and gently stir. Bottle and cap the beer.

Allow the beer to bottle condition for another 10 days and it should then be ready to drink.

COURTESY OF JERRY FRANKLIN FROM 3RD WAVE BREWING COMPANY IN DELMAR, DE

MARYLAND HOMEBREW

6770 Oak Hall Ln., Columbia, MD 21045; (410) 290-3768; mdhb.com; @MDHomeBrew

From Chris Anderson, general manager, Maryland Homebrew: "Maryland Homebrew began as a basement start-up business in June of 1992 and has now grown to be a double warehouse of 6,750 square feet—packed to the gills with everything you would need for beer- and winemaking, but also all the supplies and equipment for cheese, vinegar, mead, kombucha, and more. We cover all the basics, but also stock the harder-to-get items like firkins, barrels, hardware, and fun beer shirts.

"We also partner with the local clubs to sponsor beginner and all-grain classes at least once a month, which are usually taught by members of the local clubs. This is a great opportunity for them to raise funds for their own club events. Maryland Homebrew sponsors just about all local beer events, including the Freestate Homebrew Club's annual holiday charity party, Chilibrew, and Mashout, which is a large homebrew camping weekend."

Anderson is "a member of two local clubs, treasurer of the guild, and a cofounder of Baltimore Beer Babes, part of Barley's Angels. Maryland Homebrew is represented all around Baltimore City and surrounding counties with this club, and my activities help to educate more women not only about craft beer in general but also about how to make it."

She passed along a local favorite clone receipe for DuClaw's Devil's Milk Barleywine in all-grain format and an alterntive for extract. By design, since it was first production brewed in 1998, the Devil's Milk recipe has had a rotating set of hops—always US varieties only—at the beginning of boil, with 15 minutes remaining, at knockout, and in dry-hopping. For example, the 2014 version used Nugget for bittering and both Centennial and Simcoe at each remaining stage.

CLONE BEER RECIPE: DEVIL'S MILK

YIELD: 5 GALLONS

Ingredients

16.25 pounds English pale malt
0.65 pound CaraWheat
0.20 pound Crystal 60L
0.40 pound Melanoidin
3.25 ounces Chinook hop pellets (11.5% AAU)
2 ounces Willamette hop pellets
0.65 ounce Columbus hops

1 teaspoon Irish moss
White Labs California Ale yeast or S-05
1¼ cups dry malt extract for priming or ¾ cup priming sugar
OG: 1.099 FG: 1.020 ABV: 10.5% IBU: 88.3 Efficiency: 75%

Brewing Instructions
Mash at 152°F and do a 120-minute boil.

1½ ounces of Chinook for full 120 minutes.

1 teaspoon Irish moss for last 15 minutes of boil along with 0.70 ounce Willamette, 0.47 ounce Chinook, and 0.29 ounce Columbus.

At knock-out, 0.59 ounce Chinook, 0.59 ounce Willamette, and 0.35 ounce Columbus.

Pitch yeast when wort temperature is between 70–80°F. Allow to sit in the fermenter at 68–72°F for about 7 days, then use a sanitized hydrometer to ensure that the beer has reached its final gravity.

Rack to a secondary fermenter (glass carboy) after 7 days. Dry hop with 0.70 ounce Chinook and 0.65 ounce Willamette. Let sit another week.

Prime and bottle. When priming, dissolve corn sugar or dry malt extract in 2 pints of boiling water for 5 minutes. Pour this mixture into the empty bottling bucket and siphon the beer from the fermenter over it. This method ensures that the priming sugar will disperse evenly through your beer.

For proper carbonation, store your beer at 75°F for at least the first week after bottling. This will allow the yeast to feed on the priming sugar and produce the necessary carbon dioxide needed for carbonation. It's ready to drink, but it will improve if you age your beer another 2 to 3 weeks.

For extract version: Omit the English pale ale malt and use 9.9 pounds of light liquid malt extract and 2 pounds dry malt extract. Steeping the grains for 30 minutes at 155°F in 1½ gallons of water. Do a 5½-gallon boil if at all possible.

COURTESY OF CHRIS ANDERSON FROM MARYLAND HOMEBREW IN COLUMBIA, MD, AND DUCLAW BREWING COMPANY FROM BALTIMORE, MD

In the Kitchen

eer is liquid food. That could be a touch of oversimplification but when you consider the carbohydrates, vitamins, and a bit of protein and minerals found in beer, it's definitely something to consider. Plus the process lends itself to the food and cooking relationship: Boil water; add grains and flavoring; and instigate fermentation.

Perhaps it's no wonder that many professional chefs have a deep appreciation for the combination of beer with their culinary creations, both as an ingredient and as a pairing element on the dining room table. Following are five examples of beer and food served up from kitchens that demonstrate a tasty curiosity about the intersection of these two worlds.

BAXTER FARMS SWEET & SASSY CORN MUFFINS WITH 16 MILE CHEDDAR & OLD COURT PEPPER JAM

Hobo's is a Rehoboth Beach gem where owner Gretchen Hanson—whose culinary exploits go back to her "little catering business" as a 12-year-old—believes that alcohol should be an "enhancer on the table, not the centerpiece." To that end, the restaurant serves an eclectic menu of creative food, a well-stocked bottle list of approximately 25 food-friendly beers, many from local breweries, and is aiming to provide draft beer in the future. She has worked with 16 Mile Brewery and other local chefs on *Chefs Designing Beers,* helped create an Asian-influenced beer with tangerine, and competed in *Top Chef—Delaware.*

She believes that "cooking from scratch is the way that God intended . . . food as love, food as healing, and food as community." She provides this tasty recipe for your enjoyment.

From Gretchen Hanson, owner, Hobo's: "If you are lucky enough to be a friend of Jay Baxter's, show up at his farmhouse early one morning. Take a hayride across the turnip fields with his cute as a button 4-year-old, bounce on his in-ground trampoline with the 4-year-old, tour the antique tractors, and when you have almost but not quite worn out your welcome, have him grind (by hand, mind you, the way his grandfather did) some of his special GMO-free white cornmeal. The rest is easy."

Muffins

1 cup unsalted butter, softened

1 cup evaporated cane juice (regular sugar will do)

2 free-range eggs

1 (15-ounce) can cream-style corn

2 cups white cornmeal, finely ground

2 tablespoons baking powder

1 teaspoon sea salt

1 cup 16 Mile cheddar, grated

6 ounces cream cheese

Sweet pepper jam (recipe below)

Preheat the oven to 350°F. Soften butter and beat at high speed with cane juice or sugar until fluffy, add in eggs one at a time and beat some more. Beat in cream-style corn and dry ingredients and then stir in grated cheddar. Put in prepared mini muffin pans and pop in oven for four minutes. Pull out (they will not be done and put an almond-size piece of cream cheese right in the top center and push down softly. Put back in the oven for 5 more minutes and pull out again. Top with a teaspoon of pepper jam and put back in oven for maybe 3 more minutes. Pull out and serve.

Sweet Pepper Jam

1 cup diced Fresno chiles

2 cups diced red onion

2 (12-ounce) bottles 16 Mile Old Court Ale

1 cup organic sugar or evaporated cane juice

2 tablespoons agave nectar

Pinch sea salt

1 teaspoon cornstarch mixed to a paste with warm water (optional)

Make sure that chiles and onions are diced very finely and cover with the beer in a medium saucepan. Bring to a slow boil and add the sugar, agave, and salt. Stir constantly! When beer is thick and gooey, lower heat and whisk in cornstarch ONLY if needed—if you reduce enough you will not need to use the cornstarch as a thickener. I add it to the recipe because a lot of people lose their nerve the last few minutes and the jam ends up watery.

COURTESY OF GRETCHEN HANSON FROM HOBO'S IN REHOBOTH BEACH, DE

SMOKED & BRAISED PORK CHEEKS OVER CREAMY POLENTA WITH QUESO FRESCO & CILANTRO GREMOLATA

Jeff Miller runs one of the most acclaimed beer programs in the Philadelphia suburbs. Beer events at TJ's, particularly the anniversary party each December, are known to attract beer geeks from states away and on a daily basis the constantly changing electronic draft board shows off a wide range of styles and coveted beers. His kitchen has kept its end of the deal in providing plates of food that work well with the draft and bottle list. The weekly specials menu has been known to include very beer-pairworthy items like duck sliders, smoked spare ribs, steamed pork buns, and sticky toffee pudding. Here, he offers up this succulent dish of meat from which any leftovers would make a great cemita sandwich, also occasionally found on the restaurant's specials menu.

From Jeff Miller, co-owner, TJ's: "I'm a self-taught chef who started as a dishwasher at a French bakery and cafe in 1984. I never gave myself the title 'chef' until recently. I now feel after 30 years of hard work and constant learning that I have garnered the skills, ability, palate, and creativity to be worthy of the title. I have worked my way up through this industry and have worked with A LOT of people. I can honestly say I am currently working with the most dedicated staff in my career. TJ's wouldn't be what it is today without them."

SERVES: 5–8

For the pork cheeks

- 5 pounds pork cheeks (easy substitutions for pork cheeks include short ribs, veal cheeks, lamb neck, or brisket)
- 2 tablespoons brown sugar
- 2 tablespoons ground black pepper
- 1 tablespoon granulated garlic
- 1 tablespoon salt
- 1 tablespoon ground cumin
- 1 tablespoon smoked paprika
- ½ quart beef stock
- ¼ cup fish sauce
- 2 teaspoons oyster sauce
- 2 teaspoons sriracha (you could add more or less depending on how hot you like it)
- 1 teaspoon fresh minced garlic
- 6 ounces doppelbock, Belgian quadrupel, or strong stout
- Queso fresco or feta cheese (for garnish)

Rub pork cheeks liberally with the dry rub (made up of the next six ingredients) and smoke at 275°F for 2 hours on hickory wood chips. While the pork cheeks are smoking, move on to the gremolata (recipe below).

After 2 hours, remove pork cheeks from smoker and transfer to a large stockpot.

Over high heat, add to pork cheeks the beef stock, fish sauce, oyster sauce, sriracha, minced garlic, and beer.

For a unique twist you could also use a dark oud bruin such as Goudenband that would add a bit of funkiness to the cheeks.

Bring the pork cheeks and the braising liquid to a boil. Reduce to a simmer for 2 hours without a lid. Ninety minutes into the braising time, move on to the polenta (recipe below).

To plate use a bowl or deep lip plate. Spoon the polenta into the bowl. Top the polenta with 3 or 4 pork cheeks. Add a little of the braising liquid.

Crumble some queso fresco or feta cheese over top of the cheeks and top that with a bit of the gremolata.

For the cilantro gremolata
½ cup loosely packed fresh cilantro leaves, finely chopped (or mint or flat-leaf parsley)
1 clove garlic, minced
Zest of one lemon
¼ teaspoon kosher salt
1 tablespoon extra-virgin olive oil
Mix all of the ingredients and refrigerate until pork cheeks are finished.

For the polenta
2 cups vegetable stock
2 cups heavy cream
½ teaspoon salt
1 teaspoon ground black pepper
1 cup cornmeal
½ cup freshly grated Parmesan cheese, good quality
2 tablespoons butter
Combine stock, cream, salt, and pepper in a heavy stockpot. Bring to a slow boil. Slowly whisk in cornmeal. Turn the heat down to low.

Simmer and whisk constantly for 20 minutes, until all grains of polenta are soft. Add Parmesan cheese and butter.

(Easy substitutions for the polenta include mashed potatoes, parsnip puree, or cauliflower puree.)

COURTESY OF JEFF MILLER FROM TJ'S IN PAOLI, PA

STILLWATER CLASSIQUE & CITRUS-BRINED GRILLED SHRIMP WITH VIETNAMESE GREEN MANGO SALAD

Brian Strumke may not have his own physical brewery to call home, but his pub Of Love & Regret (OLAR)—conveniently and somewhat ironically—sits on Brewers Hill across from the old Natty Boh facility and serves as the unofficial base camp.

Chef Keith Curley heads the kitchen at OLAR and finds a menu full of ways to set the stage for great beer and food pairings. In this contributed recipe from him, Curley finds a suitable use for Stillwater's Classique, the brewery-described "post-Prohibition" beer.

From Keith Curley, chef, Of Love & Regret: "I am a Maryland native and grew up on the Chesapeake Bay. I spent time cooking in Key West and Richmond before returning home to attend culinary school.

"With the quality and complexity of flavor that modern brewers are able to achieve, along with the public's renewed interest in traditional old-world brews, beer no longer plays second fiddle in the world of food and drink pairings.

"The important thing to remember when cooking with beer is that adding heat changes the flavor profile drastically. I think we have all come to that conclusion when we decided to try that beer that had been somewhere too warm too long. Whenever possible, add your beer 'raw' to your recipe toward the end. This will allow the beer to come through and make the food taste more like the beer you are using and ties nicely into pairing the dish with the same beer."

SERVES: 6

For the shrimp
  4 ounces sugar cane vinegar (available in Asian markets)
  ⅓ cup sugar
  1½ tablespoons kosher salt
  Juice and zest of 2 oranges
  1 tablespoon black peppercorns

2 sprigs thyme

8 ounces Stillwater Classique

20 head-on Gulf shrimp, middle part of shell removed, leaving tail and head on

Combine vinegar, sugar, salt, orange juice and zest, and peppercorns in a saucepan. Bring to a boil, add thyme, and turn off. Allow to cool. Add the Classique beer. Cover shrimp with marinade and allow to sit for 4 hours minimum. Grill shrimp on both sides and serve atop the chilled salad (recipe below).

For the salad

2 green mangoes, peeled and julienned

2 cucumbers, peeled, seeded, and julienned

½ cup julienned red onion

4 scallions, cut on a bias

1 small Thai chile, minced (more if you enjoy heat)

Basil, cilantro, and mint, roughly chopped

½ tablespoon fish sauce

2 tablespoons rice wine vinegar

Juice of 2 limes

2 tablespoons olive oil

1 teaspoon soy sauce

Salt and white pepper

Combine all ingredients in bowl and toss. Keep chilled until ready to serve, at which point top with grilled shrimp hot off the grill.

COURTESY OF KEITH CURLEY FROM OF LOVE & REGRET IN BALTIMORE, MD

BELGIAN MEATBALLS WITH BEER BRAISED RED CABBAGE & BELGIAN ALE SAUCE

Throughout this book, you likely noticed that Iron Hill Brewery & Restaurant has a good portion of the population of the four states covered with soon-to-be twelve locations. Is it the beer? Is it the food? If you've been to an Iron Hill, you realize that it's both. Each Iron Hill location puts on a display of food and beer each month with pairing dinners, beer releases with coordinated food specials, and exclusive food and beer events for their King of the Hill Club members.

With the company since 1996, Dan Bethard served most recently as executive chef of the West Chester, PA, location prior to taking the title of assistant director of culinary operations for the entire company.

He offers the following advice from experience when working with beer and food: "I've had a particular love for making sauces with beer. I began using lighter styles with fish and shellfish. I found that a Belgian-style wit worked wonders with low-acid fish like flounder and mussels. A saison, which is a really great pairing with most seafood, does not work as well in the sauce.

"I then moved on to braising meats with beer. I always use the braising liquid to make my sauce. A stew of beef, pork, lamb, or venison really shines when using a sweet, malty, fruity, complex, dark ale. The beer complements the sweetness of the root vegetables in the dish and the caramelization of the meat. Some beers are too sweet for the meat being used so knowing the type of sauce that complements the choice in meat is vital. A nice brown ale works well if you don't want such a sweet sauce.

"When drinking beer with food, I recommend choosing a beer that will complement the food. Choosing a beer that contrasts can be difficult and often leads to a subpar pairing. Always start with lighter styles with lighter types of food and heavier styles with heavier types of food. I also like to pair beers with food that will cleanse the palate and get me ready for the next bite. The carbonation from a pilsner will help cut through the richness of a fattier, grilled steak. I do not recommend a hoppy beer with food. The bitterness from the hops destroys the palate and makes the experience unpleasant."

Here is a contribution from Bethard, and keep in mind that when he recommends using a Vienna-style lager and a quadrupel, that Iron Hill does a multiple award–winning "house" Vienna Red Lager on draft and a 750-milliliter bottled quad that would work perfectly in this recipe. The recipe may look long, but take the time to read it. If you enjoy the process of making from-scratch food for a large party, this recipe of easy to find and use ingredients will pay off. Halving the recipe is just as easy.

For the Belgian meatballs (shelf life 4 days)

White bread, half loaf, crust removed

2 cups heavy cream

5 pounds ground beef

3 pounds ground veal

2½ pounds ground pork

1¼ cups sweet onions, minced

6 ounces Belgian endive, minced

1½ teaspoons dried thyme

1 tablespoon dried oregano

2 tablespoons fresh rosemary, minced

1 tablespoon black pepper, ground

1½ tablespoons kosher salt

1½ ounces garlic, minced

2 ounces liquid egg or 2 fresh eggs, beaten.

Remove crust from bread, cut into medium-size dice, and in stages fill the bowl of a food processor fitted with the "S" blade. Grind into breadcrumbs and place in a medium-sized mixing bowl. Pour heavy cream over bread and thoroughly incorporate using a large spoon. Reserve.

Add the other ingredients to a large mixing bowl and then add the breadcrumb and cream mixture. Place gloves on your hands and mix thoroughly. Cover the large mixing bowl and refrigerate until ready to cook meatballs.

Cook the meatballs at 350°F for 15 to 20 minutes in a convection oven, or 20 to 25 minutes in a standard oven. Top with Belgian Ale Sauce and serve with Beer-braised Red Cabbage (recipes follow).

For the beer-braised red cabbage (shelf life 6 days)

6 pounds red cabbage

¼ pound butter

1 quart thinly sliced Spanish onions

⅜ cup sugar

2 cups Vienna-style lager

½ cup cider vinegar

1 gallon chicken broth

1 tablespoon black pepper, ground

1 tablespoon kosher salt

Quarter each head of cabbage, remove the core, and slice all the cabbage.

In a pot, melt the butter and then sauté the onions until they begin to caramelize.

Add the remaining ingredients. Bring to a boil, lower to a simmer, and cook until the cabbage is soft. If the mixture becomes too dry, add a little more chicken broth. Check seasoning.

Place in a container and cool.

For the Belgian ale sauce (shelf life 6 days)
- 1 tablespoon bacon grease
- ½ cup minced carrots
- ½ cup minced Spanish onions
- ½ cup minced celery
- 1 tablespoon minced garlic
- 1 tablespoon tomato paste
- ½ teaspoon ground black pepper
- ¼ teaspoon ground nutmeg
- 2 bay leaves
- ⅙ cup brown sugar
- 1 cup Belgian quadrupel
- 2 quarts demi-glace
- 1 teaspoon fresh thyme, minced
- 1 tablespoon red wine vinegar
- 1 tablespoon Dijon mustard

In a medium-sized pot, heat the bacon grease and sauté carrots, onions and celery until onions are translucent.

Add minced garlic and sauté for 1 minute. Add the tomato paste, pepper, nutmeg, bay leaves, and brown sugar and sauté for 1 minute longer. Add the beer and reduce by half.

Add the demi-glace, bring to a boil, reduce to a simmer and cook for approximately 30 minutes.

Stir in the thyme and vinegar and cook for 3 minutes longer. Turn off the heat and stir in the Dijon mustard. Strain the sauce through a fine mesh strainer.

COURTESY OF DAN BETHARD FROM IRON HILL BREWERY & RESTAURANT IN WEST CHESTER, PA

SHIRRED EGG WITH BRAISED SHORT RIBS, DOUBLE-CREAM & ONION STEW

Memphis Taproom was opened in 2008 by Brendan Hartranft and Leigh Maida on the principle of great beer with great food in a true honest-to-goodness Philadelphia neighborhood. Executive Chef Jesse Kimball was at the helm from the beginning. Since then, the beer has kept pace with the food, which has kept pace with the beer. And the neighborhood has treated them as one of its own.

Vintage Beer Brunches have been hugely successful events where the kitchen begins with the chosen beers from the cellar and finds food to match.

From Jesse Kimball, executive chef, Memphis Taproom: "I started working in restaurants and drinking craft beer on the Maine coast in the 1980s. In the '90s I lived in Portland, OR, and couldn't help being immersed in the vibrant craft beer and food culture. In 2000 I moved to Brooklyn, where I became very serious about cooking and beer. Just down the street was the Brooklyn Brewery, where there was a burgeoning craft beer bar scene, *Garrett Oliver's Brewmaster's Table* came out, and Spuyten Duyvil opened. I spent my weekends in the Catskills preparing tasting menus with local vegetables, meats, cheeses, beers, and wines from day excursions. I have spent the last decade in Philadelphia working professionally with food and craft beers.

"This recipe is from the tasting menu from the Vintage Beer Brunch held the first Beer Week we were open. You can make the short ribs and onion stew a day or two ahead of time. When they are cool, portion them. Then on the morning of the brunch, simply reheat, assemble, and bake the dish. Pair with whatever dark beer in which you braised the short ribs.

"The Imperial Porter to me is the black coffee alongside a plate of eggs and meat, in this case short ribs braised in the porter. A shot of double-cream from a Lancaster Farm is the cream in the coffee."

SERVES: 8

> 4 bone-in short ribs (approximately 5 pounds)
> ½ cup vegetable oil
> 3 onions, julienned
> Kosher salt
> Freshly ground black pepper
> 1 tablespoon minced garlic
> 2 (12-ounce) bottles dark and flavorful beer such as Flying Dog Gonzo Imperial
>   Porter

Sachet of parsley stems, bay leaf, cinnamon stick, five allspice berries, 1 tablespoon black peppercorns, 3 sprigs thyme—tied up together in a little baggie of cheesecloth

16 eggs

1 cup of double cream (if you cannot find double cream from a farm you can use heavy cream and reduce by 1/3)

Heat oven to 350°F.

The short ribs will be in one large brick with 4 bones. Dry ribs well and season with salt and pepper. In a pan, get the oil smoking hot. Sear the ribs flesh-side down getting them nice and dark. Flip over and brown bone-side down. Remove from oil.

Saute onions until they soften. Add garlic. When fragrant, deglaze with beer. Bring to a boil. Add short ribs back to the pot with the sachet, and reduce to a simmer. Cover and bake in oven at 350°F for 2 hours or until meat falls off bones. Let ribs and onions cool overnight in the liquid.

The next day skim the fat off the top and discard. Remove short ribs—cut meat away from bones and tendons and cut into four even ribs, then cut each rib in half and you will have eight nice squares of meat. Bring the braising liquid and onions to a boil, reduce to a simmer, and reduce until it is a nice onion stew, about 30 minutes.

PHOTO COURTESY OF LEIGH MAIDA

Final preparation and plating

Heat oven to 375°F.

Heat the short rib portions in the onion stew. Butter eight 6-ounce (3.25") porcelain ramekins. Place one short rib portion in each ramekin and spoon onion stew around until level. Crack two eggs into each dish. Season with salt and pepper. Bake eggs for 10 minutes until they are just starting to set up. Spoon 2 tablespoons cream over each dish of eggs. Return to oven and bake another 10 minutes until the eggs are set but yolks are still runny. Serve immediately.

Optional: Garnish the dish with your favorite grated cheese, roasted mushrooms (as pictured), crispy onions, micro greens, or fresh herbs.

COURTESY OF JESSE KIMBALL FROM MEMPHIS TAPROOM IN PHILADELPHIA, PA

Appendix A: More to Come

I've been fond of saying that this book project would have been much easier to write 10 years ago. Not only is the number of potential and actual brewery openings—from the smallest nano size to the much larger endeavors—growing by the week, but the number of establishments serving great beer is keeping its own intense pace. The following list of brewing establishments is broken down by state for those that are already open or are on the horizon for 2015.

The ones that are listed as "open now" are those where I was not able to give a comprehensive enough visit and review to include them in the body of the book. Those under the heading "on the horizon" are ones that, by the time you are reading this, should have opened in late 2014 or will likely be opening in 2015, based upon known conditions. It's a big and crazy brewing world out there and we're all just trying to keep up.

Delaware

ON THE HORIZON

Blue Earl Brewing Company—projected early 2015; 210 Artisan Dr., Smyrna; (302) 359-7373; blueearlbrewing.com; @BlueEarlBeer. Two homebrewers with 45+ years of combined homebrewing experience; old-world style with an American twist.

Dewey Beer and Food Company—projected spring 2015; 2100 Coastal Hwy., Dewey Beach; @DeweyBeerCo. Craft beer and food at the beach.

Maryland

OPEN NOW

Denizens Brewing Company—2014; 1115 East-West Hwy., Silver Spring; (301) 557-9818; denizensbrewingco.com; @DenizensBrewing. European-style lagers, American-style ales, Belgian-inspired beers, sour beers, and barrel-aged beers; just steps from the Metro station.

Mad Science Brewing Company—2014; 1619 Buckeystown Pike, Adamstown; (240) 409-8723; madsciencebrewing.com; @MadScienceBrew. Farm brewery on Thanksgiving Farms using their own homegrown hops, fruits, vegetables, and other products from the farm.

Ocean City Brewing Company—2014; 5509 Coastal Hwy., Ocean City; (443) 677-3075; ocbrewingcompany.com. Full-scale craft brewery with a family restaurant, sports pub, and gift shop; brewer Mark Fesche started with Deschutes and has 20 years of commercial brewing experience.

Realerevival Brewing (RAR)—2013; 504 Poplar St., Cambridge; (443) 225-5664; realerevival.com; @Reale_talk. Open-air taproom and brewery in a 1930s-era building in downtown setting. Nanticoke Nectar and Bucktown Brown are two early hits.

Red Shedman Farm Brewery & Hop Yard—2014; 13601 Glissans Mill Rd., Mt. Airy; (301) 831-5889; redshedman.com; @RedShedman. Located adjacent to Linganore Winecellars with a 15-barrel brewhouse, a tasting room with light fare, and a hop field on over 200 acres of farmland.

Scorpion Brewing Company—2014; 929 Skinners Turn Rd., Owings; scorpionbrewing.com. Locally sourced ingredients. Named after the War of 1812 flagship of the Chesapeake Flotilla. Scuttled in Patuxent River in 1814.

ON THE HORIZON

Brewer's Alley—projected 2015; 124 N. Market St., Frederick; (301) 631-0089; brewers-alley.com; @BrewersAlley. Installation of 3-barrel system to resume small-batch brewing on-site at the restaurant.

Federal Brewing Company—projected late 2015; 102 S. Main St., Federalsburg; thefederalbrewingcompany.com. 1918 bank building. Specializing in small-batch craft beers, locally roasted coffees, and high-quality pub food.

Independent Brewing Company—projected 2015; 418 N. Main St., Bel Air; (410) 960-2042; independentbrewingco.com. An extensive beer menu focusing on creativity and a limited food menu committed to quality not volume. The place will have a rustic industrial theme with the brewing equipment within view of the bar.

Manor Hill Brewing Company—projected early 2015; 4411 Manor Ln., Ellicott City; (443) 742-4712; manorhillbrewing.com. A farm brewery in Howard County from the Marriner family behind Victoria Gastro Pub in Columbia (see profile in The Rest of Maryland chapter).

New Jersey

OPEN NOW

Belford Brewing Company—2014; 84 Leonardville Rd., Belford; (732) 769-7168; belfordbrewing.com. Theme is all local Belford.

Forgotten Boardwalk Brewery—2014; 1940 Olney Avenue, Cherry Hill; (856) 437-0709; forgottenboardwalk.com; @ForgottenBoards. Sparking curiosity through craft beer and folklore. In the former home of Flying Fish.

Glasstown Brewing Company—2013; 10 Peterson St., Millville; (856) 327-7770; glasstownbrewingco.com; @GlasstownBrew. Lunch Pale, Cedar Swamp IPA, and Main Street Porter are three winners from a brewery that pays homage to the local glass industry.

Little Dog Brewing Company—2014; 141 Steiner Ave., Neptune City; (732) 361-3555; littledogbrewing.com; @LittleDogBeer. Two flagship interpretations of traditional German beers, Steinerweiss (unfiltered wheat) and Gesundheit (altbier/brown ale). Gretchen Schmidhausler has 20 years of professional brewing experience.

Lunacy Brewing Company—2015; 214 Davis Rd., Magnolia; lunacybrewingcompany .com; @LunacyBrewery. In the town known for its "one square mile of friendliness," Lunacy aims to deliver the same along with a "square mile of hoppiness."

Pinelands Brewing Company—2015; 140 S. 7th Ave., Little Egg Harbor; (609) 296-6169; pinelandsbrewing.com; @BrewInThePines. Hand-crafted ales of historic character right from the edge of the Pines.

Spellbound Brewing Company—2014; 10 Lippincott Ln., Unit 12, Mount Holly; (609) 744-0665; spellboundbrewing.com; @SpellboundBrew. A mix of styles from IPA to the more extreme, like coffee, coconut, and vanilla imperial stouts and even less common styles like gruits.

ON THE HORIZON

Berlin Brewing Company—projected spring 2015; 220 S. White Horse Pike, Berlin; berlinbrewco.com. A 5-barrel brewery with a turn-of-the-century baseball theme and an emphasis on local artisans.

Cypress Brewing Company—projected winter 2014-15; 30 Nixon Ln., Edison; (732) 243-9565; cypressbrewing.com; @CypressBrew. Opening with a dozen beers centered around American ales like classic amber, nut brown, and IPA and European interpretations like hefeweizen and rye saison.

Departed Soles Brewing Company—projected early 2015; 150 Bay St., Ste. 2A, Jersey City; departedsoles.com; @DepartedSoles. To be located in the heart of downtown Jersey City and serving not "a good gluten-free option, but a great beer that happens to be gluten-free."

Garden State Brewing Company—projected summer 2015; 247 E. White Horse Pike, Galloway; (609) 232-2337; gardenstatebeerco.com; @GardenStateBeer. Making highly drinkable well-balanced beers, using skills as a PhD chemist to ensure quality control and balance.

Hoboken Brewing Company—projected mid-2015; Hoboken; hobokenbrewing.com; @HobokenBrewing. Beginning their regional craft beer business by contracting through another brewery to produce full-flavored craft beers for both the common beer drinker and the experienced craft beer enthusiast alike.

Jugtown Mountain Brewing Company—projected spring 2015; 5 Clubhouse Dr., Stes. 8 & 9, Washington Township; jugtownmountainbrewing.com; @JugtownMtnBeer. Focus will be on sessionable American and English ales as well as crisp, refreshing farmhouse ales. Using high-quality local ingredients when possible and sustainable business practices.

Man Skirt Brewing Company—projected spring 2015; 144 Main St., Hackettstown; (908) 989-0286; manskirtbrewing.com; @ManSkirtBrew. Laid-back, retro tasting room in an old bank building with vault.

Sea Isle Brewing Company—projected summer 2015; Sea Isle City; seaislebrewingco.com; @SeaIsleBrewCo. The first and only brewery in Sea Isle City. Offering a wide selection of lagers and ales.

Screamin' Hill Brewery—projected early 2015; 81 Emleys Hill Rd., Cream Ridge; (609) 752-4271; screaminhill.com; @ScreaminHill. A 7-barrel barn brewery on a 100-acre family farm using their own hops, grain, and other ingredients.

Third State Brewing Company—projected winter 2014-15; 352 High St., Burlington City; thirdstatebrewing.com. In addition to brewing great beer, serves as a catalyst of recovery for the Historic District and the city.

Triumph Brewing Company—projected 2015; Bridge Ave., Red Bank; triumphbrew .com. Third location serving their own craft beer and locally grown foods.

Pennsylvania

OPEN NOW

Aldus Brewing Company—2014; 555 Centennial Ave., Hanover; (717) 634-2407; aldusbrewing.com; @AldusBrewing. Named after a 15th-century Venetian printer and housed in the former Snyders of Hanover pretzel factory. Brewery contains a taproom with an industrial copper-top bar and American Keepsake Ale (AKA) Kölsch as the signature beer.

Armstrong Ales—2013; 1000 Hollingsworth Dr., Phoenixville; (484) 639-7607; armstrongales.com; @ArmstrongAles01. Small-batch brewer doing a constant variety of English, German, Belgian, and American beers.

Aurochs Brewing Company—2014; 8321 Ohio River Blvd., Emsworth; (724) 260-8737; aurochsbrewing.com; @AurochsBrewing. They exclusively brew great-tasting, naturally gluten-free craft beers in a gluten-free facility and aspire to change the way people experience gluten-free beer.

Baldy Beard Brewing Company—2014; Lancaster; baldybeard.com; @BaldyBeardBrew. From the hop-heavy American ales to the sweet and spicy Belgians, the brewery honors the craft and strictly bottle conditions its beers in 12-ounce and 750 milliliter packages.

Boxcar Brewing Company—2015; 142 E. Market St., West Chester; boxcarbrewingcompany.com; @BoxcarBrewery. They plan to get the community involved in crafting their own beer via homebrew contests during which contestants will be able to use their small-scale pilot brewing system.

Brew Gentlemen Beer Company—2014; 512 Braddock Ave., Braddock; (412) 871-5075; brewgentlemen.com; @BrewGentlemen. Creates an ambitious variety of high-quality beers, operates a comfortable taproom and lounge in which to serve them, and is a part of the ongoing reinvention of Braddock.

Broken Goblet Brewing Company—2014; 1500 Grundy Ln., Bristol; (609) 868-6385; brokengoblet.com; @Broken_Goblet. A brewery and brewpub for beer lovers who are ready for a twist on the traditional tasting.

Chatty Monks Brewing Company—2014; 610 Penn Ave., West Reading; (484) 818-0176; chattymonks.com; @ChattyMonks. Their beers respect the Belgian brewing techniques yet carry the distinct mark of their own conclave. Featuring in-house yeasts, homegrown hops.

Conshohocken Brewing Company—2014; 739 E. Elm St., Conshohocken; (610) 897-8962; conshohockenbrewing.com; @ConshyBrewing. In addition to making beer they love, they have big plans to give back to the community and create a socially responsible brewery.

Crooked Eye Brewery—2014; 13 E. Montgomery Ave., Hatboro; (267) 246-5046; crookedeyebrewery.com. A family-owned and -operated 3-barrel brewery making beers that "aren't intended to slap you in the face with outlandish concoctions."

Crystal Ball Brewing Company—2014; 1612 W. King St., York; crystalballbrewing.com; @CrystalBallYork. Using the finest and freshest ingredients possible, combined with traditional brewing techniques and the latest technology, they produce world-class beer ranging from traditional offerings to the more experimental.

Do Good—2013; 3245 Amber St., Philadelphia; (267) 752-3548; dogoodbrewing.com; @DoGoodBrewing. Philanthropic business model where every beer produced is connected to a cause and a percentage of the proceeds from the beer goes to its given cause.

Funk Brewing Company—2014; 19 S. Sixth St., Emmaus; (610) 421-8270; funkbrewing.com; @FunkBrewing. Their goal is to create unique and complex hop-accentuated ales along with wonderfully creative farmhouse style beers.

Hitchhiker Brewing Company—2014; 190 Castle Shannon Blvd., Pittsburgh; (412) 343-1950; hitchhikerbrewing.com; @HitchhikerBrew. Committed to brewing the best beer possible with the lowest environmental impact.

Hop Farm Brewing Company—2013; 5601 Butler St., Pittsburgh; (412) 408-3248; hopfarmbrewingco.com; @HopFarmBeer. 10-barrel system and sourcing own-grown hops. One of nearly 20 stops on the loosely organized Allegheny River Libation Trail.

Iron Hill Brewery & Restaurant—2014; 60 Greenfield Ave., Ardmore; ironhillbrewery.com/ardmore; @IronHillArdmore. The company's 11th location. Stay tuned for a forthcoming 12th location in the early planning stages.

Kennett Brewing Company—2015; 109 S. Broad St., Kennett Square; (717) 529-2727; kennettbrewingcompany.com; @KennettBrewingC. Through a combination of replicating traditional styles and creating innovative interpretations, KBC provides customers the opportunity to affordably enjoy authentic European and innovative American ales.

Milkman Brewing Company—2014; 2517 Penn Ave., Pittsburgh; milkmanbrewing.com; @MilkmanBrewing. Multiple brewmaster approach executes new projects with a battery of personalities and ideas for every new brew.

Molly Pitcher Brewing Company—2014; 10 E. South St., Carlisle; mollypitcher.com; @MPBrewing. A 7-barrel brewery and tasting room honoring the historic role that Molly Pitcher played in the Revolutionary War.

Moo-Duck Brewery—2014; 79 S. Wilson Ave., Elizabethtown; mooduckbrewery.com; @MilkmanBrewing. Multiple brewmaster approach executes new projects with a battery of personalities and ideas for every new brew.

River Barge Brewing Company—2013; 71 Grovedale Ln., Wyalusing; riverbargebrewing.com. Offering a local beer to complement the local fine wine available at Grovedale Winery and Vineyards, which is adjacent to the brewery.

Roundabout Brewery—2013; 4901 Butler St., Pittsburgh; roundaboutbeer.com; @RoundaboutBrew. Opened in burgeoning Lawrenceville section by former award-winning brewer, Steve Sloan, at Church Brew Works.

2nd Story Brewing Company—2014; 117 Chestnut St., Philadelphia; (267) 314-5770; 2ndStoryBrewing.com; @2ndStoryBrewing. German lagers, hop-forward beers, classic English and Belgian styles, and seasonals.

ShuBrew—2013; 210 S. Main St., Zelienople; (724) 766-4426; shubrew.com; @ShuBrew. Handcrafted foods, 2-barrel brewery, plus local wines and ciders in a Main Street atmosphere. Production brewery on the horizon.

Snitz Creek Brewing Company—2014; 7 N. Ninth St., Lebanon; (717) 450-4467; snitzcreekbrewery.com; @SnitzCreekBeer. Creating a place for a community of good, hardworking people to come together, celebrate, and share their experiences, centered around great, handcrafted beer.

Spoonwood Brewing Company—2015; 5981 Baptist Rd., Bethel Park; spoonwoodbrewing.com; @SpoonwoodBrewin. At the heart of the operation is a 15-barrel brewhouse, fully complemented by an authentic wood-fired oven and premium wines on tap.

St. Benjamin Brewing Company—2014; 1710 N. 5th St., Philadelphia; (215) 232-4305; stbenjaminbrewing.com; @StBenjaminBrew. A 3-barrel brewery bringing uniquely flavored, quirky, and well-crafted beers to the beer drinkers of Philadelphia. Planning to add a pub room in 2015.

St. Boniface Craft Brewing Company—2013; 1701 W. Main St., Ephrata; (717) 466-6900; stbonifacebrewing.com; @StBonifaceBrew. A growing nanobrewery that serves pints and fills growlers in its tasting room. Food is available from a rotation of food trucks and Little Nicky's, a local Italian restaurant.

Victory at Magnolia—2015; Cypress and Mill Streets, Kennett Square; victorybeer .com; @VictoryBeer. A 7-barrel extension of the brewery offering Victory standards plus "test brews." Uniquely fresh and local menu.

Wacker Brewing Company—2014; 417 W. Grant St., Lancaster; (717) 617-2711; wackerbrewing.com; @WackerBrewing. The opening represented the rebirth of a local family brewing name from the 19th century.

Wild Side (Full Pint Brewing Company)—2015; 5310 Butler St., Pittsburgh; fullpintbrewing.com; @FullPintBrewing. No brewing, but a pub serving as an extension of the brewery and giving cellaring capabilities.

ON THE HORIZON

Brewtus Brewing Company—projected spring 2015; 23 Chestnut Ave., Sharon; brewtusbrewers.com. The complex will have a speakeasy look from the 1920s Prohibition era, serving six beers, root beer, and food, all prepared in-house.

Butler Brewing Company—projected early 2015; 101 S. Main St., Butler; (724) 264-KEGS; butlerbrewworks.com; @ButlerBrewWorks. A 5-barrel brew house with "adventurous ales" and sourcing nontraditional ingredients as well as changing up the usual brewing processes. As such, expect adventurous beer names like Amelia, Machete, River Runner, and Totem.

Crime & Punishment Brewing Company—projected early 2015; 2711 W. Girard Ave., Philadelphia; crimeandpunishmentbrewery.com. A Brewerytown 7-barrel brewpub brewing beers based on the name Crime and Punishment. The pub will comfortably seat 35–40 and have a unique atmosphere.

5 O'Clock Brewing Company—projected mid-2015; 2301 Washington Ave., Philadelphia; (484) 319-7901; 5oclockbrew.com; @5_OClockBrewCo. After a personal brush (his father) with celiac disease, owner Cory McDonald has set off to "give people great beer, both gluten-free and gluten full, and to those who have lost it, bring back the joy of beer." Tasting room and a 15-barrel system, plus ½-barrel gluten-free setup.

Levante Brewing Company—projected early 2015; 208 Carter Dr., Ste. 2, West Chester; levantebrewing.com; @LevanteBrewing. A 15-barrel system with a taproom and beers balanced between "solid," "bold," and seasonal ales and lagers. Next door to the Artisan Exchange market.

Ship Bottom Brewing Company—projected mid-2015; Wallingford; shipbottombrewery.com; @ShipBottomBrew. Nanobrewing one barrel at a time since 2012—and Beach Patrol Hefeweizen contracted at Free Will—Ship Bottom looks to move into its own 15- or 30-barrel facility in 2015. Barnacle Bottom Stout, The Shack IPA, and Double Overhead IPA are three year-round favorites that can currently be found most regularly at Capone's and Pinocchio's.

Stable 12 Brewing Company—projected early 2015; 368 Bridge St., Phoenixville; (610) 764-0250; stable12.com; @Stable12Brewing. Originally starting their business in the family barn, Stable 12 will continue with their theme "from barn to bottle, beer with a kick" in their new brew house and tap room.

Tired Hands Brewing Company—projected spring 2015; 35 Cricket Ter., Ardmore; tiredhands.com; @TiredHandsBeer. An extension of the original brew cafe in a 13,000-square-foot facility with a 20-barrel brewhouse, canning line, and a kitchen focusing on tacos and crudo.

Two Rivers Brewing Company—projected spring 2015; 542 Northampton St., Easton; (610) 829-1131; tworiversbrewing.com. A casual pub featuring 14 taps of artisan-brewed beer and farm-to-table food.

Zeroday Brewing Company—projected early 2015; Harrisburg; zerodaybrewing.com. A small-batch artisanal brewery attached to a local independent movie theater. Five year-round brews accompanied by rotating seasonal and "fun" selections. Locally sourced food offerings, gallery space for local artists, and a venue for live acoustic music.

Appendix B: Beer Lover's Pick List

Flying Fish Brewing Company, Exit 4, American Trippel, 124

Fordham & Dominion Brewing Company, Dominion Oak Barrel Stout, American Sweet Stout, 21

Four Seasons Brewing Company, Dark Side of the Pint, Oatmeal Stout, 192

Free Will Brewing Company, Free Will I. Am. Fergie Black Eyed Stout, Dry Irish Stout, 277

Frey's Brewing Company, Backwoods Brigade, Smoked American Farmhouse Ale, 82

Full Pint Brewing Company, Chinookie IPA, India Pale Ale, 193

Grist House Brewing, Crouching Porter, Hidden Chocolate, Chocolate Porter, 194

Gunpowder Falls Brewing Company, Pilsner, German-style Pilsner, 233

Heavy Seas Beer, Loose Cannon, India Pale Ale, 41

Helltown Brewing, Barleywine, English-style Barleywine, 195

High Point Brewing Company, Golden Lager, German-style Helles Lager, 156

Jailbreak Brewing Company, Welcome to Scoville, IPA, 83

Kane Brewing Company, Night To End All Dawns, Imperial Stout, 125

Lavery Brewing Company, Devil Bird Holiday Ale, Imperial Porter, 196

The Lion Brewery, Stegmaier IPA, India Pale Ale, 234

Milkhouse Brewery at Stillpoint Farm, Coppermine Creek, Dry Stout, 85

Mispillion River Brewing Company, Double Chin, Double IPA, 23

Mully's Brewery, Shucker Stout, Dry Stout, 87

Neshaminy Creek Brewing Company, Trauger Pilsner, German-style Pilsner, 279

New Jersey Beer Company, Garden State Stout, American Stout, 157

Nimble Hill Brewing Company, Bonczek, Double IPA, 236

Peabody Heights Brewery, Full Tilt Camden Cream, Cream Ale, 43

Philadelphia Brewing Company, Fleur De Lehigh, Golden Ale, 318

Prism Brewing Company, ParTea, Pale Ale, 280

Rinn Duin Brewing, The River Toms, English IPA, 127

River Horse Brewing Company, Blonde, American Blonde Ale, 129

Rivertowne Brewing Company, Hala Kahiki Pineapple Ale, Fruit beer, 198

Round Guys Brewing Company, Original Slacker, Brown Ale, 282

Ruhlman Brewing Company, IPA, American India Pale Ale, 89

ShawneeCraft Brewing Company, Double Pale Ale, India Pale Ale, 237

16 Mile Brewing Company, 1872 Licensing Porter, English Porter, 25

Sly Fox Brewing Company, Saison Vos, Belgian-style Farmhouse Ale, 283

Straub Brewery, Straub IPL, India Pale Lager, 199

Susquehanna Brewing Company, Pils-Noir, Black Pilsner, 238

3rd Wave Brewing Company, 1st Wave IPA, India Pale Ale, 27

Tröegs Brewing Company, Sunshine Pils, German-style Pilsner, 240

Tuckahoe Brewing Company, New Brighton Coffee Stout, Coffee Stout, 130

Twin Lakes Brewing Company, Greenville Pale Ale, Pale Ale, 3

Union Craft Brewing Company, Balt Alt, Altbier, 45

Village Idiot Brewing Company, Thong Remover Tripel, Belgian-style Tripel, 132

Weyerbacher Brewing Company, Last Chance IPA, India Pale Ale, 285

Yards Brewing Company, Saison, Saison, 320

Yuengling Brewery, Porter, Porter, 242

Index